1000

AutoCAD
Tips and Tricks

Third Edition

Updated for Release 12

George O. Head & Jan Doster Head

VENTANA
PRESS

AutoCAD Reference Library™

1000 AutoCAD Tips and Tricks, 3rd Edition Updated for Release 12
Copyright© 1993 by George O. Head & Jan Doster Head

Library of Congress Cataloging-in-Publication Data

Head, George O., 1945-
    1000 AutoCAD tips and tricks / George O. Head & Jan Doster Head. -- 3rd ed.
    p. cm.
    "For releases 11 & 12"
    Includes index.
    ISBN 1-56604-007-8
    1. Computer graphics. 2. AutoCAD (Computer file) I. Head, Jan Doster. II. Title.
    III. 1000 AutoCAD tips and tricks. IV. Title: One thousand AutoCAD tips and tricks.
T385.H37 1992
620'.0042'02855369--dc20   92-31100 CIP

Book design: Karen Wysocki
Cover design: Nancy Frame Design; John Nedwidek, Sitzer:Spuria
Technical editor: Brian Matthews, Architectural Technology Dept. Head, Wake Technical Community College
Editorial staff: Diana Cooper, Patricia Frederick, Jean Kaplan, Linda Pickett, Pam Richardson
Production staff: Rhonda Angel, Midgard Computing, Karen Wysocki

Third Edition 9 8 7 6 5 4 3
Printed in the United States of America

Ventana Press, Inc.
P.O. Box 2468
Chapel Hill, NC 27515
919/942-0220
FAX 919/942-1140

Trademarks

Trademarked names appear throughout this book. Rather than list the names and entities that own the trademarks or insert a trademark symbol with each mention of the trademarked name, the publisher states that it is using the names only for editorial purposes and to the benefit of the trademark owner with no intention of infringing upon that trademark.

About the Authors

George O. Head is president of Associated Market Research, a business and management consulting firm for architects and engineers. He is the developer of Integrated Management Systems, a project management and financial accounting software package for architects and engineers. He coauthored the *AutoCAD Productivity Book* and is the author of *AutoLISP in Plain English* and *AutoCAD 3D Companion* (all published by Ventana Press). He is also coauthor of *Managing, Marketing, & Budgeting for the A-E Office*.

Jan Doster Head worked for many years as business manager of a large Texas-based A/E firm. As the designer of A/E Solutions for architectural, engineering and design firms, she now focuses on implementation and training of the project management and accounting software. She is also coauthor of *Managing, Marketing, & Budgeting for the A-E Office*.

CONTENTS

CHAPTER 2   Basic Editing   29

CHAPTER 5   Basic Inquiry, Text, Annotation   101

CHAPTER 6   Basic Utilities   127

CHAPTER 8   Miscellaneous (Basic)   171

CHAPTER 9 Basic Release II 181

CHAPTER 10   Basic Release 12   195

Section II: Intermediate

CHAPTER 12   Intermediate Editing   235

CHAPTER 17   Intermediate 3D   329

Section III: Advanced

CHAPTER 2I   Advanced Drawing   425

CHAPTER 32   System Variables   593

Section IV: Windows

CHAPTER 33   AutoCAD for Windows   621

Introduction

If you're like most AutoCAD users, you are too busy drawing and designing to become a full-blown expert on how to get the most from your system. In addition, AutoCAD is so complex and ever-changing that few users venture beyond its basic commands and features.

Yet some of AutoCAD's most precious features—and biggest time-savers—are either buried in the *AutoCAD Reference Manual* or aren't mentioned at all.

That's where *1,000 AutoCAD Tips and Tricks* comes in. We've been working with AutoCAD since its first release, yet we're still discovering ways of using the program that make our work more efficient.

With Release 12, AutoCAD offers more power and productivity than ever. Its ease-of-use and efficiency take giant strides forward with the program's improved interface, which includes new pull-down menus and dialog boxes. It also features links to SQL database, as well as a Windows add-on.

1,000 AutoCAD Tips and Tricks (now more than 1,200!) telescopes years of trial and error into a well-organized compendium of techniques, shortcuts and tidbits that can save you a lot of hair-pulling. In short, the information in this book will help you go a good deal further with AutoCAD by learning at a glance what it's taken others years to accomplish.

Who Needs This Book?

As the world of AutoCAD grows more complex, with additional platforms being introduced, books that help AutoCAD users must address the new as well as the older releases. If you have used AutoCAD over the last several years, you're probably comfortable with the features of one of the earlier versions of this powerful program. But you may be eager to move up to Release 12 and/or Windows. Regardless of what release you're using, all the tips featured in this book are invaluable in working with AutoCAD.

This edition of *1,000 AutoCAD Tips and Tricks* addresses AutoCAD Release 10, Release 11 *or* Release 12. If you have worked with Release 11, you'll want to jump straight to Chapters 10, 20 and 30, which provide more than 130 power-packed tips for Release 12.

How Well Do You Need to Know AutoCAD?

1,000 AutoCAD Tips and Tricks is organized from the basic to the advanced so that any AutoCAD user can immediately put it to use. The book assumes you have AutoCAD up and running and are familiar with its basic commands and features.

How to Use This Book

Obviously, your level of AutoCAD expertise determines how you will use *1,000 AutoCAD Tips and Tricks*. New users should begin with Section I, reading it in conjunction with AutoCAD's reference manual and a good tutorial, such as *AutoCAD: A Concise Guide to Commands and Features*, by Ron Leigh, also published by Ventana Press. Much of Section I will help you use basic AutoCAD commands more efficiently. As you gain experience and confidence, you'll want to read the entire section to pick up things you may have missed; then go on to Sections II and III.

If you're an intermediate or advanced user, skimming Section I may give you a good refresher course of AutoCAD's basic commands. This section can also provide you with ideas you might have missed (or know you should implement but haven't yet!). Then you can continue to explore more advanced techniques covered in later sections.

The AutoLISP programs in each chapter provide useful productivity enhancements that will complement your knowledge.

In addition, *1,000 AutoCAD Tips and Tricks* provides a handy reference when you encounter a problem or need to find a shortcut for a particular task. We've spent a good deal of time organizing the book so that beginners and power users alike can quickly access specific information about AutoCAD.

Before beginning, please take time to examine the Table of Contents and *both* indexes—one organized alphabetically and the other by numerical entry. If you'd like to know more about a certain entry, say Tip 5.2, simply refer to the Numerical Index, and you'll find all other related entries without having to wade through an alphabetical index! If you know the specific command or feature, refer to the Alphabetical Index or to the Table of Contents.

What's Inside

For easy reference, *1,000 AutoCAD Tips and Tricks* is organized into three sections—basic, intermediate and advanced. These sections are divided into ten chapters, each addressing a major subject area of AutoCAD:

- Drawing
- Editing
- Viewing
- Layers, Blocks, Attributes
- Inquiry, Text, Annotation
- Utilities
- 3D
- Miscellaneous
- Release 11
- Release 12

Each chapter is organized into three parts:

How Do You...

More Steps to Success

AutoLISP Programs

Each "How Do You..." section asks questions on that chapter's topic and then provides the answers. The "More Steps to Success" sections offer invaluable tips, techniques and shortcuts that help you achieve increased productivity in each subject area. The chapters conclude with AutoLISP programs relating to the topic. These programs efficiently perform a tip described earlier in the chapter.

Near the end of the book, in Chapter 31, "Advanced AutoLISP," is a section of 150 tips, tricks and "How Do You..." questions on AutoLISP itself.

And new to this edition is a timely section of 40 tips specifically for the Windows user—Chapter 33, "AutoCAD for Windows."

The Table of Contents and two indexes let you quickly find the sections that discuss a particular topic.

Hardware/Software Requirements

1,000 AutoCAD Tips and Tricks was written for AutoCAD Releases 10 through 12 for DOS, although most of the features and commands apply to previous versions and all other operating system platforms.

1,000 AutoCAD Tips and Tricks assumes that your equipment and software are fully installed, configured and ready to draw.

A Note About AutoLISP

AutoLISP, AutoCAD's internal programming language, is a tremendous productivity tool. However, it's not for everyone. If you want to learn basic AutoLISP, read *AutoLISP in Plain English* (Ventana Press). This and other references will help you learn enough about AutoLISP to solve basic drawing problems unique to your discipline.

If you don't plan to create AutoLISP programs, refer to Appendix A of this book. You'll learn how to load AutoLISP files into your AutoCAD system and use them in your daily work.

Please note that you don't have to know a single AutoLISP command to take advantage of the many useful programs featured throughout the book. These AutoLISP programs are big productivity enhancers; you'll be glad you took the time to learn the simple procedure of loading and using AutoLISP files.

Don't Forget the Disk

The *1,000 AutoCAD Tips and Tricks* companion diskette, an optional, self-installing, IBM-compatible disk available from Ventana Press, contains all the AutoLISP programs listed in the book. The diskette saves considerable typing time, and it's handy for quickly loading a tailor-made solution that will become a permanent part of your system. Depending upon your discipline, these programs could dramatically boost your output, and Ventana tells me they'll return your money if you're not satisfied.

Rules of the Road

The book makes extensive use of an easy-to-use tutorial format. When you see **Type:**, you're to type what follows. This is generally followed by **Response:**, which is the system's response that you see at the Command line.

<RETURN> means you should press the Enter or Return key. In most cases while in AutoCAD, you can also press the space bar to get the same results.

Finally, if you see a plus sign at the end of a line of AutoLISP code, it indicates that the line continues. Don't type the plus sign; it's simply there because the code wouldn't fit on one line.

Moving On

When using a program as complex as AutoCAD, it's easy to get to a certain level and stay there. We think this book will prove to be a uniquely easy reference for users who want to go further with AutoCAD and challenge their abilities to get more out of their work each day.

Try to get into the habit of picking up this book whenever you have a question or hit a snag—if you think something could be done a little easier, chances are you're right!

Let's get started.

George O. Head and
Jan Doster Head

BASIC

CHAPTERS 1 - 10

CHAPTER 1

Basic Drawing

How Do You . . .

1.1 How do you change the size of a point?

A point is a single entity. Like an ordinary line, it generally has no size. But it's possible to give a size to all points in a drawing—this makes it easier to identify the point or to snap to it.

The size of a point is controlled by the system variable **PDSIZE**. Therefore, you could use the command **SETVAR PDSIZE 20** <RETURN> to set a point's size to 20 units.

Remember that the system variable **PDSIZE** changes the size of all the points in a drawing. To change their size back and make the points invisible, reset **PDSIZE** to 0.

 RELEASE 12   The DDTYPE dialogue box lets you set a style for points. The new dialogue boxes featured in Release 12 allow you greater flexibility and faster response time. They even let you correct your mistakes. And they're easy to use, whether you activate them from the pull-down or sidebar menus or from the keyboard. See Tips 10.28 and 10.29.

1.2 How do you draw a node?

There's an Object Snap mode that lets you snap to a node. Basically, a node is the same as a point. (Because you can't even look up the word "node" in the index, I wonder why AutoCAD didn't make it easier by calling Object Snap mode "snapping to a point.")

There are many reasons to create nodes or points. You can place a point on certain strategic areas of an object or block, and then snap to these areas.

Also, certain AutoLISP programs take advantage of points (nodes) that are added to objects.

1.3 How do you repeat a command?

The space bar and the <RETURN> key work essentially the same way in AutoCAD, with the exception of **TEXT**. Any time you want to repeat a command, simply press the space bar or the <RETURN> key.

Even though this is a simple concept, a few commands operate a little differently when they're repeated:

TEXT   When you repeat the **TEXT** command by pressing the space bar or the <RETURN> key twice, it's assumed that you want to use the next line under the current line of text. All height and rotation defaults remain constant.

LINE   When you repeat the **LINE** command, you get the normal responses. If you press the space bar or <RETURN> key twice, it's assumed you want to continue the line from the endpoint of the last line or arc, depending on which was drawn last.

ARC   As with the **LINE** command, you can continue from the last **LINE** or **ARC** by simply pressing the space bar or <RETURN> key twice.

FILLET   This is a little special. The default inherent in this command is the radius. Once the radius is set, each time the command is issued it uses the previous radius. Therefore, if you want to set a 0 radius, issue the **FILLET** command, choose **radius** and set it to 0. Then press the space bar or <RETURN> key, and the **FILLET** command will be repeated, but with a 0 radius.

CHAMFER   Like the **FILLET** command, **CHAMFER** maintains the previous distance and thus can be repeated.

INSERT   The name of the last block inserted becomes the default for future insertions. Press the space bar or <RETURN> key twice to continue inserting the same block.

1.4 **How do you draw an ellipse?**

In older versions of AutoCAD, an ellipse was drawn by inserting a block of a circle and distorting the distance of the X, Y points.

An ellipse is now drawn using the **ELLIPSE** command. You can draw an ellipse from either the center, as with a circle, or from one of the endpoints.

If you want to use the endpoints, you're first asked to pick two points (see Figure 1-1). The angle of the two points determines the angle of the ellipse. You're then rubber-banded from the midpoint of the two points. The distance from this midpoint determines the minor axis of the ellipse. In other words, when you pick the third point you're determining the width of the ellipse.

Figure 1-1: Drawing
an ellipse

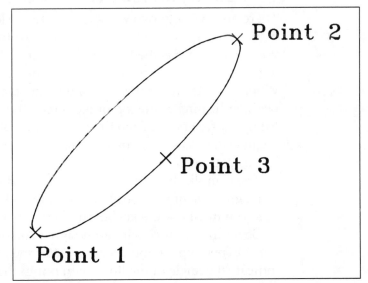

There's an option to picking the third point: you can respond with **Rotation**. AutoCAD then assumes that the first two points are the major axis. You now need to tell AutoCAD the rotation around the major axis; 0 degrees will draw a circle and 90 degrees will draw a straight line. But AutoCAD won't let you enter a degree greater than 89.4.

You can also draw an ellipse by specifying the center point and the endpoint of one axis followed by the length of the other axis.

Type: `ELLIPSE <RETURN>`

Response: `<Axis endpoint 1>/Center:`

Pick a point at one end of the ellipse.

Response: `Axis endpoint 2:`

Pick a second point at the other end of the ellipse.

Response: `<Other axis distance>/Rotation:`

The third point you now pick will determine the width of the ellipse.

1.5 How do you draw a line a specified distance?

There are basically two ways to specify the length of a line or the distance between two points when you're using AutoCAD. The easiest way is to set your snap to a specified interval that's a multiple of the distance you wish to draw. Then turn coordinates on by using Ctrl-D or the F6 function key. When you pick the first point of the line, the coordinates revert to 0 and begin indicating at the top of the screen the distance you move the cursor from that first point. Each time you pick a point, the coordinates again begin at 0. In this way you can draw from point to point, measuring each line as you draw.

The complication occurs when you need to draw a line that's not an exact multiple of your snap. Try to draw a line 14' 3 - 5/16". In order to do this, you must use the keyboard; there's no other way.

Begin the distance with an @ sign. (You can use Relative Polar Coordinates.) Then type in the distance. After the distance, use the < sign to indicate the angle of the line. Then put in the angle. Remember that unless you've changed it, 0 is to the right, 90 to the top, 180 to the left and 270 toward the bottom. Therefore, using our example above, the following will draw a line 14' 3 - 5/16" straight up. Make sure your units are set to architectural feet and inches on the following exercise.

Type: `LINE <RETURN>`

Response: `From point:`

Pick a point.

Response: `To point:`

Type: `@14'3-5/16" <90 <RETURN>`

See LISP5 in Tip 1.37 for a quick and easy way to enter LINE distances. For further use of points relative to another point, see Tip 1.7.

1.6 **How do you draw a wide line?**

When you use the **LINE** command alone, you're drawing a line with no specific width. You can always designate which pen the plotter is to use by assigning a specific color to a wide-point pen. But this isn't the best way to specify an exact width for a line.

To do this, you can use the **PLINE** command, since polylines can be any width. But setting this width isn't straightforward. Before the width can be set, you must first pick a point. Once the first point is picked, you can, of course, continue to pick points.

When the first point is picked, you have several edit options. One of these is **Width**. By typing W you can then specify the beginning and ending width of the lines you're about to draw—generally, make these the same (this is the default if you haven't previously set the width). The width you set becomes the new width for all subsequent polylines.

Type: `PLINE <RETURN>`

Response: `From point:`

Pick a point.

Response: `Arc/Close/Halfwidth/Length/Undo/Width/<Endpoint of line>:`

Type: `W <RETURN>`

Response: `Starting width <0.0000>:`

Type: `.25 <RETURN>`

Response: `Ending width <.02500>:`

Type: `.25 <RETURN>`

Now pick the second point of the line and continue with the polyline.

If the width is wrong or was drawn initially using a 0 width, you can change it by using the **PEDIT** command. When you use **PEDIT**, simply pick a line or a polyline. If the line you pick isn't a polyline, you're asked if you want to change it into one. You can then edit the line by changing its width.

1.7 How do you pick a point relative to another point?

Let's assume you wanted to begin a line two units up and three units to the right of a given intersection. There are two basic ways to do this. The first works with any version of AutoCAD.

AutoCAD permits a relative coordinate system from the last point picked, but you must first pick a point. Therefore, give the **LINE** command and pick the point to which you wish to be relative. If the prompt says **To point:** type **@3,2**, this will draw the line to a point three units in the X direction and two units in the Y direction. You can then continue drawing the lines. When you're through, erase the first construction line you drew.

The second method is a modification of this. Rather than drawing a construction line relative to the first point, use the **UCS** command. What you want to do is to reset the point of origin to that intersection. So, as a subcommand of **UCS**, choose **Origin**. Point to the intersection. The intersection is now your new 0,0. Immediately issue the **LINE** command. When the prompt says **From point:** enter the absolute coordinates 3,2. This begins the **LINE** command at that point. When you're through, use **UCS Previous**, which sets the User Coordinate System back to the World Coordinate System. See Figures 1-2 and 1-3.

Figure 1-2 (left):
New point of origin

Figure 1-3(right):
Point relative to origin

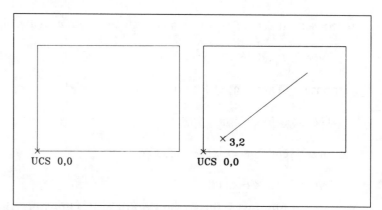

UCS 0,0

× 3,2

UCS 0,0

Type: `UCS <RETURN>`

Response: `Origin/ZAxis/3point/Entity/View/X/Y/Z/Prev/Restore` →
`/Save/Del/?/<World>:`

Type: `O <RETURN>` (This is the letter O, not zero.)

Response: `Origin point <0,0,0>:`

Pick the intersection at the new point of origin.

Type: `LINE <RETURN>`

Response: `From point:`

Type: `3,2 <RETURN>`

Response: `To point:`

Pick the next point and terminate the **LINE** command. See Tips 4.34, 6.35, 7.7 for further ways to pick the last point.

1.8 How do you HATCH in a crowd?

Hatching can and should be performed only on closed entities; there shouldn't be any open spaces. But sometimes there is more than one entity in an area; you have to have a way to control which entity gets hatched.

As an exercise, draw four concentric circles, as illustrated in Figure 1-4. If you use **HATCH** with no options and pick the outer circle, it will hatch through every other entity, as in Figure 1-5.

Figure 1-4 (left):
Entities to be

Figure 1-5 (right):
Hatching alternate
hatched entities

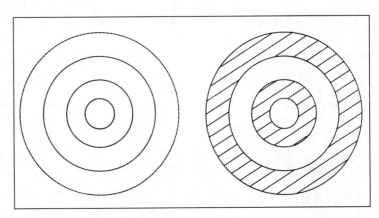

Type: HATCH <RETURN>

Response: Pattern (? or name/U,style):

Type: U <RETURN>

Response: Angle for crosshatch lines:

Type: 30 <RETURN>

Response: Spacing between lines:

Type: 1 <RETURN>

Response: Double hatch area?

Type: N <RETURN>

Response: Select objects:

Put a window around all the circles.

If you use the **O** option, it will hatch only the outermost entity, as in Figure 1-6.

Figure 1-6: Hatching outside an entity

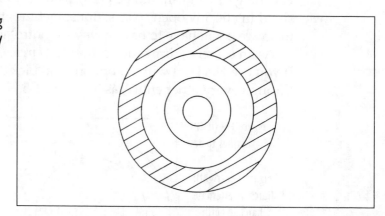

Type: HATCH <RETURN>

Response: Pattern (? or name/U,style):

Type: U,O <RETURN>

Response: Angle for crosshatch lines:

Type: 30 <RETURN>

Response: Spacing between lines:

Type: 1 <RETURN>

Response: Double hatch area?

Type: N <RETURN>

Response: Select objects:
            Put a window around all the circles.

            If you use the **I** option, the command will hatch all the way through
            each entity in the selection set.

Type: HATCH <RETURN>

Response: Pattern (? or name/U,style):

Type: U,I <RETURN>

Response: Angle for crosshatch lines:

Type: 30 <RETURN>

Response: Spacing between lines:

Type: 1 <RETURN>

Response: Double hatch area?

Type: N <RETURN>

Response: Select objects:
            Put a window around all the circles.

            The above will hatch the entities as shown in Figure 1-7.

Figure 1-7: Hatching
inside an entity

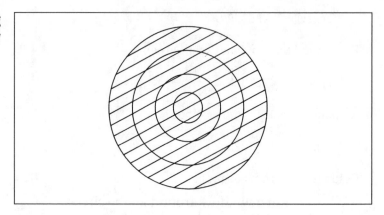

 RELEASE 12   A new alternative to HATCH, BHATCH lets you use a
dialogue box option to set your hatch requirements. See Tips 20.73
and 20.74.

1.9 How do you draw parallel lines?

There are many ways to do this; more sophisticated methods are detailed
in the intermediate section of this book. The standard way to draw parallel
lines is with the **OFFSET** command.

   With the **OFFSET** command, you can choose the offset distance and the
side to offset. It will copy the entity at that distance and on the side selected. This command is far superior to the **COPY** command, which was used
before the **OFFSET** command came into being. See Figures 1-8 and 1-9.

Figure 1-8 (left): Begin
first line

Figure 1-9 (right):
Lines offset

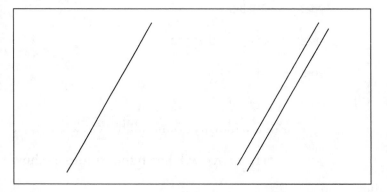

Start by drawing a line.

Type: OFFSET <RETURN>

Response: Offset distance or Through:

Type: 1 <RETURN>

This is the distance between the lines.

Response: Select object to offset:

Pick the line.

Response: Side to offset?

Pick the side to which you want it offset.

12   RELEASE 12   Provides a new double line command, located under the DRAW pull-down menu. See Tip 10.34.

1.10 How do you fill a circle?

Drawing a filled circle is easy using the **DONUT** command, which asks for the circle's inside and outside diameters. The outside diameter determines the diameter of the circle. The inside diameter determines the diameter of the hole in the doughnut. If the inside diameter is 0, the circle will fill.

Type: DONUT <RETURN>

Response: Inside diameter:

Type: 0 <RETURN>

Response: Outside diameter:

Type: 3 <RETURN>

Response: Center of donut:

Pick a point. You can now insert as many circles as you want. Press <RETURN> to exit the command.

Figure 1-10 shows the filled circle as drawn with an inside diameter of 0. Figure 1-11 shows the filled circle as drawn with an inside diameter of 1.

Figure 1-10 (left):
Filled circle

Figure 1-11 (right):
Unfilled circle (donut)

RELEASE 12   Gives you increased versatility with curved linetypes. A SETVAR of **PLINEGEN** can be reset from **0** to **1**, creating a continuous curved pattern around the curved area of a vertex. See Tip 30.18.

1.11 How do you draw a smooth curve?

Arcs, of course, form curved lines. But often you want a smooth curve that doesn't fit the specific center points and radii of an arc. Here's a better way.

Begin by drawing a polyline in the direction you want the smooth curve to go. Pick as many points as possible; this adds vertices along the curve. Then use **PEDIT** and pick the polyline.

You now have two options: **FIT** or **SPLINE**. The **FIT** command will make sure the curve goes through each of the vertices. The **SPLINE** command will produce a much smoother curve, since the curve doesn't have to pass through each vertex.

If you need to uncurve the line, you can use the **DECURVE** command in **PEDIT** for either **FIT** or **SPLINE** curves.

Use **PLINE** and start by drawing line segments, picking points at random. Draw about five of them, as in Figure 1-12.

Figure 1-12: PLINE
vertices

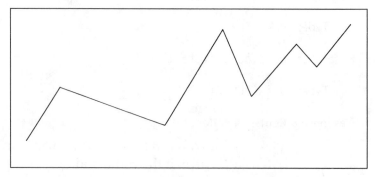

Type: `PEDIT <RETURN>`

Response: `Select polyline:`

Pick any point on the polyline.

Response: `Close/Join/Width/Edit vertex/Fit curve/Spline curve/Decurve →`
   `/Undo/eXit <X>:`

Type: `F <RETURN>`

Fit curve forms a curve pattern as shown in Figure 1-13.

Figure 1-13: Fit curve

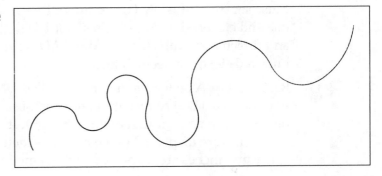

Response: `Close/Join/Width/Edit vertex/Fit curve/Spline curve/Decurve →`
   `/Undo/eXit <X>:`

Type: `S <RETURN>`

Spline curve forms a curve pattern as shown in Figure 1-14.

Figure 1-14: Spline
curve

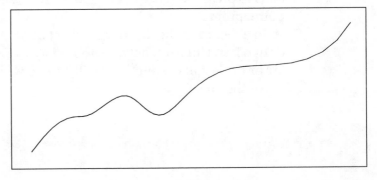

Type: `<RETURN>`

This terminates the **PEDIT** command.

1.12 **How do you know when to use a hyphen for feet and inches?**

This confuses even long-time AutoCAD users, but the answer's simple: Never use a hyphen between feet and inches. Use a hyphen only between inches and fractions of inches, regardless of what the AutoCAD display looks like.

The logic behind this is that you can't use spaces when entering feet and inches. Therefore, the hyphen is used instead of·a space to separate the inch from the fraction. Thus, three feet, four and three-quarter inches would be 3'4 - 3/4".

Actually, often you don't have to use the hyphen at all, but this can cause severe confusion. For example, 1'1 - 11/16" is very clear. It's one foot, one and eleven-sixteenths inches. But 1'111/16" will produce one foot, six and fifteen-sixteenths inches. AutoCAD is interpreting the fraction as one hundred eleven-sixteenths inches.

 RELEASE 11   A new system variable called **UNITMODE** was introduced with Release 11, to reduce the confusion of seeing one method of display on the screen and a different one for input. If **UNITMODE** is set to 0, feet and inches are displayed in the previous method. If **UNITMODE** is set to 1, feet and inches are displayed in the same format as the required input.

1.13 **How do you continue a line from a previously drawn line or arc?**

After you've issued the **LINE** or **ARC** command, you have the option of continuing from the endpoint of the last arc or line drawn. You choose this option by picking **CONTINUE** from the screen menu. An alternate method is to press the space bar or <RETURN> key when you receive the **From point:** prompt.

In either case, the line or arc will start at the endpoint of the line or arc drawn last. Unfortunately, there's no way to specify which one—the last arc or the last line. AutoCAD will choose whichever was drawn last, the arc or the line.

1.14 **How do you draw a polyarc?**

There's no specific command for drawing a polyarc; it's really a subfunction of the **PLINE** command. Start with the **PLINE** command and pick the first point of the polyline. You then have several suboptions to choose from. Choose **Arc**. This begins the polyarc command. Once you're in the polyarc mode, you have several additional options, which are similar to the **Arc** options. See Figure 1-15.

Figure 1-15: Polyarc

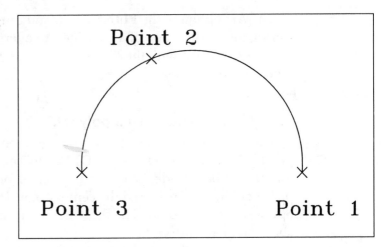

Type: `PLINE <RETURN>`

Response: `From point:`

Pick a beginning point.

Response: `Arc/Close/Halfwidth/Length/Undo/Width/<Endpoint of line>:`

Type: `ARC <RETURN>`

Response: `Angle/CEnter/CLose/Direction/Halfwidth/Line/Radius/Second pt →`
`/Undo/Width/<Endpoint of arc>:`

Type: `SECOND <RETURN>`

Response: `Second point:`

Pick the second point of the arc.

Response: `End point:`

Pick the endpoint of the arc.

The **Arc** option of the **PLINE** command can be invoked at any point during the construction of a polyline. An alternate method is to draw an ordinary arc, then with the **PEDIT** command, turn the arc into a polyarc when asked.

1.15 How do you draw a polygon?

Of course, you can always draw a polygon with regular lines or with polylines, but AutoCAD has a **POLYGON** command. You're first asked for the number of sides. Your next option is for center point or edge. If you pick a point, it's considered the center point. There are now two other options. The polygon will be drawn either inscribed in or circumscribed about an imaginary circle.

If you choose the edge instead of the center point, you're asked for the first and second points along one of the edges of the polygon. The polygon is then constructed counterclockwise. See Figure 1-16.

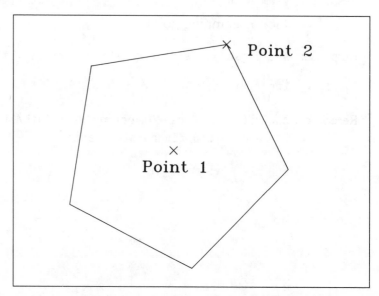

Figure 1-16: Two points of a polygon

Point 2

×
Point 1

Type: POLYGON <RETURN>

Response: Number of sides:

Type: 5 <RETURN>

Response: Edge/<Center of polygon>:

Pick a point

Response: Inscribed in circle/Circumscribed about circle (I/C):

Type: I <RETURN>

Response: Radius of circle:

Pick a point or enter the radius of the circle from the center of the polygon.

One interesting point about polygons constructed in this way is that they're seen as single, closed polylines. AutoCAD takes no account of how they were initially created. If you explode a polygon, it's exploded into individual lines (see LISP4 in Tip 1.36).

 RELEASE 12   Check out BPOLY, an advanced command that uses a dialogue box similar to BHATCH. See Tip 20.75, about creating using a boundary.

1.16 How do you draw with TRACE without leaving a notch in the corner?

First and foremost, don't ever use the **TRACE** command; it's been replaced by the **PLINE** command. But if you must use it, here's how to use it correctly.

If you try to draw a four-sided figure using the **TRACE** command, it will close each corner except the last one—there, it will leave a notch. To avoid this, start a little to the right of where you want to end up. Draw five line segments rather than four, so the close is along a straight line segment. See Figures 1-17 and 1-18.

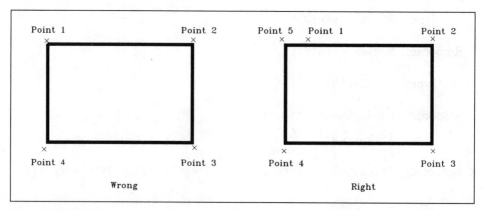

Figure 1-17 (left): Wrong way to use TRACE   Figure 1-18 (right): Right way to use TRACE

In the early versions of AutoCAD, many users tried to use **TRACE** as a parallel line function by turning **FILL** off. The problem with this method is that there's absolutely no way to get rid of these notch lines.

1.17 **How do you compute an arc clockwise?**

Normally when you draw an arc, it's constructed in a counterclockwise direction, unless you specify clockwise measurement as an option with the **UNIT** command. But this isn't the best way to do it.

AutoCAD now has a direction subcommand. After you have given the first two points of an arc, you're prompted with several options. One of these is **Direction**, which lets you point to the direction of the arc relative to the starting point. See Figure 1-19.

Figure 1-19:
Clockwise arc

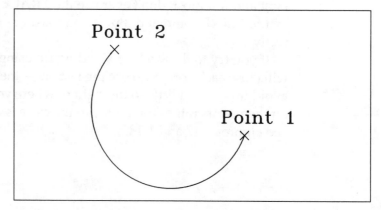

Type: ARC <RETURN>

Response: Center/<Start point>:
           Pick a point.

Response: Center/End/<Second point>:

Type: E <RETURN> (Don't type END; it won't work.)

Response: End point:
           Pick point 2.

Response: Angle/Direction/Radius/<Center point>:

Type: D <RETURN> (You will now show the direction.)

Response: Direction from start point:

Type: 250 <RETURN>

1.18 How do you draw in isometric?

Beginning with Release 10, drawing in isometric is generally not the preferred method of drawing isometric constructions. Even though AutoCAD has an isometric function, if you have Release 10 or later, you'll want to use the 3D functions to construct the model, then use **DVIEW** or **VPOINTS** to view the design in isometric. See Chapter 17.

AutoCAD's isometric function is accessed by the **SNAP** command. The suboption **Style** controls the isometric mode. Under this option you can choose standard or isometric modes. Once you're in isometric mode, Ctrl-E toggles across the top, right and left planes. Once you have the correct plane, entities can be drawn.

The difference between the 3D functions and isometric snap mode is that the 3D functions produce models that have true dimensions. Isometric snap mode distorts the actual entity, not just its view.

1.19 **How do you erase a line while staying in the LINE command?**

There's an erasing function that works transparently in the **LINE** command. While you're in the **LINE** command, drawing from point to point, type U as many times as necessary to erase the previous lines. You can then continue with the **LINE** command until you exit.

Type: LINE <RETURN>

Response: From point:

Draw three or four lines as in Figure 1-20.

Figure 1-20: Use U to
erase last line

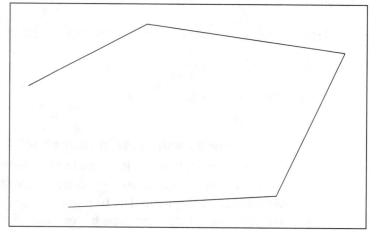

Response: From point:

Type: U <RETURN>

The last line drawn will be erased, and you're left in the **LINE** command. Continue erasing previous lines.

1.20 **How do you continue a line in the same direction and at the same angle?**

There are several ways to do this. One way is to **LIST** the line and secure the angle. Then use the **SNAP** command with the suboption **Rotate**. Enter the angle you secured from the **LIST** command. The crosshairs will rotate along the line. Turn on your **ORTHO** options with Ctrl-O or F8. You can now continue the line along the current crosshairs. When you've finished extending the line, reissue the **SNAP ROTATE** command and set the angle back to 0. This will return the grid to normal. See LISP49 in Tip 12.22.

More Steps to Success

1.21 **Changing the shape of points**

The system variable **PMODE** lets you change the shape of a simple point.

When accompanied with variations in **PDSIZE**, points are tempting to use as standard symbols. The problem with this is that you then can't use points as points, since every point in your drawing will change to the same shape.

Therefore, if you need certain shapes as standard symbols, draw and write them out as blocks, inserting them when needed.

1.22 **Temporary change in units**

Sometimes you need to indicate angles in a format different from the one initially set up by the **UNITS** command. For example, civil engineers who've set up their units as surveying units (bearings) find it very inconvenient to use bearings to measure ordinary angles, such as those in text.

Regardless of what your angle units are set to, they can be overridden. When **angles** are requested, enter the prefix **<<** before you enter the angle. This tells AutoCAD to treat the angle < as decimal. Therefore, <<180 is the equivalent of West, or 9 o'clock.

1.23 **Drawing specific line lengths**

One of the easiest ways to draw a line (or any other entity) a specific length is to turn your coordinates on with Ctrl-D or F6. Then set your snap to a multiple of the distance you wish to draw. When you pick a point for a line, center of circle, etc., the coordinates are then reset to 0. Now the coordinates will show on the screen exactly how far your cursor has moved.

1.24 **TRACE replaced**

Never use the **TRACE** command; it's left over from an earlier version of AutoCAD. For all practical purposes, it's been totally replaced by the **PLINE** command. (If you must use **TRACE**, see Tip 1.16.)

1.25 **Solids can be tricky**

The **SOLID** command lets you draw any polygon shape with a solid fill. The problem with the **SOLID** command is the order in which each side is drawn. If you do it incorrectly, you'll get a bow-tie effect. See Figures 1-21 and 1-22 for the correct way to draw a four-sided solid.

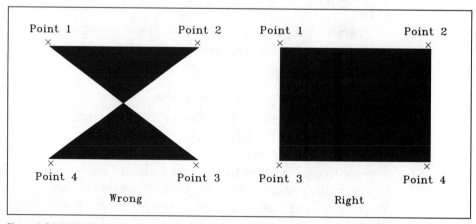

Figure 1-21 (left): Wrong way to draw a solid   Figure 1-22 (right): Right way to draw a solid

1.26 **Last point**

Whenever you're asked for a point, you can indicate the last point simply by typing an @ sign, followed by the space bar or <RETURN>.

1.27 **Offset single entities**

If you're drawing a floor plan and want to include parallel lines, use the **OFFSET** command. Before doing so, turn the lines you wish to offset into a single polyline. Then the lines will offset perfectly, and you won't have any corner cleanup to do.

To convert lines into polylines, issue the **PEDIT** command and pick the line you want to convert. If it's not already a polyline, you'll be asked if you want to turn it into one. When you answer Y, the line will be turned into a polyline. You now must join the line to other lines in the floor plan.

Choose the **Join** subcommand. Now touch each of the lines you want to join together. As long as each of the lines or entities is contiguous, they'll be joined as a single polyline, even if they weren't a polyline to begin with.

Now you can issue the **OFFSET** command.

RELEASE 12   Lets you create multiple offsets using *Grips*, small squares that appear at certain definition points of an object. Grips can be activated through the DDGRIPS dialogue box. See Tips 20.38, 20.39 and 20.41.

1.28 **Problems with SKETCH**

There can be severe problems with the **SKETCH** command; one is its use in freehand drawing. The problem is that **SKETCH** can produce literally thousands of individual entities, which overload the drawing file and make regenerations far too slow. The general rule with **SKETCH**: Try not to use it.

1.29 **A smooth trick**

There's one trick you *can* do with the **SKETCH** command. If you want a very smooth, curved line, use the **SKETCH** command to outline the curved surface. This will produce more vertices than you'd ever want to produce manually. When you're through, convert the **SKETCH** entities into a single polyline with the **PEDIT** command, converting the first entity into a polyline and then joining the rest by windowing the curve. Once the lines are converted and joined, you can use **SPLINE** or **FIT CURVE** to round them out. All of this is done while you're still in **PEDIT**.

CAUTION: Use **SKETCH** very sparingly.

1.30 **Why use the grid?**

Many people draw in AutoCAD without using the grid. Although there's no real problem with this, be aware that the grid is more than just dots on the screen used in conjunction with **SNAP**. The grid is a representation of the drawing limits.

The problem most users run into is that they forget to set their drawing limits with the **LIMITS** command. Many AutoLISP programs rely on system variables to tell them the size of the drawing area—the limits. If the limits aren't correctly set, these AutoLISP programs won't work.

1.31 **Too many arcs**

The **ARC** command is generally overused. **ARC** has specific uses: to construct well-defined arcs with specified radii, for example. But there are better ways to define smooth, curved areas. **FILLET** is often a better solution than **ARC**, especially when the element you're connecting must be tangent to two lines. The other method is to use **PLINE**, then either curve-fit the vertices with **PEDIT** or use **SPLINE**.

1.32 **Layers make construction lines a snap!**

One mistake a beginning user makes is to work out solutions without drawing construction lines. An AutoCAD construction line is drawn so that it creates an entity to which you can object snap. Construction lines don't always have to be lines; they can be circles, arcs, fillets, etc.

The problem with construction lines is that they need to be erased when you're through with them. But sometimes the area can become so crowded, you can't tell which are the regular lines and which are the construction lines. The best solution is to draw all of your construction lines on a special layer designed for them. Then, when you're through, you can erase the entire layer. See LISP45 and LISP46 in Tips 11.30 and 11.31.

AutoLISP Programs

1.33 **Line closing (LISP1)**

This simple little program draws a line between the endpoints of two lines.
It can be used as a closing routine.

Listing:
```
(defun c:lisp1 (/ os pt1 pt2)
    (setq os (getvar "osmode"))
    (setvar "osmode" 33)
    (setq pt1 (getpoint "\nPick first line "))
    (setq pt2 (getpoint "\nPick second line "))
    (command "line" pt1 pt2 "")
    (setvar "osmode" os)
)
```

To Use: Load LISP1.LSP.

Start with an unclosed group of lines as in Figure 1-23.

Figure 1-23: Closing a
group of lines

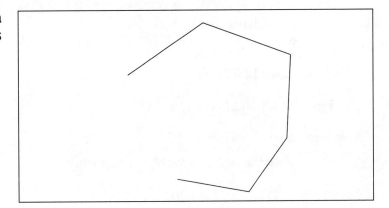

Type: `LISP1 <RETURN>`

Response: `Pick first line:`

Pick the line at about point 1. It doesn't have to be on the endpoint.

Response: `Pick second line:`

Pick the second line at about point 2. The endpoints will be connected.

1.34 Make a line longer (LISP2)

This program will lengthen a line in the same direction and at the same angle. The program doesn't attach an additional line, but maintains the original line as a single, longer entity.

Listing:
```
(defun c:lisp2 (/ ent pt1 a dis pt2 ent1)
    (setq ent (entget (car (entsel))))
    (setq pt1 (cdr (assoc 11 ent)))
    (setq a (angle (cdr (assoc 10 ent)) (cdr (assoc 11 ent))))
    (setq dis (getdist "\nAdditional length "))
    (setq pt2 (polar pt1 a dis))
    (setq ent1 (subst (cons 11 pt2) (assoc 11 ent) ent))
    (entmod ent1)
)
```

To Use: Load LISP2.LSP.

Type: `LISP2 <RETURN>`

Response: `Select objects:`

Pick the line you want to lengthen.

Response: `Additional length:`

Type: `3 <RETURN>`

The line will be lengthened by three units.

1.35 **Single-letter commands (LISP3)**

The following program is an example of how you can use AutoLISP to create a series of one- or two-letter commands for the most commonly used AutoCAD commands. It beats commercial keyboard redirectors—it's free and uses no memory.

Listing:
```
(defun c:l ()
    (command "line")
)
```

To Use: Load LISP3.LSP.

Now any time you want to use the **LINE** command, all you have to do is type L and press the space bar or <RETURN>. Each of your most commonly used AutoCAD commands should be set up as single- or double-letter commands; by using AutoLISP, you won't have to use Ctrl or Alt keys.

1.36 **Polygon entities (LISP4)**

The problem with the **POLYGON** command is that it creates a single entity. There are times when you'd like to create a polygon easily but be able to edit any single side. This program draws a polygon, then explodes it, leaving you with the individual lines.

Listing:
```
(defun c:lisp4 ()
    (command "polygon" pause pause pause pause)
    (command "explode" "l")
)
```

To Use: Load LISP4.LSP.

Type: `LISP4 <RETURN>`

The program works exactly like the **POLYGON** command.

1.37 **Exact lines (LISP5)**

This program is a shortcut for drawing lines a specific distance. Pick a start point and either point in the direction you want the line to go, or key in the angle. Then tell AutoCAD how long you want the line to be. You can keep doing this until you press <RETURN> twice.

(Use of the plus sign at the end of a line in AutoLISP code indicates that line is wrapped.)

Listing:
```
(defun c:lisp5 (/ r pt1 a dis pt3)
   (setq r 5)
   (setq pt1 (getpoint "\nBeginning point "))
   (while r
      (setq a (getangle pt1 "\nPick point in direction of +
        line or enter angle "))
      (setq dis (getdist "\nEnter distance "))
      (setq pt3 (polar pt1 a dis))
      (command "line" pt1 pt3 "")
      (setq pt1 pt3)
   )
)
```

To Use: Load LISP5.LSP.

Type: LISP5 <RETURN>

Response: Beginning point:

Pick the beginning point of the line.

Response: Pick point in direction of line or enter angle:

You can enter the angle from the keyboard or pick a point in the direction you want the line to go.

Response: Enter distance:

Enter the distance from the keyboard. The program will loop around and ask you to pick a point in the direction of the line. Press <RETURN> twice, and the program will terminate.

CHAPTER 2

Basic Editing

How Do You . . .

2.1 How do you select objects?

Any time you select objects, you're creating a selection set. The items in this set are highlighted with dots as they're selected. Then you confirm the selection set by pressing the space bar, <RETURN> or (generally) the second button on your digitizer puck or mouse.

There are four basic selection techniques:

1. Simply pick the entity. Initially, a small pick box is set at your crosshairs when you're to select objects.

2. Type W to begin a window. Pick a corner and then move your cursor across the screen. Any entity that's 100 percent inside the window will be selected.

3. Type C to begin a crossing (this also is a type of window). The difference between a window and a crossing is that the entity doesn't have to be completely inside the window to be selected. In a crossing, the entity simply has to touch or "cross" the window to be selected.

4. Type L to select the very last entity drawn.

RELEASE 12   With **DDSELECT**, a new **Entity Selection** dialogue box, you don't have to use W or C. Simply pick a space, then move from left to right to create a window. See Tips 20.6 and 20.7 regarding selection set options. Tips 20.62 through 20.67 give additional information on the same subject.

2.2 How do you add and remove entities from the selection set?

It's useful to select a whole group of entities with a window or crossing. But, unfortunately, you often catch too many entities. The commands **ADD** and **REMOVE** let you add or subtract from the selection set; simply type A or R during the selection routine.

When you type R, any entities you select are removed from the selection set and are no longer highlighted. You remain in this **Remove** mode until you type **A** for **Add Mode**. Incidentally, when you begin selecting objects after changing to **Add Mode**, you're adding them to the selection set.

It's easy to become confused and think that **Remove** erases an object. If you use **Remove** while erasing objects, they're removed from the selection set, but they're not erased.

2.3 How do you select a group of entities that have already been selected?

If you've already selected a selection set and need to select the same set again, AutoCAD provides an easy way to do it. When you're asked to select objects, type P for **Previous**. The entire previous selection set will be chosen. You can still add or remove objects, or use any other selection set procedure until you confirm all of the selections.

Unfortunately, AutoCAD provides for only one previous selection set. See LISP56 in Tip 12.29 for a way to set up multiple selection sets.

2.4 How do you unerase an erased object?

The easiest and most effective way to unerase an erased object is with the **OOPS** command. **OOPS** will bring back the most recently erased selection set. Note that **OOPS** brings back the entire selection set, not just the last entity erased. Also, **OOPS** brings back only the last group that was erased; if you want to step back and unerase more, **OOPS** won't work.

You can get back other erased objects, but you run the risk of changing other aspects of your drawing. If you need to unerase more than one selection set of entities, try the **UNDO** command. The only problem with this is that it will undo the last commands as far back as you want to go. If in each case the last command was **ERASE**, that's fine. But there might be commands in between the **ERASE** commands that you wanted to save. So you lose either your erased items or the other commands between them.

2.5 **How do you copy objects?**

Copying objects is a simple operation—use the **COPY** command. When you first start the **COPY** command, you must select objects. Once these objects are selected and confirmed, you must choose a base point (the point on the object from which you will drag or move it). The base point doesn't have to be on the object, but it's generally best if it is. Then it's a simple operation to point to where you want the object placed, as you can see in Figures 2-1 and 2-2.

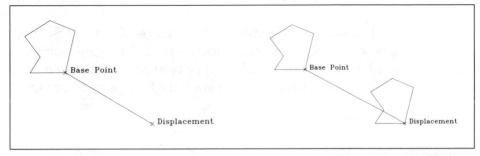

Figure 2-1 (left): Pick an object to copy   Figure 2-2 (right): New point of placement

Type: COPY <RETURN>

Response: Select objects:

Select the objects to be copied, and confirm.

Response: <Base point or displacement>/Multiple:

Pick a place on the object to be copied.

Response: Second point of displacement:

Point and pick where you'd like the object to be moved.

RELEASE 12   You can now copy using Grips, a new tool activated through the **DDGRIPS** dialogue box. See Tips 20.38, 20.39 and 20.41.

2.6 **How do you move objects?**

Basically, a move is the same as a copy, but the initial object copied is erased, thus giving the appearance of a move. The sequence is essentially the same; see Figures 2-3 and 2-4.

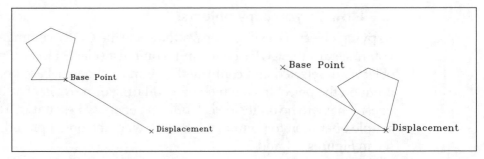

Figure 2-3 (left): Pick an object to move   Figure 2-4 (right): Move object to new point

Use the **MOVE** command. Select objects. Once these objects are selected and confirmed, you must choose a base point—the point from which you will drag or move the object. The base point doesn't have to be on the object. Now pick where you want the base point to be moved.

Type: MOVE <RETURN>

Response: Select objects:

Select the objects to be moved, and confirm.

Response: Base point or displacement:

Pick a place on the object.

Response: Second point of displacement:

Point and pick the place to which you want to move the object.

RELEASE 12   Lets you move by using Grips, a new tool activated through the **DDGRIPS** dialogue box. See Tips 20.40 and 20.41.

2.7 **How do you rotate an object?**

The **ROTATE** command begins like the **COPY** and **MOVE** commands. First, select the objects you want to rotate. Once these objects are selected and confirmed, you must choose a base point—the point around which the object will be rotated. You can now drag the rotation or type in the degree of rotation.

If you choose a point that's not on the object as the base point, it becomes the center of the circle around which the objects will be rotated. See Figures 2-5 and 2-6.

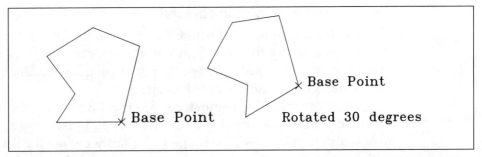

Figure 2-5 (left): Pick base point   Figure 2-6 (right): Rotate object

There's one additional option when you're asked for the angle of rotation. If an object were already rotated 45 degrees from the grid and you wanted it to be 30 degrees, you could use the **Reference** option. When you're asked for the angle of rotation, type R. You're then asked for the reference angle (this is the old angle). Next you're asked for the new angle. This is the absolute angle you want rotated from the grid (the X axis). The effect of giving the reference angle is that every angle that was referenced as the old angle becomes the new angle.

The **ROTATE** command lets you rotate the object only in an X, Y direction. If you need to rotate the object in any other direction, such as Z, see Tip 27.3.

Type: ROTATE <RETURN>

Response: Select objects:

Select the object you want to rotate.

Response: Base point:

Pick a point (generally on the object).

Response: <Rotation angle>/Reference:

Either point and pick an angle, or type in the angle.

12   RELEASE 12   Lets you rotate by Grips, a new tool activated through the **DDGRIPS** dialogue box. See Tip 20.42.

2.8 How do you mirror objects?

The **MIRROR** command in AutoCAD is actually a flip command, which means you can do a lot more than simply mirror an object. Flipping or mirroring an object means you're simply turning it over. But **MIRROR** lets you actually rotate the object as it's mirrored.

As with other editing commands, you must first select the object to be mirrored. Once it's selected and confirmed, you must draw a straight line over which the object will be flipped. The farther away the line is from the initial object, the farther it's flipped toward the other side of the line. The distance between the two objects is twice the distance from the object to the mirror line (see Figure 2-7).

Figure 2-7:
Mirrored objects

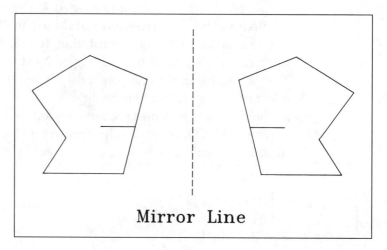

Mirror Line

You then have the option of deleting the old object. If you enter No, the original object and the mirrored object wind up right next to each other— the "butterfly" effect.

Type: MIRROR <RETURN>

Response: Select objects:

Select the object to be mirrored.

Response: First point of mirror line:

With **ORTHO** on, pick the first point of the mirror line across which you want the object to be flipped.

Response: Second point:

Pick the second point of the mirror line.

Response: Delete old objects? <N>

Answer Y or N.

 RELEASE 12   Lets you mirror by using Grips, a new tool activated through the **DDGRIPS** dialogue box. See Tip 20.44.

2.9 How do you remove part of a line?

By definition, an entity is a single unit. Therefore, a line is a single entity with beginning and ending X, Y, Z coordinates. If you want to remove part of an entity, you're really breaking it into two entities. To do this, AutoCAD uses the **BREAK** command.

Although **BREAK** seems relatively simple, it has some interesting variations. The simplest way to use the **BREAK** command is to point to two points along the entity. The entity will then be broken and the section between the two points will be removed.

But it's often not as simple as picking two points along a line. Sometimes AutoCAD can't tell which line is to be broken. For instance, if you want to break one of two intersecting lines at a point on one of the lines, you must first tell AutoCAD which line is to be broken. Therefore, to begin the **BREAK** command, first point to the line to be broken. Make sure you pick a point where there's no confusion as to which line you're picking; it doesn't have to be exactly where you want the break.

After the first point is picked to show AutoCAD the entity, you must tell it that the next point is going to be the first point of the **BREAK**. You do this by typing F. Now pick the two points, and the break will occur.

Finally, remember that most AutoCAD commands operate counterclockwise. So if you're breaking a circle or arc, the break will go from the first to the second point in a counterclockwise direction. See Figures 2-8 and 2-9.

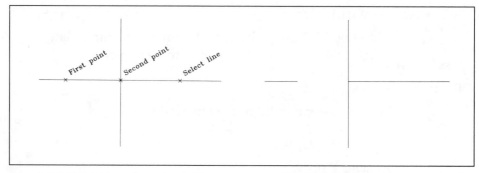

Figure 2-8 (left): Selecting points to break a line   Figure 2-9 (right): Breaking a space in a line

Type: BREAK <RETURN>

Response: Select objects:

Pick a place on the object where it's obvious which object you want to break.

Response: Enter second point (or F for first point):

Type: F <RETURN>

Response: Enter first point:

Pick the first break point.

Response: Enter second point:

Pick the second break point.

If you're using the tablet menu for the **BREAK** command, it will skip the questions. Simply pick the object and confirm, then pick two points. You don't need to specify F for the first point.

2.10 How do you divide one entity into two?

This is also done with the **BREAK** command. But instead of removing a section of the entity, all you're doing is breaking an entity into two pieces without actually separating them.

Begin the **BREAK** command as you normally would. Point to the entity that's to be broken. Now, instead of typing F for the first point of the break, type @. Pick the point where the separation is to take place. The entity is now broken in two.

Type: BREAK <RETURN>

Response: Select objects:

Select the object you want to divide, at the point you want to break it.

Response: Enter second point (or F for first point):

Type: @@ <RETURN>

2.11 **How do you change the width of a line?**

The only type of entity that can have width is a polyline. Therefore, if you want to change the width of a line, use the **PEDIT** command, even if the line you want to change isn't a polyline. If this is the case, AutoCAD will tell you that the line isn't a polyline and ask you if you want to change it into one. If you answer Y, it will become a polyline.

The option now available is width. Type W, and you'll be asked for the new width of all segments of the polyline. All segments of the polyline must have the same width when you use the **PEDIT** command.

Type: PEDIT <RETURN>

Response: Select polyline:

Pick a polyline.

Response: Close/Join/Width/Edit vertex/Fit curve/Spline curve/Decurve →
/Undo/eXit <X>:

Type: W <RETURN>

Response: Enter new width for all segments:

Type in the new width. All segments will be changed. Press <RETURN> to exit the **PEDIT** routine.

2.12 **How do you separate a group of polylines into separate lines?**

A polyline is like other lines, but it has unique features. Most editing options available for regular lines are also available for polylines. Instead of using **PEDIT**, the easiest way is to use the **BREAK @** command. What you're going to do, in essence, is to break the polyline in the middle, thus producing two lines. Of course, you could also use **BREAK** in its normal way and put an actual space between the lines.

Type: `BREAK <RETURN>`

Response: `Select objects:`

Pick the object you want to break, at the point you want to break it.

Response: `Enter second point (or F for first point):`

Type: `@@ <RETURN>`

Of course, you can always explode a polyline, which will separate it into its individual line segments. But be aware that once exploded, these segments are no longer polylines.

2.13 **How do you round corners?**

Round corners with the **FILLET** command, not the **ARC** command.

It's a simple procedure. Start with a rectangle, as shown in Figure 2-10.

Figure 2-10: Rectangle before FILLET

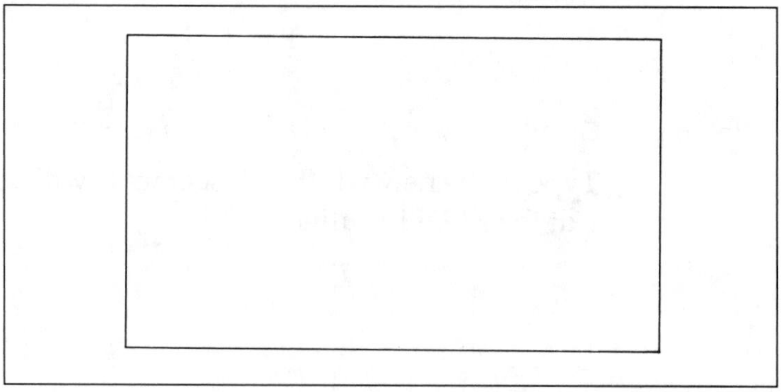

Issue the **FILLET** command and choose R for radius. Then enter the radius for the rounded corner. You'll be returned to the Command line. If you press the space bar or <RETURN>, the command will be repeated. Then pick each of the two lines that form the corners. They'll now be filleted as in Figure 2-11.

Figure 2-11: Use FILLET
with radius

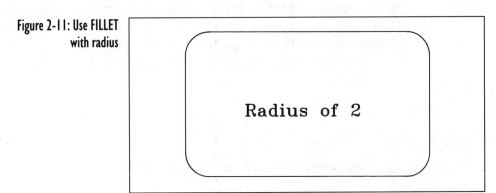

FILLET maintains the radius for that drawing until the radius is changed. Therefore, if you want to fillet multiple corners, just continue with the command and pick pairs of lines. Conversely, if the radius is 0, you can make lines extend to their intersection by picking two nonparallel lines. Therefore, if you want to re-intersect these lines while maintaining the filleted arc, use the **FILLET** command with a radius of 0 and pick the same two lines. Be very careful not to touch the filleted arc, as it's now a separate entity. The two lines will now be rejoined as before. See Figure 2-12.

Figure 2-12: FILLET
radius of 0

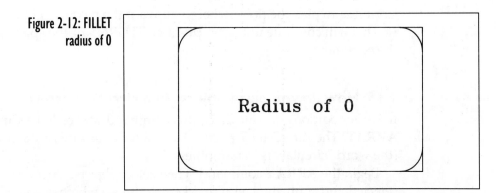

2.14 How do you make multiple copies of an object?

Of course, to make a single copy of an object, you use the **COPY** command. You're asked to select objects, and once the objects are selected and
confirmed you're given the choice of base point or multiple. The default is
generally **base point**, and you pick a point on the object before moving it.
But by entering M for multiple instead, you turn the multiple mode on.
The command continues by asking you for the base point, then the displacement. From then on, continue picking points where you want to place
the object, and pick as many points as necessary. End with <RETURN> or
the space bar.

Type: `COPY <RETURN>`

Response: `Select objects:`

Select the objects you want to copy, and confirm.

Response: `<Base point or displacement>/Multiple:`

Type: `M <RETURN>`

Response: `Base point:`

Pick any point (generally on the object to be copied).

Response: `Second point:`

Pick the point where you want the base point of the object placed.

Response: `Second point:`

Continue to pick the point where you want the next object placed.
    This will continue until you press <RETURN> or the space bar to end
the command.

2.15 How do you place objects in a circular pattern?

In earlier editions of AutoCAD, this command was called a **Circular
ARRAY**. The *AutoCAD Reference Manual* now calls this a **Polar ARRAY**
(the word "circular" is in parentheses).
    Begin the **ARRAY** command. Then select objects. Once the objects are
selected and confirmed, you're asked to choose whether you want a
rectangular or polar array. Choose P for polar. Then choose the center
point of the array. Pick a point that will be the center around which you
want the array to go.

Next, you're asked three questions: 1) the number of items in the array, 2) the angle to fill, and 3) the angle between items in the array. You must answer any two of these items. Look at the first question—the number of items in the array. AutoCAD wants to know how many items you'll have when the array is finished (this includes the one you're copying). If you don't want to answer this question, press <RETURN> or the space bar.

The next question is the angle to fill—this means how far around the circle you want the object to go. If you put in a positive number, it will go counterclockwise. If you enter a negative number, it will go clockwise. If you press <RETURN>, it defaults to 360 degrees. AutoCAD knows the distance necessary to fill 360 degrees with the number of items in the array. If you don't want to answer this question, enter 0 as the angle to fill.

The third question is the angle between items in the array. If you put in the angle as a positive number, the array will go counterclockwise. A negative number will produce a clockwise array.

AutoCAD measures the distance of the array from its center point to an arbitrary reference point, predetermined by the entity construction.

The final option is whether to rotate the objects as they're copied. This is a Yes or No question. See Figures 2-13 and 2-14.

Figure 2-13 (left): Pick center point for circular array

Figure 2-14 (right): Finished circular array

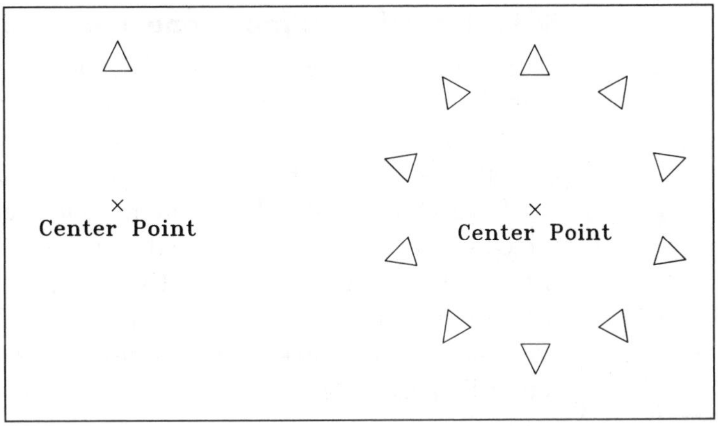

Type: ARRAY <RETURN>

Response: Select objects:

Pick the objects that you want copied, and confirm.

Response: Rectangular or Polar array (R/P):

Type: P <RETURN>

Response: Center point of array:

Pick the center point around which you want the array rotated.

Response: Number of items:

Type: 10 <RETURN>

Response: Angle to fill (+=ccw, -=cw) <360>:

Type: <RETURN>

Response: Rotate objects as they are copied? <Y>

Type: <RETURN>

Ten objects are now rotated around the selected center point.

 RELEASE 12   Lets you copy by using Grips, a new tool activated through the **DDGRIPS** dialogue box. See Tip 20.38.

2.16 **How do you move one point of a line?**

This procedure uses the **CHANGE** command. Although this procedure is simple, **CHANGE** is a powerful and sometimes complicated command, especially if you're working with 3D objects. In fact, if you're working with 3D entities, it's better to use **CHPROP** instead.

To use the **CHANGE** command as in Figures 2-15 and 2-16, select objects and confirm. You have the option to change point or properties. Most of the things you'll want to change are probably parts of properties, but unfortunately the default is **change point**. Since this is the default, all you have to do is pick the new point of the entity. To change properties, enter P <RETURN>.

Figure 2-15: Line before moving one point

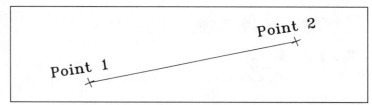

Figure 2-16: Line with new change point

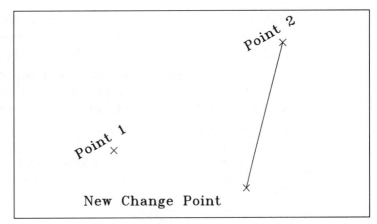

The point that's actually changed depends on the type of entity involved. If it's a line, the point that's changed is the closest point to the new point. If it's a circle, the radius is changed, since the center point of the circle remained constant. If it's text, the point that is changed is the text's location point. A block, of course, is the insertion point.

Type: `CHANGE <RETURN>`

Response: `Select objects:`

Pick the object(s) you want changed, and confirm.

Response: `Properties/<Change point>:`

Now pick the new change point.

 RELEASE 12   Lets you move one point of a line using Grips, a new tool activated through the **DDGRIPS** dialogue box. See Tips 20.40 and 20.41.

2.17 How do you smooth out a line around given points?

There are three basic ways to make curves. One is with the **ARC** command, the second is with **FILLET**. But probably the most common way to make irregular curves is with polylines. Using the **PLINE** command, pick as many points as possible around the area in the direction in which you'd like the curve to go. Now you'll have a series of lines connecting the points. Of course, AutoCAD treats the polylines as one entity.

Now use **PEDIT**, which will ask you to pick a polyline. Pick the polyline you just drew. Of **PEDIT**'s several options, **Fit curve** and **Spline curve** are the two that will smooth out a curve connecting the vertices of a polyline. The difference between **Fit curve** and **Spline curve** is that **Fit curve** produces a curve that touches each vertex of the polyline. The **Spline curve** doesn't have to touch each vertex, but must simply approach or approximate them; so **Spline curve** will generally give you a much smoother curve.

To reverse the curve, use the **DECURVE** command, which returns it to the individual vertices and lines of the polyline. See Figures 2-17 and 2-18.

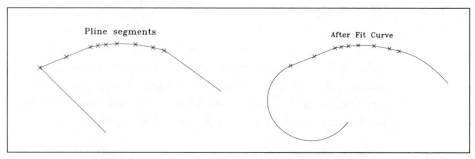

Figure 2-17 (left): PLINE vertices   Figure 2-18 (right): Fit curve

Type: PEDIT <RETURN>

Response: Select polyline:

Pick a polyline.

Response: Close/Join/Width/Edit vertex/Fit curve/Spline curve/Decurve →
               /Undo/eXit <X>:

Type: F <RETURN>

The curve will now be formed. Press <RETURN> to exit the **PEDIT** command.

2.18 How do you join two lines into a single entity?

First let's assume that the two lines or groups of lines aren't polylines but ordinary entities such as lines or arcs. Use the **PEDIT** command. When you're asked to select a polyline, pick one of the entities you want to join. **PEDIT** then tells you that the entity isn't a polyline, and asks if you want to change it into one. Answer Yes.

You'll receive the standard options for editing polylines. One of these options is **Join**. When you choose **Join**, it will ask you to select objects. You can pick the objects individually or put a window or crossing around the objects you want joined. If there's a break anywhere in the group of objects, they won't be joined.

Type: `PEDIT <RETURN>`

Response: `Select polyline:`

Pick an entity.

Response: `Entity selected is not a polyline. Do you want it to turn into one?`

Type: `Y <RETURN>`

Response: `Close/Join/Width/Edit vertex/Fit curve/Spline curve/Decurve →`
`/Undo/eXit <X>:`

Type: `J <RETURN>`

Response: `Select objects:`

Choose by windowing or crossing all the entities you want joined, and confirm. Press <RETURN> or the space bar to exit the **PEDIT** routine.

2.19 How do you make objects larger or smaller?

You can change the size of objects with the **SCALE** command. First, you're asked to select the object you want to scale. Next, choose a base point, which may be any place on the object. Now choose either a scale factor or a reference. If you choose a scale factor, the size of all the entities will be multiplied by this factor. If you want the entities made smaller, use a factor of less than 1, such as .5, to make the entity half-size. See Figure 2-19.

Figure 2-19: Scaling

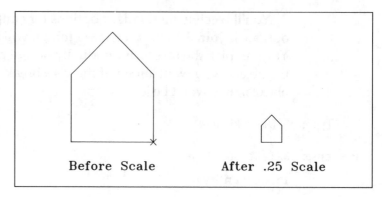

Before Scale   After .25 Scale

The **Reference** option is the most interesting one. If you choose **Reference**, you may give it any length, followed by a new length.

For example, if you wanted to enlarge an object 300 percent, you'd enter 3 for the scale factor. But what if you wanted to change the size by a ratio of 2.79 to 4.0? Well, with a good calculator you can do it. But the **Reference** option makes it much easier. Your reference length would be the old length of 2.79. The new length would be 4. AutoCAD would then automatically adjust the scale factor. Note that nothing in the drawing needs to actually be 2.79 in length; that's only a reference.

Remember that **SCALE** physically and permanently changes the size of objects, so it's a good command to use when you want multiple objects on a single sheet drawn at different scales. On the other hand, if you just want to plot your drawing out at a different scale, it's better to use the **Scale** option in the **PLOT** command.

Type: `SCALE <RETURN>`

Response: `Select objects:`

Select the objects you want to scale.

Response: `Base point:`

Pick any point on the object.

Response: `<Scale factor>/Reference:`

Type: `.25 <RETURN>`

The objects are now scaled to one-quarter of their original size.

RELEASE 12   Lets you scale by using Grips, a new tool activated through the **DDGRIPS** dialogue box. See Tip 20.43.

2.20 How do you use the STRETCH command correctly?

This has to be one of the most confusing commands in AutoCAD, but it can be one of the most useful when you use it correctly. **STRETCH** is the only command in AutoCAD that doesn't actually act on all of the points of the entities selected by using **CROSSING**. It does require you to put a crossing around the entity or part of the entity you want to stretch. Remember that **STRETCH** simply moves certain points of an entity while maintaining the connections.

The prompts for the **STRETCH** command are simple. Just remember that when it asks you to select objects, you must use a crossing to select the objects. The next prompts are for base point and new point. When these are picked, the entities are stretched from the base point to the new point.

The key to understanding **STRETCH** is that only the points captured in the window, not the entire entity, will be moved. So even though you use the **CROSSING** command, and the entire entity isn't completely inside the window, the entity points that are captured will be moved and the entity will be stretched to the location of the new points. Look at the examples in Figures 2-20 and 2-21.

Figure 2-20: Object to be stretched

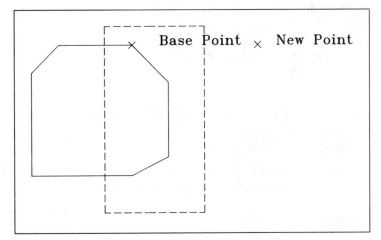

Figure 2-21: Right way to stretch an object

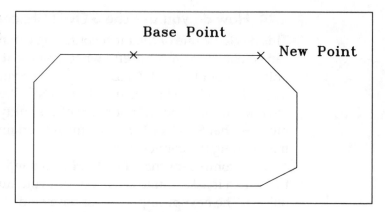

This shows a floor plan with other entities. Notice that when we put a crossing around it, the window doesn't actually include the other entities. Therefore, when the base point and new points are selected, the room is enlarged.

Type: STRETCH <RETURN>

Response: Select objects to stretch by window
...Select objects:

Type: C <RETURN> (Window by crossing)

Response: First corner:

Pick the first corner of the window.

Response: Second corner:

Complete the window, and confirm. Make sure that the window encompasses the points you want to use.

Response: Base point:

Pick a point.

Response: New point:

Pick the point to which you want the entities stretched.

One final rule: Remember that **STRETCH** operates only on the points of the entities that were in the window or crossing selected—and that it's these points that will be moved, not the entities themselves.

STRETCH maintains the original connections to the other entities that were not moved.

RELEASE 12   Lets you stretch by using Grips, a new tool activated through the **DDGRIPS** dialogue box. See Tips 20.34 and 20.37.

2.21 How do you know which way objects will go with a rectangular array?

The answer to this is easy once you learn the rules. When using rectangular arrays, you're asked two basic groups of questions—the number of rows and columns, and the distance between the rows and columns. Think of the object to be replicated as being the corner. If you enter a positive number for the distance between the rows, the number of rows replicated will go up. If you enter a positive number for the distance between the columns, the columns will go to the right. You can reverse either of these directions by entering a negative number.

Assume you want an object to be arrayed three columns to the right and four rows down.

Type: `ARRAY <RETURN>`

Response: `Select objects:`

Pick the object you want to array.

Response: `Rectangular or Polar array (R/P):`

Type: `REC <RETURN>`

Response: `Number of rows (---) <1>:`

Type: `4 <RETURN>`

Response: `Number of columns (|||) <1>:`

Type: `3 <RETURN>`

Response: `Unit cell or distance between rows (---):`

Type: `-5 <RETURN>`

Response: `Distance between columns (|||):`

Type: `5 <RETURN>`

Since the rows were entered as a negative number, they'll be replicated downward. The columns were entered as a positive number and will be replicated to the right, as in Figure 2-22.

Figure 2-22:
Rectangular array

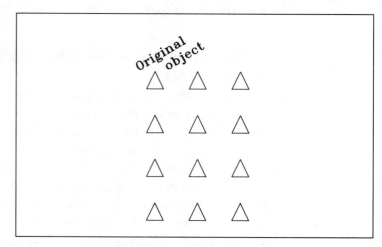

2.22 How do you move an entity to another layer?

You change an entity's layer with the **CHANGE** command, using the **Properties** option. One option within **Properties** is **Layer**, which asks you for the new layer. When you enter the layer name and confirm, entities are changed to the new layer.

One confusing fact about this is that you generally expect entities to change color when moved to another layer. This may or may not occur, depending on whether an entity was originally drawn with its color by layer or by entity. If the entity color didn't change, you can use the same **CHANGE** command with **Properties** and change the color. Then the command asks you for the color. Type in **BYLAYER,** and the entity will change to the color of that layer.

Type: CHANGE <RETURN>

Response: Select objects:

Select the object or objects you want changed.

Response: Properties/<Change point>:

Type: P <RETURN>

Response: Change what property (Color/Elev/LAyer/LType/Thickness)?

Type: LA <RETURN>

Response: New layer:

Type: LAYER-3 <RETURN>

Type: <RETURN> (This terminates the CHANGE command.)

2.23 How do you use CHAMFER?

A **CHAMFER** is similar to a **FILLET** except that a **CHAMFER** draws a straight line connecting two lines, instead of drawing a curve.

As with the **FILLET** command, it's wise to set the distance before the command is issued.

The first time you use **CHAMFER**, enter D for distance. This lets you set the first and second **CHAMFER** distances. For example, in Figure 2-23 the first distance is labeled distance A and the second is labeled distance B.

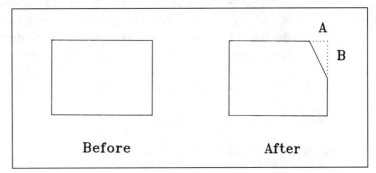

Figure 2-23:
Using CHAMFER

Before   After

You can reenter the **CHAMFER** command by repeating the last command.

Pick the first and second line, and the corners will be properly trimmed. The previous distances selected remain the default.

Type: CHAMFER <RETURN>

Response: Polyline/Distances/<Select first line>:

Type: `D <RETURN>`

Response: `Enter first chamfer distance:`

Type: `2 <RETURN>`

Response: `Enter second chamfer distance:`

Type: `4 <RETURN>`

Type: `<RETURN>` (This repeats the CHAMFER command.)

Response: `Polyline/Distances/<Select first line>:`
Pick the first line.

Response: `Select second line:`
Pick the second line.

2.24 How do you FILLET a polyline?

If you're working with a closed polyline entity, the **FILLET** command has a shortcut that lets you fillet an entire polyline at once. Assuming that you've already selected the radius, type P for polyline when you're asked to select two objects. All vertices of the closed polyline will be filleted; if they aren't, it's probably because the polyline wasn't closed.

Type: `FILLET <RETURN>`

Response: `Polyline/Radius/<Select two objects>:`

Type: `P <RETURN>`

Response: `Select 2D polyline:`
Pick the polyline.

2.25 How do you CHAMFER a polyline?

Chamfering a polyline is the same as filleting a polyline. When you're asked to select two lines, enter P for polyline.

Type: `CHAMFER <RETURN>`

Response: `Polyline/Distances/<Select first line>:`

Type: P <RETURN>

Response: Select 2D polyline:

Pick the polyline.

More Steps to Success

2.26 Use TRIM or FILLET to clean corners

Although you can use **BREAK** to clean up corners and break lines from intersections to the end of the line, it's often easier and quicker to use **TRIM** and **FILLET** with the fillet radius set to 0.

2.27 Automatic erasing

When you select objects, you usually confirm with a <RETURN>. This gives you a chance to add and remove entities from the selection set. But it's possible to use specialized commands that let you just pick an object and have it selected immediately.

These special commands work only within menu commands. Look at this example, which would be part of your menu:

```
^c^cerase single auto
```

The phrase "single auto" after a command gives you special selection options. The moment any entity is selected, it's automatically confirmed; if you simply pick an entity, it's erased immediately.

If you point to a blank space on the screen and move the cursor to the right, it automatically starts a window. If you move to the left, it automatically starts a crossing. When the window or crossing is terminated, everything captured there is selected immediately. AutoCAD uses this feature with the **ERASE** command in the pull-down menus.

2.28 Setting commands to automatically repeat

AutoCAD lets you set up an automatic repeat of a command, including the options you chose with it. For example, let's say you wanted to have the **ARC** command specified as center, start, angle. You could place the command in a menu structure and repeat it by pressing <RETURN> or the space bar. But that method would only repeat the generic **ARC** command.

If you place an asterisk (*) in front of **ARC C**, the command will be repeated at the command line until it's terminated by a Ctrl-C. As with "single auto" in Tip 2.27 above, this works only as part of your menu.

2.29 **OOPS versus UNDO**

Because the **OOPS** command unerases only the last erased group of entities, you may want to use **UNDO** instead. This is generally a mistake unless it's absolutely necessary; and you should definitely not use **UNDO** on a routine basis. Even though **UNDO** will bring back a group of entities that were inadvertently erased, it undoes absolutely everything, step by step. **OOPS** works only on the last erased group of entities, so try it first.

2.30 **BREAKing to the end of a line or arc**

There are several commands for breaking to the end of a line, but if you use the **BREAK** command, you don't need to be really careful where you place the second point. After you've chosen the first point, pick any place past the end of the line where there are no entities. The rest of the line will be erased.

2.31 **COPY or MOVE using relative displacement**

As a shortcut when using the **COPY** or **MOVE** commands, you have the option of using a relative displacement rather than giving a base point and pointing to a displacement. Suppose you wanted to copy or move an object to the right four units and up two units:

Type: MOVE <RETURN>

Response: Select objects:

Select the entities, and confirm.

Response: Base point or displacement:

Type: 4,2 <RETURN> (Notice that this is the displacement.)

Response: Second point of displacement:

Type: <RETURN>

When you press <RETURN> at the second point, AutoCAD interprets the first point as a relative displacement, not an absolute coordinate.

2.32 **MIRROR distances**

In the **MIRROR** command, the base line or mirror line determines how far away the second object will be from the first. Therefore, if you want the object mirrored to be adjacent to the original object, the mirror line should touch the original object. As you move away from the object, the second object will be placed twice the distance of the displacement of the mirror line.

2.33 **FILLET can be confusing**

For beginning users of AutoCAD, the **FILLET** command can be a little confusing. When you enter R for radius and then give a radius, nothing seems to happen. Actually, nothing is going to happen until you repeat the **FILLET** command so that you can then point to the two lines. Press <RETURN> or the space bar to repeat the command.

2.34 **MEASURE vs. DIVIDE**

MEASURE and **DIVIDE** are ideal commands for breaking up a line, depending on how you want it segmented. **MEASURE** lets you place an infinite number of points an equal distance from a beginning point. **DIVIDE** splits a line into an infinite number of equal parts. Both of these commands place points along the line. If you can see these points, you can object snap to them.

Use the system variables **PDMODE** and **PDSIZE** to give shape and readable size to the points that are being placed. **PDMODE** sets the shape of a point; **PDSIZE** sets the size.

2.35 **Cutting a hole in a hatch**

You can cut a hole in a hatched object once the object is exploded by editing the individual lines. But there are better ways to cut around the center of a hatch pattern, so this should be the last alternative. Be aware that when you explode a hatched object, you could be creating literally thousands of individual entities. The best way is to draw the outline of a hole inside the object. Hatching won't hatch the hole; the outline can then be erased.

2.36 **EXPLODE** explained

EXPLODE can be a very useful command, but you should know a few of its idiosyncrasies. Whenever you explode an object, you're returned to the Command line if the object was explodable. But this doesn't mean that the object was completely exploded.

If the object was a nested block, the first **EXPLODE** explodes only the outermost part of the block. All inner blocks are left intact.

If you want to explode all the entities, continue to **EXPLODE** until you no longer get a Command line.

2.37 **Closing a polyline**

It's possible to close an existing polyline after the fact, with the **PEDIT** command. If you use this command's **Close** option, a line will be drawn between the last point of the polyline and the first.

2.38 **Repeating commands with <RETURN> or the space bar**

Be careful when you use <RETURN> or the space bar to repeat the last command. If the command was from AutoCAD's standard tablet menu, it will act as a standard command normally would, not as it did when it was first called up by the tablet pick.

A good example of this is the **BREAK** command on the tablet. There are two of these: **BREAK @** and **BREAK FIRST**. They both operate very effectively, saving you several steps. But if either of these is repeated with <RETURN>, they no longer work as they did on the tablet menu; they repeat as generic **BREAK** commands.

You can work around this by substituting your own AutoLISP **BREAK** and **BREAK @** commands on the tablet menu. Then when they're repeated with <RETURN>, you're really repeating your own AutoLISP program, not the generic AutoCAD **BREAK**.

2.39 **TRIM** explained

The **TRIM** command can sometimes be confusing. The confusion lies in the terms and questions that are asked about the "cutting edge" and "the object to trim." The easy way to remember the difference is that the cutting edge won't disappear, but the object to trim will.

RELEASE 12   Use the new **Fence** option to trim multiple oblects at one time. See Tip 30.6.

AutoLISP Programs

2.40 Automatic erase (LISP6)

This is a simple routine that places you in automatic erasure mode: pick an object, and it's erased. If you pick a blank area and move your cursor to the right, you're in **ERASE WINDOW**; to the left, you're in **ERASE CROSS-ING**. Everything chosen will be erased without confirmation.

Listing:
```
(defun c:lisp6 ()
    (command "erase" "single" "auto")
)
```

To Use: Load LISP6.LSP.

Type: `LISP6 <RETURN>`

Pick an object or a blank area of the screen to start the crossing or window.

2.41 Change properties (LISP7)

This program is a shortcut to **CHANGE PROPERTIES**, leaving out the **Change Point** option. This is a useful routine, since changing properties is possibly the more common option.

Listing:
```
(defun c:lisp7 (/ ent)
    (setq ent (ssget))
    (command "change" ent "" "p")
)
```

To Use: Load LISP7.LSP.

Type: `LISP7 <RETURN>`

2.42 **Erase last (LISP8)**

This program is a quick way to erase the last item drawn. We suggest that you change **c:lisp8** to **c:e** so that you can use it as a single-letter command.

Listing:
```
(defun c:lisp8 ()
    (command "erase" "l" "")
)
```

To Use: Load LISP8.LSP.

Type: LISP8 <RETURN> (or E and the space bar, if you've changed it to a single letter)

You can continue by pressing the space bar or <RETURN> to erase the last several entities drawn.

2.43 **Multiple copy (LISP9)**

This program places you directly into multiple copy mode. It works just like the **COPY** command, except that you can continue placing the object.

Listing:
```
(defun c:lisp9 (/ ent)
    (setq ent (ssget))
    (command "copy" ent "" "m")
)
```

To Use: Load LISP9.LSP.

Type: LISP9 <RETURN>

2.44 **Break intersection (LISP10)**

This program provides you with a specialized break command for intersections. The **TRIM** command is an alternative, but this program is especially useful for cleanup without regard to the direction of the lines. It also provides preselected object snaps for intersections.

Listing:
```
(defun c:lisp10 (/ os pt1 pt2 pt3)
     (setq os (getvar "osmode"))
     (setvar "osmode" 512)
     (setq pt1 (getpoint "\nPick object to be broken "))
     (setvar "osmode" 33)
     (setq pt2 (getpoint "\nBreak from 1st point "))
     (setq pt3 (getpoint "\nEnter second point "))
     (setvar "osmode" 0)
     (command "break" pt1 "f" pt2 pt3)
     (setvar "osmode" os)
)
```

To Use: Load LISP10.LSP.

Type: `LISP10 <RETURN>`

Response: `Pick object to be broken:`

This works just like the **BREAK F** command. The difference is that object snap is chosen for you. All you have to do is pick the line to be broken (anywhere along the line), then pick the two intersections or endpoints where the break is to take place.

2.45 Corner cleanup (LISP11)

This program performs a special kind of corner cleanup by touching the intersection of the corner. The program works only on corners that look like those in Figure 2-24.

Figure 2-24: Cleaning
up a corner

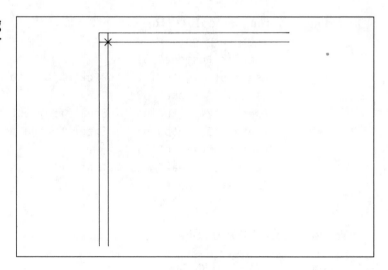

Listing:
```
(defun c:lisp11 (/ os fr pt1)
    (setq os (getvar "osmode"))
    (setq fr (getvar "filletrad"))
    (setvar "osmode" 32)
    (setvar "filletrad" 0)
    (setq pt1 (getpoint "\nPick intersection to clean  "))
    (command "fillet" pt1 pt1)
    (setvar "osmode" os)
    (setvar "filletrad" fr)
)
```

To Use: Load LISP11.LSP.

Type: LISP11 <RETURN>

Response: Pick intersection to clean:

Pick the intersection at point 1. The corners will be cleaned.

CHAPTER 3

Basic Viewing

How Do You . . .

3.1 **How do you drag objects?**

There's a system variable—**DRAGMODE**—for this purpose. It may be on, off or Auto. If it's off, dragging the object isn't permitted. If it's on, you can drag the object only if you type in the word **DRAG** each time. Auto will automatically drag the object whenever **DRAG** is permitted. Auto is the default unless changed.

 RELEASE 12   You can make AutoCAD work like a Mac by using the new **DDSELECT** command, which lets you pick and drag an object into place. See Tip 10.19.

3.2 **How do you synchronize SNAP and GRID?**

SNAP and **GRID** may have different settings, but it's often desirable for them to be identical. You'll also want both to change when you alter the setting of one.

You can do this by setting the grid to **SNAP** rather than to a specific distance. In this way, each time a new snap is set, the grid is automatically adjusted to equal it.

Type: `GRID <RETURN>`

Response: `Grid spacing(X) or ON/OFF/Snap/Aspect:`

Type: `S <RETURN>`

From now on, the grid will automatically follow the snap until it's changed. AutoCAD has a dialogue box, found under **Settings**, option **Drawing aids**, that lets you change the snap and grid settings.

3.3 **How do you get into isometric mode?**

This is done through the **SNAP** command's **Style** option. Once this is chosen, you can choose **Standard** or **Isometric**. By choosing one or the other, you toggle back and forth between the two modes.

Type: `SNAP <RETURN>`

Response: `Snap spacing or ON/OFF/Aspect/Rotate/Style:`

Type: `S <RETURN>`

Response: `Standard/Isometric:`

Type: `I <RETURN>`

Response: `Vertical spacing:`

Type: `<RETURN>`

You're now in isometric mode. The crosshairs should be slanted, letting you draw isometrically.

3.4 **How do you change isometric planes?**

Once you're in isometric mode, there are three isometric planes on which you can draw: top, left and right.

To switch between these planes, you can use either the short or long form. The long form is to type **ISOPLANE**, then type Left, Right, Top or <RETURN> to toggle between them. Almost no one uses this method.

It's easier to use Ctrl-E, which toggles you between the planes. Your computer might also have a function key specifically for this purpose.

3.5 **How do you move objects that are outside the screen viewing area?**

Depending on the depth of zoom, all of the drawing area may not be on the screen at one time. Your screen is like a window from which you can see part of a drawing—but you need to have a way of moving that window around the drawing area. The command for this is **PAN**.

PAN asks for a base point and a displacement—the distance and direction the window will be moved. This may seem backward at first, since the displacement direction is always opposite to the apparent movement of the objects. But remember that you're moving the window, not the objects. Therefore, if you want to move the window to bring in objects to the right of the viewing area, make your first and second points go from left to right.

3.6 How do you get rid of the segmented arcs and circles each time you zoom?

Depending on how your system is set up, this phenomenon can be a bit disconcerting at first. When you zoom in on an area of a drawing that has circles or arcs, they no longer look like circles or arcs. They're a series of straight line segments. They'll become good-looking arcs and circles again only when the drawing regenerates or you type **REGEN**, but this can cause a long delay. AutoCAD's set up this way by default, and you can change it. But first, let's look at the reason for the default.

When you zoom in on a drawing section, the screen can redraw a lot faster if it has to draw only straight lines. So there's a parameter you can set that tells AutoCAD the percentage of a circle to draw in order to speed up this redraw time; it's controlled with the command **VIEWRES**.

Type: `VIEWRES <RETURN>`

Response: `Do you want fast zooms? <Y>:`

Type: `<RETURN>`

Be careful here. If you type N, all zooms will require a regeneration and your productivity will go into a tailspin. So let's assume you answered Y.

Response: `Enter circle zoom percent (1-20000):`

If you set the circle zoom percent to 100, AutoCAD will use its own internal logic to determine the optimal number of vectors necessary to draw the circle without a regeneration. You can decrease the redraw time by setting the percentage at less than 100, but the circles and arcs will appear more segmented. If you set the percentage above 100, AutoCAD will draw more vectors than necessary, thus slowing you down. No matter how low you set it, a circle will always have at least eight sides. We suggest that you set the zoom to 2000 percent or less.

Be aware that fast zooms also affect line types. A change in line type may not become apparent until the next regeneration.

3.7 How do you draw straight lines parallel to the grid?

There's a drawing aid for this called **ORTHO**. When it's activated **(ORTHO On)**, all lines drawn can be made either vertically or horizontally parallel to the existing grid by moving the cursor up and down or left and right. The easiest way to turn **ORTHO** on or off is with Ctrl-O or one of the function keys on your computer. Remember, this is a toggle switch that's transparent to your current command; you can turn it on or off without affecting the command you're in.

3.8 How do you adjust the size of the Object Snap window and the pick box when asked to select objects?

AutoCAD draws one of two little boxes on the screen, depending on the function. First, whenever you're asked to select objects, the crosshairs disappear and are replaced with a small square called a *pick box*. All you need to do is to touch this square anywhere on the entity and it will be selected.

The other small box appears around the center of the crosshairs when you activate **Object Snap**. As long as the type of object requested through **Object Snap** appears in the square, you're snapped to the object. The square is called the *aperture*.

The size of the aperture is changed with the **APERTURE** command.

Type: APERTURE <RETURN>

Response: Object snap target height (1-50 pixels):

Type: `15 <RETURN>`

The larger the number, the larger the square. The actual physical size will differ, depending on your graphics card and monitor and its resolution. You change the pick box with the system variable **PICKBOX**.

Type: `SETVAR <RETURN>`

Response: `Variable name or ?:`

Type: `PICKBOX <RETURN>`

Response: `New value for PICKBOX:`

Type: `30 <RETURN>`

As with the aperture, this is the number of pixels high. The larger the number, the larger the box.

RELEASE 12   You can adjust the size of the aperture box through **DDOSNAP**. A slide bar within the new dialogue box lets you alter dynamically the size of the pick box. See Tip 10.14.

3.9 How do you make a slide?

An AutoCAD slide is simply a screen representation of a specific view of the drawing. There are no entities in a slide. You can't change a slide or zoom in on it. If you issue any AutoCAD command such as **ZOOM**, **LINE** or **ERASE**, the slide will disappear and the original drawing will reappear.

Even with all their limitations, slides are still very useful when you want to show a client different views of a drawing. They appear on the screen very quickly, with no regenerations. They can be especially useful if you want to show views of 3D objects with hidden lines.

Slides are created using the **MSLIDE** command. You must first set the view of the object you want on the screen.

Type: `MSLIDE <RETURN>`

Response: `Slide file:`

Type: `SLIDE1 <RETURN>`

The name **slide1** is what we've given in our example; of course, you can name your slide anything you want.

The slide is now made. You can view it with the **VSLIDE** command.

Type: VSLIDE <RETURN>

Response: Slide file:

Type: SLIDE1 <RETURN>

The slide appears on your screen on top of the current drawing. It disappears and your original drawing returns when you issue any AutoCAD command that changes the current view.

 RELEASE 11   Whenever a file name is asked for, a dialogue box appears for the file name entry if the system variable, **FILEDIA**, is set to 1. If the system variable is set to 0, the file name prompt appears at the command line without the dialogue box. See Tip 9.10.

3.10 How do you turn coordinates on and off?

Coordinates are updated dynamically as the crosshairs are moved around the screen. You can toggle coordinates on or off by using Ctrl-D or a function key for your specific computer.

In the early days of AutoCAD, having the coordinates on all the time could cause a jerky cursor movement. Therefore, most people kept them on only when needed. In these days of fast computers, it's really not necessary to toggle the coordinates off unless you want to.

 RELEASE 12   Use the middle button of the mouse to automatically activate the cursor menu. See Tip 10.18.

3.11 How do you do multiple object snaps?

It's possible to tell AutoCAD to accept the first of any one of a group of object snap entities it finds. For example, you can program the tablet or function key to find either the endpoint or the intersection. These combinations of object snaps can be initiated by simply separating them with commas.

This can be done manually with the **OSNAP** command.

Type: OSNAP <RETURN>

Response: Object snap modes:

Type: `END,INT <RETURN>`

This becomes your standard object snap mode until changed. You can do the same thing on an item-by-item basis by typing in the object snaps, separated by commas as needed, within a given command.

3.12 How do you turn SNAP on and off?

SNAP is a toggle switch that's turned on and off with Ctrl-B or a special function key on your computer. It simply toggles it on and off; it doesn't set the snap. That's set with the **SNAP** command.

3.13 How do you turn GRID on and off?

GRID is a toggle switch that's turned on and off with Ctrl-G or a special function key on your computer. It simply toggles it on and off; it doesn't set the distance between the grid points. That's set with the **GRID** command.

3.14 How do you create multiple windows?

Windows in AutoCAD are called viewports, and they're created with the **VPORT** command. You may have up to four viewports active at one time. The settings for each of the viewports, and their configurations, can be saved and recalled at any time. You can create an unlimited number of configurations.

Type: `VPORTS <RETURN>`

Response: `Save/Restore/Delete/Join/SIngle/?/2/3/4:`

Type: `3 <RETURN>`

Response: `Horizontal/Vertical/Above/Below/Left/Right:`

If you choose three viewports, you can choose **Horizontal** or **Vertical**. These options split the screen into three equal parts. If you want one of the screens to be larger than the other two, you must tell AutoCAD whether you want the larger screen to be above, below, to the left or to the right of the two smaller screens (see Figure 3-1).

Figure 3-1: Multiple viewports (windows)

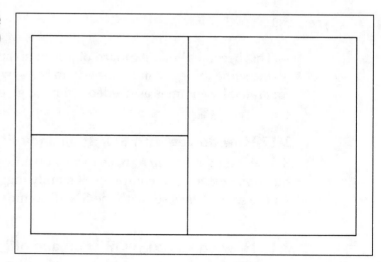

Type: R <RETURN>

You now have two small screens on the left and one large screen on the right.

Type: VPORTS <RETURN>

Response: Save/Restore/Delete/Join/SIngle/?/2/3/4:

Type: S <RETURN>

This lets you save your viewport configuration. Give it the name of your choice. When you restore a viewport configuration, you restore the specific views and settings that were active at the time of the save.

 RELEASE 11   The concept of Paper Space has been added, letting viewports be treated as entities. See Tip 29.1 for more on Paper Space.

3.15 **How do you avoid regens (regenerations)?**

Avoiding regens is the most productive thing you can do, and of course you don't want AutoCAD to regenerate a drawing inadvertently.

The **REGENAUTO** system variable can protect you. If **REGENAUTO** is set to off, you'll be informed that a regen is about to take place and asked if you want it to proceed.

 RELEASE 11   See Tip 9.13 concerning **Vmax**.

 RELEASE 12   Thanks to 32-bit Vector Space, you can now zoom without regens. See Tips 20.71, 20.72.

3.16 **How do you get blips off the screen?**

You may want the little blips on your screen as you pick points, or you might see them as a nuisance requiring additional redraws to get them off the screen.

The system variable **BLIPMODE** controls whether AutoCAD draws the blips. If **BLIPMODE** is set to 1, blips are turned on; set to 0, blips are turned off. There's also a **BLIPMODE** command that has **On** and **Off** options.

3.17 **How do you REDRAW or REGEN in all viewports at the same time?**

Each individual viewport is controlled independently. If you issue the **REDRAW** or **REGEN** command, only the active viewport will be affected. If you want all the viewports to be redrawn or regenerated at once, use **REDRAWALL** or **REGENALL**.

3.18 **How do you use Dynamic ZOOM?**

Dynamic ZOOM can be a highly productive tool if used effectively, and its effectiveness is determined by the last zoom and regeneration, which establish the display list limits.

Type: `ZOOM <RETURN>`

Response: `All/Center/Dynamic/Extents/Left/Previous/Window/Scale(X):`

Type: `D <RETURN>`

The zoom window (or *view box*) must now be sized for the area you want to zoom. When you press the pick button, an arrow on the right side of the view box appears. As you move the cursor, the view box will get larger or smaller (see Figure 3-2).

Figure 3-2: Sizing the
view box

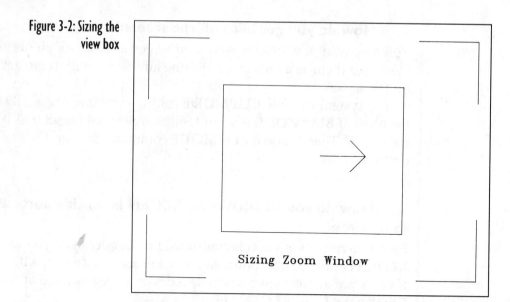

By pressing the pick button, you can toggle between the sizing option and the moving option. You can move the view box when an X appears in it (Figure 3-3). Move the box over the area where you want to zoom.

Figure 3-3: Moving the
view box

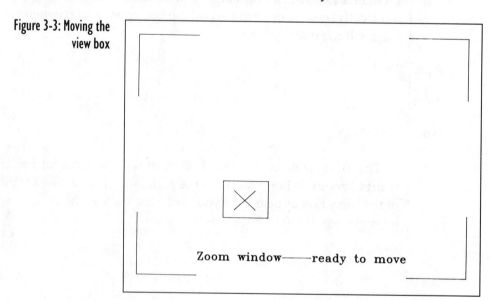

When you have the view box in position, press <RETURN> or use your confirm button. It will now zoom in on the area. When **Dynamic ZOOM** begins, the drawing begins regenerating on the screen. You don't have to wait for a full regen; when enough has regenerated on the screen for you to see what you're doing, you can activate the view box and zoom in again.

The areas of the drawing are outlined in either white or red. The white area represents the entire drawing extents. The red area represents the area of drawing for which AutoCAD will let you use **Dynamic ZOOM**. If your view box ventures outside the limits of the red area, an hourglass figure will appear in the corner of the screen. This is a warning that if you proceed to **ZOOM**, you'll force a regen, which will then redefine the area outlined in red.

 RELEASE 12   Now you can use **ZOOM** options with **PLOT** preview.

3.19 **How do you change viewports?**

Only one viewport can be active at once, but it's easy to go from one viewport to another. The active viewport displays the standard crosshairs as the cursor moves into that viewport. If the viewport is inactive, an arrow appears when the cursor moves into it. See Figure 3-4.

Figure 3-4: Active
viewport with
crosshairs

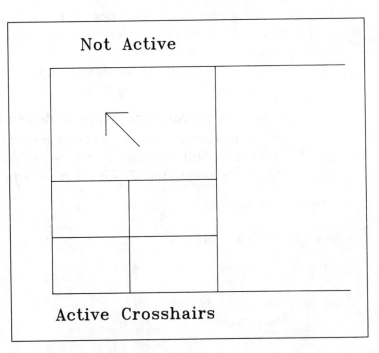

To make a viewport active, simply press your pick button while the cursor's in the viewport. The crosshairs will appear. You may toggle from one viewport to another while in other commands, such as **LINE**.

3.20 How do you create a view?

A view and a viewport configuration are two different things. A view is simply what appears on the screen at any given time. It can be a zoomed-in area on the main screen or in one of the viewports. You can save a view by giving it a user-defined name, and you can recall it with that same name.

Type: `VIEW <RETURN>`

Response: `?/Delete/Restore/Save/Window:`

Type: `SAVE <RETURN>`

Response: `View name to save:`

Type: `VIEW1 <RETURN>`

In the above example, **view1** stands for a name you choose. You can also save a view with the **Window** option, which lets you zoom in on an area and save it at the same time.

To recall a view, use the **Restore** option under **VIEW**.

3.21 How do you change the angle of the grid and crosshairs?

It's often necessary to change the rotation of the grid to the angle of an entity, especially if you want to draw parallel or at 90 degrees to it. Once the grid is rotated, use **ORTHO On** to do this.

Type: `SNAP <RETURN>`

Response: `Snap spacing or ON/OFF/Aspect/Rotate/Style:`

Type: `R <RETURN>`

Response: `Base point <0,0>:`

Type: <RETURN>

Response: Rotation angle:

Type: 20d14' <RETURN>

The crosshairs and the grid will be rotated. To return it to its original configuration, reissue the command and use 0 as the angle. See LISP59 in Tip 13.22.

3.22 How do you set a different height and width for the grid or snap?

If the width of a grid point needs to be 2 and the height needs to be 1, use the **Aspect** option for either the **GRID** or **SNAP** commands.

Type: GRID <RETURN>

Response: Grid spacing(X) or ON/OFF/Snap/Aspect:

Type: A <RETURN>

Response: Horizontal spacing(X):

Type: 1 <RETURN>

Response: Vertical spacing(X):

Type: 2 <RETURN>

3.23 How do you zoom to just a little less than the ZOOM extents?

ZOOM Extents will make a drawing as large as possible and still get everything on the screen. This is a valuable feature, but unfortunately many of the entities go to the absolute edge of the screen. This makes it difficult to use a window or crossing to capture the entities at the edge.

To work around this problem, first issue a **ZOOM Extents** command, then do a **ZOOM .9X**. Adding the X to the scale makes the scale relative to what's on the screen. See LISP15 in Tip 3.39 later in this chapter.

Type: `ZOOM E <RETURN>`

Type: `ZOOM .9X <RETURN>`
See Tip 3.26.

More Steps to Success

3.24 How to see the whole drawing

It's often important to be able to see an entire drawing on the screen.
Putting a window or crossing around the drawing will ensure that you
pick all the objects in it.

The easiest way to do this is to zoom at a scale of .5. This should put
the entire drawing in the middle of the screen.

Type: `ZOOM .5 <RETURN>`

3.25 When to use X after the ZOOM factor

Being able to zoom at a scale factor is very important. But there are two
ways to use the scale factor. First is the method described in the section
above: simply enter a number after the **ZOOM** command, and the drawing will be increased or reduced in size by that factor. The problem with
this method is that the scale is based on the original **ZOOM All** size, not
what you see on the screen at any given time.

If you want to scale the zoom to what's apparent on the screen, add the
letter X after the scale factor. For example, after a **ZOOM Extents** you
might want to reduce the image size just slightly.

Type: `ZOOM E <RETURN>`

This zooms you to the extents of your drawing.

Type: `ZOOM .9X <RETURN>`

This reduces the image on the screen by 10 percent.

RELEASE 12   The new 32-bit Vector Space of Release 12 has an unlimited
factor for the **ZOOM** command.

3.26 **A shortcut to ZOOM Extents**

Tip 3.25, above, is very useful, but it can be shortened by saving the final image as a view. Then you can restore that view instead of using **ZOOM Extents**.

3.27 **Draw in 3D, not isometric**

As you know, AutoCAD has an isometric function, but if you have Release 10 or later, you really shouldn't be using this function. It's better to design in 3D, then set the view to an isometric view. That way, the design isn't distorted, and you can get many other views from the same drawing. See the LISP86 program in Tip 17.34.

3.28 **Find the endpoint anywhere on a line**

When you use **OBJECT SNAP**, a small, square box called the *aperture* is drawn around where the crosshairs meet. It's usually best to place the object you're snapping to inside the aperture—but if you're snapping to an endpoint, this isn't always necessary. Sometimes it's best to keep the endpoint outside the aperture, since it might get confused with other objects. All you have to do is touch the line closest to the endpoint, and AutoCAD will find the correct endpoint for you.

3.29 **Transparent ZOOMS**

Transparent **ZOOM**, **PAN** and **VIEW** are functions that aren't used nearly enough. By preceding these commands with an apostrophe ('), you make them transparent to the command you're currently working with.

What this means is that you can be in the **LINE** command in one part of your drawing and zoom to another part of the drawing while remaining in the **LINE** command; see the following example.

Type: LINE <RETURN>

Response: From point:

Pick a point.

Response: To point:

Type: `'ZOOM W <RETURN>`

Place a window around the area you'd like to zoom to.

Response: `To point:`

You can now continue with the **LINE** command. Adding an apostrophe in front of **PAN** and **VIEW** makes them work the same way. **ZOOM**, **PAN** and **VIEW**, found on the tablet menu, are transparent commands.

3.30 Use two or more viewports

Using transparent **ZOOM**, **PAN** and **VIEW** doesn't always work. Sometimes you might be zoomed in so deeply that you must regenerate a drawing in order to **ZOOM** or **PAN** to another part of it.

This can create a problem if you need to continue a line from one point to another. But all is not lost. Set up two viewports zooming in to the two areas where you want to draw the line. Then begin the line in one viewport and use the pick button to toggle to the other viewport and continue the line.

3.31 Use VIEW Restore instead of ZOOM

You can save a lot of zooming and possibly some regenerations if you set areas of your drawing as views. Then pop between them with a **VIEW Restore** instead of first doing a **ZOOM All** and a **ZOOM Window**.

3.32 The grid and snap can be independent for each viewport

Remember that you can set up the grid size and the snap distances independently for each viewport.

3.33 Use Dynamic ZOOM

This is a simple little tip, but you'd be surprised how many users don't really understand **Dynamic ZOOM**. **Dynamic ZOOM** begins by regenerating a drawing on the screen, but you don't have to wait for it to regenerate before picking the area where you want to zoom. In fact, the area you want to zoom to doesn't even have to be on the screen when you pick it.

3.34 **Use ZOOM Previous instead of ZOOM All**

Use **ZOOM Previous** instead of **ZOOM All** even if you have to do it a couple of times to get back to the entire drawing. It's faster.

11 RELEASE 11   With this version, a new option was added to the **ZOOM** command. **ZOOM Vmax** is a **ZOOM All** to the limits of your virtual screen without forcing a regen. Since **ZOOM All** is an unconditional regen, it should rarely be used. This gives you an alternative that will work in most cases. See Tip 9.13.

3.35 **Use the Quick option in Object Snap (OSNAP)**

You can speed up the **OSNAP** selection process considerably by setting the mode to **Quick**. It will stop searching once it finds an object that matches the criteria requested. Without this option, AutoCAD continues to search for all entities within the aperture and selects the one closest to the point selected.

Be aware that **Quick** changes the way AutoCAD selects snap points and must be used only in conjunction with one or more other modes.

Type: OSNAP <RETURN>

Response: Object snap modes:

Type: QUI,ENDP

This sets your object snap mode to **Quick** and **Endpoint**.

AutoLISP Programs

3.36 **Set ZOOM Extents (LISP12)**

You should run this program when enough entities are in the drawing to set the extents. The program first does a **ZOOM Extents**, then a **ZOOM .9X**. Finally, it saves the drawing as a view called ZE. From then on, you should use **LISP13** instead of **ZOOM Extents**.

Listing:
```
(defun c:lisp12 ()
     (command "zoom" "e")
     (command "zoom" ".9x")
     (command "view" "s" "ze")
)
```

To Use: Load LISP12.LSP.

Type: LISP12 <RETURN>

3.37 A better ZOOM All (LISP13)

This program should be used instead of **ZOOM Extents**. Run it only after LISP12 has been run. It restores the view that was set up in LISP12.

Listing:
```
(defun c:lisp13 ()
     (command "view" "r" "ze")
)
```

To Use: Load LISP13.LSP.

Type: LISP13 <RETURN>

3.38 Object Snap none (LISP14)

AutoLISP programs sometimes leave you in an undesirable object snap. This is a quick little program that resets your object snap back to none.

Listing:
```
(defun c:lisp14 ()
     (setvar "osmode" 0)
)
```

To Use: Load LISP14.LSP.

Type: LISP14 <RETURN>

3.39 **A faster ZOOM Extents (LISP15)**

LISP12 and LISP13 set and recall views as **ZOOM Extents**, depending on what entities are in place at the time. If there are no entities, such as at the beginning of the drawing, it's saved as a **ZOOM All**. By drawing some entities around the middle of your drawing and running LISP12, you can control the zoom area and, often, the regeneration.

LISP15 is a quick **ZOOM Extents** with a .9 reduction.

Listing:
```
(defun c:lisp15 (/ pt1 pt2 dis a dis1 pt3 pt4)
    (setq pt1 (getvar "extmin"))
    (setq pt2 (getvar "extmax"))
    (setq dis (distance pt1 pt2))
    (setq a (angle pt1 pt2))
    (setq dis1 (* dis 0.1))
    (setq pt3 (polar pt1 a (* dis1 -1)))
    (setq pt4 (polar pt2 a dis1))
    (command "zoom" "w" pt3 pt4)
)
```

To Use: Load LISP15.LSP.

Type: LISP15 <RETURN>

As entities are added, this works like **ZOOM Extents**. If entities are removed, the extents won't be reduced until the next **ZOOM All**.

Basic Layers, Blocks, Attributes

 How Do You . . .

4.1 How do you create a layer?
You can use the **LAYER** command for most operations involving layers.

Type: `LAYER <RETURN>`

Response: `?/Make/Set/New/ON/OFF/Color/Ltype/Freeze/Thaw:`

Type: `N <RETURN>`

Response: `New layer name(s):`

Type: `LAYER-1 <RETURN>`

Type: `<RETURN>`

The last <RETURN> terminates the **LAYER** command. You can create more than one layer by separating the names of the layers with commas.

 RELEASE 12   Create layers easily with the new **Layer Control** dialogue box. See Tip 20.11.

4.2 How do you change layers?
Changing from one layer to another is done with the **Set** subcommand within the **LAYER** command.

Type: `LAYER <RETURN>`

Response: `?/Make/Set/New/ON/OFF/Color/Ltype/Freeze/Thaw:`

Type: `S <RETURN>`

Response: `New current layer:`

Type: LAYER-1 <RETURN>

Type: <RETURN>

The last <RETURN> terminates the **LAYER** command. You're now changed to **layer-1**. The name of this layer should be on the status line.

 RELEASE 12   Change layers easily with the new **Layer Control** dialogue box. See Tip 20.12

4.3 **How do you create and change a layer at the same time?**

There are two basic commands for creating a layer: **New** and **Make**. Both of these are subcommands of the **LAYER** command. The difference between the two is that **New** creates a new layer while leaving you on the current layer. **Make**, on the other hand, creates a new layer and then puts you on that layer.

4.4 **How do you turn a layer off and on?**

Appropriately enough, this is done with the **Off** and **On** subcommands of the **LAYER** command. There are pros and cons to using **Off** and **On**. Those layers that are turned off don't appear on the screen, but it still takes the same amount of time to regenerate a drawing.

On the other hand, **Off** and **On** don't automatically start a regeneration when you leave the **LAYER** command. This makes them ideal if you have a display-list processing board with its own fast zoom.

Another drawback to using **Off** and **On** is that it will continue to hide lines in 3D even though nothing appears on the screen. This can create some very confusing images.

 RELEASE 12   Use the new **Layer Control** dialogue box to turn layers off and on speedily. See Tip 20.10.

4.5 **How do you move an object from one layer to another?**

The easiest way to move an object to another layer is through the **CHANGE** command. One of the subcommands is **Layer**.

Type: CHANGE <RETURN>

Response: Select objects:

Select the object or objects you want moved, and confirm.

Response: Properties/<Change point>:

There are two basic functions to the **CHANGE** command. Most of the options you'll want are under **PROPERTIES**.

Type: P <RETURN>

Response: Change what property
           (Color/Elev/LAyer/LType/Thickness)?

Type: LA <RETURN>

Response: New layer:

Type: LAYER-1 <RETURN>

Type: <RETURN>

The second <RETURN> terminates the **CHANGE** command. Otherwise, you can continue to choose other options. If **layer-1** doesn't already exist, you must first create it before you can move any objects to it. See LISP64 in Tip 14.48 for a program that changes objects to another layer by pointing to the new layer.

4.6 **How do you find out what layer an object is on?**

An object's layer is one of many pieces of information available through the **LIST** command. It's easy to use—type **LIST**, then pick the object or objects you want listed. The object's layer name is at the top of the listing.

Type: LIST <RETURN>

Now pick the object and confirm. You can use your F1 key to return to the graphics screen.

4.7 **How do you find out what layers are available in a drawing?**

When you issue the **LAYER** command, one of the options is **?**. The question mark lists all of the layers in the drawing and tells you if they're on or off, frozen or thawed.

Type: `LAYER <RETURN>`

Response: `?/Make/Set/New/ON/OFF/Color/Ltype/Freeze/Thaw:`

Type: `? <RETURN>`

You can use your F1 key to return to the graphics screen.

4.8 **How do you get rid of a layer?**

Getting rid of a layer isn't a simple, one-command task. First, decide what you really want to do: Make the layer disappear? Get rid of all the entities on the layer? Or do you want to totally delete the layer, so if you ever needed it again you'd have to re-create it?

Let's take these options one at a time. If you just want the layer to disappear, use the **Freeze** or **Off** subcommands of **LAYER**.

If you want to get rid of all entities on a layer, use the following procedure. First, change to the layer you want to get rid of. Next, freeze all other layers.

Type: `LAYER <RETURN>`

Response: `?/Make/Set/New/ON/OFF/Color/Ltype/Freeze/Thaw:`

Type: `FREEZE <RETURN>`

Response: `Layer name(s) to freeze:`

Type: `* <RETURN>`

Type: `<RETURN>` (This gets you out of the LAYER command.)

By typing *****, you're freezing all of the layers in the drawing. AutoCAD won't let you freeze your current layer; that's why you changed to that layer first.

Now use the **ERASE** command and put a crossing around all the entities in the drawing that are on the screen. If you can't see all the entities, you might want to zoom to a .5 factor so all the entities are in the center of the screen. Now they can all be erased very easily. You can return to where you were by doing a **ZOOM Previous**. The final step is to thaw all the frozen layers.

Type: `LAYER <RETURN>`

Response: `?/Make/Set/New/ON/OFF/Color/Ltype/Freeze/Thaw:`

Type: `T <RETURN>`

Response: `Layer name(s) to thaw:`

Type: `* <RETURN>`

Type: `<RETURN>` (This gets you out of the LAYER command.)

See LISP115 in Tip 24.17 for a program that quickly gets rid of all the entities on a given layer.

The third possibility is to get rid of the layer completely. To do this, you must first erase all the entities on that layer, as shown above. Next, you have to save the drawing and then re-enter the drawing.

The first command you issue after you re-enter the drawing is **PURGE**. One of the options to purge is **Layers**. It will then take you through all the layers that have no entities on them and ask if you want to delete each one. Answer Y, and the layer will be deleted.

Remember, you can't make any changes to the drawing before the **PURGE** command is issued. See LISP39 in Tip 8.22.

4.9 How do you change the name of a layer?
The name of a layer is changed with the **RENAME** command.

Type: `RENAME <RETURN>`

Response: `Block/LAyer/LType/Style/Ucs/VIew/VPort:`

Type: `LA <RETURN>`

Response: `Old name:`

Type: LAYER-1 <RETURN>

Response: New name:

Type: LAYER-1A <RETURN>

   As you can see, there are quite a few other things you can change using
the **RENAME** command.

 RELEASE 12   Use the new **Layer Control** dialogue box as described in Tip
20.15.

4.10 How do you change line types?

As with colors, line types can be controlled either as parts of a given layer
or independently. If you assign a line type to a specific layer, all entities on
that layer will have the same line type. If you want the line type to be independent of the layer, use the **LINETYPE** command.

Type: LINETYPE <RETURN>

Response: ?/Create/Load/Set:

   If you're using standard AutoCAD line types, use the **Set** option.

Type: S <RETURN>

Response: New entity linetype (or ?):

Type: DASHED <RETURN>

   You should now be able to draw using dashed lines; see Figure 4-1. If
you begin drawing and the line stays continuous, you may need to change
the **LTSCALE**. See LISP19 in Tip 4.41 and LISP67 in Tip 14.51.

Figure 4-1: Line type
changed to dashes

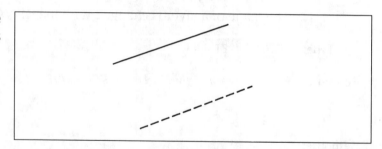

4.11 How do you know which line types are available and what they're called?

As for many AutoCAD commands, you can issue the command and then use the **?** suboption.

Type: `LINETYPE <RETURN>`

Response: `?/Create/Load/Set:`

Type: `? <RETURN>`

All the available line types, and their names, will be listed.

4.12 How do you make the line type look right?

It's confusing to see a line that you know is dotted appear as a continuous line. There are a few causes for this. **VIEWRES** may be obstructing the scale (this will clear up with the next regeneration of the drawing); or your **LTSCALE** isn't set correctly; or both.

   LTSCALE controls the scale of the line type. By increasing the size of the scale, you're increasing the physical separation of the lines or dots on the screen and on your ultimate plot. See LISP19, Tip 4.41, for a program that automatically sets **LTSCALE** based on your chosen drawing limits.

4.13 How do you make a block?

A block is a group of entities that AutoCAD treats as a single entity. A block can be specific only to a given drawing or it can be written out to disk to be shared by other drawings.

   Start by drawing the object you want to block.

Type: `BLOCK <RETURN>`

Response: `Block name (or ?):`

Give the block a name of your choice. In the future, you'll refer to it by this name when you want to insert it.

Type: PART-1 <RETURN>

Response: Insertion base point:

Pick a point on the block that will be used as a reference point for insertion in the future; see Figure 4-2.

Figure 4-2: Creating a block

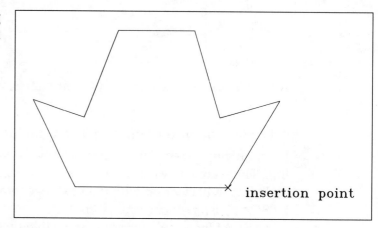

insertion point

Response: Select objects:

Select all the entities in the block, and confirm. If you are successful, the entire block will disappear. Now insert it anywhere in the drawing.

 RELEASE 11 With this release came an entirely new variation of blocks, called Reference Files. These act like blocks, except they're not actually saved as part of the drawing, nor can they be modified. See Tips 19.4 and 19.30.

 RELEASE 12 For a new variation of external reference files, see Tip 30.11.

4.14 **How do you insert a block?**

Now that you've created a block (see Tip 4.13 above), you might be ready to insert it in your drawing. Use the **INSERT** command.

Type: `INSERT <RETURN>`

Response: `Block name (or ?):`

Type: `PART-1 <RETURN>`

Response: `Insertion point:`

Pick a point where you want the block inserted. If you have **DRAG** on **Auto,** an image of the block should be dynamically dragging across the screen.

Response: `X scale factor <1>/Corner/XYZ:`

If you want the block inserted just as you drew it, SIM press <RETURN>, since the default is a scale factor of 1. Of course, you can make the block larger or smaller by increasing or decreasing the scale factor. You have the option of scaling the X and Y factors differently.

Type: `<RETURN>`

Response: `Y scale factor (default=X):`

The default of the Y scale factor is the X scale factor you just entered.

Type: `<RETURN>`

Response: `Rotation angle <0>:`

You can rotate the block as it's inserted.

Type: `<RETURN>`

The block should now be inserted just as you drew it.

RELEASE 12 You can now insert blocks by choosing the new **DDINSERT** dialogue box from the DRAW pull-down menu. See Tip 20.48.

4.15 **How do you edit a block?**

One of the first things you'll find when working with blocks is that you can't edit them until you change them back into their individual, original entities. This is done with the **EXPLODE** command.

Type: `EXPLODE <RETURN>`

Response: `Select block reference, polyline, dimension, or mesh:`

Pick the block, and confirm. The block is now exploded and should be ready to edit. Remember that it's now no longer a block.

4.16 **How do you correct a block?**

Let's suppose you wanted to make the same change to all the blocks in a drawing. The first thing you do is explode one of the blocks in the drawing so you can edit it. Then make whatever corrections need to be made on the block. Now you need to reblock the changed group of entities, using the same block name as before.

Type: `BLOCK <RETURN>`

Response: `Block name (or ?):`

Type: `PART-1 <RETURN>`

Response: `Block PART-1 already exists.`
           `Redefine it? <N>`

Type: `Y <RETURN>`

Answer the rest of the questions, selecting the objects to be blocked. The drawing will begin to regenerate, changing the referenced blocks by that name to the new definition of the modified block.

4.17 **How do you change the name of a block?**
Use the **RENAME** command to change the name of a block.

Type: `RENAME <RETURN>`

Response: `Block/LAyer/LType/Style/Ucs/VIew/VPort:`

Type: `B <RETURN>`

Response: `Old block name:`

Type: `PART-1 <RETURN>`

Response: `New block name:`

Type: `PART-1A <RETURN>`

4.18 **How do you get the entities back after blocking?**
When you issue the **BLOCK** command, the entities that were successfully blocked disappear. But sometimes you want to create a new block for future use without disturbing the existing entities.

Type **OOPS**, as you would if you'd erased something and then wanted it back. The entities return to the screen as individual entities, not a block.

4.19 **How do you get rid of a block?**
Getting rid of a block is basically the same as getting rid of a layer. If all you want is not to see the block, just erase all of that block in the drawing. The drawing still has the definition of the block.

To permanently get rid of the block definition, you must issue the **PURGE** command before anything in the drawing is changed—**Purging blocks** is one of the options. There must be no visible blocks currently in the drawing by that name. (Blocks you can see are called *referenced* blocks.)

4.20 How do you insert a block with its entities already exploded?

You can explode a block after it's inserted, but it's often easier to bring a block into a drawing already exploded. This might be especially true when you're bringing in another entire drawing.

To do this, place an asterisk in front of the block's name.

Type: `INSERT <RETURN>`

Response: `Block name (or ?):`

Type: `*PART-1 <RETURN>`

Response: `Insertion point:`

Pick a point.

Response: `Scale factor <1>:`

Type: `<RETURN>`

Response: `Rotation angle:`

Type: `0 <RETURN>`

Note that you don't have the option of giving different X and Y scale factors when you bring in an already exploded block.

4.21 How do you know what blocks already exist?

When you issue the **INSERT** command and are asked for a block name, answer with a **?**. All blocks defined in the drawing will be listed for you.

4.22 How do you share a block with other drawings?

When you first created the block, you created a block definition in one drawing only. You could return to that drawing at any time and insert the block as often as you wanted. But no other drawing knows anything about your block.

In order to share the block with other drawings, you must first write it out to disk. To do this, use the **WBLOCK** command.

Type: `WBLOCK <RETURN>`

Response: `File name:`

Type: `PART-1 <RETURN>` (This is the name of the .DWG file that will be created when you write the block out to disk.)

Response: `Block name:`

Type: `PART-1 <RETURN>`

You might think that the block name and the file name should be one and the same; practically speaking, this is true. AutoCAD will let you give a file a different name from the block definition it's going to use. But for all practical purposes, you should always give the file and the block the same name. If you don't, you'll have a block in one drawing with a different name than the name it has in other drawings. Also, you won't be able to globally change the block by changing the WBLOCK file.

The block is now written out to disk, and you can insert it into any other drawing. The inserted drawing creates its own block definition, which it uses from then on.

More Steps to Success

4.23 By layer or independently

Both line types and color can be set to a given layer or they can be set independently. From a practical standpoint, you need to decide how you're going to assign them; it can be confusing if you aren't consistent.

4.24 **Organizing layer names for wild cards**

One of the features of the **LAYER** command with **Freeze** and **Thaw** or **On** and **Off** is that you can use wild cards to name layers. For example, you could give all your text layers names beginning with the letter T and access them all at once by typing t*.

 RELEASE 11   The wild card option was greatly enhanced with this release. See Tip 19.1.

4.25 **Presetting layers in a prototype drawing**

As you develop your own way of using AutoCAD, it'll become your standard operating procedure. For example, you might find yourself continually using 22 standard layers, set with specific colors and line types. You could place layers in a standard prototype drawing such as ACAD.DWG, so whenever you begin a new drawing they'll already be set up and ready to use.

4.26 **The transparent layer**

Whenever you block an object, it permanently takes on the characteristics of the layer on which it was created. If there are multiple layers in the object when it's blocked, the object maintains the color and line type of its original layer. This can be really helpful—whenever that block is inserted, it'll have the same color and line type as the layer on which it was created.

But sometimes you'd like to be able to insert a block that takes on the characteristics of and resides on the layer on which it's being inserted. This is possible, too.

Layer 0 is a transparent layer. This means that blocks created on **layer 0** won't carry the characteristics of that layer with them; instead they will reside on and have the characteristics of the layer they are inserted on.

4.27 **Freeze and Thaw or On and Off?**

Whether to use **Freeze** and **Thaw** or to use **Off** and **On** really depends on the type of graphics board you have. Some graphics boards use display-list processing, which lets you zoom in on any part of your drawing in only a second or two, no matter how large your drawing or how slow your machine.

Freezing layers helps you when you regenerate a drawing. But regens occur most frequently during zooms. So if you have a display-list processing board, you don't really need to freeze layers.

You might simply want to make certain layers invisible. **Freeze** and **Thaw** have the unfortunate trait of doing a regen whenever they're issued. **Off** and **On** doesn't do regens.

What all this means is simple: if you have a display-list processing graphics board, use **Off** and **On**. If you don't have a display-list processing board, use **Freeze** and **Thaw**.

 RELEASE 11   With a new command, **VPLAYER**, you can control the visibility of layers on a viewport-by-viewport basis. See Tip 29.10.

4.28 Turning a layer off when assigning a color

When you assign a color to a layer, you can turn the layer off at the same time by putting a minus sign in front of the layer color number.

4.29 Creating multiple layers

AutoCAD lets you create more than one layer at a time. After entering the **LAYER** command, use the subcommand **New** to lift the layers you want to create, separating the names with commas. Then press <RETURN>.

4.30 Blocks with mixed colors and line types

If you mix colors and line types in blocks on any layer other than **layer 0**, they'll always have the same color and line types when they're inserted.

4.31 Another node

The insertion base point is also a node, so you can object snap to it.

4.32 Inserting a mirror image

When you're inserting a block into a drawing, you can insert it as a mirror image by using a negative scale factor. If you want it to be the same size as well as a mirror image, use a scale factor of –1.

4.33 **Every WBLOCK is a drawing**

Whenever you use **WBLOCK** to write a block out to disk, it creates an ordinary drawing (.DWG file). This file is the same as any other file; it can be brought into another drawing just as a block can. The only difference between the two files is that when you did the **WBLOCK** you had to supply a base point.

A drawing that was never written out as a **WBLOCK** generally doesn't have a default insertion point. If this is the case, the insertion point (by default) is 0,0 or the point of origin. You can give a drawing a base point, without writing it out as a **WBLOCK**, by using the **BASE** command.

4.34 **Insert at point of origin**

Since any drawing without an insertion point or a base point defaults to the point of origin, you can insert it into another drawing. Assuming that the **UCS** is the World Coordinate System, drawings without an insertion point should be inserted at 0,0,0. This makes them overlay your current drawing perfectly.

4.35 **You can't explode some blocks**

A word of caution when using the **INSERT** command: if you assign different values to the X and the Y scale factors, you can't explode a block. There are other entities and/or blocks that can't be exploded, such as mirrored blocks and MINSERTs.

4.36 **A problem with MINSERT**

There are times when you'll want to first insert a block and then array it. There's a command that does just that in one operation—**MINSERT**. The only problem with **MINSERT** is that all of the objects in the array are treated as a single entity that can't be exploded. Therefore, you can't change or delete a single object in the array. You'd have to delete all the objects, then insert one and issue an **ARRAY** command, then delete or change the object with **EXPLODE**.

4.37 **MINSERT problem solved**

An alternative to the **MINSERT** command is to insert a block once, then array it in separate operations. Although this takes two steps, it's what you should do if there's any chance that an object in the array will need to be changed or deleted. This also avoids problems for someone else working on the drawing later who doesn't know that the objects were inserted using the **MINSERT** command. See LISP117 in Tip 24.19 for a good program that replaces the **MINSERT** command and makes each block separate and explodable.

AutoLISP Programs

4.38 **Set layer (LISP16)**

This program sets you to a layer by letting you point to another entity that's on your target layer:

Listing:
```
(defun c:lisp16 (/ ent entlist lname)
    (prompt "\nPick an entity on the target layer ")
    (setq ent (entsel))
    (setq entlist (entget (car ent)))
    (setq lname (cdr (assoc 8 entlist)))
    (command "layer" "s" lname "")
)
```

To Use: Load LISP16.LSP.

Type: LISP16 <RETURN>

Response: Pick an entity on the target layer:

When you pick an entity that's on the target layer, the layer is changed.

4.39 **Thaw or On (LISP17)**

If you don't know whether layers are **Off** or **Frozen** and you simply want to make sure they're **On** or **Thawed**, use this program.

Listing:
```
(defun c:lisp17 ()
    (setq lname (getstring "\nLayer name(s) "))
    (command "layer" "on" lname "thaw" lname "")
)
```

To Use: Load LISP17.LSP.

Type: `LISP17 <RETURN>`

Response: `Layer name(s):`

Type in the name of the layer you want **On** or **Thawed**. You can use * or separate the layer names with commas.

4.40 **Layer status (LISP18)**

This program will list only the layers that are **Off** or **Frozen**. It's especially useful when you have a large number of layers. (Use of the plus sign at the end of a line in AutoLISP code indicates that line is wrapped.)

Listing:
```
(defun c:lisp18 (/ k a bl th onoff thl onoffl)
    (textscr)
    (setq k 5)
    (setq a nil)
    (princ "\nLayers                Status") (terpri) (terpri)
    (while (setq bl (tblnext "layer" k))
        (setq k nil)
        (setq th (assoc 70 bl))
        (setq onoff (assoc 62 bl))
        (setq thl (cdr th))
        (setq onoffl (cdr onoff))
```

```
(if (or (= th1 65) (= th1 1))
    (progn
       (setq a 5)
       (princ (cdr (assoc 2 b1)))
       (princ "              ") (princ "Frozen")
       (terpri)
    )
)
(if (< onoff1 0)
    (progn
       (setq a 5)
       (princ (cdr (assoc 2 b1)))
       (princ "              ") (princ "Off")
       (terpri)
    )
)
)
(if (= a nil)
   (prompt "There are no Frozen or Off layers in the +
     database \n")
)
(prin1)
)
```

To Use: Load LISP18.LSP.

Type: LISP18 <RETURN>

4.41 Set line type scale (LISP19)

This program automatically sets your **LTSCALE**, based on your limits. Run this program at least once before changing line types or if line types fail to appear.

Listing:
```
(defun c:lisp19 (/ dis)
    (setq dis (- (car (getvar "limmax")) (car (getvar limmin"))))
    (command "ltscale" (/ dis 32))
)
```

To Use: Load LISP19.LSP.

Type: LISP19 <RETURN>

4.42 Block insert prototype (LISP20)

This is a prototype program that shows how to insert a block using Auto-LISP. It's especially good if used on a tablet menu.

Listing:
```
(defun c:lisp20 (/ part r scale1 scale2)
    (setq part "door")
    (setq r "0")
    (setq scale1 "1")
    (setq scale2 "1")
    (command "insert" part pause scale1 scale2 r "")
)
```

To Use: Load LISP20.LSP.

Type: LISP20 <RETURN>

Modify this program and enter the name of your block where it says "door." An angle rotation should be substituted for "0." The X and Y scale factors should be assigned to **scale1** and **scale2**.

CHAPTER 5

Basic Inquiry, Text, Annotation

How Do You . . .

5.1 How do you make text fit in an area?

There are two ways to make sure that text fits within a defined area: you can use **Align** or **Fit**. But it's important to know the difference.

If you use **Align**, you'll be asked for a beginning and ending point. AutoCAD then forces the text to fit between these points by adjusting the height of the text. Naturally, the more text you try to fit into an area, the smaller the text will become.

If you use **Fit**, you'll also be asked for a beginning and ending point. The text is forced to fit between these points; AutoCAD adjusts the width of the letters, but each letter has the same height. So the more text you try to fit into an area, the more crowded the letters will look.

Figure 5-1 shows text using **Align** and Figure 5-2 shows text using **Fit**.

Figure 5-1: Align text

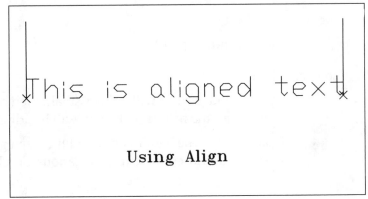

Figure 5-2: Fit text

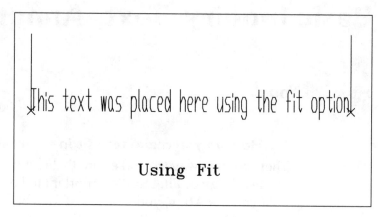

Type: DTEXT <RETURN>

Response: Start point or Align/Center/Fit/Mid/Right/Style:

Type: A <RETURN>

Response: Start point:

Pick a beginning point.

Response: End point:

Pick an ending point.

Response: Text:

Type in your text. It will appear small, then be aligned between the two points, and the height of the text will be adjusted.

 RELEASE 11 The **TEXT** command has been greatly expanded to encompass a wide variety of text justifications. See Tip 9.12.

5.2 How do you edit a line or word of text?

AutoCAD considers a line of text to be a single block. So if you want to change anything on a line of text, you must erase the line and then retype it. The main problem you run into is getting the line back into position. Also make sure that it's the same height, the same color, and that it stays on the same layer.

Each of these problems can be taken care of visually, but a better method is to use the **CHANGE** command and its option **Change Point**. If you press <RETURN> when it asks you for the new change point, and the object you've selected is **Text**, you'll be given a series of choices. One of the choices is **Change Text**.

Once you're in change text mode, a series of questions will come up along with the current default. These questions include changing the style, height, rotation and the text itself. Each question will have the current status as the default. If you want to keep that status, just <RETURN>. When you get to the text itself, you can change it, too; see LISP21, Tip 5.34, for an easier way to change the content of a line.

If you're using a style with a fixed height, your responses may be slightly different from those below until the prompt asks for **New Text**.

Type: `CHANGE <RETURN>`

Response: `Select objects:`

Pick a line of text, and confirm.

Response: `Properties/<Change point>:`

Type: `<RETURN>`

Response: `Enter text insertion point:`

Type: `<RETURN>`

Response: `Text style:STANDARD`
               `New style or RETURN for no change:`

Type: `<RETURN>`

Response: `New height <0.25>:`

Type: `<RETURN>`

Response: `New rotation angle <0>:`

Type: `<RETURN>`

Response: `New text <Left door swing>:`

Type: RIGHT DOOR SWING <RETURN>

The text will now be changed from Left door swing to Right door swing.

 RELEASE 11   A new command called **DDEDIT** lets you edit text using a dialogue box. It can be used on only one line at a time, but it gives you a full-screen editor on that line, complete with insertions, deletions and backspaces. See Tip 9.9.

5.3 How do you change fonts?

Fonts are an integral part of text style, so each font you want to use should be set up within a given style. The other options within the **STYLE** command may vary, so you can have more than one style for a given font (you must have at least one style per font).

Type: STYLE <RETURN>

Response: Text style name (or ?):

Type: R25 <RETURN> (This is a name you make up.)

Response: New style:
Font file:

Type: ROMANT <RETURN> (This is the name of the AutoCAD font.)

Response: Height:

Type: <RETURN>

Response: Width factor:

Type: <RETURN>

Response: Obliquing angle:

Type: <RETURN>

Response: Backwards?

AutoCAD® 2000

Type: <RETURN>

Response: Upside-down?

Type: <RETURN>

Response: Vertical?

Type: <RETURN>

Response: R25 is now the current text style.

5.4 How do you preset the height of text?

Whenever the height of text needs to be preset, answer the height question with a number other than 0 when you're creating a text style. AutoCAD will use that height as a default during the **TEXT** or **DTEXT** command.

5.5 How do you draw text dynamically on the screen?

When you use the **TEXT** command, the text appears at the AutoCAD command line until it's confirmed; it's then placed in position in the drawing. However, **DTEXT** will let you dynamically type text where you want it in a drawing. The only restrictions to this are if you want the text centered, fit or not drawn at the start point. **DTEXT** will type the text approximately where you want it, then center or fit it when the line is confirmed.

5.6 How do you change the height of existing text?

One way to change the height of existing text is through the **CHANGE** command with its **Change Point** option.

If you press <RETURN> when the command asks for the new change point, and the object you've selected is text, you'll be given a series of choices. One of the choices is **Change Text**. Once you're in **Change Text** mode, a series of questions will come up along with the current default. These questions include changing the style, height, rotation and the words themselves. Each question has the current status as the default. If you want to keep that status, just press <RETURN>. When you get to the height, change it.

One basic problem with this method is that you can change only one line at a time. See LISP22 in Tip 5.35 for an easier, more straightforward way to change the height of text within a window while leaving other objects alone.

Type: `CHANGE <RETURN>`

Response: `Select objects:`

Pick a line of text, and confirm.

Response: `Properties/<Change point>:`

Type: `<RETURN>`

Response: `Enter text insertion point:`

Type: `<RETURN>`

Response: `Text style:STANDARD`
`New style or RETURN for no change:`

Type: `<RETURN>`

Response: `New height <0.25>:`

Type: `.50 <RETURN>`

Response: `New rotation angle <0>:`

Type: `<RETURN>`

Response: `New text <Left door swing>:`

Type: `<RETURN>`

The height will now be changed from .25 to .50.

5.7 **How do you add new fonts?**

AutoCAD supplies you with a number of fonts. Of course, you may design your own fonts, but this isn't always practical or even necessary. There are many non-AutoCAD font files available from third-party vendors.

The fonts you buy may include special installation instructions, which you should follow. But remember that a font file is a file that resides on your hard disk with your standard AutoCAD font files. All these files are normally compiled as .SHX files, including the commercial fonts; so don't treat them differently unless you're so instructed. Treat new fonts as AutoCAD fonts: make them part of a text style.

Be aware that the font itself isn't made a part of the AutoCAD drawing; only the font name is referenced in the drawing. Therefore, the font must be available on disk. If you send your drawing to someone else to use on their AutoCAD system, you'll need to send them the font file, too, but be careful. You might be violating copyright laws.

If the font isn't on disk, AutoCAD will notify you, and ask for a new font name. You can use a standard AutoCAD font instead in order to see the drawing, even if the font looks different.

RELEASE 12   Choose the **DRAW/TEXT** pull-down menu and select the new **Set Style** dialogue box. See Tip 20.46.

5.8 **How do you draw text at an angle?**

Drawing text at an angle is simple. One of the questions that the **TEXT** command asks is **Rotation angle**. The text is drawn at the angle you selected; see Figure 5-3.

Figure 5-3: Angled text

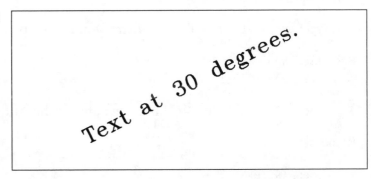

The problem is when you want text to be drawn or aligned with another entity. See the LISP23 program in Tip 5.36; it lets you point to an entity and then transfer that angle to the **TEXT** command.

5.9 How do you annotate the distance of a line along the line?

The **DIMENSION** command lets you dimension along a line; but what if you simply want to measure a line, then place that annotation along it?

This is really a two-part procedure. First, you must use the **DIST** or **LIST** command to get the distance and the angle of the entity you want to annotate. The next step is to draw text at that angle, providing the annotation description as the text, as shown in Figure 5-4. See the LISP24 program in Tip 5.37; it combines both of these steps.

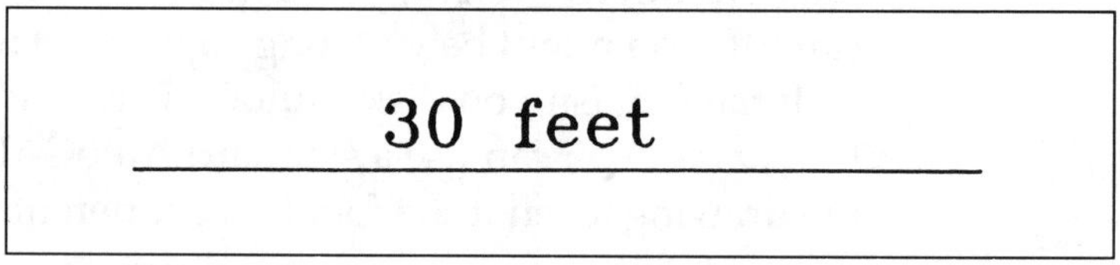

Figure 5-4: Annotated distance

30 feet

5.10 How do you write text vertically?

Writing text vertically is a function of the text style. When you get to that question, answer Y.

Type: STYLE <RETURN>

Response: Text style name (or ?):

Type: R25 <RETURN> (This is a name you make up.)

Response: New style:
Font file:

Type: ROMANT <RETURN> (This is the name of the AutoCAD font.)

Response: Height:

Type: <RETURN>

Response: Width factor:

Type: `<RETURN>`

Response: `Obliquing angle:`

Type: `<RETURN>`

Response: `Backwards?`

Type: `<RETURN>`

Response: `Upside-down?`

Type: `<RETURN>`

Response: `Vertical?`

Type: `Y <RETURN>`

Response: `R25 is now the current text style.`

See Figure 5-5.

Figure 5-5: Vertical text

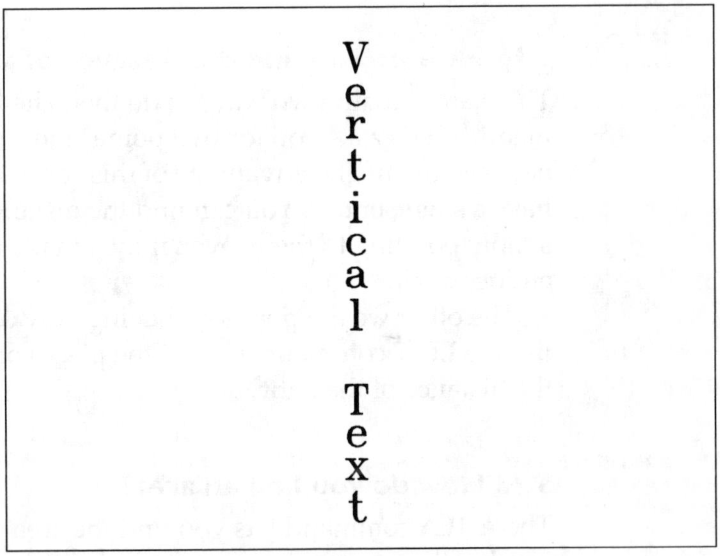

5.11 **How do you change styles?**

Before you can use a style, it must be active. A style becomes active immediately after you create it; but you can change back and forth between
styles.

To change styles, issue the **Style** subcommand within the **TEXT** or
DTEXT command.

Type: `DTEXT <RETURN>`

Response: `Start point or Align/Center/Fit/Mid/Right/Style:`

Type: `S <RETURN>`

Response: `Style name (or ?):`

Type: `R25 <RETURN>`

Now continue with the **DTEXT** command, or type Ctrl-C to abort.

RELEASE 12   You can now set Style through the new **Entity Modes**
dialogue box. See Tip 20.47.

5.12 **How do you find the distance of an entity?**

There are actually two ways to do this. The first is with the **DIST** command, which asks you for two points and then gives you the distance
between them. The advantage of this command is that you don't have to
have a single entity. You can find the distance between any two points by
simply pointing to them, even if they make up more than one entity or no
entities at all.

The other way depends on having only one entity. Then it's easier to
use the **LIST** command. One of the pieces of information it gives you is
the distance of the entity.

5.13 **How do you find an area?**

The **AREA** command lets you find the area of virtually anything. Assuming that the area you want to find isn't a single entity, pick as many points
as you can around the area. End the sequence with a final <RETURN> to
terminate the command, and you'll get the area and the perimeter.

If you want to know just the X, Y and Z coordinates of a point on the screen, the **ID** command lets you pick a point and displays only the coordinates of that point.

5.16 How do you dimension a line?

To do dimensioning in AutoCAD, you must set up the dimension variables to customize the exact appearance of the dimension lines. Once everything's set up, dimensioning a line is easy. See Figures 5-8 and 5-9.

Figure 5-8: Begin linear
dimensioning

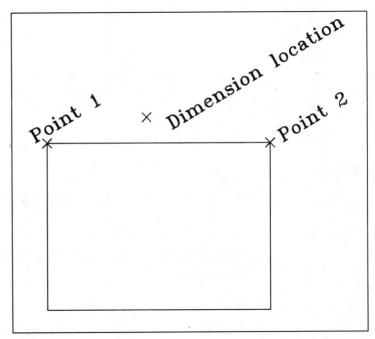

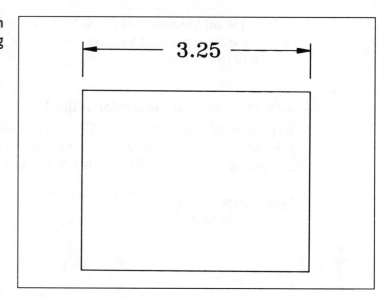

**Figure 5-9: Finish
linear dimensioning**

Type: DIM <RETURN>

Response: Dim:

Type: HORIZONTAL <RETURN> (You also might choose VERTICAL.)

Response: First extension line origin or RETURN to select:
Pick point 1 of the line you want to dimension. See Tip 25.9 for more about
the **Return** option.

Response: Second extension line origin:
Pick point 2 of the line you want to dimension.

Response: Dimension line location:
Pick where you want the dimension line to be.

Response: Dimension text <3.25>:

Type: <RETURN> to accept the dimension.

5.17 **How do you dimension an angle?**

As with dimensioning a line, dimensioning an angle is straightforward if the proper dimension variables are set.

Type: DIM <RETURN>

Response: Dim:

Type: ANGULAR <RETURN>

Response: Select first line:

Pick one of the lines that forms the angle.

Response: Second line:

Pick the second line that forms the angle.

Response: Enter dimension line arc location:

Pick the place where you want the arc.

Response: Dimension text <66.37>:

Type: <RETURN>

As with linear dimensions, AutoCAD will default on the correct value of the angle. This is called the *dimension text*. You can accept the angle or you can type in your own text, including a different angle.

Response: Enter text location:

Pick where you want the dimension text location to be. See Figure 5-10.

Figure 5-10: Angular dimensioning

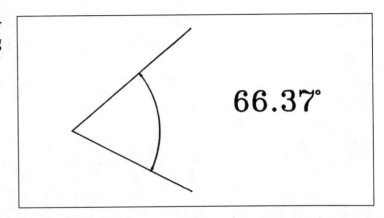

5.18 **How do you draw a leader line?**

Sometimes, you don't want to actually dimension an object; what you'd like is to draw an arrow from an object to a point where you can type in your own text. This is called a *leader line*. It's very easy to use and is part of the **DIM** command. The size of the arrow or tick mark (or even customized arrows or ticks) depends on the dimension variables in effect when the leader line is drawn.

Type: `DIM <RETURN>`

Response: `Dim:`

Type: `LEADER <RETURN>`

Response: `Leader start:`

Now begin picking points, the same way as you do with the AutoCAD **LINE** command. On the last point, press <RETURN> one extra time.

Response: `Dimension text:`

You may now type in the text to be used at the end of the leader line. See Figure 5-11.

Figure 5-11:
Leader lines

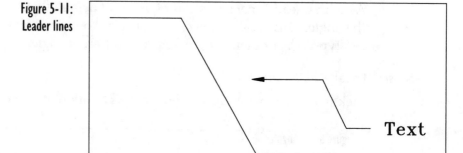

Text

5.19 **How do you do multiple dimensions?**

There are two multiple dimension options: **Base Line** and **Continuation**. After you've chosen the beginning point of origin of the first dimension, you can choose either option. **Continuation** gives you a dimension that is similar to Figure 5-12, and **Base Line** gives a dimension similar to Figure 5-13.

Figure 5-12: Multiple dimensioning with Continuation

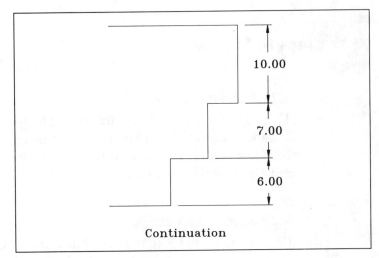

Continuation

Figure 5-13: Multiple dimensioning with Base Line

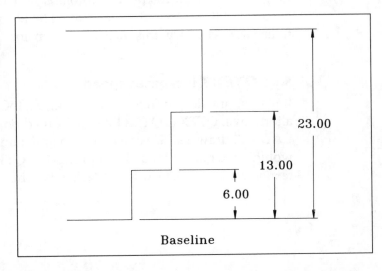

Baseline

If you want to repeat the dimension mode, such as horizontal or vertical, simply press <RETURN>.

5.20 **How do you override dimension information?**

You're supplied with dimension text in almost all of the dimension commands. This is the actual dimension as measured by AutoCAD. You can accept it by pressing <RETURN>, or you can change it to anything you want by typing in the new text. AutoCAD will place this on the dimension line.

More Steps to Success

5.21 **List any entity**

There are many ways to get information on a specific entity, such as its distance, coordinates or layers. But the easiest and fastest way is with the **LIST** command. The only prerequisite to the command is that the entity must exist and be visible on the screen.

5.22 **Save time with text**

Depending on the text fonts used in a drawing, the regeneration time ranges from barely tolerable to intolerable. The easiest and fastest way to get around this is to make sure that all text is on its own layer, so you can freeze it if necessary; this includes dimension text.

5.23 **QTEXT increases speed**

If it's not practical to freeze a text layer, AutoCAD gives you another alternative: **QTEXT**. **QTEXT** can be turned on or off. If it's on, then Auto-CAD will draw a series of enclosed parallel lines to show where the text would have gone if it had been produced. **QTEXT Off** will produce the text as usual on the next **REGEN**. See Figures 5-14 and 5-15.

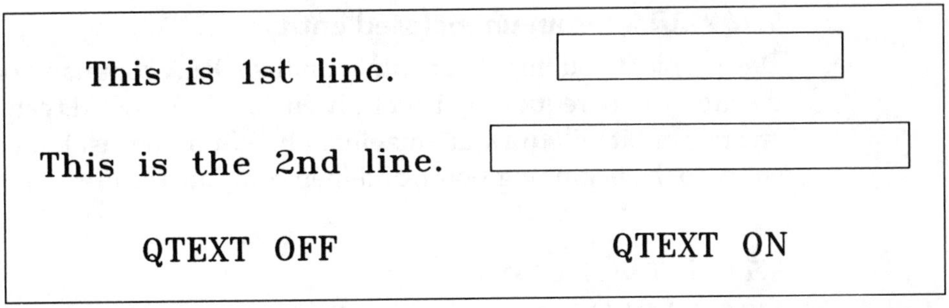

This is 1st line.

This is the 2nd line.

QTEXT OFF   QTEXT ON

Figure 5-14 (left): Text without QTEXT   Figure 5-15 (right): QTEXT On

Type: QTEXT <RETURN>

Response: ON/OFF:

Type: ON <RETURN>

5.24 **Text middle and center**

At first glance, it would seem that the **TEXT** options **Center** and **Middle** are the same. The difference has to do with the baseline of the text (the baseline is an imaginary line that's drawn right under the text). If you use the **Center** option, the text's baseline is centered left-right. The text is still drawn above the baseline. If you use **Middle**, the baseline is also centered left-right, but is also adjusted vertically, so that the point picked lies in the middle of the text.

RELEASE 11   The **TEXT** command has been greatly expanded to encompass a wide variety of text justification. See Tip 9.12.

5.25 **Preset text styles**

As you know, you need a text style in order to use a font. Although it's not hard to create a style, it's not much fun to do each time you go into a new drawing. Try setting up all of your text styles ahead of time in a prototype drawing such as ACAD.DWG.

5.26 **AREA for an unenclosed entity**

One problem you might run into with the **AREA** command occurs when the area you're requesting isn't fully enclosed. AutoCAD can't find such an area; but it will draw an imaginary line from the last known point of the entity to the beginning point, and then compute the area.

5.27 **LIST vs. DBLIST**

LIST and **DBLIST** give you virtually the same information. The difference is that with **LIST** you can select the entities you want listed. **DBLIST** will list every entity in the database, so use it only when you need such a list.

5.28 **STATUS for extended or expanded memory use**

AutoCAD's **STATUS** command lists a lot of information, most of which you may not use. But it can be used very effectively to see whether Auto-CAD is actually using extended or expanded memory, and how much it's using.

5.29 **Getting started with dimension variables**

AutoCAD provides a number of dimension variables that let you customize dimensioning almost any way you want. But without reading and studying an entire manual, it's hard to tell what variables must be set correctly to let you begin. The following list may not give you exactly the kind of dimensions you want, but most dimensions will work if these variables are set.

DIMASZ Size of the arrowheads.

DIMTSZ Size of the tick marks. Set either **DIMASZ** or **DIMTSZ**, but not both. If it's not zero, **DIMTSZ** has precedence over **DIMASZ**.

DIMEXO Extension line offset (amount the extension line is offset from the line you're dimensioning).

DIMEXE Extension line extension (amount that the extension line continues beyond the dimension line).

DIMDLI Dimension line increment for continuation with **BASELINE**.

DIMTXT Text size.

RELEASE 12   You can set dimension variables more easily by using the new **DDIM** dialogue box. See Tips 10.29 and 30.21.

5.30 **DIM and DIM1**

DIM will take you into the dimension command, then let you issue various other commands. To exit, press Ctrl-C. There's another way to get into the dimension command, perform a specific dimension and return automatically to the AutoCAD Command line. This is **DIM1**, which lets you issue one command while dimensioning.

5.31 **Adjusting dimension text**

Sometimes the position of the text in dimensioning isn't exactly right, no matter how carefully you set the dimension variables. If you don't have **Associative Dimensioning** on, the dimension text is the same as any other text and can be moved to wherever you want. If **Associative Dimensioning** is on, the text and the dimensions are treated as a single block. You can still move the text if you issue the **EXPLODE** command, but be aware that you then cannot treat the dimension as an associative dimension. However, you can move or adjust the text.

RELEASE 11 Offers new dimension options, permitting you to adjust the dimension text at will without giving up **Associative Dimensioning**. See Tips 19.11 through 19.19.

5.32 **Preset dimension variables**

Once you have the dimension variables set, they need to be in a prototype drawing, such as ACAD.DWG, so that you won't have to set them every time you start a new drawing. Do your experimenting with dimension variables in a prototype drawing. Otherwise, you'll have to get a printout of the variables' status from another drawing and reset them in the prototype.

RELEASE 11 You can now have a set group of dimension variable styles that can be saved and recalled at will within a drawing. Each style can have a complete group of variable settings. See Tips 19.11 through 19.19.

5.33 **Arrow and tick sizes conflict**

Don't give a positive number to both the arrow size and the tick size. If you want to use arrows in dimensioning, the tick size must be zero. If the tick size is a positive number, the ticks will be used no matter what size you use for the arrows.

RELEASE 12   Lets you set dimension variables more easily by using the new DDIM dialogue box. See Tip 30.21.

AutoLISP Programs

5.34 **Substitute text (LISP21)**

This program lets you quickly change a line of text without having to answer a lot of questions, as with the **CHANGE** command. If you don't like the line after it's been changed, type N and the original line will be returned. (Use of the plus sign at the end of a line in AutoLISP code indicates that line is wrapped.)

Listing:
```
(defun c:lisp21 (/ ent oldline newline ent1 yesno)
    (prompt "\nPick line of text to be changed ")
    (setq ent (entget (car (entsel))))
    (setq oldline (cdr (assoc 1 ent)))
    (terpri)
    (prompt oldline)
    (terpri)
    (setq newline (getstring 1))
    (setq ent1 (subst (cons (car (assoc 1 ent)) newline) (assoc 1 +
      ent) ent))
    (entmod ent1)
    (setq yesno (getstring "\nIs this correct <Y>"))
    (if (= (strcase yesno) "N") (entmod ent))
    (if (= (strcase yesno) "NO") (entmod ent))
)
```

To Use: Load LISP21.LSP.

Type: LISP21 <RETURN>

Response: Pick line of text to be changed:

Select object:

Pick the line of text. The line will be displayed at the Command line. Now type the new line under the old one and press <RETURN>. The new line will replace the old one.

Response: Is this correct? <Y>

Type: <RETURN> The line is made permanent. Type N, and the original line will be returned.

5.35 Change text size (LISP22)

This program globally changes the height of all text chosen. It won't change entities other than text.

Listing:
```
(defun c:lisp22 (/ ss txsize n index ent type oldsize newsize ent1)
   (setq ss (ssget))
   (setq txsize (getdist "\nEnter new text size"))
   (setq n (sslength ss))
   (setq index 0)
   (repeat n
      (setq ent (entget (ssname ss index)))
      (setq index (+ 1 index))
      (setq type (assoc 0 ent))
      (if (= "TEXT" (cdr type))
         (progn
            (setq oldsize (assoc 40 ent))
            (setq newsize (cons (car oldsize) txsize))
            (setq ent1 (subst newsize oldsize ent))
            (entmod ent1)
         )
      )
   )
   (prin1)
)
```

To Use: Load LISP22.LSP.

Type: LISP22 <RETURN>

Response: `Select objects:`

Select the text to be changed; or put a window around a large area. Don't worry if you capture entities other than text.

Response: `Enter new text size:`

Type in the new text size, or point to the size as you would in the **TEXT** command. All the text captured will change size.

5.36 **Angle text (LISP23)**

This program lets you point to a line, then aligns the text with that line. The only condition is that the current text style must let you enter the height; its style can't have been created with a fixed height. If it was, take out one of the pause statements.

Listing:
```
(defun c:lisp23 (/ ent pt1 pt2 ang)
    (setq ent (entget (car (entsel))))
    (setq pt1 (cdr (assoc 10 ent)))
    (setq pt2 (cdr (assoc 11 ent)))
    (setq ang (angle pt1 pt2))
    (setq ang (/ (* ang 180.0) pi))
    (command "dtext" pause pause ang pause)
)
```

To Use: Load LISP23.LSP.

Type: `LISP23 <RETURN>`

Response: `Select objects:`

Pick a line. LISP23 puts you in the **DTEXT** command and supplies the angle.

5.37 **Annotate (LISP24)**

Here's an example of how a simple annotation program can be written. A simple, straightforward program such as this is often better than the complicated dimensioning routine.

NOTE: If you are using a text style with a fixed height, remove the pause statement from the next to last line.

Listing:
```
(defun c:lisp24 (/ os pt1 pt2 pt3 ang txt)
    (setq os (getvar "osmode"))
    (setvar "osmode" 33)
    (setq pt1 (getpoint "\nPick 1st point "))
    (setq pt2 (getpoint pt1 "\nPick 2nd point "))
    (setvar "osmode" os)
    (setq pt3 (getpoint "\nBeginning of text "))
    (setq ang (angle pt1 pt2))
    (setq ang (/ (* ang 180.0) pi))
    (setq txt (rtos (distance pt1 pt2) 3 4))
    (command "text" pt3 pause ang txt)
)
```

To Use: Load LISP24.LSP.

Type: `LISP24 <RETURN>`

Response: `Pick 1st point:`

Pick the end point or intersection of a line.

Response: `Pick 2nd point:`

Pick the other end point or intersection of the line.

Response: `Beginning of text:`

Pick the point where the text is to begin. The distance will be calculated and aligned with the line.

5.38 Find coordinates (LISP25)

Many times, you simply need to know the coordinates of a point on the screen. You can get this information through the **LIST** command if an entity exists, but then you have to decipher which coordinate is which. And if an entity doesn't exist at those coordinates, **LIST** is worthless. This program asks you to pick a point, and gives you the coordinates.

Listing:
```
(defun c:lisp25 ()
    (getpoint "\nPick a point \n")
)
```

To Use: Load LISP25.LSP.

Type: `LISP25 <RETURN>`

Response: `Pick a point:`

Pick a point, and the coordinates will be listed.

CHAPTER 6

Basic Utilities

How Do You . . .

6.1 **How do you get help on a specific command?**

AutoCAD has an on-line help facility for all of its commands, but it can't tell which command you need help on unless you tell it. The easiest way to do this is to type HELP, followed by the command name. For example:

Type: `HELP LINE <RETURN>`

This will give you help information on the **LINE** command. If you just type HELP by itself, and then <RETURN> <RETURN>, you'll get the names of all the commands. If you type something at the Command line that AutoCAD doesn't understand, press <RETURN> or the space bar twice, and you'll get the same result as if you'd typed HELP.

RELEASE 11   You now have a context-sensitive help screen available. While in a command, you may type **'?** or **'help** to any prompt that's not asking for a text string. AutoCAD will then often display context-specific help information. This is followed by an option for more help. If you answer Y for more help, AutoCAD displays the general help screen for that command. See Tip 9.8.

RELEASE 12   Included in the new **Help...** dialogue box is an index listing all AutoCAD Commands. See Tip 20.17.

6.2 **How do you save your drawing?**

Release 11 and Release 10 users have only two ways to save a drawing in AutoCAD. When you enter AutoCAD, you give the name of a new or an existing drawing. If you issue the **END** command, the current drawing is saved under its original name and you're returned to the AutoCAD main menu. The second way is with the **SAVE** command. This command asks for the name under which you'd like to save the drawing. It will default to its original name, but you can change it. This way, you can have more than one version of the same drawing on file. **SAVE** also lets you update a drawing to disk while remaining in the drawing editor.

RELEASE 11   Any time a file name is asked for, a dialogue box appears for the filename entry if the system variable **FILEDIA** is set to **1**. If the system variable is set to **0**, the filename prompt appears at the Command line without the dialogue box. See Tips 9.10 and 9.11.

RELEASE 12   Offers alternative ways to save a drawing file. See Tip 10.6.

6.3 **How do you start over again without making your changes permanent?**

If you haven't issued the **SAVE** command using the original name of the drawing, use the **QUIT** command to quit your drawing at any time without updating your changes back to disk. You'll receive a message asking if you really want to quit the drawing without saving your changes. If you answer Y, the drawing is aborted and you're returned to the AutoCAD main menu.

RELEASE 12   Lets you use **New** and **Open** to escape from a current drawing without quitting the editor. See Tip 10.7.

6.4 How do you change units of measurement?

AutoCAD has five basic unit types:

Scientific This expresses your units in exponential notation. Example: 2.74E+01

Decimal This is not a given unit. The kind of unit is up to you; AutoCAD lets you express yourself in a whole unit and a decimal portion of that unit, such as foot, inch, meter, etc. Example: 3.25

Engineering This unit is expressed in feet and inches. The fractional portion of an inch is expressed as a decimal. Example: 3' 4.25"

Architectural This unit is expressed in feet and inches. The fractional part of an inch is expressed as a fraction. Example: 3' 4-1/4"

Fractional This is the fractional equivalent of a decimal unit. Example: 3 1/4

Issue the **UNITS** command to set the proper units.

RELEASE 12   You can now change units using the new dialogue box **DDUNITS**. See Tip 10.12.

6.5 How do you change angular measurements?

This is part of the **UNITS** command. After you've set the appropriate units, you're asked about angular measurements:

Decimal degrees These are degrees without minutes and seconds. Example: 35.215

Degrees/minutes/seconds This lets you use degrees, minutes and seconds. Example: 34d14'22"

Grads These set the angular measurement to grads. Example: 48.215g

Radians These set the angular measurement to radians. Example: 1.012r

Surveyor's units These let you use bearings. Example: N22d14'22"E

RELEASE 12   Change angular measurements easily by using **DDUNITS**, a new dialogue box. See Tip 10.12.

6.6 **How do you make angles go clockwise?**

One of the questions in the **UNITS** command is "Do you want angles measured clockwise?" The default to this question is N. Leave it that way unless you really understand all of the implications.

6.7 **How do you change 0 degrees to North instead of East?**

One of the first shockers to a new AutoCAD user is the fact that AutoCAD considers 0 degrees to be East instead of North. You can change this in the **UNITS** command. One of the questions is **Direction for angle 0?** The options are

East	3 o'clock = 0	
North	12 o'clock = 90	
West	9 o'clock = 180	
South	6 o'clock = 270	

To change the direction of 0 degrees to North, enter **90**. You're not limited to the four options above; you can enter any degree or portion you want, and it will be your new direction for 0 degrees. But be careful of your choices. If you don't have a lot of experience with AutoCAD, stick with the given options.

6.8 **How do you stop the total-elapsed-time clock?**

When you begin a new drawing, AutoCAD begins tracking the length of time you've been in the drawing since its inception. You can't stop or change this time. If you quit a drawing without saving it to disk, the time you spent in the drawing is not updated.

6.9 **How do you change the total elapsed time?**

You can't change the total elapsed time of a drawing. But you can trick AutoCAD by resetting the time to 0. Create a new drawing with the same limits and units as the existing drawing. Then insert the existing drawing, preceded by an * so that the entities come in as individual entities. Use 0,0 as the insertion point. Then save the new drawing under whatever name you wish. Since this is a new drawing, the total elapsed time will have begun again.

6.10 **How do you control the user-elapsed time?**

In addition to total elapsed time, AutoCAD lets you work with user-elapsed time. This is accessed by the **TIME** command. There are four options with this command:

Display	Displays time information
On	Starts the user-elapsed time
Off	Stops the user-elapsed time
Reset	Resets the user-elapsed time to 0

6.11 **How do you run other programs from inside AutoCAD?**

The ACAD.PGP file determines how much memory is set aside to run other programs from inside AutoCAD. Add your own special programs to this .PGP file, which you can run simply by typing the name of your program.

If you don't want to go to that trouble, AutoCAD has set up two generic commands within the .PGP file, called **SHELL** and **SH**. These commands let you issue one DOS command, which can be the name of the program you want to run. When the program finishes, you're returned to the Auto-CAD Command line.

The difference between **SHELL** and **SH** is that **SHELL** allows more memory. Thus, you can run only smaller programs with **SH**. However, with **SH**, it's easier for AutoCAD to make room in RAM for the program to run.

6.12 **How do you backtrack through a drawing?**

The **UNDO** command is one of the most powerful commands in Auto-CAD. It lets you type U any number of times to undo a command or group of commands. Or enter **UNDO 5** and go back five commands.

6.13 **How do you plot only part of a drawing?**

You have several options when you issue the **PLOT** command. If you want to plot only part of a drawing, you can zoom in on the part that you want to plot, then choose **Display** as one of the options. It will then plot only what's on the screen. If you've saved a given view as a **VIEW**, you can also plot by **VIEW**. As you enter the **PLOT** command, one of the options is **Window**, which lets you put a window around the drawing at that time.

Sometimes, what you don't want to plot is in the same display as what you want to plot. If it's on a different layer, that layer can be turned off or frozen; then it won't plot.

 RELEASE 11   With the introduction of Paper Space, other options are available for plotting only part of your drawing or rearranging parts of your drawing to appear on the same sheet. See Tip 29.1 for an overview of Paper Space.

6.14 **How do you determine which pen will be used at plotting time?**

Which pen is used by the plotter is controlled by the color of the entity. When you enter the **PLOT** command, it gives you the current settings. You're then asked if you want to change anything. Entering Y will show you your current color and pen assignments. By pressing <RETURN> you can change any of the pen numbers for any color number. All entities of a specific color will use the same pen.

 RELEASE 12   Provides you with a choice of up to 255 colors. See Tip 20.55.

6.15 **How do you adjust where AutoCAD plots on the paper?**

When you plot your first drawing, it may be a little high or low on the paper. AutoCAD picks what it considers to be 0,0 on the paper to match coordinate 0,0 in the drawing. If you want to adjust this, one of the options to change is the **Plot Origin**. This is measured in real inches on the paper. For example, if you enter 2,1 then AutoCAD moves the drawing two inches to the right and one inch up.

6.16 **How do you plot the same thing more than once?**

Sometimes in a large drawing your pen might skip or run out of ink. This usually happens at the end of the drawing. Depending on the accuracy of your plotter, you can usually plot the drawing a second time right on top of the first. With a little practice, you can turn certain layers on or off to replot only the part that didn't come out the first time.

6.17 **How do you scale when you plot?**

Actually, almost all scaling to a drawing should be done at plot time, not in the drawing itself. If you answer Y to the initial question on changing any of the plot parameters, one of the last questions AutoCAD asks you before you plot is

```
Specify scale by entering:
Plotted units=Drawing units or Fit or ?:
```

Enter the scale at which you want the drawing plotted. If you answer **FIT**, you're telling AutoCAD to use whatever scale is necessary to make the drawing fit on the size paper you have specified.

The scale factor you put in is the plotted scale=real-life units. Example: .25"=1' or 1=50

6.18 **How do you use multiple pens on a single-pen plotter?**

When you configure a plotter for AutoCAD, make sure that you've activated menu item 2 in the CONFIGURATION menu. This lets AutoCAD ask you additional questions about the equipment you're installing.

If you're installing a single-pen plotter, AutoCAD asks you if you want to be prompted for pen changes. If you answer Y, AutoCAD will prompt you to change pens during the plot.

6.19 **How do you stop a plot in the middle?**

This depends on what you mean by stopping; if you want to abort a plot, just press Ctrl-C. You can then return to your drawing.

On the other hand, some plotters can temporarily stop a plot to let you change a pen. Consult the manual for your particular plotter.

6.20 **How do you make a script file?**

A script file is to AutoCAD what the AUTOEXEC.BAT is to DOS. This isn't an exact analogy, but it's close. A script file is simply a series of keystrokes that you might type in if you were running AutoCAD.

Script files can save time in a number of situations. For example, Auto-LISP can't issue a **PLOT** command, but it can call up a script file. In the script file, you can put the commands necessary to run the plot configuration of your choice. Script files can also perform time-consuming and repetitive operations.

To create a script file, create an ordinary text file and name it anything you want as long as it has the extension .SCR. This means that it's created with a text editor such as EDLIN. Of course, EDLIN or other text editors can be run from inside AutoCAD.

Enter information in a script file exactly as you would from the keyboard. Wherever you'd normally type a space, do so on the line. Where you'd normally press <RETURN>, do so in the script file.

The following is a very simple script file that inserts a block called Part-1.

INSERT   (This is the AutoCAD command.)

part-1   (Enter block name.)

   1.1   (Insertion point.)
        (Press <RETURN> for X scale.)
        (Press <RETURN> for Y scale.)
        (Press <RETURN> for rotation.)

Notice the three blank lines at the end, which result from pressing the <RETURN> key.

6.21 **How do you run a script file?**

Now that you've written your script file, there are two ways to run it: from outside AutoCAD, or from inside. If you're already in AutoCAD, issue the **SCRIPT** command.

Type: SCRIPT <RETURN>

Response: Script file:

Type: `SC1 <RETURN>` (This assumes that the name of the file is SC1.SCR. Don't add the extension; AutoCAD adds it for you.)

If you're outside AutoCAD, you can start a script file from the DOS C: prompt:

Type: `ACAD SC1 <RETURN>`

This puts you in AutoCAD's main menu.

Make sure that the script file starts with the keystrokes necessary to get you into a drawing. A beginning script file brought up in this way might look something like this:

`2`   (Edit an existing drawing.)

`TEST1`   (The name of the drawing is TEST1.)

`VIEW R V1` (Bring up a view called V1.)

6.22 **How do you run a continuous script?**

If the script was started from DOS, and the last line in the script file was **QUIT Y**, the script file will begin again automatically when it returns to the AutoCAD main menu.

If the script was started with the **SCRIPT** command from inside Auto-CAD, make **RSCRIPT** the last command in the script file; it will keep repeating.

6.23 **How do you configure the tablet menu?**

If you use a digitizer, you can specify part of it as a tablet menu and part as the screen menu. AutoCAD comes with a very good, free tablet menu with most of the commands already programmed for you. At the top of the menu is an area where you can insert your own special AutoLISP programs, macros or blocks.

If you're using a menu developed by a third party instead of the standard AutoCAD menu, you need to know how to tell AutoCAD the menu configuration. This is done through the **TABLET** command. See LISP28 in Tip 6.48.

Type: TABLET <RETURN>

Response: Option (ON/OFF/CAL/CFG):

Type: CFG <RETURN> (This stands for "configuration.")

Response: Enter number of tablet menus desired (0-4):

Type: 4 <RETURN> (AutoCAD wants to know how many tablet menus there are. If you're using the standard AutoCAD tablet menu, there are four. Other menus may be configured differently.)

Response: Do you want to realign tablet menu areas? <N>

Type: Y <RETURN> (Whether you get the above question depends on whether AutoCAD detects that you've changed the number of menus from what's already configured.)

See Figure 6-1.

Figure 6-1:
Tablet configuration

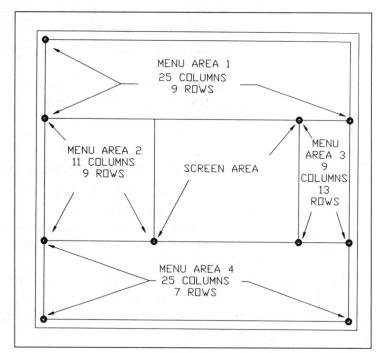

Response: `Digitize upper left corner of menu area 1:`
`Digitize lower left corner of menu area 1:`
`Digitize lower right corner of menu area 1:`

Pick the appropriate points as indicated in Figure 6-1.

Response: `Enter the number of columns for menu area 1:`

Type: `25 <RETURN>`

Response: `Enter the number of rows for menu area 1:`

Type: `9 <RETURN>`

Response: `Digitize upper left corner of menu area 2:`
`Digitize lower left corner of menu area 2:`
`Digitize lower right corner of menu area 2:`

Pick the appropriate points as indicated in Figure 6-1.

Response: `Enter the number of columns for menu area 2:`

Type: `11 <RETURN>`

Response: `Enter the number of rows for menu area 2:`

Type: `9 <RETURN>`

Response: `Digitize upper left corner of menu area 3:`
`Digitize lower left corner of menu area 3:`
`Digitize lower right corner of menu area 3:`

Pick the appropriate points as indicated in Figure 6-1.

Response: `Enter the number of columns for menu area 3:`

Type: `9 <RETURN>`

Response: `Enter the number of rows for menu area 3:`

Type: 13 <RETURN>

Response: Digitize upper left corner of menu area 4:
Digitize lower left corner of menu area 4:
Digitize lower right corner of menu area 4:

Pick the appropriate points as indicated in Figure 6-1.

Response: Enter the number of columns for menu area 4:

Type: 25 <RETURN>

Response: Enter the number of rows for menu area 4:

Type: 7 <RETURN>

Response: Do you want to respecify the screen pointing area? <N>

Type: Y <RETURN> (This gives you the chance to define your screen area. Remember, the screen area can't overlap the menu areas.)

Response: Digitize lower left corner of screen pointing area:
Digitize upper right corner of screen pointing area:

After these points are digitized, the menu is configured.

6.24 How do you use only a portion of a larger digitizer?

This depends on whether you're using a tablet menu on the digitizer or simply using the digitizer as a screen pointing area.

If you're using the tablet menu, its size and physical position on the digitizer dictate how it's configured.

On the other hand, if you're using the digitizer just for a screen pointing device, use the **TABLET** command and enter 0 for the number of tablet menus. Answer Y to respecify the screen area. Digitize the lower left-hand corner of the screen as you want it on your digitizer, then the upper right-hand corner.

6.25 **How do you undo a REDO?**

The command **REDO** will bring you back to the place of the last **UNDO**. Like **OOPS**, you can have only one **REDO** for an **UNDO** group. For example, if you enter **UNDO 8** and see that that's too much, enter **REDO** and then try an **UNDO 5**.

More Steps to Success

6.26 **SAVE under an alternate name**

Save your drawing periodically; a good backup means the difference between a catastrophe and maybe five minutes of inconvenience. If you do nothing else, at least type SAVE every half hour and press <RETURN>. This will update your latest changes to disk in case AutoCAD freezes or there's a power failure. Release 12 users have a new automatic SAVE feature; the timer is set through the SAVEFILE feature.

One way to save your drawing is under a different name than the one it was brought up under. Often, you can simply add a suffix to the name. This guards against one more risk: an AutoCAD freeze or a power failure during the save operation itself. The larger the drawing, the greater the risk.

Another method is to alternate between the real name of the drawing and its alternate name—then you're only an hour behind, even in the worst catastrophe. See LISP26 in Tip 6.46 for a save program that automatically adds a suffix to a drawing's name.

RELEASE 12   Allows you alternate ways to save drawing files. See Tip 10.6.

6.27 **Never save to floppy**

Never save to a floppy disk directly. First, floppies are unreliable at best. Second, if you fill a floppy disk, AutoCAD could freeze and not let you save your drawing.

That doesn't mean that you shouldn't use floppies for backup; you should. But save first to the hard disk, then use either the DOS copy facility or the AutoCAD copy utility to copy the .DWG file to a floppy.

6.28 **Never load from floppies**

Never load a drawing into the drawing editor from a floppy. What you must realize is that AutoCAD uses a lot more disk space than the size of the original drawing. The amount of the disk space used at any one time for temporary files varies as you work on the drawing. By bringing up a drawing directly from a floppy disk, you not only run all the risks inherent to floppies but you also increase the chance that you'll fill up the floppy.

6.29 **Always use LIMITS**

Always set and use **LIMITS**, even though AutoCAD no longer requires you to. Many people don't use **GRID** or **LIMITS**. But **LIMITS** serve a useful function: they let AutoLISP programs determine the maximum size of a drawing. They also increase AutoCAD's speed. This is useful when you want to automatically set **LTSCALE** and hatching patterns and perform fast zoom extents.

6.30 **Set reasonable limits**

If you're going to use limits, don't make them so large that you're always drawing in a small area. Make **LIMITS** no more than 20 percent larger than the largest area necessary to hold your entire drawing. Remember, you can always increase your limits.

6.31 **Set LIMCHECK to 0**

Set the system variable **LIMCHECK** to **0** (or **LIMITS Off**) so that Auto-CAD doesn't check to see whether you've drawn beyond the limits. You should use **LIMITS**, but you don't want AutoCAD to penalize you if you temporarily go beyond them.

A possible exception might be that you need **LIMCHECK** as a control to keep you from drawing out of the bounds of what will plot at a specific scale. In that case, set **LIMCHECK** to **1**.

6.32 **East—0 degrees and counterclockwise**

Be very careful if you decide to set your angle orientation to clockwise and 0 degrees to something other than East. AutoCAD's standard puts East at 0 degrees and measures angles counterclockwise.

AutoCAD will now let you change this rule, but be aware that there can be repercussions. Some AutoLISP programs rely on the standard; changing it can throw some measurements off considerably.

6.33 **Be careful when changing units**

Architectural and engineering units are interchangeable. So are fractional and decimal units. So if you start a drawing with engineering units, you can change to architectural units with no negative effects. The same is true of decimal and fractional units.

A problem arises if you want to go from decimal to architectural. Decimal isn't a specific unit of measurement; it can mean anything you want it to mean. If you decide that a decimal unit is a foot, that's fine—but if you change to architectural units, AutoCAD doesn't carry your decision through. Architectural will convert all units to its lowest form, which is the inch. Conversely, if you go from architectural to decimal, it will convert a foot to 12 decimal units.

6.34 **Converting units**

If you do change from decimal units to architectural or engineering units, you'll need to rescale your drawing after the change. This is a simple matter. After you've changed your units to engineering, issue the **SCALE** command. Put a window around the entire drawing and enter the scale factor as **12**. This will make the new drawing 12 times as large as the old one, and the conversion will be complete.

II RELEASE 11 AutoLISP enhancements include a new unit conversion command. Although this command doesn't actually convert drawing units as discussed in this section, it does provide the ability to convert any unit value to any other unit value. See Tip 19.21.

6.35 Point of origin can be changed

You aren't stuck with 0,0 as the point of origin; the **LIMITS** command will let you change it. Most often, you use the **LIMITS** command to change the upper right-hand corner limits, but the lower left-hand corner can be changed, too. For example, civil engineers or surveyors might want to change it to 10000,10000.

6.36 TIME accounting

A feature often overlooked in AutoCAD is the **TIME** command, which can tell you how much time you've spent on a specific drawing session. This can be a great help for anyone who has to fill out a time sheet.

Each time you change a drawing, reset the user-elapsed time to 0. Even if you forget to check it before you end the drawing, you can bring up the drawing and see how much time you spent in it. You can also reset the time while you're in a drawing if you want to clock something.

6.37 DOS can kill

There are certain DOS functions to avoid while you're in **SHELL**. Of course, you'd never think of using **BACKUP** or **RESTORE** from inside AutoCAD, but other functions are dangerous, too. For example, never make a new directory from inside AutoCAD. **CHKDSK/f** can be devastating. Rely on your common sense. Look at directories, copy some files and run only those programs that won't freeze AutoCAD.

6.38 SHELL can be dangerous

Running programs from inside AutoCAD can freeze AutoCAD. This isn't to say that you can't or shouldn't run them; but before you run **SHELL** and your favorite program, decide how important your most recent edits are. If you don't want to risk losing them, issue **SAVE** before you use **SHELL**.

6.39 Better OOPS than UNDO

Never use **UNDO** when you can use **OOPS**. **OOPS** brings back an erased object or group of objects. **UNDO** undoes actual commands, so you might find commands altered that you never intended to change. Use **UNDO** only if **OOPS** won't work.

6.40 **Plot without graphics**

You can use a non-graphics computer to plot; many people use an inexpensive clone computer as a plot buffer, and the machine doesn't have to be set up to run AutoCAD graphics. The minimum you need is a hard disk, close to 640k of RAM, a coprocessor and a monochrome card and monochrome monitor. You don't need a color graphics monitor, since AutoCAD lets you plot from its menu.

6.41 **Automating PLOT**

PLOT is one of the few commands that can't be automated through AutoLISP. But you can set it up using a script file accessed by AutoLISP. See LISP27 in Tip 6.47.

RELEASE 12 Starting with this release, PLOT can be accessed using AutoLISP. See Tip 30.28.

6.42 **Nested purges**

Sometimes, because of nesting, you may have to use the **PURGE** command more than once to make sure that all non-referenced items have been purged.

6.43 **PURGE can come later**

The **PURGE** command no longer has to be the very first command issued in order for it to work. You can now use any other command in AutoCAD, as long as it doesn't change the drawing database. This lets you set system variables, freeze layers, start certain AutoLISP routines, etc.

6.44 **New uses for PLOT**

Sometimes, because of interruptions in serial communications or unknown "gremlins," your crosshairs will suddenly disappear. Cursor control is gone and/or keyboard response is much slower. This can be at least temporarily corrected by using the **PLOT** command. Don't actually plot; just get to the point where AutoCAD asks you if you want to change anything. Press Ctrl-C and return to the drawing editor. Try this first; it beats having to exit and then re-enter a drawing.

RELEASE 12 Cursor loss can't be corrected this way in Release 12, but a new command—**REINIT**—rectifies this problem. See Tip 30.4.

6.45 **Check the A-B switch box before returning from PLOT**

When you're using an A-B serial switch box, turn it to the digitizer or mouse before leaving the **PLOT** command to return to your drawing. This will ensure that you have cursor control.

 **Programs**

6.46 **Alternate save (LISP26)**

This program saves your drawing to a name that's a standard suffix to the drawing's current name. This prevents overwriting your current drawing when you save it. Be sure to limit your drawing name to seven characters, since this program will add the eighth character. (Use of the plus sign at the end of a line in AutoLISP code indicates that line is wrapped.)

Listing:
```
(defun c:lisp26 (/ drwname)
  (setq drwname strcat (getvar "dwgprefix") (getvar "dwgname") +
    "1"))
  (command "save" drwname)
)
```

To Use: Load LISP26.LSP.

Type: LISP26 <RETURN>

6.47 **Automated plot (LISP27)**

You can't use an AutoLISP program to plot, but you can have an AutoLISP program call a script file to plot from. A script file is just a text file with all the keyboard entries you'd normally make. Set up a series of AutoLISP programs and script files for each type of plot you do; it will increase your efficiency.

Listing:
```
(defun c:lisp27 ()
  (command "script" "plot1")
)
```

Listing for script file:
```
plot
d
y
n
n
i
0,0
d
n
0.010
n
n
f
```

These are the answers to all the questions asked by the **PLOT** command.

To Use: Load LISP27.LSP.

Type: `LISP27 <RETURN>`

 RELEASE 12 Lets you create multiple plot configurations. See Tip 20.58.

6.48 **Configuring a tablet (LISP28)**

Configuring your tablet can be a chore, especially without a reference manual. This program supplies all the numbers necessary for the Auto-CAD standard tablet menu. LISP28 works like **TABLET CFG**, but you don't have to look up or enter column and row numbers. All that's required is for the user to pick the points.

Listing:
```
(defun c:lisp28 (/ c1 r1 c2 r2 c3 r3 c4 r4)
    (setq c1 25)
    (setq r1 9)
    (setq c2 11)
    (setq r2 9)
    (setq c3 9)
    (setq r3 13)
    (setq c4 25)
    (command "tablet" "cfg" 0 "n")
    (setq r4 7)
    (command "tablet" "cfg" 4 c1 r1 c2 r2 c3 r3 c4 r4 "y")
)
```

To Use: Load LISP28.LSP.

Type: LISP28 <RETURN>

Now pick the points on the tablet as indicated.

CHAPTER 7

Basic 3D

How Do You . . .

7.1 How do you set thickness?

Thickness isn't an AutoCAD command in itself; it's an option to the **ELEVATION** command. So if you want to set only the thickness of an object, use **ELEVATION** and default on the current elevation. The next question will ask you about the thickness. Enter the appropriate thickness at that point.

You can change the thickness of existing entities with the **CHANGE** command.

Type: ELEV <RETURN>

Response: New current elevation:

Type: <RETURN>

Response: New current thickness:

Type: 4 <RETURN>

This sets the new thickness to **4**. See LISP29 in Tip 7.38; it's a program that asks you only about thickness and leaves elevation alone. (LISP29 is like the **ELEV** command.)

RELEASE 11   Since any system variable can be used as an ordinary command, this method of setting thickness has become obsolete. The system variable **THICKNESS** should simply be typed in as an ordinary AutoCAD command followed by the set thickness value.

THICKNESS 4 <RETURN>

7.2 **How do you rotate the view of an object?**

You can view any object from anywhere in 3D space with the **DVIEW** command. When you first enter **DVIEW**, you're asked to select objects. You can select the entire object or put a window around only the part you want dynamically rotated. When you finish the **DVIEW** command, the entire object will be rotated into view, even though you selected only part of it. The advantage of doing this is that dynamic response is improved.

After you're in the **DVIEW** command with the objects selected, two options will rotate your view of the object: **Camera** and **Target**. The difference between these two is that **Camera** assumes the object is stationary and moves around the object. **Target** assumes that the camera is stationary and moves the object around the camera.

Choosing one of these options gives you control of the up and down movement of the camera. You'll see a vertical bar. As you move your cursor up and down, the object will move vertically. You may choose an angle by picking any point visually or by typing in an angle that measures from –90 to +90 degrees.

Next, you'll see a horizontal bar. This gives you control of the left-right movement of the object. You can choose an angle by picking any point visually or by typing in an angle that measures from –180 to +180 degrees.

Type: `DVIEW <RETURN>`

Response: `Select objects:`

Select with a window the objects you want to rotate, and confirm.

Response: `CAmera/TArget/Distance/POints/PAn/Zoom/TWist/CLip/Hide/Off` →
`/Undo/<eXit>:`

Type: `CA <RETURN>`

Response: `Enter angle from X-Y plane:`

Pick a vertical rotation, or

Type: `45 <RETURN>`

Response: `Enter angle in X-Y plane from X axis:`

Pick a left-right rotation, or

Type: `120 <RETURN>`

Type: `<RETURN>` (This takes you out of the DVIEW options and makes your new view permanent.)

7.3 **How do you turn perspective on?**

There's no specific command for perspective. Perspective is a subcommand of **DVIEW** called **Distance**. By setting the distance from the camera to the target, you automatically turn perspective on. See Figures 7-1 and 7-2.

Figure 7-1:
Without DISTANCE

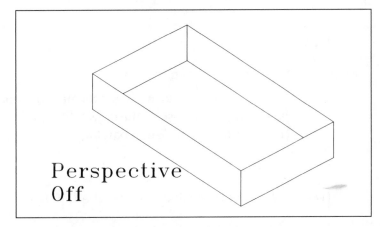

Figure 7-2:
With DISTANCE

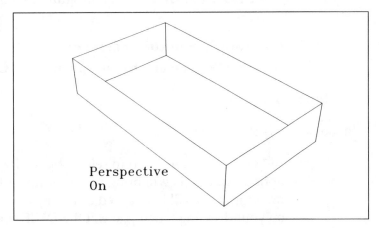

You can set this distance visually by moving your cursor back and forth, or you can enter it as a distance in your default units from the target.

Type: `DVIEW <RETURN>`

Response: `Select objects:`

Select with a window the objects you want to rotate, and confirm.

Response: `CAmera/TArget/Distance/POints/PAn/Zoom/TWist/CLip →`
`/Hide/Off/Undo/<eXit>:`

Type: `D <RETURN>`

Response: `New camera/target distance:`

Move your cursor visually for the new distance. If nothing seems to happen, you're too close to the object. Enter a large distance, then repeat the command using the slide bar. Or,

Type: `10 <RETURN>`

Type: `<RETURN>` (This exits you from the **DVIEW** command.)

See LISP34 in Tip 7.43 for a program to quickly turn perspective on.

7.4 **How do you turn perspective off?**

The **DVIEW** command has an option called **Off** that turns perspective off.

Type: `DVIEW <RETURN>`

Response: `Select objects:`

Type: `<RETURN>` (You don't need to select objects. If you press <RETURN> at this option, AutoCAD will bring up the outline of a house rather than your drawing. This will help speed things up. Any commands issued will act on your drawing when you exit the **DVIEW** command.)

Response: `CAmera/TArget/Distance/POints/PAn/Zoom/TWist/CLip →`
`/Hide/Off/Undo/<eXit>:`

Type: `OFF <RETURN>`

Type: `<RETURN>` (This exits you from the **DVIEW** command.)

See LISP35 in Tip 7.44 for a program that turns perspective off.

7.5 **How do you know where Z is?**

This is one of the major keys to working with 3D. AutoCAD will let you change your User Coordinate System, so X and Y can be placed anywhere in a drawing. So can Z, although at times it's difficult to imagine exactly where it is in relation to X and Y.

AutoCAD uses the *right-hand rule* to find the direction of Z; so can you. Hold your right hand up with your forefinger pointing up and your thumb to the right and the remaining fingers facing you. The forefinger represents the direction of X; the thumb represents the direction of Y; and the remaining fingers represent the direction of Z. See Figure 7-3.

Figure 7-3:
The right-hand rule

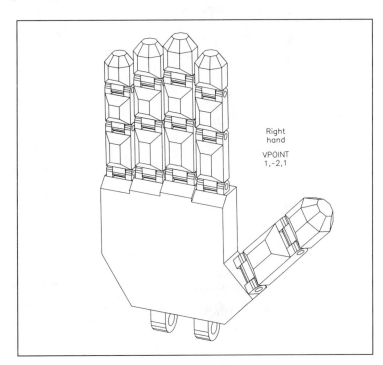

Right
hand

VPOINT
1,-2,1

7.6 **How do you know whether you're on the top or the bottom of a drawing?**

You can hide lines in order to see where you are in a drawing, but this can take time. AutoCAD gives you another way.

Look at the UCS icon in Figure 7-4. Notice how X and Y intersect with connecting lines. This means that you're on the top of the object looking down. Look at the UCS icon in Figure 7-5. Notice that X and Y don't have intersecting lines. This means that you're on the bottom looking up.

Figure 7-4: UCS icon with crossing line

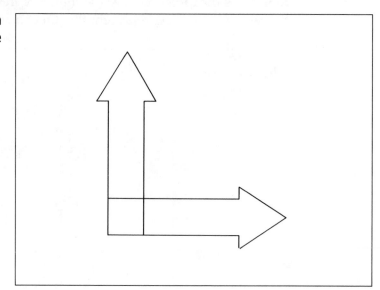

Figure 7-5: UCS icon without crossing lines

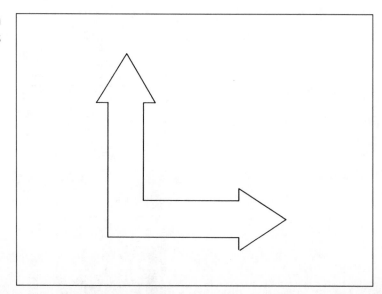

7.7 **How do you change your point of origin?**

The point of origin and the direction of X, Y and Z can all be changed to meet your needs. This is done with the **UCS** command. UCS stands for User Coordinate System; WCS stands for World Coordinate System. Before Release 10, AutoCAD used only the World Coordinate System.

Any time you change any part of the WCS, you're operating in the UCS.

Type: `UCS <RETURN>`

Response: `Origin/ZAxis/3point/Entity/View/X/Y/Z/Prev/Restore/Save →`
            `/Del/?/<World>:`

Type: `O <RETURN>`

Response: `Origin point <0,0,0>:`

Pick a new origin point on the screen. This is now your new point of origin. All absolute coordinates will be relative to this new point.

7.8 **How do you change the direction of X and Y?**

UCS has many options for changing the direction of X and Y. The most common and useful is **3point**. This lets you choose a new point of origin pointing to the direction of positive X and positive Y. See LISP31 in Tip 7.40 for a straightforward way to get to **3point**.

Type: `UCS <RETURN>`

Response: `Origin/ZAxis/3point/Entity/View/X/Y/Z/Prev/Restore/Save →`
            `/Del/?/<World>:`

Type: `3 <RETURN>`

Response: `Origin point <0,0,0>:`

Pick a new point of origin.

Response: `Point on positive portion of the X-axis:`

Point and pick the direction of the new positive X.

Response: `Point on positive-Y portion of the UCS X-Y plane:`

Point and pick the direction of the new Y plane.

7.9 **How do you turn off the UCS icon?**

The UCS icon is controlled by the **UCSICON** command, which gives you several options. **Off** turns **UCSICON** off.

Type: UCSICON <RETURN>

Response: ON/OFF/All/Noorigin/ORigin:

Type: OFF <RETURN>

7.10 **How do you attach the UCS icon to the origin?**

Origin and **Noorigin** are options to the **UCSICON** command.
Origin places the UCS icon at the point of origin. **Noorigin** places the UCS icon in the lower left-hand corner of your screen or viewport.

Type: UCSICON <RETURN>

Response: ON/OFF/All/Noorigin/ORigin:

Type: OR <RETURN>

7.11 **How do you control the UCS icon in all viewports simultaneously?**

If you issue any of the **UCSICON** subcommands, you affect only the current, active viewport. If you want to affect all viewports at once, precede the subcommand with **All**. This isn't a toggle switch; **All** must precede any **UCSICON** command when you want it to affect all the viewports.

Type: UCSICON <RETURN>

Response: ON/OFF/All/Noorigin/ORigin:

Type: A <RETURN> (This lets AutoCAD know you want to affect all viewports at the same time with the next command.)

Response: ON/OFF/All/Noorigin/ORigin:

Type: ON <RETURN>

See the LISP38 program in Tip 7.47 for **UCSICON** settings that are always preceded by **All.**

7.12 How do you go from one viewport to another?

The active viewport will always show crosshairs when you bring your cursor into it. The inactive viewport will show a little arrow.

To toggle to a new active viewport, place your cursor in that viewport and pick any point on the screen. It will then become your new active viewport. See Figure 7-6.

Figure 7-6:
Switching viewports

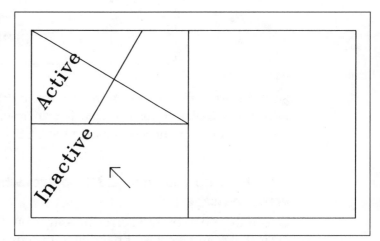

7.13 How do you draw on more than one side of an object?

The key to drawing in 3D, hence on different sides or planes of an object, is correctly setting the proper UCS. First rotate the object into view with **DVIEW** until the plane on which you want to draw is flat (parallel) to your viewing area, as though it were the X-Y in 2D.

Then use **UCS 3point** to redefine the point of origin, positive X and positive Y. See Figure 7-7. You'll notice that your UCS icon has now shifted to show you the new direction of X and Y. For all practical purposes, you're now drawing on a 2D plane on the side of the object you want.

Figure 7-7:
UCS 3point

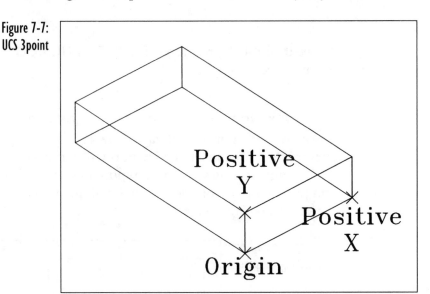

There are many other options possible by changing the UCS and using **OBJECT SNAP**, but this is the basic principle. If using **OBJECT SNAP** is possible, you don't need to change the UCS.

7.14 How do you change 3D objects when you keep getting error messages?

One of the most common error messages on the **CHANGE** command in 3D is that your object isn't parallel to the current UCS. Use the **CHPROP** command instead. It has almost all the features of **CHANGE**, and works on any 3D object, regardless of its position relative to the current UCS.

7.15 **How do you look straight on at an object from any side?**

Plan view looks from Z down at X and Y. If you're having difficulty rotating a view to look straight at the side of one object, here's the easy way to do it.

First set your UCS as indicated in Figure 7-8 by using the **3point** option. Now look at Figure 7-9. You want to turn the object so that Side 1 is facing you.

Figure 7-8: Viewing sides of an object

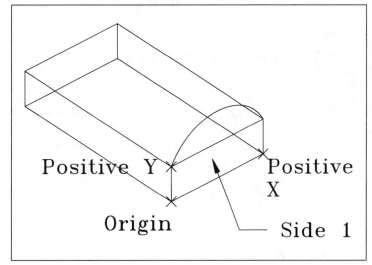

Positive Y

Positive X

Origin

Side 1

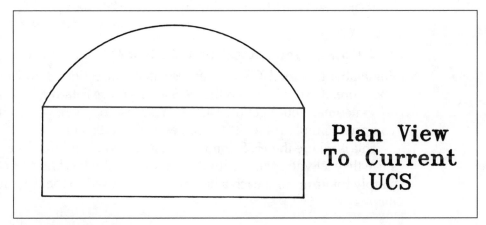

Plan View To Current UCS

Figure 7-9: UCS plan view

Type: UCS <RETURN>

Response: Origin/ZAxis/3point/Entity/View/X/Y/Z/Prev/Restore/Save →
   /Del/?/<World>:

Type: 3 <RETURN>

Response: Origin point <0,0,0>:

Pick a new point of origin.

Response: Point on positive portion of the X-axis:

Point and pick the direction of the new positive X.

Response: Point on positive-Y portion of the UCS X-Y plane:

Point and pick the direction of the new Y plane.

Now you want to change to the plan view of the object relative to the current UCS.

Type: PLAN <RETURN>

Response: <Current UCS>/Ucs/World:

Type: <RETURN>

The object will now turn as shown in Figure 7-9 above.

7.16 **How do you rotate the UCS icon?**

Remember that the UCS icon represents the direction of positive X and Y. Therefore, if you can rotate the UCS icon, you're rotating X, Y and Z.

Sometimes you'll get the UCS icon almost to where you want it, but if you could simply rotate it 90 degrees it would be perfect.

This is where the **UCS** command's **X, Y** and **Z** options come in handy, since they let you rotate around X, or Y or Z. Try it—draw an object and simply rotate around each axis until you get used to the way the icon moves.

7.17 How do you make more than one UCS icon active at one time in different viewports?

This is a commonly asked question, and the answer is simple: you can't. Remember that you have only one drawing; the viewports simply let you view that drawing in different ways. If you could set independent coordinate systems simultaneously, you wouldn't be able to begin a command in one viewport and continue that command in another.

7.18 How do you label text on the screen in 3D?

One of the easiest ways to label text in 3D is to use the **View** option of the **UCS** command. This lets you set the UCS so it's parallel with the screen, not with the object.

Type: `UCS <RETURN>`

Response: `Origin/ZAxis/3point/Entity/View/X/Y/Z/Prev/Restore/Save →`
`/Del/?/<World>:`

Type: `VIEW <RETURN>`

Now put some text on your screen. Notice in Figure 7-10 that, although the object is labeled in 3D, the text is facing the viewer.

Figure 7-10:
Text labels

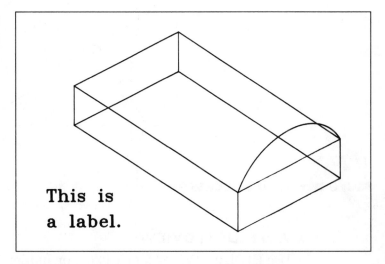

7.19 **How do you place text or dimensions along a 3D line?**

The easiest way to do this is to use the **Entity** or **3point** option of the **UCS** command. **Entity** changes the UCS to the direction of the entity being dimensioned, or to the axis where you want the text. If you use this, make sure that X is pointing in the direction you want the text to go. If it's not, you can rotate 180 degrees around Y.

Type: `UCS <RETURN>`

Response: `Origin/ZAxis/3point/Entity/View/X/Y/Z/Prev/Restore/Save →`
`/Del/?/<World>:`

Type: `E <RETURN>`

Notice the results in Figure 7-11.

Figure 7-11:
Dimensioning
a 3D line

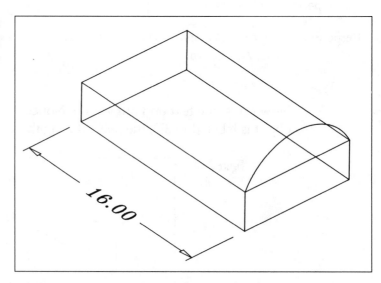

More Steps to Success

7.20 **HIDE in DVIEW**

Use **HIDE** in **DVIEW** for checking on hidden lines rather than using the regular **HIDE** command. It's faster.

7.21 **Partial HIDE**

Zoom in and hide only the area you need. This will avoid your having to hide all the lines in a drawing.

7.22 **Freeze hatching before hiding lines**

Freeze all hatching before you hide any lines. Hatching increases the workload of the **HIDE** command so that it's almost unusable. Work with hatching and **HIDE** only for the final plot or slide.

7.23 **Use Freeze, not Off, with HIDE**

Avoid using **On** and **Off** with **HIDE;** use **Freeze** and **Thaw** instead. When you use **On** and **Off,** the objects aren't actually removed from consideration by the **HIDE** command. If the objects that are turned off obstruct the view of lines that need to be hidden, the hidden objects will disappear even though there's nothing visible in front of them. This won't happen with **Freeze.**

7.24 **Use the AutoCAD house as a shortcut in DVIEW**

Use AutoCAD's house drawing to turn perspective on and off, change the zoom, distance or camera angle, or perform any other function that doesn't require that you see an object.

This feature is activated by pressing <RETURN> instead, when you're asked to select objects. AutoCAD then displays the outline of a house to provide some perspective on what you're doing. This is faster than having to wait for a real drawing on the screen to regenerate.

7.25 **Work in two viewports with perspective on and off**

When you're working with perspective, it's a good idea to set up at least two viewports. Always have the same view of the object in both viewports, but turn perspective on in one and off in the other. Since AutoCAD won't let you edit with perspective on, you can edit the view that has perspective off and see the results in the viewport with perspective on.

7.26 **Check your work with two viewports**

Never draw in 3D without at least two viewports for checking purposes. What you see using only one view in 3D isn't necessarily what you get. If you're drawing and are using an incorrect UCS for the area and function, it may look right in the active viewport—but you might get a different result in another viewport with a different viewing angle. However, if they both look right, you can assume that your drawing is correct.

7.27 **Use OBJECT SNAP instead of changing the UCS**

Whenever you use **OBJECT SNAP,** AutoCAD knows the exact coordinates of the object, so you don't have to set your UCS to define X, Y and Z. To save time, use **OBJECT SNAP** whenever possible to avoid having to constantly change the UCS.

7.28 **Select only what you need in DVIEW**

When you use **DVIEW,** you don't always have to select all the objects or even all of the objects you're interested in. In fact, the fewer entities you select that will still give you the same information and visualization for rotation, the better the dynamic response time will be. Select only what you need. When you're through with **DVIEW** and return to the Command line, all the objects in your drawing will be rotated to the proper view.

7.29 **You can still use filters**

Before Release 10, X-Y filtering was one of the few ways to pick a point in 3D space. Now that you can change the UCS and **OBJECT SNAP** to any 3D point, filters aren't the primary tool. All the same, often, the easiest way to pick a point with a given elevation is to use the filtering command.

Type: `LINE <RETURN>`

Response: `From point:`

Type: `.XY <RETURN>`

Response: `From point:`

Pick a point.

Response: Need Z:

   Type: 4 <RETURN>

Response: To point:

Pick a point.

This lets you pick a point and supply the elevation (Z) from the keyboard. Filtering is still a valuable tool in 3D.

7.30 Preset your viewport configurations

As you gain more experience working with AutoCAD in 3D, you're going to want certain standard views in each of your viewports. These should be saved as preset configurations.

7.31 Name and save your UCS

When you create a new UCS, it's a good idea to give it a name and save it. As you rotate around your drawing, the common pattern is to work on sections as needed and then return to them. You don't want to have to rebuild each UCS every time you need it. AutoCAD lets you save your current UCS and later restore it by name.

7.32 Save both the UCS and the view at the same time

When you save a UCS, you've saved only the User Coordinate System information that can be recalled at any time. You haven't saved the view that was present when the UCS was created.

Often, you'll want to match the UCS with a view of the drawing so that you can recall them both. When this is necessary, save both the UCS and the view and apply a common naming convention to them. See LISP32 in Tip 7.41 for a program that saves both the view and the current UCS simultaneously under a common name.

7.33 **Use 3DFACE to model a solid**

Before Release 10, **Thickness** was about the only practical way you could project entities into 3D space, so it was the main tool for drawing in 3D. But **Thickness** has some drawbacks. Now, with all the tools available to you, it's generally better to draw each individual entity. If you need to model a solid, use **3DFACE** instead of **Thickness.**

7.34 **Thickness shortcuts**

You should use individual entities drawn in 3D rather than using **Thickness,** but there are still some shortcuts you can take. If you needed to draw a floor plan or other object in 3D, you might be better off to first draw it with **Thickness** on a temporary layer. This is the quickest way to draw: first, in plan view and, then, use **DVIEW** to rotate it into view.

Now change to your permanent layer and, using **OBJECT SNAP,** outline the object with ordinary lines and apply 3D faces where necessary. Then erase the original entities drawn with **Thickness.** This is much faster than trying to draw everything from scratch, and it gives the same result.

7.35 **You can't hide text**

Text is transparent to the **HIDE** command, so if you need to hide text behind a solid, you have to be a little creative. Put the text on another layer and turn that layer off or freeze the layer before you hide the lines.

7.36 **Problem entities in DVIEW**

Extruded items (items with **Thickness**), circles, text, hatches, etc., can play havoc with the speed of even the fastest computers when you're working in **DVIEW.** These types of entities redraw so slowly during rotation of objects that too many entities make the **DVIEW** command far too slow. Therefore, make sure that these entities are on layers that can be frozen when you use **DVIEW.**

7.37 **Save your views if you want to get back**

Even if you haven't been saving views in the past, start now. Many times the only way to get back to where you were, short of an **UNDO,** is to save a view before you go into **DVIEW.** Then if something goes wrong or you need to get back to a specific view, you can always do a **VIEW RESTORE.**

AutoLISP Programs

7.38 Set Thickness (LISP29)

This program lets you set **Thickness,** leaving **Elevation** alone.

Listing:
```
(defun c:lisp29 ()
    (setq ev (getdist "nnew thickness:  "))
    (setvar "thickness" ev)
)
```

To Use: Load LISP29.LSP

Type: LISP29 <RETURN>

Response: New thickness:

Enter the new thickness.

7.39 Elevation and Thickness to zero (LISP30)

After you've drawn using **Thickness** and/or **Elevation,** it's very important to set both back to 0 before setting the view with **DVIEW** and drawing in 3D. This program sets both thickness and elevation to 0 at the same
time.

Listing:
```
(defun c:lisp30 ()
    (command "elev" "0" "0")
)
```

To Use: Load LISP30.LSP.

Type: LISP30 <RETURN>

7.40 **UCS 3point (LISP31)**

The most common **UCS** subcommand you'll be using is **3point.** This program takes you directly to **3point** without any questions and sets **OBJECT SNAP** to **End** and **Intersection,** then returns your snap to its original form.

Listing:
```
(defun c:lisp31 (/ os)
    (setq os (getvar "osmode"))
    (setvar "osmode" 33)
    (command "ucs" "3" pause pause pause)
    (setvar "osmode" os)
)
```

To Use: Load LISP31.LSP.

Type: LISP31 <RETURN>

Now pick the point of origin, new positive X and direction of positive Y.

7.41 **View and UCS save (LISP32)**

When you save a UCS, AutoCAD doesn't automatically save the accompanying view. As a result, if the view and the name of the UCS aren't saved and matched in some way, it's very difficult to get them back together. This lets you save a view and the accompanying UCS automatically.

Listing:
```
(defun c:lisp32 (/ name)
    (setq name (getstring"\nEnter name of VIEW and UCS "))
    (command "ucs" "s" name)
    (command "view" "s" name)
)
```

To Use: Load LISP32.LSP.

Type: LISP32 <RETURN>

Response: Enter name of VIEW and UCS:

When you enter this name, the view and the UCS will be saved together under the same name but with different suffixes.

7.42 Restore View and UCS (LISP33)

This program restores both the view and the UCS that were saved using LISP32. (Use of the plus sign at the end of a line in AutoLISP code indicates that line is wrapped.)

Listing:
```
(defun c:lisp33 (/ name)
    (setq name (getstring "\nEnter name of VIEW and +
      UCS to restore "))
    (command "view" "r" name)
    (command "ucs" "r" name)
)
```

To Use: Load LISP33.LSP.

Type: LISP33 <RETURN>

Response: Enter name of VIEW and UCS to restore:

7.43 Perspective On (LISP34)

Perspective is turned on by setting a given distance, using the **Distance** subcommand of **DVIEW**. Once the distance is set, AutoCAD needs a quick and easy toggle switch that can turn perspective on and off. This program gives you the **On** switch. One word of caution: the distance should be set at least once before this program is run. If it's not, AutoCAD chooses an arbitrary distance. Depending on how close or far away the target is from the camera, the object may seem to disappear. If this happens, go into **DVIEW** and adjust the distance.

Listing:
```
(defun c:lisp34 ()
    (command "dview" "" "d" "" "")
)
```

To Use: Load LISP34.LSP.

Type: LISP34 <RETURN>

7.44 **Perspective Off (LISP35)**

If perspective is on, this program gives you a quick way to turn it off.

Listing:
```
(defun c:lisp35 ()
    (command "dview" "" "off" "")
)
```

To Use: Load LISP35.LSP.

Type: `LISP35 <RETURN>`

7.45 **DVIEW Camera (LISP36)**

DVIEW gives you a lot of choices, as do many of the AutoCAD commands. You'll probably use the **Camera** option of **DVIEW** quite often to adjust the view. This program takes you to the beginning of this command without all the questions. It also starts you out with your object selection set to **Crossing**. Therefore, begin by picking your crossing window, then confirm, and you're in **DVIEW Camera**.

Listing:
```
(defun c:lisp36 ()
    (command "dview" "c" pause pause "" "ca")
)
```

To Use: Load LISP36.LSP.

Type: `LISP36 <RETURN>`

Begin your crossing window to select objects, and confirm. You're now in **DVIEW Camera** and can move your object vertically, then horizontally.

7.46 **DVIEW Camera left-right (LISP37)**

This program is a refinement on LISP36. As it takes you into **DVIEW Camera**, it maintains your vertical orientation and takes you straight to the horizontal orientation.

Listing:
```
(defun c:lisp37 ()
    (command "dview" "c" pause pause "" "ca" "")
)
```

To Use: Load LISP37.LSP.

Type: `LISP37 <RETURN>`

7.47 **UCSICON All (LISP38)**

This is a nice little program that can be used instead of **UCSICON** whenever you want to set the UCS icon simultaneously in all viewports. When you use the **UCSICON** command without **All**, it sets the icon for only the active viewport. **All** isn't a toggle switch.

This program begins the **UCS-ICON** command with the **All** option. Then all you have to do is tell AutoCAD your option for the icon, and it will move in all viewports.

Listing:
```
(defun c:lisp38 ()
    (command "ucsicon" "a" pause "")
)
```

To Use: Load LISP38.LSP.

Type: `LISP38 <RETURN>`

You can now enter **On**, **Off**, **Origin** or **Noorigin**.

CHAPTER 8

Miscellaneous (Basic)

How Do You . . .

8.1 How do you configure AutoCAD?

When you first installed AutoCAD it wasn't properly configured, so you performed a configuration routine. There were four main configurable devices: the video display, the digitizer, the plotter and the printer-plotter. You were asked to choose among the available options and then to answer other questions about those choices.

Once AutoCAD is configured, you can still go back and revise that configuration. This is done from the AutoCAD main menu as item number 5. AutoCAD begins by showing you its current configuration, which you see by pressing <RETURN>.

There are four main options, labeled as menu items 3, 4, 5 and 6. By choosing any of these you can change the configuration. When you're through answering the questions, item 0 exits you from the configuration. Answer Y or press <RETURN> if you want to make your changes permanent, or N if you want to abort the configuration process.

RELEASE 12 Lets you reconfigure from inside the drawing editor. See Tip 20.26.

8.2 How do you change the prototype default drawing name?

Up to Release 11, AutoCAD lets you have one default drawing name, which can act as a prototype drawing. This means that when you start a new drawing, you can use the prototype as a model so you don't have to keep setting up standard parameters.

When you receive AutoCAD, it's set up with ACAD.DWG as the default prototype drawing. This can be changed. In the configuration menu, item number 8 is Configure Operating Parameters. As a submenu, item number 2 is Initial Drawing Setup. It asks you the following:

```
Enter name of default prototype file for new drawings or . for none
<acad>:
```

At this point, enter the name of your new prototype drawing. When the configuration is updated, AutoCAD will use the new name each time you start a new drawing.

 RELEASE 12   Lets you create a prototype library. See Tip 20.3.

8.3 How do you use an ADI driver?

AutoCAD uses a generic device driver that lets manufacturers tailor their own devices for AutoCAD's use. This generic driver is called ADI. If you're going to use an ADI driver, you'll also be using a driver file furnished by the manufacturer of your particular device. This is generally an executable file.

Before going into AutoCAD, you must type in the name of the driver. Place the name in the AUTOEXEC.BAT file so it will be called up when you boot the computer. When you configure AutoCAD, choose ADI as the driver and generally default on the hexadecimal address. AutoCAD will then look for the device driver at that address and the device will work. If the driver wasn't loaded, AutoCAD will give you an error message indicating the missing driver when you try to enter the drawing editor. You'll be returned to the main menu.

 RELEASE 12   Offers a new and much improved Autodesk Device Interface (ADI) driver. See Tips 30.24, 30.26, 30.27.

8.4 How do you turn AutoLISP on or off?

If you don't have enough memory in your machine, the first thing Auto-CAD does when it boots is to disable AutoLISP. But you can do that also, if you want to.

In the CONFIGURATION menu, item number 8 lets you configure operating parameters. A submenu of this is item number 7, AutoLISP Feature. Here you can tell AutoCAD not to use AutoLISP and to allot its memory to your use.

8.5 How do you list your drawing files?

The AutoCAD main menu gives you a facility called File Utilities. This is item number 6, and its submenu item number 1 is List Drawing Files.

8.6 How do you list your drawing files while you're in a drawing?

Use the AutoCAD **FILES** command.

Type: `FILES <RETURN>`

Response:
```
0. Exit File Utility Menu
1. List Drawing files
2. List user specified files
3. Delete files
4. Rename files
5. Copy file

Enter selection (0 to 5) <0>:
```

8.7 How do you recover a .BAK file?

Whenever you edit a drawing, AutoCAD makes a backup copy of it when you **END** or **SAVE** to the same file. It gives the copy the same name, but with the extension .BAK instead of .DWG.

You can't load a .BAK file directly into AutoCAD. AutoCAD can recognize only .DWG files. It's a simple operation to rename the .BAK file with a file name that ends in .DWG. This is done through DOS. Enter

```
RENAME FILE1.BAK FILE1.DWG <RETURN>
```

Then the drawing can be loaded.

8.8 How do you set colors on VGA or EGA?

First, let's assume you have a VGA or EGA monitor and video card. When you're configuring the video from the AutoCAD configuration menu and have chosen the IBM Video Graphics Array, you're asked two questions concerning color:

```
Do you want dark vectors on a light background field?
```

If you answer Y to this question, you'll get a light gray background with dark entities. If you answer N, you'll get a black background. You'll then be asked:

```
Do you want to supply individual colors for parts of the graphics
screen?
```

If you answer Y, you're walked through various questions on the color of each screen area.

8.9 How do you turn HANDLES on?

Normally, you shouldn't concern yourself with this unless you're an AutoLISP programmer, or you've been instructed to do so in your proto-type drawing for a software product that requires it. But if you need to turn **HANDLES** on, here's how:

Type: `HANDLES <RETURN>`

Response: `ON/DESTROY:`

Type: `ON <RETURN>`

8.10 How do you turn HANDLES off?

Generally, you don't want to do this. If you had to turn the **HANDLES** on, you probably don't want to destroy them—but there's no way to turn **HANDLES** off without destroying all of the existing handles in a drawing. Therefore, the options for **HANDLES** are **On** and **Destroy**:

Type: `HANDLES <RETURN>`

Response: `ON/DESTROY:`

Type: DESTROY <RETURN>

Response: ***** W A R N I N G *****

Completing this command will destroy *all* database handle information in the drawing. Once destroyed, links into the drawing from
external database files cannot be made. If you really want to
destroy the database handle information, please confirm this by
entering (here a message will appear) to proceed, or NO to abort
the command.

Proceed with handle destruction <NO>:

This is such a dangerous command that AutoCAD doesn't use the
ordinary Y or N options. There are six random messages that will appear
in the above statement. If you want to destroy the handles, you must type
the message exactly as you see it in the warning.

8.11 How do you get rid of or modify the sign-on message?

When you first use AutoCAD, there's a sign-on message before you get
to the AutoCAD main menu. This message is stored in a file called
ACAD.MSG, which must be an ASCII file. If you want to keep a sign-on
message, you can modify this file with your favorite text editor. If you
don't want a message at all, delete the file.

8.12 How do you exchange data with other CAD systems?

AutoCAD provides several ways to exchange data with other CAD systems. If you want to convert an AutoCAD drawing to another CAD system
or vice versa, AutoCAD has pretty much become the standard.

AutoCAD freely publishes its text format so other CAD systems can
convert their drawings to AutoCAD and so you can port an AutoCAD
drawing to other CAD systems. Since the format is a text file, you can also
port other editable information to other non-CAD programs for processing. To put a drawing in DXF format, use the **DXFOUT** command; to bring
a drawing in, use **DXFIN**. Be aware that **DXFIN** should be used only as
the first command before any changes are made. Otherwise, only entities
can be imported.

Another standard supported by AutoCAD is the IGES format. The two
commands in this format similar to DXF are **IGESIN** and **IGESOUT**.

More Steps to Success

8.13 Set **ACADFREERAM=24**

For all AutoCAD IBM versions, you should set **ACADFREERAM** equal to 24 or higher; do not set higher than 32. Place the following line in your AUTOEXEC.BAT file:

```
SET ACADFREERAM=24
```

Notice that there's a space between **SET** and

```
ACADFREERAM,
```

but after that there are no spaces.

NOTE: This variable is ignored in all 386 versions of AutoCAD.

8.14 **Additional storage directory**

AutoCAD has a standard search path when looking for files. It recognizes and remembers the DOS path to its executable files. If it needs an Auto-LISP file or a .DWG file, it searches your current directory first, then it searches the AutoCAD directory.

AutoCAD also lets you give it one more directory path to search. You do this with an environment variable: a variable you set up using the DOS **SET** command. It's normally placed in the AUTOEXEC.BAT file:

```
SET ACAD=DRAWINGS
```

Placing this statement in the AUTOEXEC.BAT file tells AutoCAD that it can search one more directory, called **DRAWINGS**, for the file it needs. This lets you place **WBLOCK** drawings and AutoLISP programs in a central directory and not have to call them up with complete path names.

11 RELEASE 11   You can now set multiple directories in the same manner as the PATH command; that is, separated by semicolons.

```
SET ACAD=C:\DRAWINGS;C:\LISP;C:\PARTS
```

8.15 **Don't convert Version 2.5 or later**

One of the menu items on the AutoCAD main menu is Convert Old Drawing File. This is used only to convert drawings made before Version 2.5. If
you have drawings from 2.5 or later and want to read them into the current release of AutoCAD, simply load them; don't convert them first.
Converting them first will destroy part of the file. If this happens, the
conversion first saves the original under another name.

8.16 **An easy way to move a file**

You can move a drawing file from one directory to another using item
number 4 of the **FILES** command:

Type: `FILES <RETURN>`

Response: `0. Exit File Utility Menu`
`1. List Drawing files`
`2. List user specified files`
`3. Delete files`
`4. Rename files`
`5. Copy file`

Type: `4 <RETURN>`

Response: `Enter current filename:`

Type: `/CURRENTDIR/CURRENTFILENAME`

Response: `Enter new filename:`

Type: `/NEWDIR/CURRENTFILENAME`

Be careful how you use these functions. For example, never use them on
open AutoCAD working files or your current drawing.

8.17 **Clean up your .BAK files**

If you're like most people, you don't have a lot of extra disk space. With some drawing files approaching or exceeding a million bytes, it's a luxury to maintain a .BAK file for each of your drawing files; so you should periodically delete *.BAK files from your drawing directories. See LISP41 in Tip 8.24.

8.18 **Import entities only**

To import entities only while using **DXFIN**, draw a single line in the drawing, then erase it. Then enter **DXFIN** and confirm. This way, Auto-CAD will bring in only the entities, not the system variables and tables.

8.19 **Proper CONFIG.SYS**

For the most efficient use of AutoCAD, make sure you have the following parameters in your CONFIG.SYS file:

```
buffers=30
```

```
files=30
```

 RELEASE 11   This tip is not specific to Release 11. It really has to do with AutoCAD 386. You should follow the suggested CONFIG.SYS settings indicated by your specific platform, because these may change as Auto-CAD continues to optimize its program.

8.20 **Multiple-level subdirectories slow you down**

Avoid going too deep into subdirectories. When you make sub-sub-sub-subdirectories, you slow AutoCAD down, making it less productive.

This is important only for 80286 or slower computers. The faster the computer, the less significant the time factor for searching through the subdirectories. File organization on faster computers offers more productivity than the slower performance through the directories.

8.21 **Un-nest subdirectories**

When you're in a sub-subdirectory you can enter

```
CD .. <RETURN>
```

This will take you back one subdirectory from where you are. You can keep doing this all the way back to the root directory in DOS.

 **AutoLISP Programs**

8.22 **Purge layers (LISP39)**

Many times, numerous layers are set up in a prototype drawing in case they're needed; this is a good practice (see Tip 18.1). Once the drawing is completed, though, it's a good idea to purge the unreferenced layers from the drawing database. The problem is having to sit at your computer and enter Y or N for each layer before it's purged. This program answers Y to all questions for you and runs very rapidly.

Listing:
```
(defun c:lisp39 (/ flg cnt e)
   (setq flg 1)
   (setq cnt 0)
   (while (setq e (tblnext "layer" flg))
      (setq cnt (+ cnt 1))
      (setq flg nil)
   )
   (repeat cnt
      (command "purge" "la" "y")
   )
)
```

To Use: Load LISP39.LSP.

Type: LISP39 <RETURN>

8.23 **List drawing files (LISP40)**

This program lists all the drawing files in your current directory.

Listing:
```
(defun c:lisp40 ()
    (command "files" "1" "")
    (prin1)
)
```

To Use: Load LISP40.LSP.

Type: `LISP40 <RETURN>`

8.24 **Clean out .BAK files (LISP41)**

If you're backing up properly, the .BAK files that AutoCAD creates on each **END** or **SAVE** can eat up a lot of disk space. One extra .BAK file could result in a "disk full" error. This program gets rid of all the .BAK files in the current directory as you end a drawing, and the current .BAK file is not saved. You can use this program instead of **END**.

Listing:
```
(defun c:lisp41 ()
    (command "save" "")
    (command "shell" "del *.bak")
    (command "quit" "y")
)
```

To Use: Load LISP41.LSP.

Type: `LISP41 <RETURN>`

CHAPTER 9

Basic Release II

How Do You . . .

9.1 How do you recover a damaged file?

If a drawing file has been damaged in some way, it can still be recovered. Item nine of the AutoCAD main menu is used for recovering a damaged file. You will be asked for the name of the file. The program will proceed to go through various aspects of the file. When it's finished, you'll receive a message similar to the following:

```
total errors found 1 fixed 1
Audit accepted recovered database.
Press RETURN to continue:
```

When you <RETURN>, the drawing will be brought to the screen.

It may or may not be exactly what you expected. Depending on what needed to be fixed, AutoCAD may have made some adjustments or deleted some entities, layers, blocks, etc. At this point, nothing has happened to the original drawing on disk. You may **QUIT**, **END** or **SAVE** to another file. When you **SAVE** or **END**, you're creating a .DWG file with the errors repaired.

RELEASE 12   Automatically detects a damaged file when you **OPEN** it. See Tip 20.23.

9.2 How do you know what was wrong with the drawing?

After AutoCAD has audited or recovered a drawing, it writes out a file in the current directory. This is a text file that contains the audit information. The file is the name of the drawing with an extension of .ADT.

9.3 **How do you check to see if a file is OK before saving?**
Use the command **AUDIT**.

Type: `audit <RETURN>`

Response: `Fix any errors detected <N>`

Type: `Y <RETURN>`

AutoCAD proceeds to audit the file to check for and fix any errors found. The information on the audit is in a text file in your current directory under the drawing name .ADT.

9.4 **How do you unlock a file that's locked by mistake?**
From the AutoCAD main menu, item 6, File Utilities, there's a submenu item 6 called Unlock File. You're asked to enter locked file(s) specification. Enter one file name or use the wild card facilities to unlock multiple files. Be sure to enter the actual .DWG original file name, and include the extension .DWG as part of the name.

`File Utility Menu`

Type: `6 <RETURN>`

Response: `Enter locked file(s) specification:`

Type: `c:\acad\sample\nozzle.dwg <RETURN>`

Response: `The file: \ACAD11\SAMPLE\NOZZLE.DWG was locked by George Head at`
`10:47 on 12/21/1990.`
`Do you still wish to unlock it? <N>`

Type: `Y <RETURN>`

Response: `Lock was successfully removed.`
`1 files unlocked.`
`Press RETURN to continue:`

Type: `<RETURN>`

RELEASE 12   You can now use the **File Utilities** dialogue box to unlock files. See Tip 20.28.

9.5 **How do you know if someone is using a file?**

If you're using a network version of AutoCAD, a File Lock file is established in the same directory of the file when it is brought up in the drawing editor. It carries the same file name with the extension .DWK.

When you edit an existing file that's being used by someone else, you receive the following message:

```
Waiting for file: C:\ACAD11\SAMPLE\NOZZLE.dwg.

Locked by Jan Head at 10:47 on 12/21/1990

Press Ctrl-C to cancel
```

AutoCAD will continue to retry every few seconds for about a minute. If you enter a Ctrl-C, the retry will be cancelled, and you'll be returned to the AutoCAD main menu. After about a minute, you'll receive the following message:

```
Access denied: C:\ACAD11\SAMPLE\NOZZLE.dwg is in use.

Press RETURN to continue:
```

You'll be returned to the AutoCAD main menu.

9.6 **How do you streamline the log-in procedure?**

Each time you enter the drawing editor, AutoCAD asks you to log in with your name. The log-in name doesn't have to refer to a person. It can refer to a network node or a network identifying name or number. The name used at log-in time is used to identify who has control of a drawing.

You may find it convenient to standardize the log-in procedure by network node or by individual. AutoCAD gives you the ability to create a default log-in name, which is stored as part of the configuration of Auto-CAD. Begin by entering item five (Configure AutoCAD) from the Auto-CAD main menu.

Response: Configuration menu

Type: 8 <RETURN>   (Configure operating parameters)

Response: Operating parameter menu

Type: `10 <RETURN>`   (Log-in name)

Response: `Log-in Name:`
`Enter default log-in name or . for none`

Type: `Type in your name or computer identifier.`

Proceed to update your configuration.

When you enter the drawing editor you will get the message:

`Log-in was successful as "Your name".`

9.7 How do you create multiple default log-in names?

Since the default log-in name is stored as part of the configuration of AutoCAD, you use the same procedure to create multiple log-in names as you do to create multiple configurations using different digitizers or different ADI drivers. See Tip 18.5.

Establish a directory where the various configuration files are to be stored. Copy your most recent configuration files to this directory. The directory name might be **BOB**, if Bob is the individual that will be logging in to AutoCAD. See Tip 18.5 for the names of the files to be copied.

Point AutoCAD to that directory, so it finds that specific configuration.

Type: `SET ACADCFG=C:\BOB <RETURN>`

This statement might be put in a batch file called BOB.BAT. You can now start AutoCAD. Establish BOB as the default log-in name and save the configuration. From now on, Bob will simply type BOB to enter AutoCAD. This way he will be using his specific configuration, including his own log-in name.

9.8 **How do you get help on specific commands?**

Release 11 greatly expanded its context-sensitive help procedures. Begin by starting a command such as **LINE**. At any point in the command, you can begin the help sequence.

Type: `LINE <RETURN>`

Response: `From point`

Type: `'help <RETURN>`

Response: A short form of the help screen will come up to give you immediate information on the command you're using. If there is more expanded information, you'll receive the following message:

`>>Do you want more help for the LINE command? <N>`

Type: `Y <RETURN>`

Now a more general help screen will appear. You will also be directed to the appropriate chapter in the *AutoCAD Reference Manual*.

Type <RETURN> to resume the **LINE** command. You may need to press F1 to return to the graphics screen.

9.9 **How do you change a line of text?**

Release 11 lets you change individual lines of text using a dialogue box.

Type: `DDEDIT <RETURN>`

Response: `Select a TEXT or ATTDEF object/Undo:`

Type: `Pick a line of text`

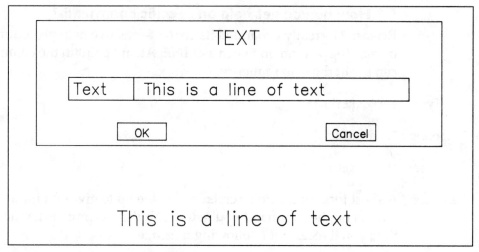

Figure 9-1: Using a dialogue box to change text

A dialogue box is brought to the screen. Place the arrow where you would like to modify the text. Notice the rectangular box that's highlighted. As you move the arrow from left to right, the rectangular box moves. This is where your cursor pointer is located.

If you simply begin typing, you'll replace the line of text. If you make a mistake anywhere along the way, press **Cancel,** and the original line of text will be returned.

When you have the cursor where you want it on the line, pick. Now, the arrow is no longer effective on the line of text. But you can move the cursor left and right with your arrow keys. You can use your backspace and delete characters to the left, or use your delete key and delete characters to the right. If you begin typing text, it will insert the text where the cursor is. <RETURN> or **OK** on the line, and the line is permanent. You still have the opportunity to **OK** the changes or **Cancel**.

After you've changed one line of text, AutoCAD continues to ask you to select another line. You may continue or <RETURN> one last time to abort the command.

You cannot select text using a **WINDOW** or **CROSSING** or in any way build a selection set. You must pick a single line of text.

9.10 How do you turn file dialogues on and off?

Anytime AutoCAD asks you for a file name, you have the option of bringing up a dialogue box listing the available files and changing directories. Whether AutoCAD uses dialogue boxes for file access is determined by a system variable called **FILEDIA**.

Type: `FILEDIA <RETURN>`

Response: `New value for FILEDIA`

Type: `0 <RETURN>`

If **FILEDIA** is 1, file dialogue boxes will be used. If **FILEDIA** is 0, file dialogue boxes will not be used.

9.11 How do you use file dialogue boxes?

In AutoCAD, when you issue a command that accesses a file, and if the system variable **FILEDIA** is set to 1, AutoCAD brings up a file dialogue box appropriate for the type of file you're accessing.

Figure 9-2: Accessing files with a file dialogue box

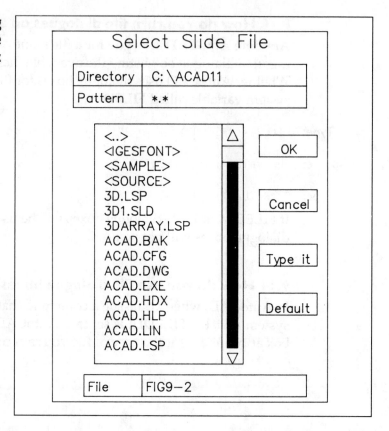

At the top of the screen is the Drive and Directory path you are currently in. By picking this area, you change drive and/or directory. Below the directory is the pattern. Even though it defaults to *.DWG if you issued the **SAVE** command, since you are saving .DWG files, you can change the pattern to *.* or anything else.

Once the pattern is established, a list of files matching the pattern is displayed on the left. If there are too many to fit on the screen, there's an arrow pointing up and an arrow pointing down. In the center is a rectangular box. By picking anywhere along the line between the two arrows, you can slide up and down the files. If you pick the top or the bottom arrow, you'll advance up or down one file at a time. When you find the file you want, pick that file, and it will be displayed at the bottom of the screen.

At this point, you can modify the file name, choose **OK**, choose **Cancel** and cancel the entire operation, or return it to the default. If you choose **Default**, any changes you've made to the file name, the directory or the pattern will be returned to their original conditions.

At the very top of the list of files, you'll see < . . >. By picking this, you'll be given the root directory of the current drive. From here you can choose other directories.

9.12 How do you control text justification?

You now have the ability to control where the insertion point of text is, in relationship to the position along the letter. Text is divided into Top, Middle and Bottom of the letter in a vertical direction, and Left, Center, Right in a horizontal direction.

Type: TEXT <RETURN>

Response: Justify/Style/Start point:

Type: J <RETURN>

Response: Align/Fit/Center/Middle/Right/TL/TC/TR/ML/MC/MR/BL/BC/BR:

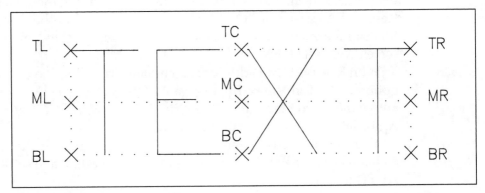

Figure 9-3: Choosing text insertion point

The first five options are the same as versions prior to Release 11. The last four refer to the vertical and horizontal positioning of the insertion point along the letter.

TL	Top Left
TC	Top Center
TR	Top Right
ML	Middle Left
MC	Middle Center
MR	Middle Right
BL	Bottom Left
BC	Bottom Center
BR	Bottom Right

9.13 How do you ZOOM All without a REGEN?

You can't, actually. But you can come close to it. At all times AutoCAD maintains what's called a virtual screen. As long as you're zooming within the current virtual screen, you will not have a **REGEN**. Prior to Release 11, it was necessary to set up a **VIEW**, perhaps called **ZA**, which was within the virtual screen, and then force a single regen. From then on, use **View Restore ZA** instead of **ZOOM All**, and you'll always zoom back to the limits of the virtual screen, as long as you haven't created another virtual screen with a **REGEN**.

With Release 11, an additional command was added to the zoom options. I's called **Vmax**. By doing a **ZOOM V**, AutoCAD will zoom you automatically to the limits of the virtual screen without a regen. This is the equivalent of the workaround using **ZA**.

You still have to be careful not to re-establish a new virtual screen with an inadvertent regen. Therefore, it's always a good idea to set **REGEN-AUTO** to **Off**.

RELEASE 12   The size of **Vmax** has changed with this release. It no longer works as a **ZOOM All**. See Tip 20.72.

More Steps to Success

9.14 Set display units to input units

In order to avoid confusion, especially for new AutoCAD users, you can now set the system variable, **UNITMODE**, to 1. This will display the units in the same format AutoCAD requires for the input. For example, feet, inches and fractional inches must be input as

3'4-1/2"

AutoCAD normally displays this as

3'-4 1/2"

With **UNITMODE** set to 1, the display will be the same as the required input.

9.15 Use any file dialogue box to move around on your disk

You can use any file dialogue box you bring up to find any file on any drive. When file names are displayed in the file dialogue box, you can change the pattern to *.* or any other specification you want. You can also change directories and drives. You're not stuck with only the pattern default of the command that activated the file dialogue box. In this way, you can move around your hard disk at will. **VSLIDE** is a safe command to use for this, since no harm will come if you accidentally pick a file.

Be careful not to use a command like **SAVE** to bring up the dialogue box for this purpose; the accidental choosing of a file will activate the command that brought it up.

9.16 File dialogues at will

The system variable **FILEDIA** controls whether the file dialogue boxes automatically are activated. If **FILEDIA** is set to 0, file boxes will not automatically appear. If **FILEDIA** is set to 1, they will automatically appear.

With **FILEDIA** set to 0, by typing ~ (tilde), you can still ask for a file dialogue box at any time during an appropriate command that would have requested one. This will bring down the file dialogue box regardless of the **FILEDIA** setting.

9.17 **REGEN vs. Vmax**

Be very careful anytime you permit or cause a regen. The **REGEN** creates and defines a new **Virtual Screen**. This means that **ZOOM V** will be able to zoom back only to the virtual screen that is in effect at that time. If you have done a regen on a small part of the drawing, that small limited part has become your virtual screen and that's as far back as you can go with **ZOOM V**.

RELEASE 12   The size of **Vmax** has changed with this release. It no longer works as a **ZOOM All**. See Tip 20.72.

9.18 **ZOOM V before END**

Always return to a **ZOOM V** before you **END** your drawing. The next time AutoCAD brings up the drawing, it will bring it up from the **ZOOM** area where it was saved. But at the beginning of a drawing session, Auto-CAD performs a regen. Therefore, to get back to a **ZOOM All** to create the virtual screen, you'll need another **REGEN**.

If, on the other hand, you had done a **ZOOM V** before you saved your drawing, when the drawing is brought up again, the first regen will create the virtual screen at the correct limits.

9.19 **Use SET ACAD for AutoLISP files and blocks**

Since the ACAD environment variable can point to multiple directories, consider placing AutoLISP files in their own directory. You can do the same thing with **WBLOCKS** and organize them in several directories, if this kind of organization helps.

By using different ACAD environment variables, you can make sure that different groups don't accidentally use each other's **WBLOCKS**. Simply include only the directories where **WBLOCKS** are part of the batch file used to call up AutoCAD.

9.20 **Use CHKDSK more often**

It's now more important than ever to periodically use **CHKDSK**. Remember not to use **CHKDSK/F** until you know that the only thing wrong with the disk is lost clusters.

An aborted AutoCAD drawing can now leave millions of bytes in lost clusters that need to be recovered.

9.21 Use meaningful log-in names

Make sure your choice of log-in name is logical. This name is used in several places to tell users who has control of given files.

9.22 Sorted files

You can control sorting of the file names displayed in the file dialogue box by using the **MAXSORT** system variable. Set **MAXSORT** to 0 for no sorting. Set **MAXSORT** to any other integer number for the maximum number of files to be sorted. If there are more files to be displayed than the value of **MAXSORT**>, sorting won't take place. This can save you some time for large groups of files. But, of course, the time-savings and capacity of **MAXSORT** will depend on the speed of your computer.

9.23 Enter decimal feet

You can now enter decimal feet even though you're in architectural or engineering units. 3'6" may be entered as 3.5'. Note that it will be displayed as 3'6".

9.24 Still need SETVAR

Even though you can type the system variable name directly without the command **SETVAR**, it works only for those system variables that don't have the same name as an AutoCAD command. For example, **blipmode** will bring up the AutoCAD **BLIPMODE** command instead of the system variable. Therefore, in cases where names are the same, you still need to enter **SETVAR** if you specifically want the system variable.

9.25 Use DDEDIT to change attributes

Attribute components can be easily changed using **DDEDIT**, the same command used to edit text. If AutoCAD sees that the text is an attribute, it will permit you to change the tag, prompt and default of the attribute.

In order for this to work, it must not be a block. If it is a block, first explode the block, then change the attribute definition. If you just want to change the value of one of the fields of the attribute, use **DDATTE**.

9.26 **File dialogue with INSERT**

The **INSERT** command does not automatically give you a file dialogue box, even if **FILEDIA** is set to 1. But you can force a dialogue box to come down by typing ~ (tilde) at the block name prompt.

9.27 **INSERT= using file dialogue box**

To force an **INSERT=** using a file dialogue box, type =~ at the block name prompt.

9.28 **WBLOCK shortcut**

When using **WBLOCK>**, if the block name and the file name are the same (which is the case most of the time), you can use = for the block name rather than retyping it; AutoCAD will use the same name.

9.29 **More text than space**

When working with a dialogue box, you can exceed the physical limitation of the dialogue box. When this happens, a > at the end of the text means there's text hidden to the right; a < to the left of the text means there's text hidden to the left.

CHAPTER 10

Basic Release 12

How Do You . . .

10.1 How do you start a new drawing?

When you begin AutoCAD Release 12, you're in a new drawing immediately. Unlike previous AutoCADs, this drawing doesn't currently have a name. You can begin the drawing without naming it. The first time you issue the **SAVE** command, AutoCAD will ask you for a drawing name. From then on, that will be the name of the drawing.

If you're already working on a drawing and want to begin a new one, enter **New** from the FILE pull-down menu. See Figure 10.1. You're then given the opportunity to save your existing drawing, because you'll automatically exit the current drawing when the new drawing is begun.

```
File Assist Draw Construct Modify View Settings Render Model    AutoCAD
                                                                * * * *
New...                                                          ASE
Open...                                                         BLOCKS
Save...                                                         DIM:
Save As...                                                      DISPLAY
Recover...                                                      DRAW
                                                                EDIT
Plot...                                                         INQUIRY
                                                                LAYER...
ASE            >                                                MODEL
Import/Export  >                                                MVIEW
XREF           >                                                PLOT...
                                                                RENDER
Configure...                                                    SETTINGS
Compile...                                                      SURFACES
Utilities...                                                    UCS:
Applications...                                                 UTILITY

About AutoCAD...                                                SAVE:
Exit AutoCAD...




Command:
```

Figure 10-1: FILE pull-down menu

When you use the **New** command and begin a new drawing, you're given a dialogue box in which to name it. See Figure 10-2. Enter the name of the new drawing in the box to the right of **New Drawing Name**. You're not required to name it at this time; simply pick OK or press <RETURN>, and the new drawing will begin.

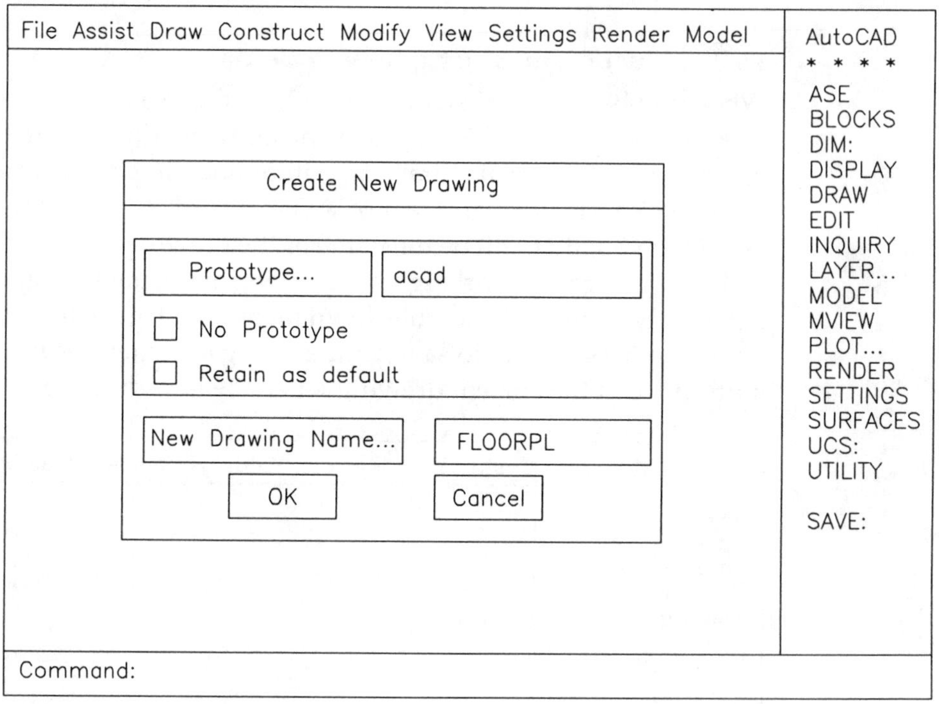

```
File Assist Draw Construct Modify View Settings Render Model    AutoCAD
                                                                * * * *
                                                                ASE
                                                                BLOCKS
                                                                DIM:
        ┌─────────────────────────────────────────┐           DISPLAY
        │          Create  New  Drawing            │           DRAW
        │                                          │           EDIT
        │   ┌──────────────────┬─────────────────┐ │           INQUIRY
        │   │   Prototype...   │  acad           │ │           LAYER...
        │   └──────────────────┴─────────────────┘ │           MODEL
        │   ┌─┐                                    │           MVIEW
        │   │ │  No  Prototype                     │           PLOT...
        │   └─┘                                    │           RENDER
        │   ┌─┐                                    │           SETTINGS
        │   │ │  Retain  as  default               │           SURFACES
        │   └─┘                                    │           UCS:
        │                                          │           UTILITY
        │   ┌──────────────────┬─────────────────┐ │
        │   │ New  Drawing  Name... │  FLOORPL    │ │           SAVE:
        │   └──────────────┬──────┴─────┬────────┘ │
        │          ┌───────┴──┐  ┌──────┴───┐      │
        │          │   OK     │  │  Cancel  │      │
        │          └──────────┘  └──────────┘      │
        └─────────────────────────────────────────┘
Command:
```

Figure 10-2: Prototype dialogue box

10.2 **How do you bring up an existing drawing?**

Since there is no main menu in AutoCAD Release 12, choose **Open** from the FILE pull-down menu. If you're in an existing drawing at the time, that drawing will be saved automatically when you exit to bring up the next drawing.

When you use the **Open** command, you get a file dialogue box that allows you to move around in your directories and find the drawing you want to work on. When you've found the one you want to open, pick it, and then pick OK (or double-click on the drawing name), and the drawing will begin. This really requires a triple click on the drawing name. The first picks the file, then a double-click activates the OK on the file.

10.3 **How do you move around in file dialogue boxes?**

There is, of course, more than one type of file dialogue box, although all file dialogue boxes have several items in common. Look at Figure 10-3, the **Open Drawing** file dialogue box. At the top is its name. Below the name is the pattern; this is the wild card and extension for the files being searched. In this case, it's *.DWG. This is exactly what you would get if you issued a directory command and asked for all files with the DWG extension; if the pattern were *.*, all files in the directory would appear.

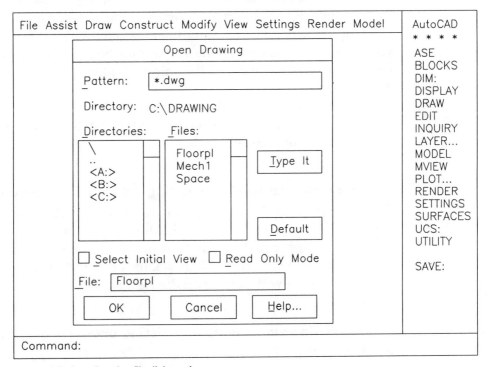

Figure 10-3: Open Drawing file dialogue box

Below the pattern is the name of the current directory. Here, it is **C:\DRAWING**. This line is changeable only by picking in the directory box below. The directory box is labeled **Directories**. In this example it begins with a \ followed by .. and each of the drive letters available on your machine. If you pick the \, you're in the root directory. If you pick the .., it will take you one directory level higher. Picking on the drive letters, of course, will change drives.

As you pick a directory, the names of the files available in that directory will appear in the box to the right, labeled **Files**. Look toward the bottom of this box, above the OK. When you pick from **Files:**, the name of the selected file will appear in the **File:** box. Of course, you can also type directly into the box. Once the correct file is in the **File:** box, <RETURN> or pick OK.

The **Type It** box lets you get rid of the file dialogue box and type the name of the file at the AutoCAD Command line.

The **Default** box sets the directories, files and other parameters back to the way they were when you first entered the dialogue box.

Many of the options have an _ (an underscore) below the first letter. If you press Alt and the letter, the appropriate box will highlight; then press <RETURN> to select the box. Use this method only if your mouse or digitizer isn't working.

Each of the file dialogue boxes has something unique about it. For example, **Select Initial View** and **Read Only Mode** are found exclusively in **Open Drawing**. See Figure 10-3.

10.4 How do you start an existing drawing in a saved view?

The **Open Drawing** file dialogue box has a **Select Initial View** option. See Figure 10-3. Once you've selected the drawing you want to open, a second dialogue box appears, showing the names of the saved views for that drawing. Select a view by double-clicking, or by picking the view and then OK. The drawing will come up in the view selected.

10.5 How do you bring up an existing drawing so you can view it but not change it?

The **Open Drawing** file dialogue box has a selection option of **Read Only Mode**. See Figure 10-3. When this box is picked, and the drawing is opened and on the screen, it looks no different from any other drawing in the box. Change it, draw on it or make any edits you want. There will be no indication that the drawing is **Read Only** until you save it, at which point you'll be alerted that the drawing file is "write protected." This means that the only way you can save the drawing to the same file is to save it by another name—or else use the same name but save it to another directory. This prevents you from overwriting the **Read Only** drawing.

10.6 How do you save a drawing?

The command for **SAVE** has changed slightly from its original meaning. Now there are two kinds of saves. If typed from the keyboard, they are **SAVE** and **QSAVE**; but if picked from the FILE pull-down menu, they are **Save...** and **Save As...** See Figure 10-1. What is confusing is that **Save...**, from the pull-down menu, is actually **QSAVE** if typed from the keyboard. Correspondingly, **Save As...**, from the pull-down menu, is actually **SAVE** if typed from the keyboard.

   QSAVE or **Save...** will not ask you for the name of the drawing. It will save the drawing under its current name and remain in the drawing. **SAVE** or **Save As...** will bring up a file dialogue box and ask you for the name of the drawing. If you change the name of the drawing during the **Save As...** operation, it will permanently change the name of the drawing in the current file. That is to say, the current name of the drawing on your screen will be the new name that you saved it under. This means that future **QSAVE**s will be with the new name.

   This is a very good change, because it permits you to save your drawing periodically under alternate names and be able to see what the last name you used was. Remember that both **SAVE** and **QSAVE** let you continue in the current drawing. Be very careful, though, with the **END** command. Remember that the last name you used with **Save As...** is the name that will be used with **END**.

10.7 How do you quit a drawing?

It depends on what you want to do when you quit the drawing. **QUIT** will not only quit the drawing but will return you to the operating system. If this is what you want to do, type **QUIT** or **END**, and you not only will quit the drawing but also will exit AutoCAD. You can accomplish the same thing by picking **Exit AutoCAD** from the FILE pull-down menu.

   Usually, the reason you'll want to **QUIT** the drawing you're in is to abort any changes to the current drawing and bring up another drawing or start a new drawing.

   The procedure for this is now slightly different. By opening another drawing or by starting a new drawing, you'll always be forced to exit the current drawing. As you exit the current drawing, you'll be given the opportunity to save it. Therefore **New** and **Open** are really ways to quit the current drawing.

10.8 **How do you lock and unlock layers?**

Locking layers is really very easy. From the command line:

Type: `Layer <RETURN>`

Response: `?/Make/Set/New/ON/OFF/Color/Ltype/Freeze/Thaw/LOck/Unlock:`

Notice that the LOck has the L and the O in uppercase. This is slightly different from other commands in that, when there are two commands that begin with the same letter, AutoCAD generally has both of them require the first two letters as uppercase. If you use only the first letter, AutoCAD will ask which one you want. In this case, if you use only the L, AutoCAD will immediately assume **Linetype**. The reason for this is that **Ltype** is an older command, and AutoCAD wanted to maintain as much compatibility for third-party software and users as possible.

Therefore locking and unlocking layers is easy.

Type: `LO <RETURN>`

Response: `Layer name(s) to Lock:`

At this point, enter the names of the layers you want to lock. Locking layers will still permit you to draw on the layers; they just won't be part of any selection set. Therefore, they are immune from being changed in any way while they're locked.

To unlock a layer or group of layers, use the unlock command in the same way.

10.9 **How do you move dialogue boxes on the screen?**

Dialogue boxes can be moved around on the screen by picking in the shaded area at the top. Hold down the pick button on the mouse and drag the dialogue box into position.

Other than that, they can't be resized, nor can they be changed in any way through AutoCAD. The user can change dialogue boxes by modifying their respective files.

10.10 **How do you know if a radio button is active?**

A radio button is generally an either/or situation, unlike a check box, where several items can be checked. A radio button sequence will light up (darken the button) when it's picked and will turn off any other related buttons. It's called a radio button because it operates similarly to radio buttons on a car radio.

10.11 **How do you know the default button or box in dialogue boxes?**

When you enter the dialogue box, there is only one default option: **OK**. But if a box is highlighted by picking or by pressing Tab or the arrow keys, that becomes the current default. This means that <RETURN> will activate that option.

10.12 **How do you change units with the Units dialogue box?**

The units dialogue box can be activated by typing **DDUNITS** from the Command line or picking **Units Control...** from the SETTINGS pull-down menu. See Figure 10-4. Here, it's a simple matter of picking the **Units** and/ or **Angle** you want to use. The precision is a pop-up list box with the available units of precision for the units and/or angles chosen. The **Direction...** box brings up a dialogue box that gives you the ability to set the 0 degree beginning angle of measurement as well as pick the radio button for clockwise or counterclockwise measurement of angles.

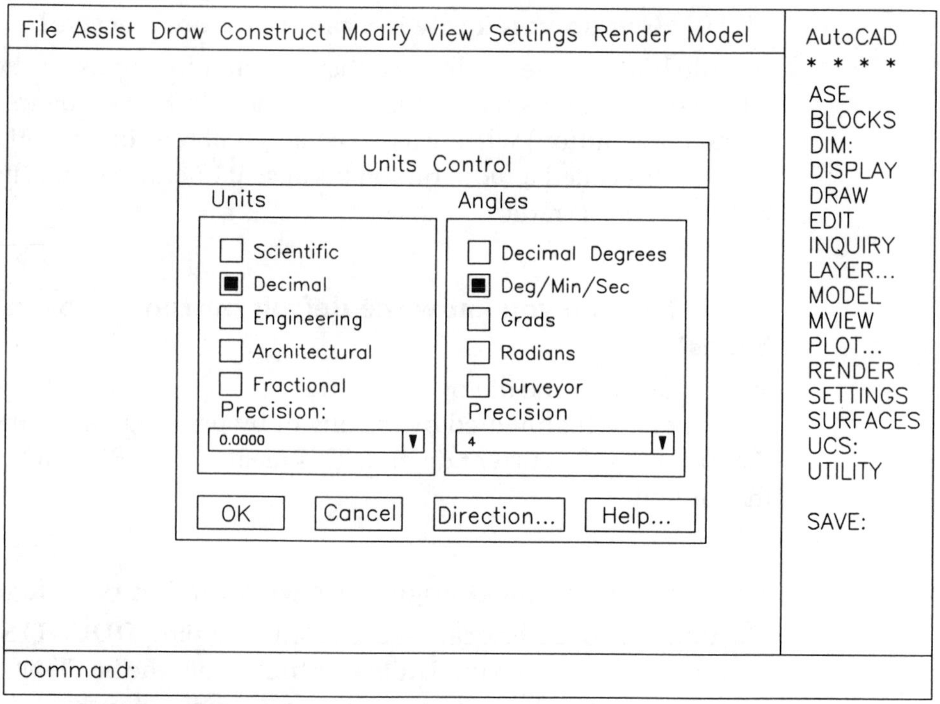

File Assist Draw Construct Modify View Settings Render Model

AutoCAD
* * * *
ASE
BLOCKS
DIM:
DISPLAY
DRAW
EDIT
INQUIRY
LAYER...
MODEL
MVIEW
PLOT...
RENDER
SETTINGS
SURFACES
UCS:
UTILITY

SAVE:

Units Control

Units

☐ Scientific
■ Decimal
☐ Engineering
☐ Architectural
☐ Fractional
Precision:
0.0000 ▼

Angles

☐ Decimal Degrees
■ Deg/Min/Sec
☐ Grads
☐ Radians
☐ Surveyor
Precision
4 ▼

OK   Cancel   Direction...   Help...

Command:

Figure 10-4: DDUNITS dialogue box

10.13 How do you set running Object Snap modes using the dialogue box?

Pick **Object Snap...** from the SETTINGS pull-down menu or type in **DDOSNAP** at the Command line. Now it is a simple case of picking one or more of the object snaps available.

10.14 How do you set the aperture-box size dynamically?

Pick **Object Snap...** from the SETTINGS pull-down menu or type in **DDOSNAP** at the Command line. At the bottom of the dialogue box is a slide bar for the aperture size. To the right is a box with a picture the size of the aperture. Sliding the bar to the left and right changes the size of the aperture.

More Steps to Success

10.15 Be careful with END; it's not what it used to be

END still saves your drawing and exits the drawing editor, but now when you exit the drawing editor you're completely out of AutoCAD. Remember there is no main menu. Also, it's tricky to know what the name of the drawing is at the time you **END** the drawing. Now that AutoCAD has added the **SAVE** and **QSAVE** commands, the permanent name of the drawing isn't so permanent anymore. It will change any time you save it under a different name. Therefore **END** will use the current name of the drawing, not the original name.

10.16 Use QUIT or END; it doesn't matter

It really doesn't matter whether you use **QUIT** or **END**. Don't worry. If you've changed the drawing since the last save, AutoCAD lets you save the drawing before it exits by using **QUIT**.

Old habits are hard to break. Just remember that the purpose of **QUIT** and **END** is to end the entire AutoCAD drawing session, not to bring up another drawing. Thus, **END** saves the drawing under its current name and exits, while **QUIT** asks you if you want to save it before it exits. Unlike the old **QUIT** that asked you if you wanted to abort all changes, this **QUIT** lets you save the changes on the way out.

10.17 Find the current name of the drawing

SAVENAME is the system variable that really counts, because it determines the current name of the drawing for saving, ending and quitting. Therefore, if you want to know the current name of the drawing, type **SAVENAME** at any time, and AutoCAD will tell you.

10.18 **Quick Object Snaps**

By giving you what is called a *cursor menu*, AutoCAD has finally done
something about making object snaps easy and quick to use. The default
cursor menu that comes with AutoCAD Release 12 is the OBJECT SNAP
menu. In order to activate the OBJECT SNAP cursor menu, pick the third
button on your mouse or digitizer puck. This places the OBJECT SNAP
menu at the cursor crosshairs, where you can choose them easily and
quickly. See Figure 10-5. If your mouse doesn't have a middle button, you
can activate the cursor menu by holding down the Shift key and pressing
the second button.

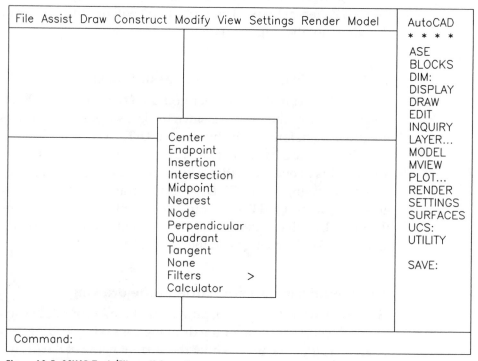

Figure 10-5: OSNAP Tools/Filters dialogue box

10.19 **Stop the window with Press and Drag**

In the **DDSELECT** dialogue box, check **Press and Drag**. This will change an **Implied Window** from two picks to pick, hold down, drag and release. This way, an accidental pick in space will not inadvertently begin creating a window.

Remember, with **Press and Drag** active, you must hold down the pick button as the window is being formed, then release it when the window is complete.

10.20 **Uppercase menu item**

If any menu item is in all-uppercase (such as DRAW), it means that the menu item has a submenu attached to it.

10.21 **Uppercase menu item followed by :**

If any menu item is in all-uppercase followed by a : (such as LINE:), it means that it has a submenu attached to it and that this command automatically cancels any previous command.

10.22 **... following a menu item**

If any menu item is followed by three dots (...), it means a dialogue box will be called.

10.23 **Lowercase or mixed-case menu item**

If any menu item is all-lowercase or mixed case, it means it has subcommands available.

10.24 **> in menu item**

This is a cascading menu item on the pull-down menus. All you have to do is to move your cursor to the right of the menu item with the >, and the sub pull-down menu will appear. (Of course, you can also pick the > and another pull-down menu will appear.)

10.25 **Icons without check boxes**

In previous versions of AutoCAD, you didn't pick the icon itself to activate it; instead, you had to pick the little check box next to it. Now you pick the actual icon itself.

10.26 **Only the pick button active in pull-down menus**

When a pull-down menu is on the screen, only the pick button on your mouse or digitizer is available. This means that none of the other programmed buttons will work until the pull-down menu disappears.

10.27 **Intelligent pull-downs**

The pull-down menus are now smart. They remember which of the items was the last you picked the last time that pull-down menu was chosen. So, the next time the pull-down menu is chosen, that item is already highlighted. To choose the item highlighted, all you need to do is pick the title of the pull-down menu.

10.28 **All dialogue boxes available from keyboard**

You can activate all dialogue boxes from the keyboard. The names of the dialogue boxes all begin with DD. Many of the dialogue boxes have the same name of the command (such as **DDCHPROP** and **CHPROP**). This means you can activate dialogue boxes through script files and AutoLISP. (Conversely, all dialogue boxes you create should always begin with DD.)

10.29 List of dialogue boxes available

DDATTDEF	Attribute definition
DDATTE	Edit Attributes in a block
DDATTEXT	Extract Attributes and write to disk
DDCHPROP	Change Properties
DDEDIT	Edit text and Attribute definitions
DDEMODES	Change settings for entity creation properties
DDGRIPS	Controls and enables Grips
DDIM	Controls dimension styles and variables
DDINSERT	Inserts a previously defined Block
DDLMODES	Control Layers
DDMODIFY	Selects a single entity and modifies properties
DDOSNAP	Sets running Object Snap modes
DDPTYPE	Sets style for points
DDRENAME	Renames blocks, styles, etc.
DDRMODES	Controls on-screen drawing aids
DDSELECT	Controls active selection modes
DDUCS	Controls User Coordinate System
DDUCSP	Selects new UCS at right angle to current UCS
DDUNITS	Sets Units
DDVIEW	Controls Views
DDVPOINT	Controls Vpoints

10.30 Dialogue box shortcuts

Rather than using your mouse or digitizer all the time when you're in a dialogue box, there are several short cuts you can use.

If the name of the box has an underscore, you can type Alt+the letter that is underscored. This will highlight the box. Then you can <RETURN>, and the box will react the same as if it were picked.

The Tab key and the left and right arrows will move you forward through the selections.

The Up arrow will move you back through the selections.

The Ins key will toggle an insert and typeover mode.

The Home key will move the text cursor to the beginning of the text.

Shift+arrow will highlight or select the text for further edit, such as deleting text.

Ctrl+X discards changes made to the text and restores the previous text.

Esc as well as Ctrl+C will cancel the dialogue box.

An arrow in the text box will activate the cursor the same as a pick.

10.31 Difference between a list box and a pop-up list

A pop-up list will generally be a single box with a Down arrow. Activate it by picking the Down arrow and selecting from the available choices. Don't type in anything. You're restricted to the available choices. On the other hand, a regular list box containing all possible selections will always be available. If the list is long, it will have a scroll bar. Generally, there is always another area where the name of the item selected will be listed. You also can type other options in this area.

10.32 Deactivating alerts

There is a new type of dialogue box that really isn't a dialogue box in the strict sense of the word: the Alert Box. An Alert Box pops up on the screen to alert you to something important. You can't proceed any further until you acknowledge the Alert. Most of the Alert Boxes have a simple OK as the only option; in this case, all you have to do is pick the OK or press <RETURN>. Other Alerts may contain a couple of choices—to abort changes, update existing files, etc. The point is, you can't continue or use any menus of any kind until one of the options on the Alert Box is chosen.

10.33 **Where's the message file?**

Previous AutoCADs began by displaying the contents of the ACAD.MSG file. Most users found it was more efficient to delete this file so as to save time beginning AutoCAD (though some found the file useful in displaying pertinent information).

Since AutoCAD now begins directly in the drawing editor, the ACAD.MSG is activated in a different manner. At the Command line, you can type **ABOUT**, and it will bring up the message file. Or you can pick **About AutoCAD...** from the FILE pull-down menu. The message file now comes up as a list box where you can scroll through the actual text of the message file.

If you're using the default installation of AutoCAD, you'll find the ACAD.MSG file in the support subdirectory under the ACAD directory. If the ACAD.MSG file doesn't exist, the **ABOUT** command will bring up the message dialogue box, but the message area will be empty.

10.34 **How you draw a double line**

Drawing a double line is easy with the new **DLINE** command. You can access it through the DRAW pull-down menu or use (load **"Dline"**) at the command prompt. Use it the same as the LINE command:

Type: `(Load "Dline")`

Type `Dline`

Response: `Break/Caps/Dragline/Offset/Snap/Undo/Width/<Start point>:`

Pick a point to start from. You can change the default width of 0.05 to any new value at the start by typing W.

INTERMEDIATE

CHAPTERS 11 - 20

CHAPTER 11

Intermediate Drawing

How Do You . . .

11.1 How do you hatch wall parts?

We're assuming that the wall parts are more complicated than simple offset polylines. When wall segments are broken by doors, windows or other elements, hatching also gets more complicated. Avoid hatching until all the doors and windows have been inserted; it's a drastic mistake to try to insert these parts into a hatched area. You could explode the hatching and try to clean out the area, but this creates too many entities. And then what will you do if you want to move a door?

The best thing to do is first make sure all of your parts have been inserted. Then make a new layer, called "Outline." Using **PLINE**, trace over the wall area, making sure you stop where the window or door begins. Then close the polyline. Continue this until all of the area to be hatched has been traced with a closed polyline. Figures 11-1 and 11-2 show how this is done.

Figure 11-1:
Outline layer

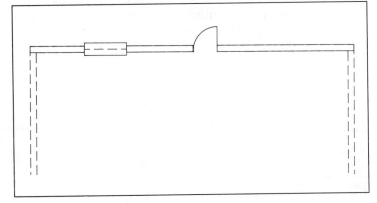

Figure 11-2: Outline
layer with hatching

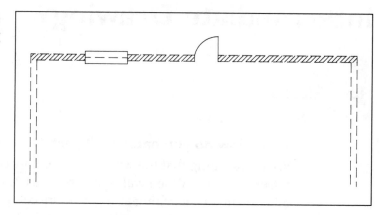

Now that the area to be hatched is totally enclosed, it's simple to hatch each segment. Make sure the hatching is done on a separate layer from the outline layer, so you can control the visibility of both.

RELEASE 12   With the new BHATCH command, you get a complete hatching environment. See Tip 20.73.

11.2 How do you outline irregularly shaped areas for hatching?

It's easy to trace over an area with a polyline so you can enclose it on another layer for hatching. But if that area is irregularly shaped, the easiest way to handle it is to copy the irregular portion to another layer. See Figure 11-3.

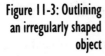

Figure 11-3: Outlining an irregularly shaped object

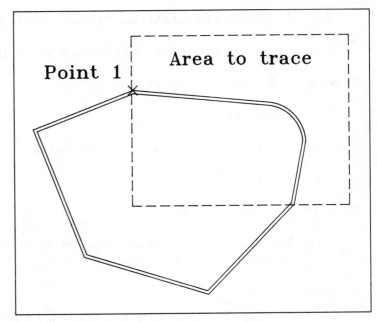

The area you need to trace over is curved, so use the **COPY** command.

Type: COPY <RETURN>

Response: Select objects:

Pick the objects you want to copy, and confirm.

Response: <Base point or displacement>/Multiple:

Pick a point at point 1. Make sure you use **OBJECT SNAP**, because you'll have to pick this exact same point again.

Response: Second point of displacement:

Pick the same point as point 1.

It will appear that nothing happened. But you've actually made a copy of the same entities in exactly the same position. Of course, they're on the same layer. Your next step is to move them to another layer.

Type: CHANGE <RETURN>

Response: Select objects:

Type: P <RETURN> (This stands for "previous selection set.")

Type: <RETURN> (This second <RETURN> is to confirm the objects selected.)

Response: `Properties/<Change point>:`

Type: P <RETURN>

Response: `Change what property (Color/Elev/LAyer/LType/Thickness) ?`

Type: `LA` <RETURN>

Response: `New layer:`

Type: `OUTLINE` <RETURN> (This assumes that you've already created this layer and that you want to move the entities there.)

Type: <RETURN>

The last <RETURN> exits you from the **CHANGE** command. See LISP72 in Tip 14.56 for a program that lets you copy entities to another layer.

11.3 How do you offset from a center line?

You're actually offsetting a center line twice, once in each direction. Doing this manually takes several steps; see LISP43 in Tip 11.28 for a program that does them for you.

Figure 11-4: Center
line before offsetting

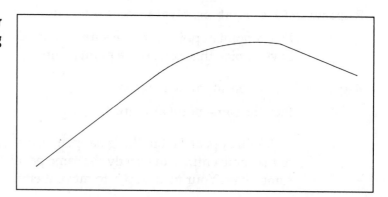

Figure 11-5: Center
line after offsetting

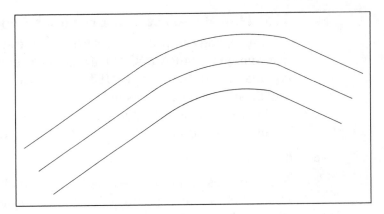

Look at Figures 11-4 and 11-5. You want to create two parallel lines on either side of the center line. Simply enter the offset distance and select the object to offset. Then point to one side. Without exiting the command, select the same object again and point to the other side. The AutoLISP program handles this in one operation, and can even be customized to change the center line to a dashed line or to erase it altogether.

11.4 How do you keep point sizes constant relative to the screen size?

The system variable **PDSIZE** lets you adjust the size of a point or node. The problem is that it's an absolute size, so when you zoom in on an area the size of the point increases too.

You can keep the point size constant relative to the screen size, regardless of the zoom factor. When you issue **PDSIZE**, make it a negative number; this tells AutoCAD not to increase the size of the point while zooming.

11.5 How do you close a series of lines drawn at different times?

Frequently, you need to close a group of lines and curves to form a completely closed entity. The easiest way to do this is to **PEDIT** one of the segments and turn it into a polyline. Then issue the **JOIN** command and window all of the entities. Finally, issue the **CLOSE** command, and AutoCAD will locate the two endpoints and draw a polyline connecting them. The group will now be a single closed polyline. See LISP44 in Tip 11.29.

11.6 **How do you stay in a command once you've entered it?**

Of course, you can press <RETURN> or the space bar again to repeat the last command, but AutoCAD offers an easier way. Simply precede the command with the word **MULTIPLE**. Once the command has finished, it will be automatically reissued.

Be careful. This can have some strange results, depending on what the command is and how it's used. For example, to move several objects,

Type: `MULTIPLE MOVE <RETURN>`

As soon as you've moved the first group of objects, AutoCAD asks you to select objects again. This will continue until you type a Ctrl-C; pressing <RETURN> won't work.

This command can be used with macros and AutoLISP programs prefaced by **C:** as well as with other AutoCAD commands.

WARNING: Don't use this command inside an AutoLISP **(command)** function; AutoCAD will ignore it.

11.7 **How do you make the CIRCLE command default to diameter instead of radius?**

There are two ways to do this. First, you can change the tablet menu for **CIRCLE** to ^c^c (command **CIRCLE** pause "d"). This forces it into diameter mode. Another way is to write a little AutoLISP program, such as the following:

```
(defun c:circle1 ()
  (command "circle" pause "d"))
```

Now if you use **CIRCLE**, it will work the way it's always worked. If you use **CIRCLE1**, it will default to diameter. But to redefine the **CIRCLE** command itself, use the **UNDEFINE** command. Let's assume that the following program is part of your ACAD.LSP file.

```
(defun c:circle ()
  (command ".circle" pause "d"))
```

One problem is that our AutoLISP program and the **CIRCLE** command have the same name, and AutoCAD gives preference to the AutoCAD command. But you can set the command aside: undefine the AutoCAD command.

Type: UNDEFINE <RETURN>

Response: Command name:

Type: CIRCLE <RETURN>

> **CIRCLE** means your AutoLISP program, not the AutoCAD command. The program executes whenever you enter **CIRCLE**. You can still use the original AutoCAD command by placing a . (period) in front of it; for example, **(.CIRCLE)**. This is why there's a period before **CIRCLE** in the command statement above.
>
> If you want to get the old command back,

Type: REDEFINE <RETURN>

Response: Command name:

Type: CIRCLE <RETURN>

Now the **CIRCLE** command acts as it used to, and your AutoLISP program ceases to function. If you want to **UNDEFINE** a series of commands each time you enter the drawing editor, you can place them in the S::STARTUP section of the ACAD.LSP file.

11.8 How do you draw an elliptical arc?

Any arc is part of a circle. Just as you can create an arc without the **ARC** command by breaking or trimming a circle, you can create an elliptical arc by breaking or trimming an ellipse.

Start by creating an ellipse, then simply break it. Where you break or trim, it will determine the arc. **BREAK** doesn't act as you might think it would on an ellipse. If it breaks in the wrong direction, try drawing one construction line at each end where you want to break the ellipse. Then use **TRIM** instead.

Remember that an ellipse is really a series of polyarcs. When you break, trim or explode an ellipse, you've reduced it to its component parts. After you've broken the ellipse, you might want to use the **PEDIT** command and join the arcs so they really do form one elliptical arc.

11.9 How do you draw a solid triangle?

The **SOLID** command in AutoCAD won't draw a solid until you've given it four points; see the triangle in Figure 11-6.

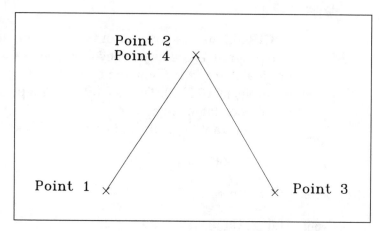

Figure 11-6: Triangle with four points

Begin the **SOLID** command. AutoCAD will ask you for points 1, 2, 3 and 4. Pick the points as indicated. When point 4 is requested, return to point 2. The solid triangle will be drawn. You can exit **SOLID** with a Ctrl-C.

An alternative method is to use **PLINE** with a beginning width of 0 and an ending width to the base of the triangle. Be aware, though, that this method will draw only an isosceles triangle.

11.10 How do you input information from a survey report?

You can change the way you measure angles whenever you want, without harming the existing drawing. When you're through with the new unit of measurement, you can return to any other method of measuring angles.

The **UNITS** command lets you use survey units, which are measured using bearings. Although it's not required, you may also want to change 0 degrees to North.

11.11 How do you draw a shape?

A shape is a special way to compress blocks on disk. Don't worry about how to draw or create a shape file. There are third-party software products on the market that can convert your block into a shape file. So let's assume that you already have a shape file.

Before you can use any of the shapes, the file must be loaded.

Type: `LOAD <RETURN>`

Response: `Name of shape file to load (or ?):`

Type in the name of the file. If you type ?, AutoCAD will list all of the shape files that are already loaded.

To use a shape, simply assume that it's another block, and use the **SHAPE** command. This has prompts similar to those of the **INSERT** command.

11.12 How do you digitize a drawing?

We'll assume here that your tablet is in digitizing mode and that your drawing is securely taped to the digitizer. Tip 16.9 of this book explains how to set up your digitizer.

You'll notice that every point on the digitizer is bit-mapped to your screen. As a general rule, don't use **SKETCH** to make your drawing; use the same tools you'd use to create the drawing from scratch. If there's a line in the drawing, issue the **LINE** command. Then position the crosshairs over the endpoint of the line and pick the point. Continue to pick the next point of the line in the same way.

Later in the drawing, use common sense. If you know that two lines should be connected, don't try to digitize back to an existing line; use **OBJECT SNAP** and connect them on the screen. This way, you can quickly input an undocumented drawing. But be prepared; even your best efforts will need some final cleanup.

The best way to input contour lines is to digitize **PLINE** points, then later curve-fit the polylines.

11.13 How do you digitize on a tablet that's too small?

Most AutoCAD users don't have large, 36-inch digitizers. If digitizing large drawings is a substantial part of your business, consider investing in a larger digitizer. If you only occasionally have this need, you can get away with a smaller one.

When you configured the digitizer (see Tip 16.9), you picked two points on the digitizer and gave absolute coordinates for each point.

When you need to move the paper, identify two known coordinates that will still be addressable when the paper is moved. You might need to place temporary points on the sheet and in the drawing. Then, when the paper is moved, recalibrate (configure) the digitizer, giving the two reference points.

More Steps to Success

11.14 Create AutoLISP macros for ARC options

You'll probably never use more than two or three of the many **ARC** command options available. To save time, turn these into AutoLISP macros in your screen or tablet menu. Here's a macro for **Center, Start, Angle**:

```
^c^c(command "arc" "c" pause pause "a")
```

"arc" begins the command. **"c"** chooses the **Center** option. The **pause pause** lets you pick two points. **"a"** chooses the **Angle** option.

11.15 New use for PLINE Length

The **Length** subcommand of **PLINE** isn't often used, since it simply draws a polyline a given distance from the last known point and in the same direction and angle as the last line or polyline. **Length** seems nothing more than an elaborate way to extend a line, but with a little imagination you can use it for more than that.

Relative commands and redefining your UCS are ways to locate points relative to other points in your drawing; but they're often inconvenient, especially if the line's at an angle.

Look at a practical example. In Figure 11-7, you've just finished drawing a series of lines or polylines. Notice the direction in which the polylines are going. Your object is to locate a point exactly three units before your last point. You might need to come off the line here, to draw another line or simply to **ID** the point so you can locate another point relative to that position.

Figure 11-7:
PLINE Length

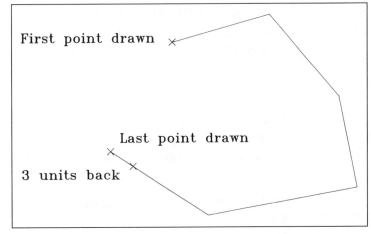

This can be a difficult task, but the **Length** subcommand of **PLINE** makes it easy. You may already be in the **PLINE** command. If you are, start at the second response line.

Type: PLINE <RETURN>

Response: From point:

Pick the last point drawn.

Response: Arc/Close/Halfwidth/Length/Undo/Width/<Endpoint of line>:

Type: L <RETURN>

Response: Length of line:

Type: -3 <RETURN> (You may enter either a positive or negative number. With a positive number, the line will continue in that direction. With a negative number, the line will backtrack that number of units over the previous polyline.)

Notice that the endpoint of the line is now three units back into the last line drawn. You can now **ID** for relative coordinates or come off the end-point of the new polyline. When you're through, erase that construction line segment. Don't worry: AutoCAD will erase it before it erases the line under it.

11.16 **Use blank areas on the tablet**

When you're using your tablet menu, you can use any of the blank areas between the blocks as a <RETURN>.

11.17 **Use coordinates only with SNAP On**

Be very careful when using coordinates to draw by. AutoCAD picks points with extreme accuracy, even though coordinates look only as accurate as the **UNITS** command can make them. Use this method only with **SNAP**.

11.18 **<RETURN> as Continue**

A <RETURN> in response to **From point:** in the **LINE** or **ARC** command is the same as **Continue**.

11.19 **How to use TTR**

The **TTR** option of **CIRCLE** can be a little confusing. First, you should choose it as your first option in the **CIRCLE** command. **TTR** stands for tangent, tangent and radius. This means you want a circle with a given radius to be tangential to two other objects. In Figure 11-8, the circle is tangent to the two lines at the points indicated, with a radius of 8.

Figure 11-8: Circle
tangent to two lines

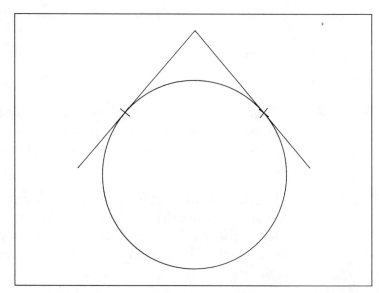

Type: `CIRCLE <RETURN>`

Response: `3P/2P/TTR/<Center point>:`

Type: `TTR <RETURN>`

Response: `Enter Tangent spec:`

This means to pick one entity to which you want the circle to be tangent. Now pick a point.

Response: `Enter second Tangent spec:`

Pick the other entity to which you want the circle to be tangent.

Response: `Radius:`

Type: `8 <RETURN>`

When you enter the radius, AutoCAD will construct a circle that matches all of the conditions. If more than one circle can be drawn, it chooses the tangent point closest to where you picked.

11.20 **The Diameter option can be confusing**

Note that when you're using the **Diameter** option of **CIRCLE**, the circle cuts through the measuring line when it's dragging, not through the endpoint of the line, as when it's measuring by radius. This can be a little confusing at first if you're dynamically dragging the circle. Remember that the circle will have a radius of 50 percent of the length of the line you're pointing with.

11.21 **Bring in a hatch exploded**

Of course you know that a hatch pattern can be exploded the same as a block. But it can also be inserted already exploded, the same as a block, if you precede it with *.

Type: `HATCH <RETURN>`

Response: `Pattern (? or name/U,style):`

Type: `*BRICK <RETURN>`

11.22 Explode a hatch without changing layers

There's an advantage to bringing in a hatch already exploded with the *, rather than exploding it later (see Tip 11.21). When a hatch pattern is exploded, it's sent to layer 0. If you want the hatch to be exploded and on a specific layer, bring it in exploded on the target layer.

11.23 Rehatch when stretching

Have you ever tried to stretch a group of entities that contained a hatch pattern? Everything stretches but the pattern, because AutoCAD places the base definition point of all hatches at 0,0, and the definition point of a hatch is never picked up.

Even if you could fool AutoCAD by crossing over the 0,0, coordinates, you'd only be moving the hatch pattern in mass from one place to another. You wouldn't stretch it. You're no better off if you explode the hatch; individual lines are stretched at the point of crossing and the other lines are moved intact. This gives you a very strange-looking pattern.

In short: If you use **STRETCH** on entities that have hatching, first complete the **STRETCH**. Then erase the hatch pattern. Finally, rehatch the entities.

11.24 HATCH first, then COPY

If you have groups of entities that need to be hatched in the same way, you should **HATCH** them first, then make copies. Or, you can make copies first, then **HATCH** one and copy the patterns to the other objects with the same relative base point.

If you **HATCH** each copy, you drastically increase the size of the file.

11.25 ID establishes last point

When you want to pick a point in absolute coordinates relative to another point in a drawing, you can use the @ command followed by the absolute coordinates. However, this makes the absolute coordinates relative to the last point picked in the drawing, and may not be the point you intended.

You could set your UCS origin to your chosen point, but it's faster to use the **ID** command and pick a point. This establishes a last point without actually placing an entity on the screen. Now you can use the point with @ for absolute coordinates relative to the correct last point.

Also, using **ID** means that you don't have to have any entities at the point you picked. See LISP48 in Tip 11.33 for a program that can be used within an AutoCAD command.

11.26 **The tablet menu includes a compass**

If you don't feel comfortable with a keyboard, or can never find the < sign for relative polar commands, don't forget that the tablet menu has a small compass on it. When you point to one of the compass directions, it automatically adds the < sign for you.

AutoLISP Programs

11.27 **Hatch cutter (LISP42)**

Sometimes after a hatch pattern has been placed, you need to take out a part of that area. Any removal of a hatch pattern requires that the pattern be exploded and then trimmed around the boundaries. This program organizes and combines some of these steps.

First, begin with a group of hatched entities and draw a polyline inside the area where you want to carve out a section, as shown in Figure 11-9. You'll be asked to pick the hatch pattern, then the polyline. Then it's easy to touch all of the lines inside the polyline you want cleaned out. See Figure 11-10.

Figure 11-9: Outline
of cutting area

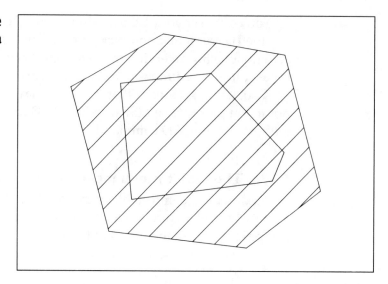

Figure 11-10:
Area after cut

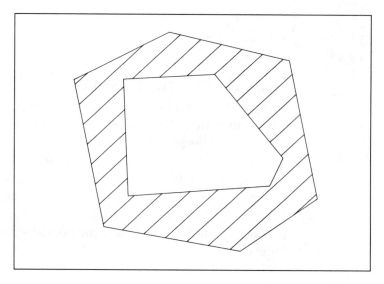

Listing:
```
(defun c:lisp42 (/ os pt1)
    (setq os (getvar "osmode"))
    (prompt "\nPick HATCH pattern ")
    (command "explode" pause "")
    (setvar "osmode" 512)
    (setq pt1 (getpoint "\nPick the polyline "))
    (setvar "osmode" os)
    (command "trim" pt1 "")
)
```

To Use: Load LISP42.LSP.

Type: LISP42 <RETURN>

Response: Pick HATCH pattern:
Select block reference, polyline, dimension, or mesh:

Pick any place on the hatch pattern.

Response: Pick the polyline:

Pick anywhere on the polyline that you drew. The polyline will now highlight.

Response: Select object to trim:

Finally, touch all of the hatch patterns inside the polyline one at a time. When you're through, press <RETURN>. You may now erase the polyline or leave it.

11.28 Offset from center line (LISP43)

The AutoCAD **OFFSET** command is the main way to draw parallel lines. But sometimes you need to offset the parallel lines from a center line; that is, you want half the distance on either side of the line you're offsetting. This program does just that.

Listing:
```
(defun c:lisp43 (/ os dis e pt1 pt2 pt3 a)
    (setq os (getvar "osmode"))
    (setq dis (getdist "\nEnter offset distance "))
    (setq dis (/ dis 2))
    (setq e 1)
    (while e
        (setvar "osmode" 512)
        (setq pt1 (getpoint "\nPick line to offset "))
        (setvar "osmode" os)
        (setq pt2 (polar pt1 3.12414 1))
        (setq pt3 (polar pt1 3.12414 -1))
        (command "offset" dis pt1 pt2 "")
        (command "erase" "l" "")
        (command "offset" dis pt1 pt3 "")
        (command "oops")
        (setq a (getstring "\nEnter to continue or <E> to stop"))
        (if (= (strcase a) "E") (setq e nil))
    )
    (setvar "osmode" os)
)
```

To Use: Begin with a line you want to offset. Then load LISP43.LSP.

Type: LISP43 <RETURN>

Response: Enter offset distance:

Remember that half this distance will be placed on either side of the line that's offset.

Response: Pick line to offset:

Pick the line.

If you're offsetting a group of connected lines that aren't a single polyline, use a **FILLET 0** to clean up the ends.

II.29 **Close area (LISP44)**

This program lets you close a series of connected lines that aren't fully closed at the ends. The program makes them all polylines, joins the polylines, then issues the **PEDIT Close** command.

Listing:
```
(defun c:lisp44 (/ os pt1)
    (setq os (getvar "osmode"))
    (setvar "osmode" 512)
    (setq pt1 (getpoint "\nPick one line "))
    (setvar "osmode" os)
    (command "explode" pt1 ^c)
    (command "pedit" pt1 "Y" "J" "c" pause pause "" "c" "")
    (command "explode" pt1)
)
```

To Use: Load LISP44.LSP.

Type: LISP44 <RETURN>

Response: Pick one line:

Pick any line in the group.

Response: First corner:

Put a window around the entire group. The lines are now closed.

II.30 **Construction line layer (LISP45)**

It's generally a good idea to put your construction lines on a separate layer so you can remove them easily. This program sets up a separate layer just for construction lines. LISP46 returns you to your previous layer and LISP47 erases all construction lines created on the construction line layer; see Tips 11.31 and 11.32.

Listing:
```
(defun c:lisp45 ()
    (setq prevlay (getvar "clayer"))
    (command "layer" "m" "const1" "")
)
```

To Use: Load LISP45.LSP.

Type: LISP45 <RETURN>

A layer called "const1" is set up, and you're changed to that layer. Now draw any construction lines you want. Use LISP46 to immediately change back to your previous layer.

11.31 Restore from construction layer (LISP46)

This program is used in conjunction with LISP45 above. It restores you to your previous layer.

Listing:
```
(defun c:lisp46 ()
    (command "layer" "s" prevlay "")
)
```

To Use: Load LISP46.LSP.

Type: LISP46 <RETURN>

11.32 Delete construction layer (LISP47)

This program provides an easy way to get rid of all of your construction lines, provided they were drawn on layer "const1."

Listing:
```
(defun c:lisp47 ()
    (setq a (ssget "x" '((8 . "const1"))))
    (command "erase" a "")
)
```

To Use: Load LISP47.LSP.

Type: LISP47 <RETURN>

11.33 Relative origin (LISP48)

This program lets you pick any point relative to any other point. The beauty of this program is that it can be used within another command.

Listing:
```
(defun i ()
    (setq pt1 (getpoint "\n Pick relative position \n"))
    (setvar "lastpoint" pt1)
    (getpoint "\n Enter relative distance or coordinates \n")
)
```

To Use: Load LISP48.LSP.

This program differs from others in that the name of the program is (i). When it's executed you must put the () around the name; this lets you use it inside an AutoCAD command.

Let's look at an example using the **COPY** command. Begin with the regular AutoCAD command.

Type: `COPY <RETURN>`

Response: `Select objects:`

Pick the object you want to move, and confirm.

Response: `<Base point or displacement>/Multiple:`

Pick a base point.

Response: `Second point of displacement:`

This is one place you may want to use the program. It could also have been used when you picked the base point. But in this example, you want the object moved two inches to the right and one inch above another intersection.

Type: `(i)`

Response: `Pick relative position:`

Pick the intersection you want as the relative point.

Response: `Enter relative distance or coordinates:`

You can now use relative coordinates, preceded by @ or relative polar coordinates where you give a distance and an angle.

Type: `@2,1 <RETURN>`

CHAPTER 12

Intermediate Editing

How Do You . . .

12.1 How do you use a different kind of spline curve?

Beginning with Release 10, AutoCAD offers you more than one type of spline curve; you control the type with system variables. Look at Figure 12-1. Example A shows a quadratic B-spline and example B shows a cubic B-spline.

Figure 12-1: Quadratic and cubic B-spline curves

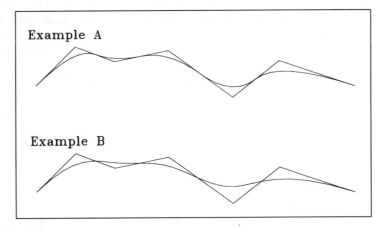

Example A

Example B

Type: `SETVAR <RETURN>`

Response: `Variable name or ?:`

Type: `SPLINETYPE <RETURN>`

Response: `New value for SPLINETYPE:`

Type: `5`

This produces example A. If it's set to 6, it produces example B.

12.2 **How do you mirror and keep the text going in the correct direction?**

This is a simple procedure that's been around for a long time. Unfortunately, AutoCAD's default is set to mirror the text, but you can change this.

The mirroring of text is controlled by the system variable **MIRRTEXT**. If it's set to **1**, then text is mirrored; if it's set to **0**, text isn't mirrored.

12.3 **How do you rotate an object an exact number of degrees relative to the grid?**

Let's assume that there's an object at a 90-degree angle to the grid that you want to rotate to 12 degrees from the grid. If you simply rotate and enter the angle it will rotate 12 degrees from its current position. Therefore, use the **Reference** option of **ROTATE**. Look at Figure 12-2.

Figure 12-2: Using
ROTATE Reference

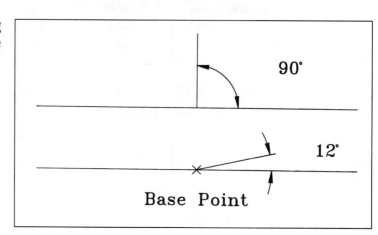

90°

12°

Base Point

Type: ROTATE <RETURN>

Response: Select objects:

Pick the object to rotate, and confirm.

Response: Base point:

Pick a base point on the object.

Response: <Rotation angle>/Reference:

Type: R <RETURN>

Response: Reference angle <0>:

Type: 90 <RETURN> (This is the current angle.)

Response: New angle:

Type: 12 <RETURN>

12.4 How do you array along an angle?

This depends on whether you want the object rotated in the same direction as the rotated array. If you do, simply create the array, then rotate the entire group. If you don't want the object rotated relative to the array, then change the rotation of the snap before you do the array.

Type: SNAP <RETURN>

Response: Snap spacing or ON/OFF/Aspect/Rotate/Style:

Type: ROTATE <RETURN>

Response: Base point:

Type: <RETURN>

Response: Rotation angle:

Type: 30 <RETURN>

Now do the array. When you're through, rotate the grid back to 0. See LISP51 in Tip 12.24.

12.5 **How do you clean up a tic-tac-toe?**

An example of a tic-tac-toe is a road intersection; see Figure 12-3. There are several ways you can attack this problem. But the one way you can't is to do a **FILLET 0**. This will send your lines in any direction but the one you want.

One method would be to break the various lines from the intersections. But that takes too many picks. The easiest way is to use **TRIM**. When asked to select the cutting edges, place a crossing window around the area to be cleaned, and confirm. Be sure it's a crossing and not a window, because you must capture all four lines. When asked to select the object to trim, pick where the Xs are shown in Figure 12-3. The results are shown in Figure 12-4.

Figure 12-3:
Tic-tac-toe

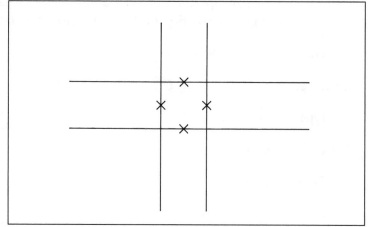

Figure 12-4:
Using TRIM

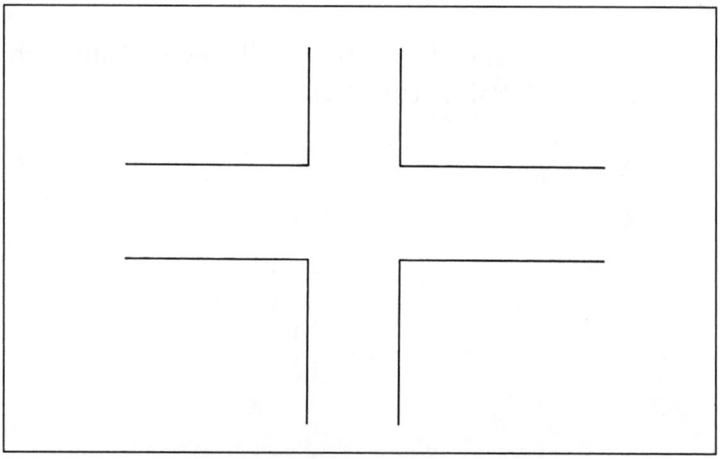

Type: `TRIM <RETURN>`

Response: `Select cutting edge(s)...`
`Select objects:`

Put a crossing window around the four intersections, and confirm.

Response: `Select object to trim:`

Pick a point at each X. When you've picked all four, press <RETURN> to end the command. See LISP53 in Tip 12.26.

12.6 How do you switch from Arc to Line in PLINE?

After you've begun the **PLINE** command and picked the first point, you have options like those for the **PEDIT** command.

`Arc/Close/Halfwidth/Length/Undo/Width/<Endpoint of line>:`

If you choose **Arc**, you draw polyarcs. Each point picked in **Arc** has a different set of options:

`Angle/CEnter/CLose/Direction/Halfwidth/Line/Radius/Second pt →`
`    /Undo/Width/<Endpoint of arc>:`

You can now choose **Line**, and toggle back and forth between **Arc** and **Line** while in the **PLINE** command.

12.7 How do you add width to a polygon?

A polygon created with the **POLYGON** command is nothing more than a closed polyline, so you can edit it with **PEDIT**. You can change the width of all line segments.

12.8 How do you make a reusable selection set?

This is a little difficult from the keyboard, but not impossible. But it's better left to a series of AutoLISP programs; see LISP56 in Tip 12.29.

Type: `(setq a (ssget)) <RETURN>`

This sets up selection set "A."

You can do this for any group of selection sets you want to create. You're limited to a maximum of six selection sets. When you're ready to use one, give this command:

Type: SELECT !A <RETURN>

This makes selection set A your previous selection set, and you can now use it in any command that says "Select objects:" and permits multiple object selection. When asked for selection objects,

Type: P <RETURN>

and the previous selection set will be chosen.

Another method would be to enter !a any time you're asked to select objects.

12.9 How do you use UNDO Marks?

When you issue the **UNDO** command, you have several options.

Auto/Back/Control/End/Group/Mark/<number>:

If you enter M for **Mark**, then a mark is placed there. You now proceed to work in AutoCAD. You may place another mark any time you want to. Each **UNDO Back** will undo back to the closest mark. When you run out of marks, be careful. You'll be advised that this will undo everything. If you answer Y, everything in your drawing will be undone from the time you entered the drawing editor.

12.10 How do you use UNDO Group?

Normally, you don't; this should be reserved for menu commands, so that they can be undone as a group. If you have **UNDO Auto** on, this is taken care of automatically. Every time you issue a menu command, it's treated as a group regardless of how complicated it may be. When you do an **UNDO**, then the entire group is undone.

More Steps to Success

12.11 **Extend a line in either direction**

Here's a good way to extend a line, because the line can go in any direction or angle.

Let's say you want to extend a line three units in a given direction. Draw a circle with a radius of three units, with the endpoint of the line as the center of the circle. Then use the **EXTEND** command to extend the line to the end of the circle. Be sure to erase the circle. The circle is the boundary edge, and the line is the object to extend.

See LISP49 in Tip 12.22 for a program that does this for you.

12.12 **Move objects using STRETCH**

You can use the **STRETCH** command to move objects, even doors and windows in broken parallel lines. See LISP50 in Tip 12.23.

Figure 12-5: Object before STRETCH

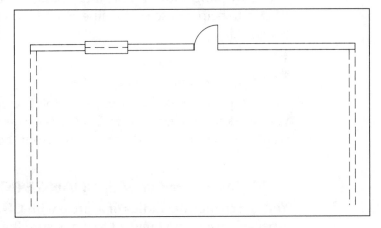

Look at Figure 12-5. Put a **STRETCH** crossing window around the door. Pick the base point at the intersection of the wall line and door, and move it down to the end of the wall as in Figure 12-6. Be sure you do this before you hatch the area or you'll have a mess on your hands.

Figure 12-6: Object
after STRETCH

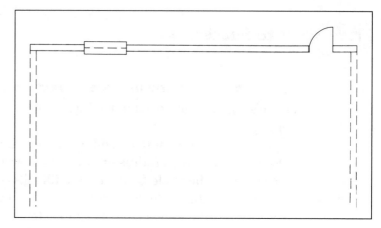

12.13 **Set width to zero when selecting polylines**

Sometimes it's hard to get AutoCAD to confirm when you're selecting polylines with width. It keeps returning **zero found**, because you have to hit the center line of the polyline. Try changing the width to zero while you're working with the line, then change it back later. Use a crossing in **PEDIT** to help you select the line. See LISP54 and LISP55 in Tips 12.27 and 12.28.

12.14 **Use Previous frequently**

Don't forget to make frequent use of the **Previous** subcommand when you're asked to select objects. Even if those aren't exactly the objects you want, you can usually add or remove from the selection set.

12.15 **Change radius with CHANGE POINT**

You can change the radius of a circle with **CHANGE POINT**. This can be especially useful if you want to make sure the circle cuts through a given point after it's drawn.

12.16 **Move blocks using CHANGE POINT**

MOVE isn't the only command you can use to move things. You can move a block with **CHANGE POINT** with fewer picks.

12.17 **Use Through for offset distance**

The offset distance doesn't have to be keyed in from the keyboard; you can measure it by picking a first and second point. If you pick T for **Through**, you can simply pick one point that the new offset will pass through.

12.18 **Different fit-curves**

SPLINES and **FIT CURVE** can be a little confusing. First, let's explain the difference between a fit-curve and a spline. A fit-curve must pass through each vertex of a polyline. A spline approaches the vertices, but doesn't have to actually pass through them. How close the spline must come to the vertices is determined by the degree of the polynomial. This also is the difference between the two types of splines.

12.19 **How many points do you use with SPLINE?**

You can control the smoothness of a curve using **SPLINE** by adjusting the number of segments in the curve. If the number is set too low, the curve will still look angular. If the number's too high, it will slow down regeneration time.

Once the number is set and the spline is drawn, changing that number won't change the curve on the next regeneration—it's fixed. The only way to get **SPLINE** to use the new number is to uncurve the curve and **SPLINE** it again. You set the number of segments with the system variable **SPLINESEGS**.

12.20 **Using BOX**

You might prefer to see what's happening when you move points in a drawing. By using **BOX** instead of **WINDOW** or **CROSSING** you can actually see the motion of points from left to right **(WINDOW)** or from right to left **(CROSSING)**. **BOX** can't be abbreviated to B.

12.21 **SPLINES forever**

If you've fitted or splined a polyline, be careful of the edit you perform on it. If you use **BREAK** or **TRIM** on it, you're stuck with the curve—you can't uncurve it.

AutoLISP Programs

12.22 **Extend either end of a line (LISP49)**

There are many ways to extend a line once it's drawn. This program is very flexible; you can extend a line from either end, even if it's at an intersection.

Listing:
```
(defun c:lisp49 ()
     (setq os (getvar "osmode"))
     (setvar "osmode" 512)
     (setq pt1 (getpoint "\nPick point near end of line "))
     (setvar "osmode" os)
     (setq dis (getdist pt1 "\nDistance to extend "))
     (command "circle" "endpoint" pt1 dis)
     (command "extend" "last" "" pt1 "")
     (command "erase" "last" "")
)
```

To Use: Load LISP49.LSP.

Type: LISP49 <RETURN>

Response: Pick point near end of line:

You don't have to pick the actual endpoint of the line. Just show AutoCAD which end of the line you want.

Response: Distance to extend:

You're now tied to the point you've picked. You can point to the distance to extend the line, or type it in from the keyboard. AutoCAD will draw a circle from the endpoint of the line with a radius the distance of the extension. It will then use the **EXTEND** command to lengthen the line to the edge of the circle. Then the circle is erased.

Make sure that the circle doesn't cut through the point on the line that's selected, since AutoLISP won't know which entity to extend.

12.23 **Position doors and windows (LISP50)**

This program is handy for repositioning doors and windows once they are inserted into walls. You don't have to worry about the object's exact position. (Use of the plus sign at the end of a line in AutoLISP code indicates that line is wrapped.)

Listing:
```
(defun c:lisp50 (/ pt1 pt2)
    (setq pt1 (getpoint "\nPick relative position "))
    (setq pt2 (getpoint pt1 "\nEnter relative distance or +
       coordinates "))
    (command "stretch" "c" pause pause pause pause pt2)
)
```

To Use: Load LISP50.LSP.

Begin with a drawing like Figure 12-7. Now move the door swing four inches to the left of the right wall intersection, as in Figure 12-8.

Figure 12-7: Door ready to be moved

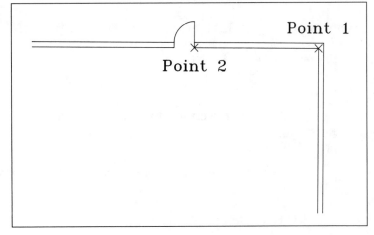

Point 1

Point 2

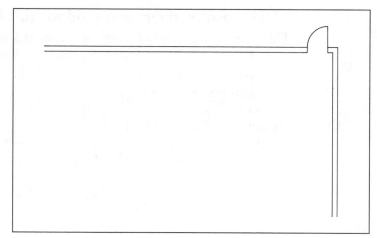

Figure 12-8: Door after being moved

Type: LISP50 <RETURN>

Response: Pick relative position:

            Pick the intersection at point 1.

Response: Enter relative distance or coordinates:

Type: @4<180 <RETURN>

Response: First Corner:

            Window the entire door, and confirm.

Response: Base point:

            Pick the base of the door at point 2. The door will now move into position.

12.24 **Array at an angle (LISP51)**

This program lets you array objects at an angle.

Listing:
```
(defun c:lisp51 (/ a ang)
    (prompt "\nSelect objects to array ")
    (setq a (ssget))
    (command "select" a "")
    (setq ang (getangle "\nEnter angle for array rotation "))
    (setq ang (rtd ang))
    (command "array" "previous" "" "r" pause pause pause pause)
    (setvar "snapang" ang)
    (setvar "snapang" 0)
)
(defun rtd (a1)
    (/ (* a1 180.0) pi))
```

To Use: Load LISP51.LSP.

Type: LISP51 <RETURN>

Begin with a single object such as in Figure 12-9.

Figure 12-9: Object
to be arrayed

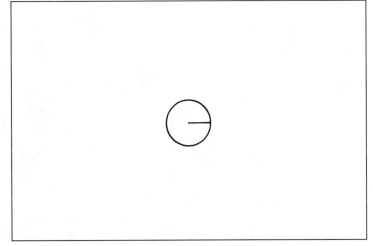

Response: Select objects to array:
Select objects:

Select the entities, and confirm.

Response: Enter angle for array rotation:

Type: 45 <RETURN>

Response: Number of rows (---):

Type: 5 <RETURN>

Response: Number of columns (|||):

Type: 4 <RETURN>

Response: Unit cell or distance between rows (---):

Type: 3 <RETURN>

Response: Distance between columns (|||):

Type: -3 <RETURN>

**Figure 12-10: Object
arrayed at an angle**

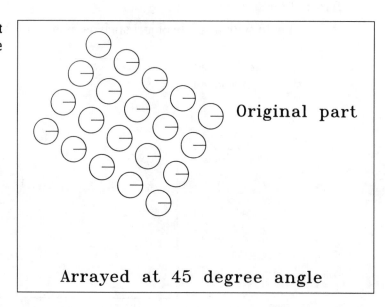

Original part

Arrayed at 45 degree angle

12.25 Explode **MINSERT (LISP52)**

The problem with the **MINSERT** command is that all of the arrayed objects are treated as a single object, so you can't explode them. This program lets you explode one block and leave the others unexploded. You can explode them later as individual blocks with the AutoCAD **EXPLODE** command.

Listing:
```
(defun c:lisp52 (/ a el p ip s r c dr dc angl)
    (setq a (entsel))
    (setq el (entget (car a)))
    (setq p (cdr (assoc 2 el)))
    (setq ip (cdr (assoc 10 el)))
    (setq s (cdr (assoc 43 el)))
    (setq r (cdr (assoc 71 el)))
    (setq c (cdr (assoc 70 el)))
    (setq dr (cdr (assoc 45 el)))
    (setq dc (cdr (assoc 44 el)))
    (setq angl (cdr (assoc 50 el)))
    (command "erase" ip "")
    (command "insert" p ip s "" (rtd angl))
    (setvar "snapang" angl)
    (command "array" "l" "" "r" r c dr dc)
    (command "explode" (cadr a))
    (setvar "snapang" 0)
)
```

To Use: Load LISP52.LSP.

Type: LISP52 <RETURN>

Start with a series of blocks that were inserted using MINSERT.

Response: Select objects:

Pick the entity you want to explode. The program then explodes only the object you picked. The entities are now blocks, not **MINSERT** single entities, except for the one exploded.

12.26 **Tic-tac-toe cleanup (LISP53)**

A very common wall cleanup is a "tic-tac-toe" as shown below.

Listing:
```
(defun c:lisp53 ()
    (command "trim" "c" pause pause "" )
)
```

To Use: Load LISP53.LSP.

Type: `LISP53 <RETURN>`

Response: `First corner:`

Pick the first and second corners as shown in Figure 12-11. Do not confirm.

Figure 12-11:
Tic-tac-toe cleanup

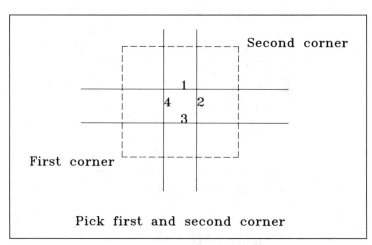

Response: `Select object to trim:`

Pick lines 1, 2, 3 and 4. Press <RETURN> to terminate the program.

Figure 12-12: Finished intersection

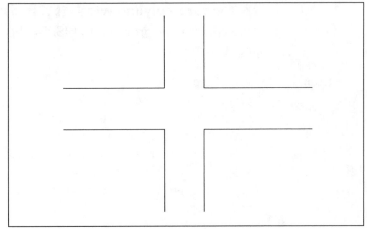

12.27 Reduce polylines to 0 (LISP54)

Polylines are difficult to select if they have width and **FILL** is on. It's often easier to reduce them to 0, then restore their width. This program reduces them to 0 and the next program, LISP55, restores their width.

Listing:
```
(defun c:lisp54 (/ a d1)
    (setq a (entget (ssname (ssget) 0)))
    (setq bw (cdr (assoc 40 a)))
    (setq ew (cdr (assoc 41 a)))
    (setq d1 (subst '(40 . 0.0) (assoc 40 a) a))
    (setq d1 (subst '(41 . 0.0) (assoc 41 a) d1))
    (entmod d1)
)
```

To Use: Load LISP54.LSP.

Type: `LISP54 <RETURN>`

Response: `Select objects:`

Put a crossing window around any segment of the polyline, and confirm. The polyline chosen will be reduced to 0 width.

12.28 **Restore polyline width (LISP55)**

This is a companion program to LISP54 above. It restores a polyline to its original width.

Listing:
```
(defun c:lisp55 (/ a d0 d1 e1)
    (prompt "\nPick polyline \n")
    (setq a (entget (car (entsel))))
    (setq d0 (cons (car (assoc 40 a)) bw))
    (setq d1 (cons (car (assoc 41 a)) ew))
    (setq e1 (subst d0 (assoc 40 a) a))
    (setq e1 (subst d1 (assoc 41 a) e1))
    (entmod e1)
)
```

To Use: Load LISP55.LSP.

Type: `LISP55 <RETURN>`

Response: `Select objects:`

Pick the polyline that was reduced. This program can also add the width of one group of polylines to the width of others.

12.29 **Create a reusable selection set (LISP56)**

This program lets you make reusable selection sets. You'll need a similar program for each selection set you want to use; the variable will change (**s2, s3,** etc.) for each additional program.

Listing:
```
(defun c:lisp56 ()
    (setq s1 (ssget))
)
```

To Use: Load LISP56.LSP.

Type: LISP56 <RETURN>

Response: Select objects:

Use any selection method you wish. The selection set is assigned to variable **s1**. The next time you're asked to select objects in a command, type in **!s1>**. This tells AutoCAD to use the AutoLISP variable **s1**. For example,

Type: ERASE <RETURN>

Response: Select objects:

Type: !s1 <RETURN>

Notice that your saved selection set is highlighted.

CHAPTER 13

Intermediate Viewing

How Do You . . .

13.1 How do you do a transparent zoom if you're too deep?

This is one of the biggest problems with transparent zooms. Transparent zooms let you **ZOOM**, **PAN** and **VIEW Restore** while working in a command; simply precede the command with an apostrophe. The only problem is that AutoCAD performs a regen when you've zoomed in too far.

Starting with Release 10, you have a way to overcome this problem: use your viewports. You can set up one viewport deeply zoomed in on one area of your drawing, and another viewport zoomed in on another area. Without having to use a transparent zoom, you can begin your command in one viewport and toggle to the other to finish it, regardless of how deeply you've zoomed.

RELEASE 12   With Release 12 it is rare that you will be too deep in the ZOOM, if you're using a 32-bit 4.2 video driver. Even so, the above method is a valuable and time-saving tip.

13.2 How do you switch from one tablet underlay to another?

This is as easy as switching from one menu to another. First, let's assume that we're talking only about Menu Area One, the area at the top of the tablet that's labeled A-H vertically and 1-25 horizontally.

Menu items are entered as part of the ACAD.MNU file in the TABLET1 area. Commands positioned here control the menu blocks regardless of how they're labeled, so if you have more than one menu underlay, you must control which one is active. (Normally, the reason for numerous underlays is for working with detailed parts or specific programs relating to a single discipline.)

First, make as many copies of ACAD.MNU as you have underlays. You might want to call them ACAD1.MNU and ACAD2.MNU, assuming that you have three sets of underlays. These three menus are exactly alike except for the TABLET1 area, where each will have its own specific commands and programs. The menus may have some symbols and AutoLISP programs in common, so these should remain constant from menu to menu. See Tip 23.2 for another method that uses submenus rather than creating separate menu files.

Use the AutoCAD **MENU** command to call up the appropriate menu.

Type: `MENU <RETURN>`

Response: `Menu file name or . for none:`

Type: `ACAD1 <RETURN>` (This will call up ACAD1.MNU.)

13.3 How do you switch tablet underlays by picking from the tablet?

This is like calling up the **MENU** command from the AutoCAD command line, but you build the macros that do this for you on the tablet menu area.

At the last three blocks on each menu, you should have listed ACAD, ACAD1 and ACAD2 or any block you choose. Place this macro in the appropriate part of each Tablet1 area of the menus:

```
^c^cmenu acad
^c^cmenu acad1
^c^cmenu acad2
```

Don't put all of these in the same menu block area. H23 might have the first one call up ACAD.MNU, H24 might use the second, and H25 the third; you simply pick one of the menus in order to change templates. Be sure, though, to physically change the template by sliding one under the top transparent area. Some people use a flip-chart mechanism to do this.

13.4 How do you create the squares for a standard tablet underlay?

Start with engineering units. Draw a crossgrid that's 9.6" by 3.2". Each of the grid squares will be .4" apart in both directions. This will fit very closely as an underlay in the TABLET1 area. You can then use this drawing to put in your symbols or directions for each of the blocks; see Figure 13-1. You can plot at a scale of 1 to 1.

Figure 13-1:
Tablet grid

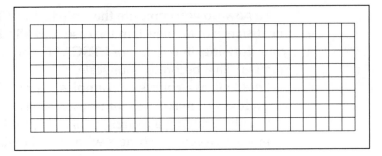

See LISP62 in Tip 13.25 for a program that draws crossgrids.

13.5 How do you control the frequency of redraws during dragging?

Use two system variables, **DRAGP1** and **DRAGP2**, which control how often AutoCAD checks the new coordinates while dragging an image. The larger the value, the more image AutoCAD will draw before it checks to see where the image is. This lets you see more of the image before Auto-CAD erases and starts to draw it at another point, but the process is sluggish. If the number is smaller, cursor response improves, but less of the object is drawn.

13.6 How do you know whether you can use pull-down menus?

Just put your cursor at the top of the screen and see if they're there. But if you really want to be sure, you can check a read-only system variable called **POPUPS**. If your display supports pull-down menus, **POPUPS** has a value of **1**. If it doesn't support them, **POPUPS** has a value of **0**.

13.7 How do you convert scale factors to your drawing?

AutoCAD requires scale factors rather than sizes for many things, such as dimensions, **LTSCALE** and **HATCH**. But most of these are based on a *unit factor*, which means that they were created as one unit in size.

Let's look at several functions that request a scale factor. **LTSCALE** is global for the entire drawing. **HATCH**'s scale factor depends on what is being hatched and its size in relation to the rest of the drawing.

So how do you compute the scale factors? The easiest way is to measure the distance of an object, in the case of **HATCH**, or measure the limits of your drawing, in the case of **LTSCALE**, and divide this distance by a fixed number. That becomes your scale.

Let's look at a couple of examples. Using a little AutoLISP at the Command line will make the math easier; see LISP63 in Tip 13.26.

Start by drawing a rectangle, as in Figure 13-2 below. Measure the distance between the corners with the following typed in at the Command line.

Type: (setq d (getdist)) <RETURN>

Response: Nothing appears to happen; AutoLISP is waiting for you to pick two points. Pick point 1 and point 2 in Figure 13-2. **d** now contains the distance.

Figure 13-2: Object to be scaled

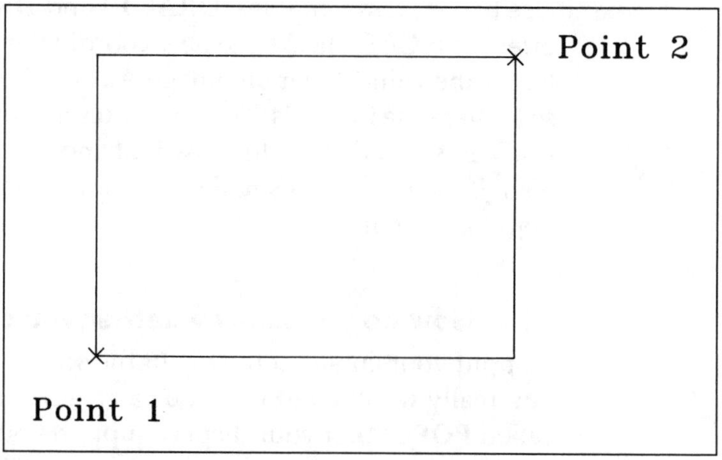

Point 2

Point 1

Type: (/ d 40) <RETURN>

This will produce your scale. You may want to use a larger or smaller number than 40.

Now do a **HATCH U** using the scale you just produced. Create larger or smaller objects with the same technique, and you'll see that the hatch and the object are about the same size.

Line type scales, which are global for an entire drawing, need a measurement that's the limits of the drawing. You can secure those limits with the system variables **LIMMIN** for the lower left and **LIMMAX** for the upper right. The following AutoLISP command does this for you:

```
(setq d (distance (getvar "limmin") (getvar "limmax")))
```

The next line would read:

```
(/ d 40)
```

This is the scale for **LTSCALE**.

13.8 **How do you use dialogue boxes?**

Dialogue boxes are mostly self-explanatory, but there are a couple of tricks to using them:

1) You can't get out of them by pressing <RETURN>. A Ctrl-C will exit you from a dialogue box and abort the changes.

2) You must choose the part of the box where the data are stored; you can't choose the area where the text explaining the data is located.

3) Once you've picked the data to change, you may change it from the keyboard.

4) You don't then have to pick the OK box, you can simply press <RETURN>.

5) To terminate the dialogue box and update the changes, you must pick **OK**; <RETURN> won't do this for you.

 RELEASE 12   See Tips 10.28, 10.29, 10.30. New dialogues and shortcuts.

13.9 **How do you create your own dialogue boxes?**

 RELEASES 10 AND 11   You can't create dialogue boxes. AutoCAD has hard-coded the dialogue boxes as part of the program. Dialogue boxes aren't like icons and pull-down menus.

 RELEASE 12   This is no longer true. You can create your dialogue boxes with text files. Refer to *The AutoCAD Productivity Book* by Ventana Press (1992 edition).

13.10 **How do you create multiple ORTHOS?**

Some CAD systems let you turn **ORTHO** on at whatever angle you want. AutoCAD permits only 90 degrees to the current grid. The best you can do is to change the rotation of your crosshairs with a system variable.

If you want a 45-degree **ORTHO**:

Type: `SETVAR SNAPANG <RETURN>`

Response: `New value for SNAPANG:`

Type: `45 <RETURN>`

Notice that the crosshairs are at a 45-degree angle. If **ORTHO** is on, then all lines drawn will be at 45 degrees to the grid. See LISP61 in Tip 13.24 for a program that does this for you.

RELEASE 12   Lets you use dialogue boxes to choose multiple options of a command. See Tips 10.28, 10.29, 10.30.

More Steps to Success

13.11 **Use the whole screen for your drawing**

You may want to fill your entire screen with only one drawing. To photograph the screen, or for some other reason, you may not want the status line, menu area and Command line visible.

For most graphics cards (this is not universal), these items can be turned off by reconfiguring AutoCAD (item 5 of the AutoCAD main menu). Stay in your same video driver, but answer N to **Do you want status line, command line and screen menu?** Your AutoCAD drawing will take up the entire screen.

BE CAREFUL: You won't have a command line, but you can use function key F1 to see what you're typing in.

13.12 Use VIEW Window

You don't have to bring up a view on the screen in order to save it. You can use **VIEW Window**, and AutoCAD will ask you the name of the view to save. Then it will prompt you for a first corner and another corner. The screen won't redraw or regenerate, but the view will be saved. To test this, do a **VIEW Restore**; you can set up a lot of rough views ahead of time. You could also give the view window exact coordinates for the first and other corner.

13.13 Use SNAPANG instead of SNAP Rotate

A lot of users successfully use **SNAP Rotate** for a variety of reasons. Try using the system variable **SNAPANG** and supplying the angle instead of using **SNAP Rotate**. It often works better because it rotates only the cross-hairs, not the grid itself. It also has fewer picks and keystrokes.

Also try using UCS Entity. It's even quicker.

13.14 Group object snaps

As you probably know, object snaps can be grouped, such as Endpoint with Intersection or Center with Midpoint. This usually works well. For a line, AutoCAD chooses Midpoint, since lines can't have centers and circles can't have midpoints. But arcs can have both. If you want the midpoint chosen, point toward the midpoint of the arc. If you want the center chosen, point toward the end of the arc.

13.15 Use OBJECT SNAP only on entities you can see

OBJECT SNAP is effective only on visible entities. Be careful with entities like dashed lines. You can find the midpoint of a dashed line, but your aperture must actually touch part of the line itself. If it fits between the spaces, it will miss the entity.

13.16 If you have trouble displaying the grid, use AXIS

Some display list graphics cards might give you a little trouble displaying the grid. This could actually slow you down rather than make you more productive. If this is the case with your graphics card, try using **AXIS** instead of **GRID**. In Release 12, **AXIS** is not available; it's been discontinued.

13.17 Pull-down commands can differ from screen or tablet menus

Be careful when using pull-down menus. To some extent, screen menus, pull-down menus and tablet menus are interchangeable. But similar commands often act differently on each menu. **ERASE** on the pull-downs is an **ERASE Auto**. **BREAK** on the tablet menu is either a **BREAK F** or a **BREAK @**. These differ greatly on the screen menu.

13.18 ZOOM Left

ZOOM Left produces a zoom of your drawing limits if you're in **WCS** and enter 0,0 and the height of your limits. **ZOOM All** gives you everything in the drawing. This can cause a problem if you have a small object outside your drawing limits.

13.19 Use F7 to redraw

A quick way to redraw your screen is to quickly turn **GRID** off and on, or on and off. This can be done on most machines by pressing F7 twice quickly. It's much faster than searching for **REDRAW**. Be careful using this if you have a dense grid, since it can slow redraw time.

AutoLISP Programs

13.20 Reposition grid (LISP57)

This program is a quick and easy way to reposition the grid to the end-point, intersection, etc., of any entity.

Listing:
```
(defun c:lisp57 (/ os pt1)
    (setq os (getvar "osmode"))
    (setvar "osmode" 33)
    (setq pt1 (getpoint "\nPick endpoint or intersection"))
    (setq pt1 (list (car pt1) (cadr pt1)))
    (setvar "snapbase" pt1)
    (setvar "osmode" os)
    (command "redraw")
)
```

To Use: Load LISP57.LSP.

Type: `LISP57 <RETURN>`

Response: `Pick endpoint or intersection:`

Pick any point, and the grid will be repositioned to that point.

13.21 Set grid back (LISP58)

This program returns the grid back to its 0,0 origin.

Listing:
```
(defun c:lisp58 (/ pt1)
    (setq pt1 '(0 0))
    (setvar "snapbase" pt1)
    (command "redraw")
)
```

To Use: Load LISP58.LSP.

Type: `LISP58 <RETURN>`

13.22 Set angle of crosshairs to object (LISP59)

This program sets the crosshairs to the angle of any entity in your drawing that has a beginning and ending point. This can be especially useful if you want to come off that object at 90 degrees.

Listing:
```
(defun c:lisp59 ()
    (setq el (entget (car (entsel))))
    (setq pt1 (cdr (assoc 10 el)))
    (setq pt2 (cdr (assoc 11 el)))
    (setvar "snapang" (angle pt1 pt2))
)
```

To Use: Load LISP59.LSP.

Type: `LISP59 <RETURN>`

Response: `Select objects:`

Pick any object, and the crosshairs will be repositioned. Use LISP60 (below) to get them back.

13.23 Reposition crosshairs (LISP60)

This is a companion program to LISP59. It returns the crosshairs to their normal orthogonal position to the grid.

Listing:
```
(defun c:lisp60 ()
     (setvar "snapang" 0))
```

To Use: Load LISP60.LSP.

Type: LISP60 <RETURN>

13.24 User-defined ORTHO command (LISP61)

This program lets you define the angle of your **ORTHO** command. It moves the crosshairs and puts you in **ORTHO** mode. Enter **(OT)** to use the command within another AutoCAD command.

Listing:
```
(defun ot ()
     (setvar "orthomode" 1)
     (setq ang (getorient "\nAngle for ortho \n"))
     (setvar "snapang" ang)
)
```

To Use: Load LISP61.LSP.

Begin a **LINE** command, for example, as you normally would. When you want to draw the next line at 33 degrees, do this:

Type: (OT) <RETURN>

Response: Angle for ortho:

Type: 33 <RETURN>

Now continue with the **LINE** command. You can turn **ORTHO** on or off as needed; it remains at 33 degrees until you change it.

13.25 Tablet grid (LISP62)

This program lets you draw a crossgrid to any specifications you want. The example given here draws one that will fit in tablet area 1 so you can create your own underlays.

Listing:
```
(defun c:lisp62 (/ h1 v1 dh dv nh nv pnt c p1 p2)
    (setq h1 (getdist "\nLength of horizontal "))
    (setq v1 (getdist "\nLength of vertical "))
    (setq dh (getdist "\nDistance between horizontal "))
    (setq dv (getdist "\nDistance between vertical "))
    (setq nh (getint "\nNumber of horizontal lines "))
    (setq nv (getint "\nNumber of vertical lines "))
    (setq pnt (getpoint "\nStarting point "))
    (setq c 0)
    (repeat nh
        (setq p1 (list (car pnt) (+ (cadr pnt) c)))
        (setq p2 (list (+ (car p1) h1) (cadr p1)))
        (command "line" p1 p2 "")
        (setq c (+ c dh))
    )
    (setq c 0)
    (repeat nv
        (setq p1 (list (+ (car pnt) c) (cadr pnt)))
        (setq p2 (list (car p1) (+ (cadr p1) v1)))
        (command "line" p1 p2 "")
        (setq c (+ c dv))
    )
)
```

To Use: Load LISP62.LSP.

Type: LISP62 <RETURN>

Response: Length of horizontal:

Type: 9.6

Response: Length of vertical:

Type: 3.2

Response: Distance between horizontal:

Type: .4

Response: Distance between vertical:

Type: .4

Response: Number of horizontal lines:

Type: 9

Response: Number of vertical lines:

Type: 25

Response: Starting point:

Pick a starting point on your screen.

13.26 Scale factors (LISP63)

This program gives you the standard scale factor for any entity or for a drawing as a whole. When obtained for a drawing as a whole, the scale factor can be used for **LTSCALE**. For entities it can be used to determine the scale factor for hatch patterns. This program will give you the unit scale factor. Some hatch patterns must be multiplied by 2.

Listing:
```
(defun c:lisp63 ()
    (setq a (getstring "\n<L> for limits or <RETURN> for object "))
    (if (=(strcase a) "L")
        (progn
            (setq d (distance  (getvar "limmin")  (getvar "limmax")))
            (setq d (/ d 40))
            (princ "\nThe scale factor is ") (princ  d)
        )
    )
    (if (= (strcase a ) "")
        (progn
            (setq d (getdist "\nMeasure corners of object "))
            (setq d (/ d 40))
            (princ "\nThe scale factor is ") (princ d)
        )
    )
    (princ)
)
```

To Use: Load LISP63.LSP.

Type: LISP63 <RETURN>

Response: <L> for limits or <RETURN> for object:

If you type L, you get the scale factor for your current limits. **Limits** must be set for this to work. If you press <RETURN>, you must measure the corners of an object; then you'll get the scale factor for the distance selected.

Intermediate Layers, Blocks, Attributes

How Do You . . .

14.1 How do you plot just certain layers?

Only layers that are on or thawed can be plotted, so you must turn off or freeze layers that you don't want plotted. See LISP65 in Tip 14.49 for a program that asks for only the layers you want plotted and freezes all others.

11 RELEASE 11 With the introduction of Paper Space, options are available for plotting only part of your drawing or rearranging parts of your drawing to appear on the same sheet. See Tips 29.1, 29.5, 29.9 and 29.16.

14.2 How do you know how many blocks of the same kind are in your drawing?

First, you need to know the name of the block that you want to count. The following one-line AutoLISP program can be typed in from the Command line; it tells you how many of that same kind of block are in your drawing.

```
(setq n (sslength (ssget "x" (list (cons 2 "block"))))) <RETURN>
```

Substitute the enquoted name of your block for "block."

For ready-to-run programs that count blocks for you, see LISP69 and LISP70 in Tips 14.53 and 14.54.

14.3 **How do you get back to color by layer after you've changed it?**

If you want your drawing to key in on the layer for **LINETYPE** and **COLOR**, you normally assign the color or line type to a specific layer. If you use the **LINETYPE** or **COLOR** command and assign a color directly while you're working on the drawing, your color assignments by layer will no longer work. To return to assigning colors by layer, issue the **COLOR** command, but instead of giving a color, type **BYLAYER**.

Type: COLOR <RETURN>

Response: New entity color:

Type: BYLAYER <RETURN>

14.4 **How do you control the X and Y scale factors at the same time when inserting a block?**

If the scale factor is numeric and the Y scale factor is the same as the X, simply enter the X scale factor and press <RETURN> when it asks you for Y. Or point to the scale factor by using the **CORNER** command, which ties the first corner to the insertion point. To enter **CORNER**, either type the command or simply pick another point on the screen.

The purpose of either method is to let you point to both the X and Y scales simultaneously. You should use these methods only when you have **SNAP** on, or you'll be issuing absolute or relative and/or polar coordinates. For example, enter any of these to indicate the other corner:

3,1
@3,1
@3<45

NOTE: You're not scaling the block to fit within the other corner. The distance you measure to the other corner will be the scale multiplier times the X and Y distance values.

WARNING: Blocks inserted with different X and Y scale factors can't be exploded in AutoCAD. There are third-party programs that let you explode these blocks.

14.5 How do you insert objects between parallel lines?

This can become rather complicated, but here's the procedure:

1) You must know the distance between the parallel lines.

2) Insert the object on the first line, rotating the object at the same angle as the parallel lines.

3) Scale the object using **REFERENCE** by pointing to the distance of the object and using the distance between the parallel lines as the new distance.

This procedure assumes that you don't know the exact size of the block you're inserting; if you do know it, you can scale at the same time.

14.6 How do you globally update all blocks with a new definition?

Let's assume you're updating only blocks that are defined within the current drawing, not blocks that have been **WBLOCK**ed to disk. If you want all the blocks with the same name in the drawing to have the same change, use the procedure in Tip 14.7.

Let's look at blocks that haven't been **WBLOCK**ed but are referenced in the current drawing. First, insert the block you want to change anywhere in the drawing. Then explode the block. If you try to reblock a non-exploded block, you'll get an error message saying that the block references itself. When you have the block the way you want it, block it again. You'll be asked if you want to redefine it. Answer Y. On the next regeneration of the drawing, all blocks of the same name will be redrawn and redefined.

14.7 How do you globally update blocks that have been changed on disk?

First, bring up the actual drawing of the block; this will be a .DWG file. Make any changes you want and save the file. Now bring up the drawing that references that disk block. Insert the changed block as follows:

Type: `INSERT <RETURN>`

Response: `Block name (or ?):`

Type: `BLOCKNAME= <RETURN>` (**BLOCKNAME** is the name of your block.)

Type: `Ctrl-C`

The block is redefined as soon as you press <RETURN> after entering the = sign. You don't have to continue with the **INSERT** command. Enter Ctrl-C to cancel.

14.8 How do you create an attribute?

Use the **ATTDEF** command and start with a block to which you want to assign information on size, price, material, vendor, description or anything else you'd like to know. The eventual purpose of these attributes will differ, depending on your needs. But generally the information is extracted from the drawing to another file, which can be used by another program.

When you begin the command, you have four choices: Invisible, Constant, Verify and Preset. These choices aren't mutually exclusive; an attribute may be invisible as well as constant. Beside each choice is the current value if you choose to do nothing. By entering I, C, V or P, you toggle the Y-N option. When the choices are as you want them for the particular attribute, press <RETURN>, and the command continues. Let's look at each of the choices.

Invisible   The attribute's value won't appear on the screen, nor will it be plotted.

Constant   The attribute has a built-in value for each block that's inserted in the drawing; AutoCAD doesn't prompt you for the value.

Verify   AutoCAD asks you to verify the entry after it's made. You can change it or press <RETURN> to accept it.

Preset   This is similar to Constant, but may be changed during a dialogue box session when the block is inserted. If you don't use the dialogue box, it acts the same as Constant.

Let's create a block with one attribute. Start with a block as in Figure 14-1.

Figure 14-1: Attribute attached to block

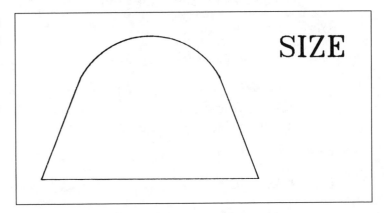

Type: `ATTDEF <RETURN>`

Response: `Attribute modes—Invisible:N Constant:N Verify:N Preset:N`
`Enter (ICVP) to change, RETURN when done:`

If everything's the way you want it, press <RETURN> or toggle any of the choices by entering its first letter.

Type: `<RETURN>`

Response: `Attribute tag:`

This is the label by which the attribute will be known. You can think of this as a field in a database program.

Type: `SIZE <RETURN>`

Response: `Attribute prompt:`

This is the question you're asked when you insert the block. If you simply press <RETURN>, AutoCAD will use the tag as the prompt.

Type: `WHAT IS THE SIZE? <RETURN>`

Response: `Default attribute value:`

You can now give AutoCAD a default attribute value, or <RETURN> if there is none. This is the value AutoCAD uses if you press <RETURN> when asked the attribute prompt questions when you insert the block.

Type: `14 <RETURN>`

Response: `Start point or Align/Center/Fit/Middle/Right/Style:`

This tells AutoCAD where to print the attribute value if it's visible. Even if it's not visible, AutoCAD needs to know where to put the attribute tag for the initial block. Pick a point near the block.

Response: `Rotation angle:`

Type: `<RETURN>`

The first attribute tag is now created as shown in Figure 14-1. You can continue to create additional attribute tags for this block by repeating the entire procedure. To complete the attribute, you must **BLOCK** and/or **WBLOCK** the entire area, including the attribute tags. See Tip 14.46 for more information on changing text with attributes.

 RELEASE 12   Use the new **DDATTDEF** dialogue box to create attributes. See Tip 20.50.

14.9 How do you make attributes part of a block?

Attributes should usually be part of a block, since this is how they get their value when inserted. If you're just creating a block, create the attributes at the same time. When you block the item, be sure to include the attribute tags as well.

If a block already exists and you want to add attributes to it, first insert it somewhere in your drawing. Explode the block. Use the **ATTDEF** command and create the attributes. Now reblock the block and answer Y when asked if you want to redefine it.

Be aware that at this point only the block redefined will have attributes. Other blocks in the drawing by the same name will be redefined as blocks but won't automatically have the attributes. Release 10 AutoLISP provides a routine that takes care of this; it's called **ATTREDEF**.

14.10 **How do you make special attribute prompts?**

When you create an attribute using **ATTDEF**, you'll be asked for an attribute tag. This is the name under which the attribute will go. The next question is **Attribute prompt**. If you don't give AutoCAD an attribute prompt, it will prompt with the name of the attribute tag. If you want a special attribute prompt, enter it at this question.

14.11 **How do you make attributes invisible?**

You can make attributes invisible by entering I at the first question in **ATTDEF**. This acts as a toggle for Y or N as to invisibility. If you want all attributes to be invisible regardless of their settings, use the **ATTDISP** command. If it's set to off, all attributes will be invisible.

14.12 **How do you make attributes visible?**

You can make attributes visible by entering I at the first question in **ATTDEF**. This acts as a toggle for Y or N as to invisibility. If you want all attributes to be visible regardless of their settings, use the **ATTDISP** command. If it's set to on, all attributes will be visible.

14.13 **How do you change attributes once they're in a drawing?**

This is done with the **ATTEDIT** command. Let's look at each of the questions asked.

Type: `ATTEDIT <RETURN>`

Response: `Edit attributes one at a time? <Y>`

Type: `<RETURN>`

This lets you edit the attributes one at a time rather than globally.

Response: `Block name specification <*>:`

This requests the name of the block or blocks you want to edit. Press <RETURN> for all blocks regardless of name, or specify a single block name.

Response: `Attribute tag specification <*>:`

Press <RETURN> for all tags regardless of name, or specify a single tag name.

Response: `Attribute value specification <*>:`

Specify a specific value you want changed, or press <RETURN> for any value.

Response: `Select attributes:`

Select one or more attributes by pointing on the screen. When you're through, confirm. Attributes don't highlight when selected, so keep selecting and confirming. AutoCAD will tell you how many have been selected and will place an X on the one it's selecting for change.

Response: `Value/Position/Height/Angle/Style/Layer/Color/Next <N>:`

Choose one of the items to change, or press <RETURN> to go to the next selected item. The X will advance on the screen to the next item. AutoCAD gives you a dialogue box to edit attributes; see Tip 14.18.

14.14 How do you globally change attributes on the screen?

First, see Tip 14.13 for changing one attribute at a time. Start by answering N to the first question, to put you into the global mode.

Type: `ATTEDIT <RETURN>`

Response: `Edit attributes one at a time? <Y>`

Type: `N <RETURN>`

Response: `Edit only attributes visible on screen? <Y>`

You may answer Y or N to edit attributes that are visible on screen or to globally edit all attributes that match your criteria. As before, you can limit the block name specification and the attribute tag specification. If you press <RETURN> on **Attribute tag specification**, it asks you:

Response: `String to change:`

Now type in the old string or value.

Response: `New string:`

Type in the new string or value. Everything that matches will be changed.

14.15 How do you change attribute definitions in a block?

First, explode the block. When you do, the tags will become visible on the screen. Now use the **CHANGE** command. Point only to the tag you want to change. Press <RETURN> for **Change Point**. It will ask you for New style, insertion point, etc., as well as for New tag, New prompt and New default value. When you're through, reblock the block and attributes and redefine them.

RELEASE 11   A new command called **DDEDIT** lets you edit text as well as attribute definitions using a dialogue box. See Tips 9.9 and 9.25.

14.16 How do you change a constant attribute?

A constant attribute can't be changed once it's in a drawing, but you can change the initial block (see Tip 14.15). When it's reblocked, all blocks by the same name will change their constant values to the new value.

14.17 How do you use dialogue boxes to enter attribute values?

This is controlled by the system variable **ATTDIA**. If it's set to 0, the dialogue box won't come down. If it's set to **1**, it will come down each time a block with attributes is entered.

14.18 How do you use dialogue boxes to edit attributes?

This is not part of your pull-down menus. To activate the dialogue box for editing attributes, type **DDATTE**.

14.19 How do you use Verify with attributes?

One of the options at the beginning of **ATTDEF** is **Verify:** N or Y. This may be toggled by entering V. **Verify** lets you verify or change the value one last time after it's entered. You can then accept the value by pressing <RETURN>.

14.20 How do you set defaults for attributes?

This is one of the questions asked with **ATTDEF**. At the question, enter a value or press <RETURN> if there's no default for this tag.

14.21 How do you combine attribute modes?

When you first enter **ATTDEF,** you're given four attribute modes: Invisible, Constant, Verify and Preset. Except for Constant and Preset, the choices aren't mutually exclusive. In the case of Constant and Preset, if both are set to Y, Constant is chosen instead of Preset. You may continue to change any of these. When you're through, press <RETURN>. The command will continue.

14.22 How do you change the attribute text or tag?

First insert a block with the attributes. Then use the **CHANGE** command with **Point** (the default) and select the tag you want to change. Continue to press <RETURN> until you're prompted for a new tag.

14.23 How do you continue defining attributes after the first?

If they're all done at the same time, press <RETURN> after the first and you'll continue with the last command, which was **ATTDEF**. The advantage of this is that when you're asked to pick a point for the text, you can simply press <RETURN>, and the attribute text will continue under the last text, just as in the **TEXT** command.

See Tip 24.14 for a way to line up attribute tags after the fact.

14.24 **How do you control text display with attributes?**

The text that's displayed with attributes isn't ordinary text. You can change the value with **ATTEDIT**, assuming that it's not constant, but it's hard to change the position on a single item. First you must explode the block. Then use the **CHANGE Point** command and change the position or rotation of the tag that relates to the text. Next, reblock and redefine the block. This creates a new definition for the attribute. If you've changed only non-constant items, other blocks in the drawing won't change.

14.25 **How do you combine attributes with a single block?**

Which attributes go with which block are controlled when the block is created. When you're asked to select objects for the block, be sure to include the tags of any attributes you want for that block.

14.26 **How do you control the order of the attribute prompts?**

AutoCAD uses the order in which they're picked when you're selecting objects for blocking. Be careful using **Window**—then objects are selected in reverse order from the way they were created.

14.27 **How do you assign attributes to a drawing without associated blocks?**

Sometimes you simply want to get information into a drawing that doesn't necessarily pertain to specific blocks. You still have to block the attribute tags. First create the attributes using **ATTDEF**. Then block the tags as though they were a block in and of themselves. Now insert the block you just created. If the tags are invisible, nothing will show on the screen, but the attributes will be in the drawing.

14.28 **How do you change attributes you can't see?**

First use the **ATTDISP** command to make all attributes visible. Then use a change or edit facility. When you are through, change **ATTDISP** back to **Normal**.

14.29 How do you avoid answering attribute questions when you don't need them?

This is controlled by the **ATTREQ** system variable. If it's set to **0**, no attribute questions or prompts are asked. Constants and presets and any defaults are still inserted. If it's set to **1**, all questions are asked. Note that defaults act like presets if **ATTREQ** is off.

14.30 How do you plot attributes?

This depends on whether they're visible; if you can see them on the screen, they'll plot.

More Steps to Success

14.31 Off and On may be better than Freeze and Thaw

If you have a display-list-processing graphics board, avoid regenerations as much as possible. Use **Off** and **On** instead of **Freeze** and **Thaw**.

14.32 Set COLOR and LINETYPE back to BYLAYER when you're finished

You can become confused by **COLOR** and **LINETYPE** if you use these commands and don't set them back to **BYLAYER** when you're through. The next time you're on a layer that you expect to be a certain color, it will be the last color set. Setting **COLOR** and **LINETYPE** back to **BYLAYER** when you're through with them avoids this problem.

14.33 Invisible blocks

A block inserted on a layer that's later frozen is made invisible, even if other parts of the block are on thawed layers.

14.34 Nested blocks share outer blocks' characteristics

If the outer blocks are created on a certain layer, they maintain the characteristics of that layer. Inner blocks created on layer **0** will take on the characteristics of the outer blocks.

14.35 **Pre-scaling blocks**

Type in the word **SCALE** at the insertion point when you're inserting blocks, to smooth the dragging and placement of the blocks. The X-Y scale factors must be the same. See LISP71 in Tip 14.55.

Type: `INSERT <RETURN>`

Response: `Block name (or ?):`

Type: `BLOCKNAME <RETURN>` (Enter the name of your block here.)

Response: `Insertion point:`

Type: `SCALE <RETURN>` (Do this instead of picking the insertion point.)

Response: `Scale factor:`

Enter the scale factor, and the insertion command will continue without the X-Y scale questions.

Response: `Insertion point:`

Now pick the insertion point; you'll see that the dragging is smoother.

14.36 **WBLOCK without BLOCK**

You don't have to **BLOCK** a part first in order to do a **WBLOCK**. When you're asked for the name of the block, just press <RETURN>.

14.37 **Unit blocks**

Blocks can be created as one unit in size, then scaled when they're inserted. This way, you won't have to create a block for every possible size. The disadvantage is that you can't later explode the block if the X and Y scale factors differ. If there are many possible sizes, consider writing an Auto-LISP program for parametric processing that asks you questions on the size of the object and then creates it from scratch.

14.38 Block libraries

You might consider storing groups of blocks as a single drawing. Then insert that drawing at 0,0. Once the drawing is inserted, enter **ERASE Last** and the actual blocks will disappear, but their definitions will be active. This way, you don't have to have large numbers of .DWG files out on disk.

You can have one library file or several files, depending on the types of blocks. Another method is to use **INSERT** with **blockname=** <RETURN>. Then do a Ctrl-C. The block never actually appears on the drawing.

For your final production drawing, be sure to **PURGE** any unreferenced blocks.

14.39 Blocks controlled by insertion point

Be careful if you use nested blocks on a frozen layer. The insertion point controls the freezing of the whole block.

14.40 Freeze across layers

If you've ever wanted to turn off or freeze parts of a drawing that don't correspond to a given layer, here's how to do it (this is especially useful for plotting).

BLOCK the items you want to turn off. Give them an insertion point of 0,0. They'll disappear, and you can plot. Insert them with an * at 0,0 to bring them back. This is a little safer than using **ERASE**, especially if you accidentally save your drawing. Of course, you can insert a block without the * and then erase it whenever you need to freeze it.

14.41 Tags on separate layers

If you place attribute tag data on separate layers, you can control it more easily than with **ATTDISP**. **ATTDISP** is global for all attributes. Using layers lets you see what tag goes on what layer and control its visibility.

14.42 Keep tags short

Attributes have no set limit. But if you want to use the dialogue box, make them less than 24 characters long for the prompt or tag and 34 characters long for the value.

14.43 **Tags should be visible to edit**

If you want to use the **ATTEDIT** command and edit attributes one at a time, they must be visible. This isn't true for global editing or if you use the **DDATTE** dialogue box for editing.

14.44 **Window selects tags in reverse order**

Be careful using **Window** or **Crossing** to select attributes when you're blocking them. They select in reverse order.

14.45 **Tags as prompts**

You don't always have to use a prompt with an attribute. The tag will be the prompt if you press <RETURN> at that question.

14.46 **Attributes make changing text easier**

When you make a title block as part of your prototype drawing, make the block with attributes, presets and defaults. This way it's easier to answer questions using the dialogue **DDATTE** box than trying to zoom in and place the variable text where you want it. You can apply and expand this tip for any group of variable text.

14.47 **Use Preset, not Constant**

Unless you're sure you'll never change a value in an attribute, always use a Preset instead of a Constant.

AutoLISP Programs

14.48 **Change layers (LISP64)**

This program lets you change a group of entities to another layer by simply pointing to any entity on the new layer.

Listing:
```
(defun c:lisp64 ()
    (prompt "\nSelect entities to be changed ")
    (setq f6 (ssget))
    (prompt "\nPoint to entity on target layer ")
    (setq f7 (entsel))
    (setq n (sslength f6))
    (setq i 0)
    (setq g7 (entget (car f7)))
    (setq i7 (assoc 8 g7))
    (repeat n
        (setq g6 (entget (ssname f6 i)))
        (setq i6 (assoc 8 g6))
        (setq g8 (subst i7 i6 g6))
        (entmod g8)
        (setq i (1+ i))
    )
)
```

To Use: Load LISP64.LSP.

Type: LISP64 <RETURN>

Response: Select entities to be changed:
Select objects:

Pick the entities you want changed, and confirm.

Response: Point to entity on target layer:
Select objects:

Pick an object that's already on the target layer. The other entities will be moved to the target layer.

14.49 Layer plot (LISP65)

This program lets you choose the layers you want plotted. It freezes all layers, then thaws only the layers you name.

Listing:
```
(defun c:lisp65 ()
    (setq crlyr  (getvar "clayer"))
    (command "layer" "m" "xxxtemp" "")
    (command "layer" "f" "*" "")
    (command "layer" "t" pause)
)
```

To Use: Load LISP65.LSP.

Type: LISP65 <RETURN>

Your screen should be blank now, and you're on layer XXXTEMP.

Response: Layer name(s) to Thaw:

You may use any wild-card method that AutoCAD permits. Each group or layer name must be separated by a command without spaces, as in

Type: WIN*,DIMEN,FLOOR

14.50 Return to current layer (LISP66)

This is a companion program to LISP65. It returns you to your current layer and thaws it at the same time.

Listing:
```
(defun c:lisp66 ()
    (command "layer" "t" crlyr "s" crlyr "")
)
```

To Use: Load LISP66.LSP.

Type: LISP66 <RETURN>

14.51 **Change line type (LISP67)**

This is an example program that automatically changes to a given line type and sets **LTSCALE** at the same time. LISP68 is a companion program that changes the line type back to continuous. You should copy this program and change the name of the line type for each line type you use.

Listing:
```
(defun c:lisp67 (/ lower upper d scal)
    (setq lower (getvar "limmin"))
    (setq upper (getvar "limmax"))
    (setq d (- (car upper) (car lower)))
    (setq scal (/ d 40))
    (command "ltscale" scal)
    (command "linetype" "s" "dashed" "")
)
```

To Use: Load LISP67.LSP.

Type: LISP67 <RETURN>

14.52 **Continuous line (LISP68)**

This is a companion program to LISP67. It changes you back to a continuous line. The program leaves out the code that sets LTSCALE.

Listing:
```
(defun c:lisp68 ()
    (command "linetype" "s" "continuous" "")
)
```

To Use: Load LISP68.LSP.

Type: LISP68 <RETURN>

14.53 Block count (LISP69)

Give this program the name of a block, and it tells you how many blocks of that name are in a drawing. (Use of the plus sign at the end of a line in AutoLISP code indicates that line is wrapped.)

Listing:
```
(defun c:lisp69 (/ bloc d a n)
    (setq bloc (getstring "\nEnter name of block you want +
      counted "))
    (setq d (cons 2 bloc))
    (setq a (ssget "x" (list d)))
    (if (/= a nil)
        (progn
            (setq n (sslength a))
            (prompt "There are ") (prin1 n) (prompt " in the +
              database \n")
        )
    )
    (if (= a nil)
        (prompt "There are none in the database \n")
    )
)
```

To Use: Load LISP69.LSP.

Type: LISP69 <RETURN>

Response: Enter name of block you want counted:

Type in the name of your block.

14.54 **List all blocks (LISP70)**

This program gives you a listing of all the blocks in a drawing and tells you how many there are.

Listing:
```
(defun c:lisp70 (/ flag g6 g a g7 n sp sp1 b)
    (setq b nil)
    (princ "\nNumber        Block Name \n")(terpri)
    (setq flag "flagset")
    (setq sp "")
    (setq sp1 "")
    (while (setq g6 (tblnext "block" flag))
       (setq flag nil)
       (setq g (assoc 2 g6))
       (setq a (ssget "x" (list g)))
       (if (/= a nil)
          (progn
             (setq b 1)
             (setq n (sslength a))
             (setq g7 (cdr (assoc 2 g6)))
             (if (<n 1000) (progn (setq sp " ") (setq sp1 " ")))
             (if (<n 100) (progn (setq sp " ") (setq sp1 " ")))
             (if (<n 10)  (progn (setq sp " ") (setq sp1 " ")))
             (prompt sp1)(princ n) (prompt sp) (princ g7)(terpri)
          )
       )
    )
    (if (= b nil)
       (prompt "There are none in the database \n")
    )
    (princ)
)
```

To Use: Load LISP70.LSP.

Type: `LISP70 <RETURN>`

14.55 **Insert scale (LISP71)**

When you insert objects, the scale is usually a fixed amount. But the scale questions make the dragging awkward. This program sets the scale right away so that dragging of an object is natural.

Listing:
```
(defun c:lisp71 ()
    (if (= scal "") (setq scal "1"))
    (command "insert" pause "scale" scal pause)
)
```

To Use: Load LISP71.LSP.

Type: LISP71 <RETURN>

Response: Enter scale or <RETURN> for 1:

Type: <RETURN>

Response: Block name (or ?):

The rest of the questions are the same, but you are not asked for the X and Y scale.

14.56 **Copy entities to another layer (LISP72)**

This program lets you copy entities to another layer. You won't be able to see them immediately, because they're right on top of the original entities. Test this by moving one of the entities; upon the next **REDRAW** you'll see there are two. This program can be especially useful when you're creating an outline layer for area or hatching.

Listing:
```
(defun c:lisp72 ()
    (setq layr (getstring "\nEnter target layer name "))
    (setq a (ssget))
    (command "copy" a "" "0,0" "0,0")
    (command "change" a "" "p" "la" layr "")
)
```

To Use: Load LISP72.LSP.

Type: `LISP72 <RETURN>`

Response: `Enter target layer name:`

Type in the name of the layer to which you want to copy.

Response: `Select objects:`

Select the objects you want copied, and confirm. You can freeze one of the objects in order to control the color.

14.57 Freeze across layers (LISP73)

It always seems that the objects we want to freeze or turn off are on a layer with other objects that we don't want to turn off. This program lets you select the objects you want turned off. You could, of course, erase them and **OOPS** them back. But this is dangerous. What happens if you erase something else in the meantime? The objects are lost forever. The next program, LISP74, is a companion program that lets you thaw the objects you've frozen. These programs give you only one set of frozen objects. If you freeze other objects without thawing the frozen ones, you'll lose the original objects; but this is still a lot safer than erasing them.

You can modify this program for named sets of objects.

Listing:
```
(defun c:lisp73 ()
    (prompt "\nSelect items you want frozen \n")
    (setq frzblk (ssget))
    (setq a (tblsearch "block" "freezeblk"))
    (if (= a nil)
       (command "block" "freezeblk" "0,0" frzblk "")
    )
    (if (/= a nil)
       (command "block" "freezeblk" "Y" "0,0" frzblk "")
    )
)
```

To Use: Load LISP73.LSP.

Type: `LISP73 <RETURN>`

Response: `Select items you want frozen:`
`Select objects:`

Select the objects, and confirm. They'll disappear, but they've been stored in a block called FREEZEBLK. You can insert this at any time at 0,0 or use LISP74 to bring them back.

14.58 Thaw across layers (LISP74)

This program will thaw the objects frozen by LISP73.

Listing:
```
(defun c:lisp74 ()
    (command "insert" "freezeblk" "scale" "1" "0,0" "0")
    (command "explode" "last")
)
```

To Use: Load LISP74.LSP.

Type: `LISP74 <RETURN>`

CHAPTER 15

Intermediate Inquiry, Text, Annotation

How Do You . . .

15.1 How do you underline and overscore text?

Insert the following codes before and after the text that's to be underlined and overscored; these codes are embedded within the line of text.

%%u	Underline on and off
%%o	Overscore on and off

For example, This <u>word</u> is underlined. should be typed in as follows:

```
This %%uword%%u is underlined.
```

13.2 How do you use the degree symbol and other standard symbols?

The following are codes for the various symbols available:

%%d	Degrees symbol
%%p	Plus or minus symbol
%%c	Circle diameter

15.3 How do you put a percent sign into text?

Since the percent sign (%) is used in most special symbols, use three percent signs (%%%) if you want to print just a percent sign. One percent sign works in most cases, but three signs always work.

15.4 **How do you change text justification?**

Whenever you place text in a drawing, you give it a starting point and a justification, which can be left, right, center, middle, etc. The starting point can be identified using **OBJECT SNAP INSERTION**. The only way to change the justification is to re-enter the text at the same insertion point using the new justification.

The best way to pick this insertion point is to ID the point before the original text is erased using **OBJECT SNAP INSERTION**. Now when the **TEXT** command asks for the insertion point, give it @0,0—which are the absolute coordinates of the last point picked.

See LISP75 in Tip 15.35 for a program that lets you automatically change the justification of text.

15.5 **How do you find the angle formed by two lines?**

Without an AutoLISP program, the easiest way to find the angle of two lines is to **DIMENSION** the lines and abort the dimension once the default text appears on the screen.

See LISP78 in Tip 15.38 for a program that's a more straightforward way to find the angle between two points.

15.6 **How do you globally change text fonts?**

All text fonts are controlled through **STYLE**, so if you want to change one you must change the style. This can be done with the **CHANGE Point** command. **Style** is one of the options if the entity is text.

However, it's hard to change large groups of text with the **CHANGE** command without inadvertently picking up other entities. This can be a disaster. If you can change the style definition, then all text in a drawing that has the same style will have its fonts changed. So use this method only if you want to change all of the text.

15.7 **How do you control the distance between lines of text?**

One problem in AutoCAD is that the **TEXT** command continues the next line of text, using its own algorithm for the distance between lines. You might prefer to set this as a variable, but this can be difficult—you have to pick a polar coordinate such as @2<270 each time you enter another line of text. See LISP76 in Tip 15.36 for a program that lets you set the distance.

15.8 How do you find the area for an area that's not a single entity?

Except for simple areas such as polygons with snappable endpoints or intersections, don't try to find the area of any group of entities without using the **Entity** option of the **AREA** command.

First, use the **PEDIT** command to make the group of entities a joined, single polyline. If the lines aren't already polylines, you can make them so by answering Y. Then **JOIN** all the lines with a window or crossing. Now you can use the **AREA Entity** command. When you're through, you can explode the lines.

See LISP77 in Tip 15.37 for a program that gives the area of any group of closed entities.

15.9 How do you create associative dimensioning?

Associative dimensioning is controlled by the system variable **DIMASO**, which can be set to on or off. If dimensions are created with associative dimensioning on, they can't be moved directly.

If they're exploded, they lose their associative dimensioning properties.

 RELEASE 12   Use the new DDIM dialogue box for setting dimension variables. See Tip 30.21.

15.10 How do you set tolerances in dimensioning?

Tolerances are appended to the default text and are controlled by three system variables. **DIMTP** holds the value of the plus tolerance. **DIMTM** holds the value of the minus tolerance. **DIMTOL** turns the tolerances on and off.

15.11 How do you create center-mark lines?

You create a center-mark line in dimensioning with the **DIMCEN** system variable. If the variable is set to zero, center marks aren't drawn. If it's greater than zero, the value entered determines the size of the center mark. If the value is negative, center lines are drawn instead of center marks.

15.12 How do you safely change the text of associative dimensions?

Using ordinary commands, it's almost impossible to change the text of an associative dimension without harming the associative dimension itself. You can explode the dimension and make the changes, but then you can't restore the characteristics of the associative dimension.

But the **DIM** command has an option called **Newtext** that lets you change the text in an associative dimension without changing its other aspects. If an entity is stretched or moved, the dimensions move with it but the text remains constant. If you want to change associative dimensioning back to its normal condition (associative calculations), again use **Newtext**; but when you're asked for the new text, press <RETURN>. It will revert back to the current value of the dimension.

15.13 How do you get dimension text back to its relative position after it has been stretched or moved?

Associative dimensioning lets you move and stretch already dimensioned areas and have the dimensions updated automatically. But text often isn't positioned correctly. The command in **DIM** called **HOMETEXT** re-centers the text.

15.14 How do you get the existing dimension to reflect changes in dimension variables?

When you change the system variables that control dimensions, some dimensions aren't changed; you must choose the ones you want to update. Use the **Update** subcommand of **DIM** and select only the dimensions that you want to reflect the new changes.

15.15 How do you add your own text to the default dimension text?

When the default dimension text comes up and you want to add an additional string, type in the text you want. When you want AutoCAD to use the actual dimension text, type <>. You can then continue typing. This makes use of the default text plus the additional string you've typed in front of and/or behind it. The associative dimension will be automatically updated along with the string you added.

Assume that 11.12 is the dimension text.

Response: `Dimension text <11.12>:`

Type: `AROUND <> MORE OR LESS <RETURN>`

This will produce:

`Around 11.12 more or less`

15.16 How do you add a standard suffix to all dimension text?

Any standard suffix you want added to all dimension text is stored in the system variable **DIMPOST**. Use **DIMAPOST** for the alternate dimension suffix.

15.17 How do you add a standard prefix to all dimension text?

Any standard prefix you want added to all dimension text must be typed in each time, using the method described in Tip 15.15. There's currently no system variable that controls this.

15.18 How do you draw all dimension text above the dimension line?

The system variable **DIMTAD** controls text drawn above the dimension line. If this is set to off, the text is centered between the dimension lines. If the system variable is on, the text is drawn above the dimension line and the dimension line is drawn solid.

RELEASE 11   Offers new options that let you adjust the dimension text at will without giving up **Associative Dimensioning**. See Tip 19.12.

15.19 How do you align dimension text with the line to be dimensioned?

Use the system variables **DIMTIH** and **DIMTOH** to force text in the direction of the line, whether it's vertical or horizontal. **DIMTIH** controls text that's drawn inside the dimension lines and **DIMTOH** controls text drawn outside the dimension lines. If these system variables are on, the text is always drawn horizontally. If they're off, the text is drawn at the same angle and in the same direction as the dimension line.

15.20 How do you rotate a dimension line?

You can control the rotation of a dimension line by choosing from the options **Horizontal**, **Vertical** or **Aligned**. **Horizontal** and **Vertical** position a dimension line at 90 degrees in each direction. **Aligned** positions the dimension line at the angle of the points picked. The other option, **Rotated**, lets you give an angle for the dimension line, thus overriding Auto-CAD's default.

15.21 How do you make your own arrows for dimensioning?

If you don't like the AutoCAD arrows, you can create a block with your own arrowhead, drawn at one unit. Tell AutoCAD which block to use with the system variable **DIMBLK**. You can even tell AutoCAD to use one block for the left arrow and another block for the right arrow—use **DIM-BLK1** for the left and **DIMBLK2** for the right.

15.22 How do you force text to fit inside dimension lines?

AutoCAD has its own algorithm to determine whether text will fit within dimension lines, but you can tell AutoCAD to force text to fit regardless of the algorithm. Use the system variable **DIMTIX**; if it's on, dimension lines aren't drawn at all. If its companion command **DIMSOXD** is on, Auto - CAD won't draw dimension lines outside of extension lines.

15.23 How do you force dimension lines inside, even if text is outside?

Just as you can force text inside dimension lines, you can tell AutoCAD to always place dimension lines inside, regardless of the position of the text. Use the system variable **DIMTOFL**.

15.24 How do you round dimensions?

You tell AutoCAD to round dimensions by placing a value for the rounding in the system variable **DIMRND**. If the value is **0**, no rounding takes place. Enter the precision of rounding you want. If you enter **.1**, rounding is done to the tenth of a unit.

15.25 How do you control whether text is above or below a dimension line?

AutoCAD has a system variable **DIMTVP**, which works only if **DIMTAD** is off. If **DIMTVP** is positive, text is placed that distance times the size of the text above the dimension line. If **DIMTVP** is negative, text is placed that distance below the dimension line.

15.26 How do you suppress zeros in dimensioning?

By setting the system variable **DIMZIN** to a number between **0** and **3**, you control how AutoCAD works with feet and inches. Numbers higher than **3** control decimals.

0   Suppress zero feet and zero inches.
1   Include zero feet and zero inches.
2   Include zero feet and suppress zero inches.
3   Suppress zero feet and include zero inches.
4   Suppress leading zeros.
8   Suppress trailing decimal zeros.
12 Suppress both leading and trailing zeros.

15.27 How do you change fonts for dimension text?

All fonts, whether they're for regular text or dimension text, are controlled by the **STYLE** settings in effect when the text is drawn. You can modify your dimension text the same way as any other text by changing the style definition.

More Steps to Success

15.28 **Delta X and Y**

Whenever you use **LIST** on an entity or group of entities, you're told the beginning X,Y and ending X,Y coordinates and the distance of the entity. You're also given the delta X and the delta Y—these are the coordinates of the slope from the beginning X,Y coordinate. For a line, the ending point is X units left or right and Y units up or down from the beginning X,Y coordinates.

15.29 **The DEFPOINTS layer**

Whenever you use associative dimensioning, AutoCAD draws the points it uses to identify where the dimension points are located. It stores these points on a layer called **DEFPOINTS**. You can see these points by turning on that layer and turning off other layers. These points can also be plotted if the layer is on. Don't try to erase these points; they're part of the dimensioning and are treated as a block.

15.30 **Use TEXT on the tablet**

One advantage to using the standard AutoCAD tablet menu is that the tablet **TEXT** command automatically takes you into the **DTEXT** command.

15.31 **A trick to temporarily change fonts**

You can temporarily change a drawing's text font: rename or remove the appropriate .SHX file. If AutoCAD can't find a specific font on disk, it asks for an alternate font. If the font on disk has the same name as the FONT.SHX it's expecting, AutoCAD will use that font regardless of how it was originally created.

15.32 **A warning about fonts**

Be careful when you're changing **STYLE** and fonts. The font's pitch may be different or it may be wider or thinner than the original; text may not fit.

15.33 **Change only one dimension variable**

Don't try to set all of the dimension variables for each prototype drawing or scale. AutoCAD lets you set up your dimension variables once, for the smallest scale. Then use the system variable **DIMSCALE**, which multiplies all the dimension variables by that scale. This way, you have to change only one system variable for dimensioning each drawing.

15.34 **Use script files to import text**

There are all kinds of programs for bringing in text from an outside ASCII source, but there's a simple way to bring in text that doesn't require an AutoLISP program. First make sure that your text file ends with the extension .SCR. Then use a text editor to place the appropriate AutoCAD commands at the beginning of the text you want imported.

See LISP79 in Tip 15.39 for an AutoLISP shell that prompts you for the beginning point. See Tip 25.11 for a complete program for importing text files into AutoCAD without modification.

AutoLISP Programs

15.35 **Text justification (LISP75)**

Whenever you begin a **TEXT** sequence, you determine whether the text is left-, center-, middle- or right-justified. Changing this justification after the text is input can be difficult, but this program lets you do it.

Listing:
```
(defun c:lisp75 (/ j e p11 p10 f en p11n p10n fn y)
    (setq j (getstring  "\nLeft/Center/Middle/Right "))
    (setq j (strcase j))
    (setq e (entget (car (entsel))))
    (setq p11 (assoc 11 e))
    (setq p10 (assoc 10 e))
    (setq f (assoc 72 e))
    (setq en e)
    (if (= (cdr f) 0) (setq p11n (cons 11 (cdr p10))))
    (if (= (cdr f) 0) (setq en (subst p11n p11 en)))
    (if (and (= j  "L") (/= (cdr f) 0))
        (progn
            (setq p10n (cons 10 (cdr p11)))
            (setq en (subst p10n p10 en)
        )
    )
    (if (= j "L") (setq fn 0))
    (if (= j "C") (setq fn 1))
    (if (= j "M") (setq fn 4))
    (if (= j "R") (setq fn 2))
    (setq fn (cons 72 fn))
    (setq en (subst fn f en))
    (entmod en)
    (setq y (getstring "\nIs this correct <Y> "))
    (if (= (strcase y) "N") (entmod e))
    (if (= (strcase y) "NO") (entmod e))
)
```

To Use: Load LISP75.LSP.

Type: `LISP75 <RETURN>`

Response: `Left/Center/Middle/Right:`

Choose the first letter of any of these for a new justification.

Response: `Select objects:`

Pick a line of text, and the justification will be changed. You'll then be asked if it's correct If it is, press <RETURN>, and the change is permanent. If it's not, enter N, and the old text justification will be restored.

15.36 **Control the distance between lines (LISP76)**

AutoCAD lets you determine the height of text but not the distance between lines of text. This program tests to see whether the current text style has a fixed height and adjusts for that variation.

Listing:
```
(defun c:lisp76 (/ pt1 c d sty tb siz a)
    (setq pt1 (getpoint "\nStarting point "))
    (setq c (getdist pt1 "\nLine Spacing "))
    (setq d "T")
    (setq sty (getvar "textstyle"))
    (setq tb (tblsearch "style" sty))
    (setq siz (cdr (assoc 40 tb)))
    (if (= siz 0.0)
        (progn
        (princ "\nHeight <")(princ (getvar"textsize")) (princ">")
        (setq a (getdist pt1))
        (if (= a nil) (setq a (getvar "textsize")))
        )
    )
    (While d
        (setq e (getstring 1 "\nText:   "))
        (if (= e "") (setq d nil))
        (if (= siz 0.0) (command "text" pt1 a "0" e))
        (if (/= siz 0.0) (command "text" pt1 "0" e))
        (setq pt1 (list (car pt1)(- (cadr pt1) c)))
        )
    )
```

To Use: Load LISP76.LSP.

Type: LISP76 <RETURN>

Response: Starting point:

Pick the starting point for the text.

Response: `Line spacing:`

Point to or enter the distance for the line spacing. If you're using a style that presets the height of the text, you may not be asked to input the height.

Response: `Text:`

Now type in the text. <RETURN><RETURN> will terminate the program.

15.37 All-purpose area command (LISP77)

This program finds the area of any enclosed group of entities. All you have to do is pick a point and put a window around the area.

Listing:

```
(defun c:lisp77 (/ os pt1 a)
    (setq os (getvar "osmode"))
    (setvar "osmode" 512)
    (setq pt1 (getpoint "\nPick any point on area "))
    (setvar "osmode" os)
    (prompt "\nNow WINDOW area ")
    (setq a (ssget))
    (if (= (sslength a) 1)
        (progn
            (command "area" "e" a)
        ))
    (if (> (sslength a) 1)
        (progn
            (command "pedit" pt1 "y" "j" a "" "")
            (command "area" "e" pt1)
            (command "explode" pt1)
        )
    )
)
```

To Use: Load LISP77.ISP.

Type: `LISP77 <RETURN>`

Response: `Pick any point on area:`

Touch any of the lines.

Response: `Now WINDOW area:`
`Select objects:`

Put a window around the entire group of entities, and confirm. You may have to flip to the text screen. The area has been calculated for you.

CAUTION: This program converts all lines to polylines, then computes the area. At the end, all entities are exploded. If the group contained polylines to begin with, the program will work fine; but if it didn't, you may want to modify the program.

15.38 Angle formed by two lines (LISP78)

This is one of the most accurate angle-measuring programs around. Most programs give you different answers depending on the order in which you choose the lines, or they go crazy if the objects chosen aren't lines. The best way to measure the angle between two lines is with the DIM command in AutoCAD, but this is too cumbersome. This program uses the DIM command in an AutoLISP program, combining the best of both worlds.

Listing:
```
(defun c:lisp78 (/os pt1)
    (setq os (getvar "cmdecho"))
    (setq pt1 (getpoint "\nPick a point between the lines "))
    (setvar "cmdecho" 1)
    (command "dim" "angular" pause pause pt1  ^c ^c)
    (setvar "cmdecho" os)
    (textscr)
)
```

To Use: Load LISP78.1SP.

Type: LISP78 <RETURN>

Response: Select first line:

Pick either line to measure.

Response: Second line:

Pick the second line. You'll be flipped to a text screen. The angle measured will appear in brackets as "dimension text."

15.39 Text in a script file (LISP79)

This program is an easy way to import text into AutoCAD, and it's really a combination of two files. The file LSPP79.LSP runs the program that brings text in to LISP79.SCR. The first two lines of the ASCII file must be

Listing: text
            @

Also the text must be triple-spaced. This program simply shows what can be accomplished using script files in combination with AutoLISP. Your imagination and needs might spark other ideas.

Listing: text
            @

```
Now is the time for all good men <RETURN>
<RETURN>
<RETURN>
to come to the aid of their country.
```

Listing:
```
(defun c:lisp79 ()
    (prompt "\nPick beginning point for text ")(terpri)
    (command "id" pause)
    (setq a (getstring "\nEnter name of script file "))
    (command "script" a)
)
```

To Use: Load LISP79.ILSP.

Type: `LISP79 <RETURN>`

Response: `Pick beginning point for text:`
`ID Point:`

Pick the beginning point where you want the text to go.

Response: `Enter name of script file:`

Type: `LISP79 <RETURN>`

Enter the name of your script file here; LISP79 is simply an example. The prepared file must have .SCR as its extension, but you don't enter the extension at this point.

CHAPTER 16

Intermediate Utilities

How Do You . . .

16.1 How do you plot different scales on the same sheet?

All drawings should be drawn using real-life dimensions. When you plot, the scale is given to the plotter. If you want to plot areas of a drawing at two different scales, you must compose a master drawing that contains the two areas.

You might start by creating a new drawing, using **newdrawing=olddrawing** where **newdrawing** is the name of the plotting drawing and **olddrawing** is the name of the original drawing with the largest area of those that you want to plot.

Once the new drawing is created, it will have begun with **olddrawing**. Now scale the entire drawing to the scale you want to plot.

The next step is to insert the other drawings into the master plot drawing. When asked for the insertion point, type **SCALE** and enter the scale for that part of the drawing. Continue to insert and scale for each part of the drawing you want composed. When all the drawings are composed and positioned on the sheet, plot it out at **1=1**.

 RELEASE 11   With the introduction of Paper Space, other options are available for plotting only part of your drawing or rearranging parts of your drawing to appear on the same sheet and at different scales. See Tips 29.1, 29.5, 29.9 and 29.16.

16.2 How do you turn UNDO off?

The **UNDO** command stores the information it needs on disk so that it can backtrack later. This can use up a lot of disk space, which is later recaptured when the drawing is ended; but like many users, you may be short on disk space. You can turn off or limit **UNDO**, only to its last command, by using the **Control** option.

Type: `UNDO CONTROL <RETURN>`

Response: `All/None/One <All>`

Choose **All** for the **UNDO** command to work normally, **None** to turn it off completely or **One** to undo only the last command.

16.3 How do you make a slide library?

AutoCAD lets you group all of your slides into a single file. Generally this doesn't save disk space, because the single file is about as large as all the individual files. But it does let you organize slide files and cuts down on operating system overhead. The single file is called a *slide library*.

The first step is to create a DOS text file with the names of the slides you want to include. Don't add the extension .SLD. You can shell out and use EDLIN or type EDIT if EDLIN is available and your .PGP file is set up to use it. The text file is simply a list of slide names with a <RETURN> at the end. The names of the slides might be

```
area1
fside
bside
feleva
3dlevel
```

Now that the slide list is created as a DOS text file, you'll need to convert the slides into a slide library. Let's assume that the slide list is called SLDLIST and the name of the slide library is SLD1. The next step must be done from DOS, or you can shell out to AutoCAD.

Type: `SLIDELIB SLD1 <SLDLIST <RETURN>`

SLIDELIB is an external program that will work from inside or outside AutoCAD. Of course, you must have a path to the directory in which it resides (normally, it will be in your regular AutoCAD directory unless you've deleted it). Don't forget the < before the name of the slide list.

The file has now been created. There's no way to edit it, but you can edit the slide list and remake the file. All slides must be available in order for the program to work.

16.4 **How do you view a slide that's part of a slide library?**

Use **VSLIDE** as you would to view any slide. Let's assume the name of the slide is 3DLEVEL and it's located in a slide library called SLD1. To view the slide,

Type: `VSLIDE <RETURN>`

Response: `Slide file:`

Type: `SLD1(3DLEVEL) <RETURN>`

Notice that the name of the slide library comes first and the name of the actual slide is in parentheses.

16.5 **How do you customize the help screens?**

Some users want to customize the help screens in order to add or change instructions for their training programs. All of the help information is stored in a DOS text file called ACAD.HLP, which can be edited with a text editor.

The first part of the file contains general help information. Lines that begin with a backslash (\) separate and label the sections. For example, a section called \DIM1 would begin the information about that command. Feel free to add or delete information, but be sure to keep the labels.

AutoCAD maintains another file called ACAD.HDX as an index file to find an area quickly; it's re-created the first time you use HELP. If you make any changes to ACAD.HLP, be sure to delete ACAD.HDX.

16.6 **How do you get help while in a command?**

You can type HELP and the name of the command, or use AutoCAD's context-sensitive help facility. If you're in the middle of a command and need help, type '? and AutoCAD will give you the help screen(s) for the command you're in. Don't forget the apostrophe.

16.7 How do you run a script file from a batch file?

You can start a script file from outside AutoCAD by simply adding the name of the file to **ACAD** when you call it up. Let's assume that the name of the script file is STARTER.SCR. From a DOS prompt

Type: `ACAD STARTER <RETURN>`

AutoCAD will start. When you get to the AutoCAD main menu, the script file will take over. Make sure you include whatever's necessary to call up the drawing, new file, etc., in your script.

16.8 How do you purge VPORTS, VIEWS and UCS?

Don't use the **PURGE** command with these. Each of these commands has its own delete function as an option to the command.

16.9 How do you configure a tablet for digitizing?

Before you can use a tablet for digitizing, you must calibrate it with the **TABLET** command. Calibration is coordinating two known points on a paper drawing with two coordinates on the screen.

Type: `TABLET <RETURN>`

Response: `Option (ON/OFF/CAL/CFG):`

Type: `CAL <RETURN>`

Response: `Calibrate tablet for use ...`
`Digitize first known point:`

Pick a point on your paper.

Response: `Enter coordinates for first point:`

Type: `3,5 <RETURN>` (These would be the first known coordinates for the paper being digitized.)

Response: `Digitize second known point:`

Type: `8,7 <RETURN>` (These would be the second known coordinates for the paper being digitized. The second coordinates can be anywhere in the drawing; they don't have to be those of the upper right-hand corner.)

16.10 **How do you toggle back and forth from digitizer to menu?**

This can be done by turning **TABLET** on or off and using Ctrl-T to toggle it back and forth. Also, F10 on most computers will do the same thing if you haven't changed it.

16.11 **How do you determine scale factors to set up a drawing?**

Although in AutoCAD you should be using actual dimensions of the items you're drawing (not scaling), you still must make sure that the drawing will fit on the eventual scale for the size paper you'll be using. The easiest way is to use the AutoLISP program SETUP.LSP—or MVSETUP.LSP in Release 11 and Release 12—on the AutoCAD screen menu.

But if you want to set up your own limits and units, here's some math that will help you. Let's start with an easy one. If you want 1/4 inch to equal 1 foot (plotted on paper that's 24" x 36"), first set up a ratio as a simple word problem. If you get 1 foot for every 1/4 inch, how many feet do you get with 24 inches?

$$\begin{array}{c|c} 1 & X \\ \hline 1/4 & 24 \end{array}$$

Now, cross-multiply.

1 * 24 = 24
1/4 * X = X/4

Therefore, X/4=24. Solve for X. X=96'. Do the same thing for 36 inches. X=144'. Therefore, set your limits to 144',96'.

If you were using decimal units at a scale of 1 to 50 on 24" x 36" paper, it would be

$$\begin{array}{c|c} 50 & X \\ \hline 1 & 24 \end{array}$$

or X/50=24 or 24 * 50=1200. Therefore, your limits would be 1800,1200. Check it out with the SETUP.LSP program. They should match if your calculations are correct.

16.12 How do you set the user scale in SETUP.LSP and MVSETUP.LSP?

If you're working in architectural or engineering feet and inches, the wording of the **Other** option can be a little confusing. In all the other options, you have to choose 1/4"=1' or 1"=50'. But what if you wanted 1"=200'? You can't enter the scale that way; you'd get the error message "Requires numeric value."

Instead, you must enter a scale factor. The scale factor 1"=200' would be 2400. (What times 1"=200'? can be expressed as "what times one inch equals 200 feet?" The answer is 2400.)

16.13 How do you plot on a printer?

Making a printer plot is really no more difficult than plotting with a plotter, but you must use the printer-plotting command **PRPLOT**. You also must have a printer-plotter configured for AutoCAD. Except for those on pen choices, the questions are pretty much the same. If you write the plot out to a file, it will have the extension .LST instead of .PLT.

RELEASE 12   Starting with Release 12, **PRPLOT** is no longer available. Simply choose the printer as your plotter device.

16.14 How do you set up multiple paths and recover old paths?

When you boot your computer, there's probably a path statement in your AUTOEXEC.BAT file that looks something like this:

```
PATH = C:\;C:\ACAD;C:\DOS;C:\TRC
```

You might want to change the statement or add a path to it that's active only while you're in AutoCAD. But you'd like to be able to change it back to the original path statement when you're finished. You don't want to have to change your AutoCAD batch file whenever you change the standard path.

The following line will save the old path statement to a batch file called OLDPATH.BAT. When you want to restore the old path, just type **OLD-PATH** or make **OLDPATH** the last item in the batch file.

Type: `PATH > OLDPATH.BAT`

16.15 How do you plot as close to the edge of the paper as possible?

One of the most frustrating things about plotting with AutoCAD is trying to plot on all of the paper. As a matter of fact, it can't even be done on most plotters because the pinch wheels take up some room. But that's only half the story.

When you enter the AutoCAD plotting command, AutoCAD allows a certain standard size such as A, B, C, D or E, and MAX as the area of plotting. AutoCAD then tells you the maximum plotting area. Most plotters are capable of a little more than this; by readjusting the point of origin and entering your own size, you can increase the plotting area. Note that this is true for *most* plotters. Some drivers seem to have a maximum built in. Others will let you specify any amount and then truncate the area they can't plot. Playing with these numbers will generally get you as close to the edge of the paper as possible.

16.16 How do you adjust the starting point or align the plotter with the paper?

Some plotters can automatically line up the plotter before plotting. Use that feature when it's available—but when it's not, here's another way.

After the paper is in the plotter, turn off all layers except **LINEUP**. On the **LINEUP** layer is a single point, placed at 0,0. First, plot that layer only. Physically measure how much to the right or left, up or down the dot needs to come to be aligned with the paper. Plot it again and change the plot origin by the X and Y values (note that these values are in inches or decimal inches). You may have to do this a couple of times. Now turn on the other layers and plot. The origin will still be the default.

16.17 How do you reprogram function keys?

To reprogram the function keys, you must have the following statement in the root directory, in a text file called CONFIG.SYS:

```
device = ansi.sys
```

316 AutoCAD TIPS AND TRICKS

You must also have a file called ANSI.SYS in your root directory. You'll find ANSI.SYS on your DOS disk. Once this is set up, you can enter ANSI codes that will reprogram certain keys. The model for all key redirection is

```
ESC[0;59;'int,end';13p
```

0;59 is the keyboard code for F1. **'int,end'** is what you want it to say when you press the F1 key. **13** is the code for a <RETURN>. These codes must begin with Esc and end with **p.** Case (upper or lower) makes a difference.

The only problem is that Esc can't be entered this way; nor can it be entered with the Esc key on the keyboard.

If you're using BASIC, the line above would be

```
print chr$(27)+"[0;59;'int,end';13p"
```

chr$(27) is the control code for Esc.

If you're writing in AutoLISP, the line would read

```
(prompt "\e[0;59;'int,end';13p")
```

\e is the AutoLISP code for Esc.

You can also put this in a batch file. If you do, the line will be

```
prompt $e[0;59;'hello';13p
```

$e is the DOS code for Esc.

The following are the function key codes:

0;59	F1
0;60	F2
0;61	F3
0;62	F4
0;63	F5
0;64	F6
0;65	F7
0;66	F8
0;67	F9
0;68	F10

See LISP80 in Tip 16.42 for a program that uses function keys.

16.18 **How do you program Alt keys?**

Tip 16.17 explains how to program keys through ANSI.SYS. To use Alt keys, you press and hold down the Alt key as you press another key. For example, Alt-L equals the **LINE** command. The codes for the Alt keys are as follows:

0;120-0;131	1,2,3,4,5,6,7,8,9,–,=
0;16-0;25	Q,W,E,R,T,Y,U,I,O,P
0;30-0;38	A,S,D,F,G,H,J,K,L
0;44-0;50	Z,X,C,V,B,N,M
0;104-0;113	F1-F10

Example: `(prompt "\e[0;38;'line';13p")`

See LISP81 in Tip 16.43 for a program that uses Alt keys.

16.19 **How do you program the Ctrl (control) keys?**

Tip 16.17 explained how to program keys through ANSI.SYS. You use a Ctrl key by pressing and holding it down as you press another key. For example, Ctrl-P is for **PLINE**. When reprogramming control keys, don't change those that have meaning in DOS, such as Ctrl-C (^C). The codes for the control keys are as follows:

1-26	A-Z
48-57	0-9
0;94-0;103	F1-F10

Notice that A-Z and 0-9 don't have a 0; in front of them. For example,

`(prompt "\e[16;'pline';13p")`

See LISP82 in Tip 16.44 for a program that uses control keys.

16.20 **How do you set all keys back to the way they were?**

Tip 16.17 explained how to program keys through ANSI.SYS. Remember to return the keys to their original settings—otherwise, they'll continue to have the meanings you set them to while in AutoCAD. See LISP83, LISP84 and LISP85 in Tips 16.45, 16.46 and 16.47.

To reset the keys, just make the code number equal to itself. For example, to reset Ctrl-P, enter

```
(prompt "\e[16;16p")
```

To reset F2, enter

```
(prompt "\e[0;60;0;60p")
```

More Steps to Success

16.21 **Multiple UNDOs**
The **UNDO Mark** and **UNDO Back** commands let you make sure that you can undo a group exactly as you want. You can experiment, knowing full well that you can undo a group back to its beginning. **Mark** starts a group and **Back** undoes back to the mark.

16.22 **Never use UNDO Group**
Never use **UNDO Group** and **End** except in menu commands. You'll encounter problems if you try to mix the two. Use **UNDO Mark** instead.

16.23 **Leave UNDO Auto on**
Generally, leave **UNDO Auto** on so that any item selected from a menu will be undone as a group. This keeps you from having to use **UNDO Group** and **End** in menus.

16.24 **REGEN once, not ten times**
Even if you don't have groups or marks set, try to **UNDO** as a group to speed things up. For example, an **UNDO 10** will cause one regeneration, while pressing U ten times may cause ten regenerations.

16.25 **Save pen strokes when plotting**
If you have a drawing that tends to go over the same area several times, answer Y to the question, **Adjust area fill boundaries for pen width?** This will save pen strokes and possibly wear and tear on your drawing.

16.26 **A quick way to change pen assignments**

When you're plotting and changing pen assignments, you don't have to go through all of the pens to get to the one you want. Just type C and the color number. For example, **C12** will take you directly to color 12.

16.27 **S lets you review pen assignments**

If you'd like to look at all the pen assignments while choosing them before plotting, type S when asked for the pen number. AutoCAD will display the pen assignments made thus far and continue letting you make changes until you type X.

16.28 **Save your sanity—plot in UCS WORLD**

Unless you have a very good reason not to, plot only when you're in **UCS WORLD**. If your **UCS** isn't **WORLD** when you begin to plot, and you change the plotter origin, there's no telling where your plot will end up.

16.29 **Customize plot size**

Be aware that most plotters let you specify your own plot size. You're not stuck with the designations of A through E.

16.30 **Use DVIEW to rotate 3D plots**

You can rotate a plot in 3D (plotted from a **DVIEW**) 90 degrees. To do this, first rotate the **DVIEW** 90 degrees, then plot.

16.31 **Don't hide lines first**

Except for letting you see them on the screen, it does no good to hide lines before you plot. AutoCAD still must hide lines during the plot sequence.

16.32 **When an inch is not an inch**

Depending on your plotter, your scale may not be correct. You can compensate for this when the AutoCAD configuration menu asks whether you want to calibrate your plotter.

16.33 **Save time when using a printer-plotter**

When you're printing a check plot, **FREEZE** the borders and/or title block. The plot will run much faster, because the printer won't have to go to that side of the paper as it truncates any blank area.

16.34 **Two dangerous AutoCAD commands**

PLOT and **SHELL** can be the most dangerous commands in AutoCAD. If you've never frozen your computer during a **PLOT** or **SHELL**, it's only a matter of time before it happens. For safety's sake, always **SAVE** before you use either of these commands.

16.35 **How to shade areas**

If you use green ink when plotting, you'll get a nice light look for shaded areas when you make bluelines.

16.36 **Compose plotting views**

Set up plotting views for each drawing. That way, you can plot from the AutoCAD main menu without having to enter the drawing editor to compose the plot. See Tip 26.5 for more about plotting views.

16.37 **ZOOM Extents isn't the same when plotting**

Be very careful when you're plotting extents. AutoCAD does only one regeneration in **PLOT** mode, so you'll probably get a different result than **ZOOM Extents**. It's safer to store the extents as a view and then plot from the view.

16.38 **PURGE more than once**

You may have to issue the **PURGE** command several times, since some items may be nested. Save the drawing and exit. Then re-enter the drawing and issue the **PURGE** command again until no unreferenced items are found.

16.39 **Ctrl-X erases everything**

In addition to backspacing on the command line, you can use Ctrl-X to erase everything on a line and restart the command. Ctrl-X doesn't actually erase the line; it prints ***Delete*** and lets you continue from that point.

16.40 **Multiple DOS commands**

If you simply type **SHELL**, you can use only one DOS command, and then you're automatically returned to AutoCAD. But if you want to, you can remain in DOS for several commands: press <RETURN> once more. When you're through and want to return to AutoCAD, type EXIT and press <RETURN>.

16.41 **Digitizing quirks**

You can run into real problems while digitizing if you issue a **TABLET CAL** and you're still using your tablet menus. What happens is that your cursor will seem to disappear in certain areas and will reappear in others. You're effectively blocked from part of the screen.

To fix this, make sure you don't have any menus. Before you calibrate the tablet, enter **TABLET CFG** and answer 0 to the question on the number of menus.

Type:	TABLET <RETURN>
Response:	Option (ON/OFF/CAL/CFG):
Type:	CFG <RETURN>
Response:	Enter number of tablet menus desired (0-4):
Type:	0 <RETURN>
Response:	Do you want to respecify the screen pointing area? <N>:
Type:	<RETURN>

Now you can calibrate your digitizer and get all of the screen area for digitizing. But turning the tablet off won't get your menus back. To do this,

Type: `TABLET <RETURN>`

Response: `Option (ON/OFF/CAL/CFG):`

Type: `OFF <RETURN>`

Type: `TABLET <RETURN>`

Response: `Option (ON/OFF/CAL/CFG):`

Type: `CFG <RETURN>`

Response: `Enter number of tablet menus desired (0-4):`

Type: `4 <RETURN>`

You must now reconfigure the tablet area.

AutoLISP Programs

The following AutoLISP programs are examples of how you can redirect the function keys for certain AutoCAD commands. For these programs to work, you must have ANSI.SYS set up as a device driver in the CONFIG.SYS file. This is a text file that you create. You may already have one; if you do, check to see that the following line appears somewhere in the file:

`device=ansi.sys`

If you don't already have a CONFIG.SYS file, you must create one and put the above line in it. The CONFIG.SYS file and the ANSI.SYS file should both be in the root directory. They become active only when the system's rebooted. You can find the current version of ANSI.SYS for your operating system on your original DOS disk.

ANSI.SYS seems to have only one major flaw: it doesn't let you redirect an unlimited number of keys. It can redirect about 20 of the size listed in the AutoLISP programs below. If you like the convenience of using function keys, you can choose only the ones you like best and load them all as one program.

The following programs represent the function keys when pressed by themselves, when used with Alt, and when used with Ctrl. Only F2, F4, F5 and F10 are programmed as single keystrokes. This is because F1 is used as a flip screen. F3 is used a lot by EDLIN, and the rest of the function keys have current assignments in AutoCAD.

Even though all of the programs below can be used at one time, you can test them by removing one of the program reassignments, using the removal programs. This creates room for other reassignments. If you try loading all three programs, only about the first 20 will be active, depending on your version of ANSI.SYS and your operating system.

16.42 Function keys (LISP80)

F2   Object Snap Endpoint and Intersection

F4   Object Snap Center and Midpoint

F5   Erase Last

F10   Redraw

Listing:
```
(defun c:lisp80 ()
     (textscr)
     (prompt "\e[0;60;'int,end';13p")
     (prompt "\e[0;62;'cen,mid';13p")
     (prompt "\e[0;63;'erase l ';13p")
     (prompt "\e[0;68;'redraw';13p")
     (graphscr)
     (prompt "\n    ")
     (prompt "\n    ")
     (princ)
)
```

To Use: Load LISP80.LSP.

Type: LISP80 <RETURN>

16.43 **Alt function keys (LISP81)**

Alt F1	LINE
Alt F2	PLINE
Alt F3	ARC
Alt F4	CIRCLE
Alt F5	DTEXT
Alt F6	ZOOM Window
Alt F7	ZOOM Previous
Alt F8	ZOOM All
Alt F9	PAN
Alt F10	VPORTS

Listing:
```
(defun c:lisp81 ()
    (textscr)
    (prompt "\e[0;104;'line';13p")
    (prompt "\e[0;105;'pline';13p")
    (prompt "\e[0;106;'arc';13p")
    (prompt "\e[0;107;'circle';13p")
    (prompt "\e[0;108;'dtext';13p")
    (prompt "\e[0;109;'zoom w';13p")
    (prompt "\e[0;110;'zoom p';13p")
    (prompt "\e[0;111;'zoom a';13p")
    (prompt "\e[0;112;'pan';13p")
    (prompt "\e[0;113;'vports';13p")
    (graphscr)
    (prompt "\n    ")
    (prompt "\n    ")
    (princ)
)
```

To Use: Load LISP81.LSP.

Type: LISP81 <RETURN>

16.44 Ctrl function keys (LISP82)

Ctrl-F1	PEDIT
Ctrl-F2	COPY
Ctrl-F3	MOVE
Ctrl-F4	OFFSET
Ctrl-F5	ROTATE
Ctrl-F6	MIRROR
Ctrl-F7	BREAK
Ctrl-F8	TRIM
Ctrl-F9	FILLET
Ctrl-F10	ARRAY

Listing:
```
(defun c:lisp82 ()
    (textscr)
    (prompt "\e[0;94;'pedit';13p")
    (prompt "\e[0;95;'copy';13p")
    (prompt "\e[0;96;'move';13p")
    (prompt "\e[0;97;'offset';13p")
    (prompt "\e[0;98;'rotate';13p")
    (prompt "\e[0;99;'mirror';13p")
    (prompt "\e[0;100;'break';13p")
    (prompt "\e[0;101;'trim';13p")
    (prompt "\e[0;102;'fillet';13p")
    (prompt "\e[0;103;'array';13p")
    (graphscr)
    (prompt "\n    ")
    (prompt "\n    ")
    (princ)
)
```

To Use: Load LISP82.LSP.

Type: `LISP82 <RETURN>`

16.45 **Unload function keys (LISP83)**

Listing:
```
(defun c:lisp83 ()
   (textscr)
   (prompt "\e[0;60;0;60p")
   (prompt "\e[0;62;0;62p")
   (prompt "\e[0;63;0;63p")
   (prompt "\e[0;68;0;68p")
   (graphscr)
   (prompt "\n    ")
   (prompt "\n    ")
   (princ)
)
```

To Use: Load LISP83.LSP.

Type: LISP83 <RETURN>

16.46 **Unload Alt function keys (LISP84)**

Listing:
```
(defun c:lisp84 ()
   (textscr)
   (prompt "\e[0;104;0;104p")
   (prompt "\e[0;105;0;105p")
   (prompt "\e[0;106;0;106p")
   (prompt "\e[0;107;0;107p")
   (prompt "\e[0;108;0;108p")
   (prompt "\e[0;109;0;109p")
   (prompt "\e[0;110;0;110p")
   (prompt "\e[0;111;0;111p")
   (prompt "\e[0;112;0;112p")
   (prompt "\e[0;113;0;113p")
   (graphscr)
   (prompt "\n    ")
   (prompt "\n    ")
   (princ)
)
```

To Use: Load LISP84.LSP.

Type: LISP84 <RETURN>

16.47 Unload Ctrl function keys (LISP85)

Listing:
```
(defun c:lisp85 ()
    (textscr)
    (prompt "\e[0;94;0;94p")
    (prompt "\e[0;95;0;95p")
    (prompt "\e[0;96;0;96p")
    (prompt "\e[0;97;0;97p")
    (prompt "\e[0;98;0;98p")
    (prompt "\e[0;99;0;99p")
    (prompt "\e[0;100;0;100p")
    (prompt "\e[0;101;0;101p")
    (prompt "\e[0;102;0;102p")
    (prompt "\e[0;103;0;103p")
    (graphscr)
    (prompt "\n    ")
    (prompt "\n    ")
    (princ)
)
```

To Use: Load LISP85.LSP.

Type: `LISP85 <RETURN>`

CHAPTER 17

Intermediate 3D

How Do You . . .

17.1 How do you look at the other side of an object?

The **DVIEW** command lets you do a left-right horizontal rotation of 180 degrees and a vertical rotation of 90 degrees. In neither case can you turn the object completely around.

But you can do this by reversing the target and camera points so that you're looking at the other side of the object; use the **DVIEW Points** suboption.

It's difficult to secure the exact coordinates, but LISP87 in Tip 17.35 will do that for you.

17.2 How do you hatch in 3D?

Hatching in 3D isn't difficult; there are two basic rules. First, make sure that you're hatching parallel to the current UCS—use **3POINT** to make sure that **UCS** X and Y are going in the same direction as the object being hatched. Second, make sure that the object being hatched is completely closed. Putting a **3DFACE** on an object is a good way to hatch it.

RELEASE 11   If the reason you want to hatch in 3D is to create the illusion of shading, Release 11 now has a **SHADE** command for this purpose. See Tip 19.20.

17.3 How do you draw a polyline across planes?

You could give the **PLINE** command X, Y and Z coordinates and draw in 3D space, but all the vertices along the polyline must have the same Z value. This means that **PLINE** won't let you draw across planes. However, you can use another AutoCAD command to draw across planes: **3DPOLY**.

17.4 **How do you make an object parallel to the current UCS?**

Often when you're editing, you'll get a message that says an object isn't parallel to the current UCS. One way to make it parallel is to use **UCS** and select the **Entity** subcommand. Now point to the entity. Each entity stores its own UCS at the time it was created. (The *AutoCAD Reference Manual* calls this the Entity Coordinate System.) This command makes the UCS the same as the Entity Coordinate System, and thus parallel.

17.5 **How do you make a 3D block?**

Making a 3D block is no different from making a 2D block. Simply **BLOCK** and/or **WBLOCK** the group of entities. However, when you **INSERT** 3D blocks they come into your drawing in accordance with the current **UCS**.

Therefore, it's a good idea to block objects only while you're in **UCS WORLD**; then you'll have some control over how they're inserted.

17.6 **How do you change the UCS of a current block to WORLD?**

Sometimes you make a mistake and **BLOCK** an object while in another UCS. When you **INSERT** the object, you find your error. Go ahead and insert it anyway. Then **EXPLODE** the block. Make sure you're in **UCS WORLD**; then reblock the object and reinsert it. If there are other objects by the same name, they'll automatically rotate to be in alignment with **UCS WORLD**.

17.7 **How do you make 3DFACE lines and original PLINE vectors visible after SPLINE curves?**

The system variable **SPLFRAME** will make these visible, along with the curves, if it's set to **1**. If it's set to **0**, they're not visible.

17.8 **How do you change the DVIEW house default?**

When you enter **DVIEW**, you are asked to select objects. If you press <RETURN> at this point, AutoCAD puts a drawing of a house on the screen, but you may want your own drawing instead. If you do, create it as a **BLOCK** and/or **WBLOCK** called **DVIEWBLOCK**, and AutoCAD will use that. Be sure to draw your block with an area of 1 x 1 x 1 units.

17.9 How do you move inside an object?

The key to moving inside an object is to have perspective turned on. As you approach the object, walls and other barriers peel away. However, when you set the camera inside the object at a given elevation using the **DVIEW POINTS** command, AutoCAD seems to throw you outside the object. The reason for this is that if perspective isn't on, **DVIEW POINTS** changes only the angle of viewing, not the distance from the camera to the target. If **DVIEW POINTS** has **Perspective On**, both the angle of viewing and the actual distance you designate are set.

   If you've used **DVIEW POINTS** without setting perspective, you can still move in on the object from that angle of viewing. Set **Perspective On** and move your camera-to-target distance closer.

17.10 How do you stay in the plan view of the current UCS when you change your UCS?

If you set the system variable **UCSFOLLOW** to **1**, each time a new UCS is set, the view becomes the plan view of that UCS. If it's set to **0**, the view won't change and you must issue **PLAN** manually.

17.11 How do you save a UCS using the dialogue box?

It's usually easier to issue the **UCS** command from the keyboard or the screen menu, then choose **Save** and give it a name. The dialogue box is a little more difficult to use. It requires that the name be given to the UCS on the second page of the dialogue box when the UCS is created. Unless you delete the UCS and re-establish it, you can't save a UCS after the fact using the dialogue box. The reason is that the **Save** option is available only on the screen where the UCS is created.

17.12 How do you apply a 3DMESH between two objects?

The only difficult thing about meshes in 3D is which kind to use. Whenever you want to connect two objects, use **RULESURF** (see Figures 17-1 and 17-2). It doesn't matter what shape the two objects are; the example below shows two straight lines.

Figure 17-1: Two
objects before
RULESURF

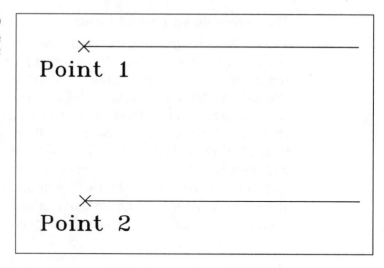

Figure 17-2: 3DMESH
using **RULESURF**

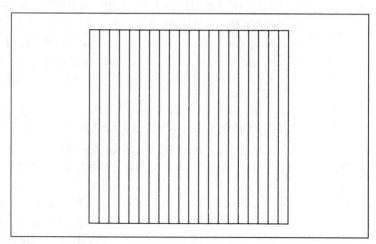

To form a surface mesh,

Type: `RULESURF <RETURN>`

Response: `Select first defining curve:`

Don't let this response confuse you; the two objects don't have to be curves. Pick a point toward the end of the line at point 1. It doesn't have to be the endpoint, but it must be more than halfway on that side of the line.

Response: `Select second defining curve:`

Pick a point toward the end of the line at point 2. It really doesn't matter which side of the lines you choose; just be sure you choose the same relative side for each line. If you don't, you'll get a cross-mesh (similar to a bow-tie effect).

Look at Figure 17-3 for other examples of how **RULESURF** can be used. Just remember that you use **RULESURF** only to connect two objects.

Figure 17-3: Other examples of RULESURF

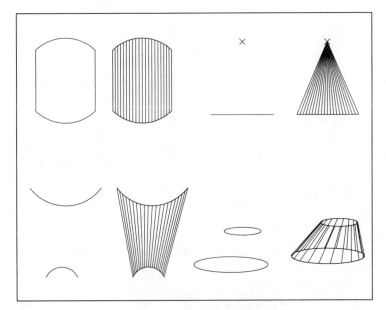

17.13 **How do you extend a mesh out from an entity?**

The key to this kind of mesh is that you have only one entity. The mesh extends from it for a given length and in a given direction, and you have to tell AutoCAD what the length and direction are.

This information is passed to AutoCAD in the form of a *direction vector*. A direction vector, an entity in and of itself, is the mesh's length and direction. The direction vector and the entity to which you apply the mesh can't be the same entity. You might even want to erase the direction vector once it's done its job.

See Figure 17-4. The entity is on the left; the direction vector is on the right.

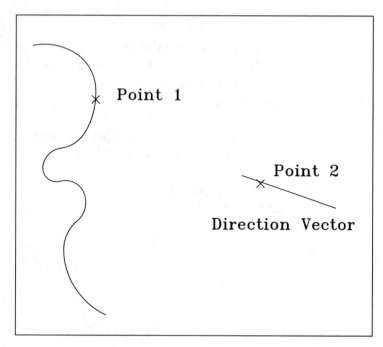

Figure 17-4:
Direction vector

Point 1

Point 2

Direction Vector

Type: TABSURF <RETURN>

Response: Select path curve:

Pick point 1. The entity doesn't have to be a curve.

Response: Select direction vector:

Pick point 2.

Look at the result in Figure 17-5. The side of the entity that the mesh projects from depends on which end of the direction vector you pick.

Figure 17-5: Mesh
using TABSURF

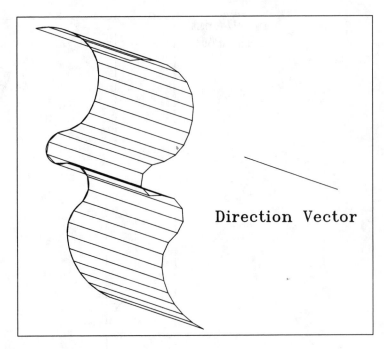

Direction Vector

17.14 How do you rotate a mesh around an object (such as to form a bowl, glass, etc.)?

Use the **REVSURF** command. The rotation is like an array and takes on the shape of the initial curve. Look at Figure 17-6. Each object starts with a curve and a line that represents the path of rotation.

Figure 17-6: Mesh
using REVSURF

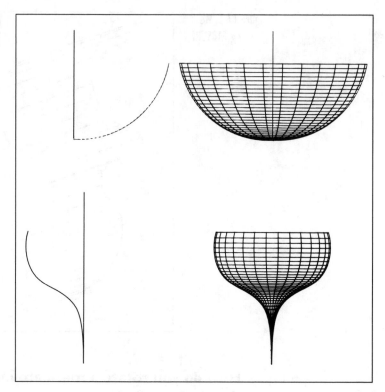

Type: `REVSURF <RETURN>`

Response: `Select path curve:`

Pick the curve, which is the object to be rotated. It doesn't have to be a curved object.

Response: `Select axis of revolution:`

Pick the object around which the curve will revolve. In Figure 17-6, the axis of revolution is the straight line.

Response: `Start angle <0>:`

You can begin the array at any degree around the revolution path. Press <RETURN> and start with the original entity.

Type: `<RETURN>`

Response: `Included angle (+=ccw, -=cw) <Full circle>:`

You can now enter the number of degrees you want the entity to revolve. If you press <RETURN>, it will make a full circle around the axis of revolution. If you enter a positive number, it will revolve counterclockwise. A negative number makes it revolve clockwise.

Type: `<RETURN>`

Look at Figure 17-7 for a tilted view of these objects.

**Figure 17-7:
Tilted view**

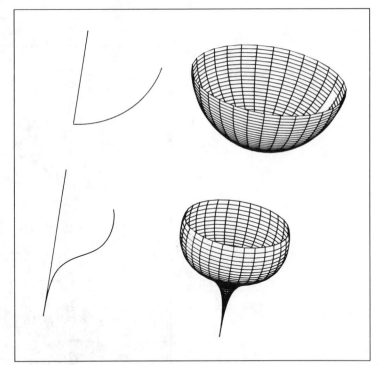

17.15 **How do you apply an EDGESURF?**

EDGESURF is a very versatile surface mesh. It requires simply that you have exactly four entities and that they be connected. Look at Figures 17-8, 17-9 and 17-10. As you can see, the entities can also be curved. This drawing began with a series of four polylines. These lines were curve-fitted and then the **EDGESURF** was applied.

Figure 17-8: Entity
with four polylines

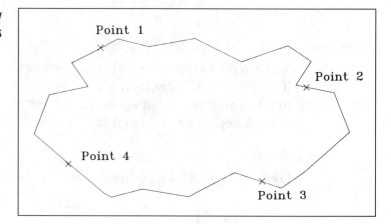

Figure 17-9:
Curve-fitted entity

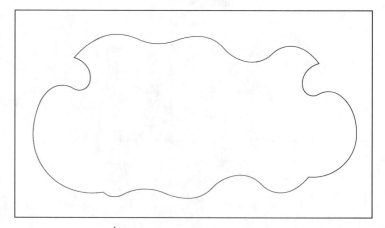

Figure 17-10: Entity
after EDGESURF

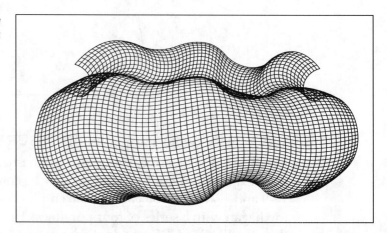

Type: EDGESURF <RETURN>

Response: Select edge 1:

Pick a point at about point 1.

Response: Select edge 2:

Pick a point at about point 2.

Response: Select edge 3:

Pick a point at about point 3.

Response: Select edge 4:

Pick a point at about point 4.

17.16 How do you connect multiple entities with a 3D mesh?

The trick to doing this is to use **EDGESURF**, but it takes a little preparation. You must make sure that there are only four groups of entities. To do this, use **PEDIT** and select entities. If they aren't already polylines, turn them into polylines. Now join as many entities as necessary until you have exactly four groups. Then use **EDGESURF** on the four groups.

Look at Figure 17-11 to see how this is done with a simple box.

Figure 17-11: Another way to use EDGESURF

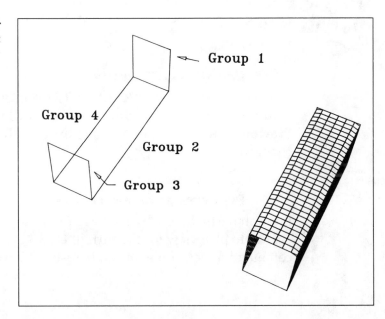

17.17 **How do you make part of a 3D face invisible?**

You can make **3DFACE** lines invisible as they're created, then make them visible again with the system variable **SPLFRAME**. AutoCAD has no edit command that will make them invisible once they're created, but you can do that through AutoLISP. See LISP88 and LISP89 in Tips 17.36 and 17.37 for programs that let you choose which part of **3DFACE** you want visible or invisible.

17.18 **How do you set the density of a mesh?**

The density of a mesh is controlled by the system variables **SURFTAB1** and **SURFTAB2**. **SURFTAB1** controls **TABSURF** and **RULESURF**, since their meshes go in only one direction. **REVSURF** and **EDGESURF** require both **SURFTAB1** and **SURFTAB2**, since they have meshes that go in both directions.

17.19 **How do you change the density of a mesh?**

You can't directly change the density of a mesh once it's been created. You must erase the mesh, change the system variable and create the mesh again under the new system variable.

More Steps to Success

17.20 **Edit with UCS Entity**

Whenever you're using **BREAK** or **TRIM** in 3D, use **UCS Entity** on the entity you're breaking or trimming. When you're through, choose **UCS Previous** and you'll be returned to the UCS that was in effect before you changed it.

17.21 **Plan view as an alternative**

If the above tip doesn't work: Save the view you're working in, then change to plan view for the current UCS. Next, try the **TRIM** or **BREAK** command. When you're through, restore the view.

17.22 **An obsolete command that still has some uses**

VPOINT can be a shortcut to **DVIEW Camera** if you already know the angle. Just remember to input the angle in **VPOINT** in reverse order to that for **DVIEW Camera**. You must use the **Rotate** option with **VPOINT**.

17.23 **TWIST can turn your world upside down**

If you use **TWIST** to rotate or view a 3D object, the UCS icon for top and bottom can be reversed, since AutoCAD can't then tell which is which. The object rotates, but your view of the current UCS doesn't.

17.24 **Don't look through the wrong end of the telescope**

Don't confuse **ZOOM** and **DISTANCE**. If you use **ZOOM** in **DVIEW** while perspective is on, you can get some strange results. Remember that **DISTANCE** actually repositions your camera to target points, while **ZOOM** is like using a telephoto lens without actually moving the camera.

17.25 **How not to hide**

You can keep entities from being hidden during the **HIDE** command. Place those entities on any layer, then create a layer called HIDDEN plus the name of the layer you want to be visible. For example, let's say you wanted all entities on a layer called FRONT to remain visible. Place the entities on that layer, then create a layer called HIDDENFRONT. All entities on the FRONT layer will be visible.

17.26 **Hide the hidden layer**

If you need to get rid of a hidden layer, rename it without using the HIDDEN prefix.

17.27 **Shortcut to thickness**

You can use **SETVAR Thickness** without going through the **ELEVATION** command; see LISP92 in Tip 17.40.

17.28 Be creative using meshes

Whenever you need to apply a surface to any area, always consider joining lines together until you can satisfy the requirements of **RULESURF** or **EDGESURF**.

17.29 The unused mesh

Never use **3DMESH** as a command. It should be used only by an Auto-LISP program that needs exact control over the vertices for the mesh.

17.30 Use polylines in 3D, not lines

Make sure that all lines are initially drawn as polylines if you plan to work in 3D. This will make things a lot easier as you do your work (for example, when you're applying 3D meshes).

17.31 Use dashed lines for hidden lines

If you want to use a line type such as dashed lines for hidden lines, trace over or copy the lines to another layer. Then break and trim the lines to look like the parts of the lines that are hidden. Now prepare a HIDDEN layer (see Tip 17.25 above). When the lines are really hidden, the dashed lines will show through the parts that are hidden.

17.32 Hatching in 3D

The easiest way to do a **HATCH** in 3D is to create a **3DFACE**, then **HATCH** the last entity.

17.33 Restrictions on 3D plotting

You have very little control over the rotation and the position of an object at plot time. First rotate the drawing using **DVIEW**, then plot.

AutoLISP Programs

17.34 Isometric (LISP86)

Even though you shouldn't use isometric mode for your drawing, this doesn't mean that you can't create isometric views from your 3D drawings. This program places you in an isometric view of a drawing.

Listing:
```
(defun c:lisp86 ()
    (command "ucs" "w" "vpoint" "1,-1,1")
)
```

To Use: Load LISP86.LSP.

Type: LISP86 <RETURN>

17.35 Reverse target and camera (LISP87)

Often, the only way to get to the other side of a drawing in AutoCAD is to reverse the current positions of the target and the camera. That's what this program does. (Use of the plus sign at the end of a line in AutoLISP code indicates that line is wrapped.)

Listing:
```
(defun c:lisp87 (/ tx ty tz tar cam)
    (setq tx (+ (car (getvar "target")) (car (getvar "viewdir"))))
    (setq ty (+ (cadr (getvar "target")) (cadr (getvar "viewdir"))))
    (setq tz (+ (caddr (getvar "target")) (caddr +
     (getvar "viewdir"))))
    (setq tar (list tx ty tz))
    (setq cam (getvar "target"))
    (command "dview" "c" pause pause pause "po" tar cam)
)
```

To Use: Load LISP87.LSP.

Type: LISP87 <RETURN>

17.36 Make 3D faces visible or invisible (LISP88)

This program will make invisible any combination of four sides of a 3D face. Simply enter the code number for the appropriate side(s). **0** will make all sides visible.

1	Side 1	
2	Side 2	
4	Side 3	
8	Side 4	
3	Sides 1 and 2	(1+2=3)
5	Sides 1 and 3	(1+4=5)
6	Sides 2 and 3	(2+4=6)
7	Sides 1, 2 and 3	(1+2+4=7)
9	Sides 1 and 4	(1+8=9)
10	Sides 2 and 4	(2+8=10)
11	Sides 1, 2 and 4	(1+2+8=11)
12	Sides 3 and 4	(4+8=12)
13	Sides 1, 3 and 4	(1+4+8=13)
14	Sides 2, 3 and 4	(2+4+8=14)
15	All sides	(1+2+4+8=15)

Listing:
```
(defun c:lisp88 (/ b i d d1 b1)
    (setq i (getint "\nEnter sum of the sides to make invisible: "))
    (setq b (entget (car (entsel))))
    (setq d (assoc 70 b))
    (setq d1 (cons (car d) i))
    (setq b1 (subst d1 d b))
    (entmod b1)
)
```

To Use: Load LISP88.LSP.

Type: `LISP88 <RETURN>`

Response: `Select objects:`

Pick the 3D face you want to work with.

Response: `Enter sum of the sides to make invisible:`

Enter the code number as indicated above.

17.37 **Find sides of a 3D face (LISP89)**

This is the companion program to LISP88. In order to use LISP88 successfully, you must know how a 3D face is drawn—which is Side One and which is Side Two.

Listing:
```
(defun c:lisp89 (/ b i d d1 b1 e)
    (setq b (entget (car (entsel))))
    (setq i 1)
    (repeat 2
        (setq d (assoc 70 b))
        (setq d1 (cons (car d) i))
        (setq b1 (subst d1 d b))
        (entmod b1)
        (prompt "\nThis is side ") (princ i)
        (setq i (+ 1 i))
        (setq e (getstring))
    )
    (terpri)
    (entmod b)
)
```

To Use: Load LISP89.LSP.

Type: `LISP89 <RETURN>`

Response: `Select objects:`

Pick the 3D face you want to know about. Side One will disappear. Press <RETURN> and Side Two will disappear. Press <RETURN> again and the 3D face will return to its normal state.

17.38 **Change to plan and save view and UCS (LISP90)**

Once you change views using DVIEW, you can't get back to a previous DVIEW unless it's saved. This program saves the current view and the current UCS. Then it takes you to the plan view of the current UCS. The companion program, LISP91, restores you to your previous UCS and DVIEW.

Listing:
```
(defun c:lisp90 ()
   (command "view" "s" "tempview")
   (command "ucs" "s" "tempview")
   (command "plan" "")
)
```

To Use: Load LISP90.LSP.

Type: LISP90 <RETURN>

17.39 **Restore previous DVIEW and UCS (LISP91)**

This is a companion program to LISP90. It restores the view and UCS saved under that program.

Listing:
```
(defun c:lisp91 ()
   (command "ucs" "r" "tempview")
   (command "view" "r" "tempview")
)
```

To Use: Load LISP91.LSP.

Type: LISP91 <RETURN>

17.40 **Set thickness (LISP92)**

AutoCAD has no direct command to set **Thickness**, but this program supplies one. Instead of going through **ELEV**, it uses **SETVAR**—the preferred way to set **Thickness** for compatibility with future AutoCAD releases.

Listing:
```
(defun c:lisp92 (/ a)
    (setq a (getdist "\nNew thickness "))
    (setvar "thickness" a)
)
```

To Use: Load LISP92.LSP.

Type: `LISP92 <RETURN>`

Response: `New thickness:`

Enter the new thickness.

17.41 **Join entities (LISP93)**

This quick little program makes a single polyline out of any singularly connected group of entities. It's ideal to use when applying meshes.

Listing:
```
(defun c:lisp93 (/ a)
    (setq a (ssget))
    (if (> (sslength a) 1)
        (command "pedit" a "y" "j" a "" "x")
    )
)
```

To Use: Load LISP93.LSP.

Type: `LISP93 <RETURN>`

Response: `Select objects:`

Select any group of objects. You can use **Crossing** or **Window**. Then confirm the selection. The items are now joined as a single polyline.

Miscellaneous (Intermediate)

How Do You . . .

18.1 How do you make a prototype drawing?

There are many variables, settings and text styles that need to be set up for an initial drawing, and you shouldn't have to do this every time you start a new drawing. It's also useful to be able to carry over blocks or floor plans from one drawing to another. There's a way to make sure that each new drawing begins with the initial setups and entities already in place.

When you install AutoCAD for the first time, you load a file called ACAD.DWG. When you configure AutoCAD, item number 8 is **Configure operating parameters**. Within this item is item number 2, **Initial drawing setup**. Here AutoCAD asks,

```
Enter name of default prototype file for new drawings or . for none
<acad>:
```

In the initial setup, AutoCAD defaults to ACAD.DWG as the prototype drawing. You can enter ACAD.DWG and make layers, load line types, set grid and snap, set units and limits, include the title block, etc. This drawing file then becomes the basis for any other new drawing.

RELEASE 12   Creating prototype drawings the new way. See Tip 20.3.

18.2 How do you specify no default prototype drawing?

When you're configuring the initial drawing, name the default drawing as a period (.). Then AutoCAD won't use any drawing as the default.

18.3 How do you use more than one prototype drawing?

Obviously, the setup you use most often should be your initial prototype drawing. It might have a set scale, such as 1 to 50 or 1"=1/4". But what if you want different scales in other prototype drawings?

You can have as many prototype drawings as you want; in fact, you can use the following technique as you create new drawings and include basic entities in them.

Let's assume you'd like a drawing called PROTO1.DWG to be the prototype for the next new drawing you do. When you give AutoCAD the name of the new drawing, enter

```
NEWDWG=PROTO1
```

This tells AutoCAD to use PROTO1 as the model when **NEWDWG** is being created.

18.4 **How do you get into AutoCAD if your default prototype drawing doesn't exist?**

When AutoCAD is first installed, the default prototype drawing is ACAD.DWG. If something has happened to that drawing, AutoCAD gives you an error message each time you try to bring up a new drawing.

There are several ways to handle this. When AutoCAD asks you for a new drawing name, enter NEWDWG=. Notice that there's nothing after the equals mark. This tells AutoCAD that there's no prototype drawing to be used. You could also change the default in the configuration to a period or the name of another existing drawing.

RELEASE 12   Beginning a drawing without a prototype drawing. See Tip 20.2. If you can't get this far, start AutoCAD as **ACAD –r**. This wil begin the configuration menu. Make your default prototype something else, or . (period), for none.

18.5 **How do you set up more than one configuration?**

As of Release 10, there are five files that control the configuration of Auto-CAD. These files are:

ACADDS.OVL

ACADDG.OVL

ACADPL.OVL

ACADPP.OVL

ACAD.CFG

NOTE: 386 versions of AutoCAD use only ACAD.CFG.

If you do nothing, these files are stored in the **\ACAD** directory or wherever your AutoCAD program files are located. The actual directory name isn't required; you can call it **\ACAD10** or **\CAD** if you want to.

You can store these files where you wish; they don't have to be in your default AutoCAD program directory. You do this by setting an environmental variable using the DOS **SET** command.

For example, let's assume you want two configurations, one for a VGA card and the other for an EGA. Make two directories: **C:\VGA** and **C:\EGA**. Now type in the following line at the DOS prompt or put it in a batch file:

```
SET ACADCFG=C:\VGA
```

When this is executed, AutoCAD thinks that its configuration files are in the directory **C:\VGA**. When AutoCAD comes up, it will take you through the configuration routine if it hasn't already been configured. When the files are updated, they'll be in the **C:\VGA** directory.

The easiest way to set up the EGA configuration is to copy all of the files from the **C:\VGA** directory to the **C:\EGA** directory. Now use the DOS **SET** command and type in the following line at the DOS prompt or put it in a batch file:

```
SET ACADCFG=C:\EGA
```

When this is executed, AutoCAD thinks that its configuration files are now in the **C:\EGA** directory. Since you copied the same configuration files from **C:\VGA** to **C:\EGA**, AutoCAD is still configured the same way. Now you can make the one change in the video graphics card from VGA to EGA. When it's updated, it's in **C:\EGA**.

Note that the directory names **C:\EGA** and **C:\VGA** have no special meaning; you can call the directories anything you want, as long as their names differ from one another.

Now it's simple to toggle between configurations to include the **SET** statement in the batch file that calls up each configuration of AutoCAD.

See Tip 18.26 for a sample batch file called LISP94.BAT.

18.6 How do you attach a program to AutoCAD?

You can run regular DOS commands or other programs by simply typing in their names directly from the AutoCAD Command line. This gives the illusion that you've attached a program or DOS command to AutoCAD.

This magic is done through a file called ACAD.PGP. This file should already exist, and you can modify it with a text editor such as EDLIN.COM. Let's look at one line in the file:

```
EDIT,EDLIN,40000,File to edit: ,0
```

This line lets you use EDLIN while inside AutoCAD. Each item in the line is separated by a comma. EDIT is the command you type in from the Command line that begins your program. The next item, EDLIN, is the actual name of the program or the word that begins the program. 40000 is the number of bytes of memory that you need to run your program. (AutoCAD doesn't actually set aside this amount of memory; it shells out and lets you use the memory. When the program is finished, the memory is recaptured for AutoCAD.)

The next item, File to edit, is the prompt statement. If this is included, whatever you enter at this prompt is added as a parameter to the program name. If you don't want the prompt, use two commas. Don't worry about the final 0. Just include it.

Let's say you want to run a program called XYZ. You'll enter XYZ in AutoCAD to call up the program. The program needs 90,000 bytes to run. Place this line somewhere in the ACAD.PGP file:

```
XYZ,XYZ,90000,,0
```

Of course, you can't run very large programs this way in AutoCAD.

18.7 How do you limit the amount of extended/expanded memory used?

You can use either of two commands, depending on whether you're using extended or expanded memory. If you do nothing, AutoCAD will use all of the extended or expanded memory available. See Tip 28.9.

To tell AutoCAD how much extended or expanded memory to make available, use the DOS **SET** command at the DOS prompt, or place it in the AUTOEXEC.BAT batch file. Enter

```
SET ACADXMEM=,512k
```

This lets AutoCAD use only 512k of extended memory.

```
SET ACADLIMEM=32
```

This also lets AutoCAD use only 512k of expanded memory. Note that 32 is a number that's to be multiplied by 16k; you don't enter the actual number of bytes.

If you don't want AutoCAD to use any extended memory, enter SET ACADXMEM=NONE. For expanded memory, enter SET ACADLIMEM=0.

18.8 How do you sort files?

You can't actually sort a directory without a commercial utility, but you can display it as though it were sorted either by **SHELL** or while you're in DOS:

```
DIR *.DWG | SORT
```

You must be pathed to SORT.EXE. This is generally in your DOS directory. You can use any valid DIR file specifications.

18.9 How do you get a printout of a directory?

This is available through **SHELL** or directly in DOS. Enter

```
DIR *.DWG > PRN:
```

The > directs the output of the directory to your printer. You could also direct it to a file and then copy the file to the printer.

18.10 How do you get a printout of your text screen?

Use Ctrl-Q or pick PRINTER at any point on the standard AutoCAD tablet menu. From then on, everything on your text screen will also be output to the printer. To turn it off, use Ctrl-Q or PRINTER again.

18.11 How do you bring in prototype layers, text style and blocks after a drawing is created?

We'll assume that there's already a prototype or other drawing that has the layers, text styles, blocks, line types, etc., already in it. Simply **INSERT** that drawing with an equal sign (=). When asked for the insertion point, enter Ctrl-C. See LISP96 in Tip 18.28.

Type: `INSERT <RETURN>`

Response: `Block name (or ?):`

Type: `PROTO1= <RETURN>`

Response: `Insertion point:`

Type: `Ctrl-C (^C) to cancel.`

All of the blocks, layers, text styles, etc., that belong to that drawing are now part of your current drawing. At your first opportunity, **PURGE** blocks so that the block definition of PROTO1 can be removed.

More Steps to Success

18.12 **SET ACAD= doesn't work with prototype drawings**

All prototype drawings should be in a default AutoCAD directory such as **C:\ACAD** so that you won't have to path to them when you enter their names. The **SET ACAD=** environment variable has no effect on them.

RELEASE 12   See Tip 20.3 for more on prototype drawings.

18.13 **Hidden options**

Try reconfiguring AutoCAD by choosing item number 2 on the configuration menu, **Allow detailed configuration.** Different peripherals will ask different questions. You may be surprised to find how much more control you have over color and other parameters.

18.14 **Plot spooling for networks**

Many third-party plotting programs can do background spool plotting. To tell AutoCAD where to put the plot file when you plot to a file, name the file AUTOSPOOL. You can designate where the plot file is to be placed when you configure AutoCAD.

Under Operating Parameters (item number 8) is item number 4. This is where you designate the directory. The file name that's actually written has a file extension whose first two letters match the designated network node name. If you haven't designated a network node name, AutoCAD defaults to **AC$**. The first letter of the file name will begin with a V if it's a plotter file, or with an R if it's a printer-plotter file. The rest of the file name is a series of numbers based on the time and date of the plot that keep the name unique.

18.15 Temporary files for RAM disks

AutoCAD uses a series of temporary files whenever you're working in a drawing. This can cause you real problems if you're networking and using the same directory. This tip won't solve the shared directory problem on a network—but you can greatly improve AutoCAD's performance if you have a RAM disk with enough memory.

AutoCAD lets you tell it where to place the temporary files. This is found in configuration menu item number 8, **Configure operating parameters**, and item number 5, **Placement of temporary files.**

You must have enough memory to hold your largest drawing, plus the memory necessary to hold the **UNDO** commands. Don't set up a RAM disk until you're sure that there's enough memory available for this. Then you can load .OVLs and temporary files into other portions of RAM. This will give you the overall best performance.

18.16 Be careful in setting temporary files for networks

Just placing temporary files in another directory doesn't solve the whole problem of networking. There are still files that must be in the drawing directory. Therefore, you should have a different configuration for each user or network node. This configuration should have a network node name, found in the configuration menu under item number 8, **Configure operating parameters**, or item number 6, **Network node name**.

You can enter up to three characters. This helps AutoCAD give a unique name to its temporary files and keeps two people from crashing in the same directory, even though they're working on different drawings.

RELEASE 11   Network control under Release 11 has been greatly expanded. See Chapter 9 for a description of the various network features.

18.17 OOPS for configuration

If after updating a configuration you discover that you want your old one back, use the backup file ACAD.BAK in the configuration directory or in the AutoCAD directory. Simply rename or copy ACAD.BAK over to ACAD.CFG.

18.18 **ACAD knows about VDISK**

If you're using a RAM disk, try to use VDISK, which is furnished on your DOS disk. AutoCAD will then give the disk enough memory to run, according to your specifications, before taking the rest of the memory. If you use a commercial RAM disk such as one that might have come with your memory card, AutoCAD may not be able to recognize it. You may then have to specify how much memory to use and where the memory is to begin. See LISP95 in Tip 18.27 for a sample batch file that sets AutoCAD up for use with a RAM disk. See also Tips 18.8 and 28.1.

18.19 **Make directories by project groups**

You should have a separate directory that holds all the drawings for a particular project. You should name the directory according to your project or project number. Don't put drawings in either the root directory or in the AutoCAD directory where your programs are located. These are usually the first to go when you're updating a version of AutoCAD, so your drawings might get overwritten.

18.20 **Beware of common names**

When you're placing projects in their own directories, don't give the directories the same names as their working order, such as **A.DWG** or **B.DWG** for Sheet A and Sheet B. Eventually, you'll be in the wrong directory when you decide to delete Sheet A. Instead, make sure all drawings have unique names. You could place part of the project number in front of the A or B—for example, **89025A.DWG**. This way, if you're in the wrong directory the worst that can happen is a **File not found** message.

18.21 **Alternate names when you're saving drawings**

Save your drawings at least every 30 minutes. This may seem like a lot, but it's nothing compared to losing a day's work. Save a drawing under at least one different name than the one you called it up by. If the power goes off during the **SAVE** operation, at least you won't destroy your only copy.

RELEASE 12   For how to set the time for automatic saving, see Tip 20.24.

18.22 **Don't forget special menus and fonts when archiving**

Eventually, you'll want to save all your project's drawings on floppy disks placed in a permanent archive. Then erase the drawings from the hard disk to recover the disk space.

Make sure you include any files that might go with the drawings, including any special fonts, menus, etc. Then, when they're restored, you'll have everything you need to reproduce them.

18.23 **The three-generation backup**

In addition to backing up your drawing files to floppy disk, you should back up the entire hard disk. We recommend the "three-generation" back-up system.

First, you'll have a series of disks or a tape that makes up the total backup of your hard disk. Each group of disks or tape that represents the entire hard disk is called a *set*.

You should have three sets: A, B and C. Let's assume that you back up every week. The first week, back up onto Set A. The next week, back up onto Set B. On the third week, back up again onto Set A, etc., alternating each week between Sets A and B.

At least once a month, back up onto Set C and remove it from the premises. Remember that the process of backing up destroys the previous backup.

18.24 **Your disk is slowing down**

AutoCAD is a vicious system when it comes to fragmenting files. Whenever a file is deleted, AutoCAD leaves a free area on the hard disk. When another file is written to hard disk, it may try to occupy that area. If the file fits, all well and good; but if it's larger, part of the file is written to the vacant area and the rest is written to another part of the disk. So if your disk seems to be getting slower with age, it's not your imagination.

There are several commercial programs that will reorganize your disk, placing the file cluster consecutively. You should run one of these often.

18.25 **Recovering disk space**

From time to time, often because AutoCAD crashed and you had to reset your machine, you'll develop "lost clusters." You can identify these by doing a **CHKDSK.**

Never do a **CHKDSK/F** (which will fix the lost cluster) without first doing a **CHKDSK** without the **/F**. The **/F** will fix whatever's wrong with the disk, but what's wrong may be more than just lost clusters.

After you've done the **CHKDSK/F**, and if it found lost clusters, tell DOS to convert them to files. These files are now in the root directory, each with the extension .CHK. Delete ***.CHK**, and you'll recover the disk space.

Another way to recover the disk space is to answer N to **Convert lost chains to files?** This keeps you from having to delete the *.CHK files.

AutoLISP Programs

18.26 **Change configurations (LISP94)**

The following is a DOS batch file that you can use to call up different AutoCAD configurations. Of course, this is only an example—you'd have a different batch file for each configuration.

Listing:
```
set acadcfg=c:\vga
set lispheap=39000
set lispstack=5000
set acad=c:\details
acad
```

To Use: Name the batch file (for example) VGA.BAT. Then you can call up Auto-CAD by typing VGA <RETURN>.

18.27 **Using a RAM disk (LISP95)**

If your largest drawing has enough space in memory and you have memory left over, you might want to use it for your overlay files. This can make AutoCAD run faster.

The following example batch file copies the necessary overlay files to a RAM disk called E: (your RAM disk-drive letter may be different). Make sure that the overlay files you're copying are in a different directory than AutoCAD, so it will accept the proper PATH statement. In this sample batch file, the overlay programs are in a directory called **C:\TEMPOVL**. Your configuration files should also be copied to this directory and deleted from **\ACAD** after the configuration has been completed.

CAUTION: If you configure AutoCAD, remember that the configuration files are in **E:** (RAM disk). When you leave AutoCAD, be sure to copy the configuration files (.OVL and ACAD.CFG) to **C:\TEMPOVL**, or they'll be lost when you turn off your machine.

Listing:
```
copy c:\tempovl\*.ovl e:\
copy c:\tempovl\acad.cfg e:\
set acadcfg=e:\
set lispheap=39000
set lispstack=5000
set acad=c:\details
acad
```

To Use: Use this batch file when calling up AutoCAD for the first time. Then you can bypass it and start with ACAD.

18.28 **Insert prototype block (LISP96)**

This program inserts a prototype block definition in your current drawing without actually inserting the block. This is good for creating layers, line types, styles, etc., after a drawing is created.

Listing:
```
(defun c:lisp96 ()
    (setq a (getstring "\nName of prototype block "))
    (setq a (strcat a "="))
    (command "insert" a ^c)
)
```

To Use: Load LISP96.LSP.

Type: LISP96 <RETURN>

Response: Name of prototype block:

Enter the name of the prototype drawing or block. It must be on disk.

Intermediate Release II

How Do You . . .

19.1 How do you use wild cards?

Release 11 offers a greatly expanded series of wild cards in a variety of commands. Here's a list of the wild cards now available to you and what they mean. In order to show you how each wild card variation operates, let's assume the target contains "ABC123XYZ\%." This, of course, would be too many characters for a single file, but it could be a variable in Auto-LISP as well.

~ (tilde)   This means not found. ~234 will give you everything that doesn't contain 234. Therefore, our sample file would be selected, since 234 is not part of the pattern.

*   This is the standard wild card that matches anything. It can now be used both before and after or anywhere else in the search pattern.

?   Matches any single character or number.

@   Matches any single character. The character cannot be a number.

Matches any single number.

. (period)

(space)   Matches one or more spaces.

[...]   (Don't actually use the periods.) This means there's a match for any one of the characters enclosed in the brackets: *[XJK]*

Our file would be found because the X is located in the string, even though the J and K are not. The characters don't have to be in a specific order, just contained somewhere within the string.

[~...]   Finds the file only if there are characters not included within the brackets. *[~JKL]* would find the file, since the string doesn't include J, K or L.

[-] (hyphen)   The hyphen used inside the brackets treats the pattern as a range. *[1-5]* would find the file, since 123 is matched as being found within the range of 1 to 5.

, (comma)   This is used as an "or": *123*,*JKL* would find the file because 123 is found within the string, even though JKL is not. The comma acted as an "or."

' (back quote)   Treats the next character literally. This is used for special characters. This should be used for all nonalphanumeric special characters.

19.2 **How do you create an odd-shaped 3DFACE?**

Prior to Release 11, the only way to put a **3DFACE** on an odd-shaped object was with a **MESH**. This is still the accepted method, especially if the object has curves. But from time to time you'll want to put various 3D faces on objects that aren't curved but have nonrectangular vertices.

PFACE is the command that gives you the ability to put a series of quick meshes over an odd-shaped area. Let's assume you want to put a mesh on Figure 19-1.

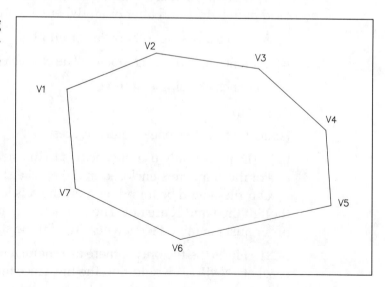

Figure 19-1: Using PFACE for nonrectangular shapes

Type: `PFACE <RETURN>`

Response: `Vertex 1`
`Vertex 2`
`Vertex 3`
`Vertex 4`
`Vertex 5`
`Vertex 6`
`Vertex 7`

At each of the above questions, pick an intersection as they are marked. What you have done is identify the various vertices by number.

Response: `Vertex 8`

Type: `<RETURN>` (When there are no more vertices to pick, <RETURN>.)

	You Type:
Response: `Face 1, vertex 1`	1
`Face 1, vertex 2`	2
`Face 1, vertex 3`	3
`Face 1, vertex 4`	4
`Face 1, vertex 5`	5
`Face 1, vertex 6`	6
`Face 1, vertex 7`	7
`Face 1, vertex 8`	`<RETURN>`
`Face 2, vertex 1`	`<RETURN>`

At this point, a single mesh has been placed on the entire object. You can prove this by placing something behind the object and hiding the lines.

Let's look at the complete command. What you did in the above example was place a single face on the entire object. The **PFACE** command lets you place multiple faces on objects from any vertex to any vertex. When we finished with Face 1, **PFACE** began asking us about Face 2, etc.

Face 1, vertex 1 is really saying, "Previously you identified various vertices by number in the first phase of the **PFACE** command. Now tell me which number you want to be the first vertex of Face 1." In essence, you're drawing **3DFACE** lines from point to point. It was convenient to use the same point number with the same vertex number. But we could have drawn multiple faces from any point or group of points to any other point. We could have even overlapped if necessary.

19.3 **How do you make PFACES invisible?**

When you're asked for Face 1, vertex 3, answer the question with a negative number. This will make the edge of the **PFACE** invisible.

19.4 **How do you make one drawing reference another?**

External reference is a feature of Release 11 that lets you use another drawing as a block, without actually having that drawing saved as part of the existing drawing. There are several advantages to this technique. First, you can save an enormous amount of disk space. If one or several large blocks were used in many drawings, the size of those blocks would be a part of each one of the drawings. This way, only one actual DWG file exists for the block, and it's simply referenced by the other drawings. Second, any changes to the original block or base external file are automatically reflected in each and every one of the drawing files that references it.

The easiest way to understand external reference is to compare it to a font shape file. The actual font shape doesn't reside in each drawing; it's merely referenced. Therefore, the font shape file must be on disk each time the drawing is brought up. If AutoCAD can't find the proper font shape file, you're asked to supply the name of another. The same applies to external reference files. They must exist on disk where AutoCAD can find them each time the drawing is brought up. At the same time, you do have the ability to convert at any time all or parts of an external file to part of the actual AutoCAD drawing file. One drawback to external files is that they can't be changed in any way within the actual drawing file. They can be changed or edited only within their own files.

Type: `Xref <RETURN>`

Response: `?/Bind/Detach/Path/Reload/<Attach>:`

Type: `<RETURN>` (This chooses Attach, the default choice.)

Response: `Xref to Attach:`

Type: `toolpost <RETURN>` (Enter the name of the file of your choice. Be sure to drive/path spec the name of the file. For example, toolpost can be found on **C:\acad\sample\toolpost**. If so, that is what should be entered.)

Response: `Attach Xref Toolpost:` (The drive/path spec will be repeated as it loads.)

The rest of the entries and the responses are exactly like the **INSERT** command. You pick an insertion point, scale the block, rotate, etc. From now on the **XREF** block looks and acts like an ordinary block. You can even explode it in a very special way.

19.5 How do you explode an external reference block?
Use the **XREF** option, **Bind.**

Type: XREF <RETURN>

Response: ?/Bind/Detach/Path/Reload/<Attach>:

Type: Bind <RETURN>

Response: Xref(s) to bind:

Type: toolpost <RETURN> (You can use any of the available wild cards to choose more than one reference block.)

Response: Scanning . . .

The toolpost is now part of the drawing. If it's made up of independent blocks, they can be exploded the same as any other blocks, otherwise they're now independent entities.

19.6 How do you remove an external reference from your drawing?
The **Detach** option of the **XREF** command performs this operation.

Type: XREF <RETURN>

Response: ?/Bind/Detach/Path/Reload/<Attach>:

Type: Detach <RETURN>

Response: Xref(s) to Detach:

Type: toolpost <RETURN> (You can use any of the available wild cards to choose more than one reference block.)

Response: Scanning . . .

19.7 How do you update changes made to the external reference file?

If you make changes directly to an external reference file, nothing special has to be done to reflect those changes in any drawing files that reference the reference file. But on a network system, a change can be made to a reference file directly by someone else on the network. It's then possible to update your existing file with the latest version of the reference file without having to exit your current drawing. To do this, use the **Reload** option of **XREF**.

Type: `XREF <RETURN>`

Response: `?/Bind/Detach/Path/Reload/<Attach>:`

Type: `Reload <RETURN>`

Response: `Xref(s) to reload:`

Type: `toolpost <RETURN>` (You may use any of the available wild cards to choose more than one reference block.)

Response: `Scanning . . .`

19.8 How do you change the path of an existing external reference file?

The path to an external reference file is established when the file is referenced with **XREF** the first time. If you need to change the path, use the **Path** option of **XREF**.

Type: `XREF <RETURN>`

Response: `?/Bind/Detach/Path/Reload/<Attach>:`

Type: `Path <RETURN>`

Response: `Edit path for which Xref(s):`

Type: `toolpost <RETURN>` (You may use any of the available wild cards to choose more than one reference block.)

Response: `Old path:\acad\sample\toolpost`
`New path:`

You can now type in the new path or leave this unchanged. If you used a wild card, AutoCAD will ask you one at a time for the new path for each **XREF** that matches the wild cards used.

19.9 How do you make only part of an external reference a permanent part of your drawing?

Any given external reference can have a series of dependent symbols. These may include blocks, text styles, layers, linetypes or dimstyles. This is done with the **XBIND** command.

Type: `XBIND <RETURN>`

Response: `Block/Dimstyle/LAyer/LType/Style:`

Type: `Layer <RETURN>`

Response: `Dependent Layer name(s):`

You can respond with the layer name or any wild card option.

19.10 How do you make abbreviated commands?

Although abbreviations can be made with AutoLISP, Release 11 offers a more direct method. You can modify the ACAD.PGP file and add the abbreviations. The ACAD.PGP is a text file provided with AutoCAD. You can create your own or modify the existing one with a text editor.

Abbreviations are called Aliases. The abbreviations are contained in two fields separated by a comma. First, type the abbreviation, then comma, then *, then the command.

`AR, *ARRAY`

The above would make the abbreviation **AR** stand for theAutoCAD command **ARRAY**. Now type **AR** instead of **ARRAY**. For command names, choose any AutoCAD command, AutoLISP program name, Auto-LISP command, ADS command, etc.

AutoCAD supplies a few of these already made to get you started. You can find them in the ACAD.PGP file.

19.11 How do you change an existing dimension variable for just one dimension variable?

You're able to change the value of any associative dimension as a one-time shot without having to make a change in the dimension variable. You do this with the dimension command **OVERRIDE**. Dimension commands can be accessed only while in the **DIM** command.

Begin first with a dimension. Assume you wanted to change the arrow size for one or a group of dimensions.

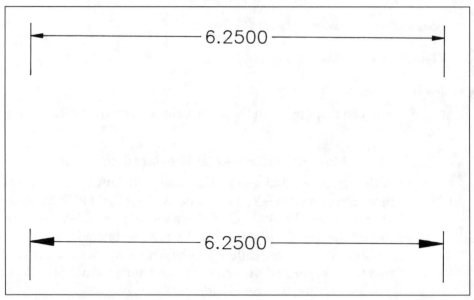

Figure 19-2: Changing one dimension with OVERRIDE

Type: `DIM <RETURN>`

Type: `Override <RETURN>`

Response: `Dimension variable to override:`

Type: `Dimasz <RETURN>`

Response: `Current value <0.1800> New Value:`

Type: `.36 <RETURN>`

Response: `Dimension variable to override`

You can continue to enter additional dimension variables. <RETURN> when you're through entering dimension variables to override.

Type: `<RETURN>`

Response: `Select objects:`

Select in any manner all dimensions you want to change. When you confirm, they'll be updated only with the variables you've indicated.

NOTE: With Release 12, all dimension variables can be set with the new **DDIM** dialogue box. See Tip 30.21.

19.12 **How do you move dimension text around?**
Within **DIM**, the **Tedit** subcommand lets you place associative dimension text anywhere you want it.

Type: `DIM <RETURN>`

Type: `Tedit`

Response: `Select dimension:`

Pick the dimension you want to move. You can also use a **WINDOW** or **CROSSING**. But AutoCAD will do only one dimension at a time. Therefore, **WINDOW** or **CROSSING** is a convenience only. They don't actually select multiple dimensions. Picking is generally the preferred method.

Response: `Enter text location (Left/Right/Home/Angle)`

Pick where you would like the text to be. You may also choose any of the above options. Left moves it to the left. Right moves it to the right. Angle lets you enter an angle for the text. Home returns it to its default position.

NOTE: With Release 12, all dimension variables can be set with the new **DDIM** dialogue box. See Tip 30.21.

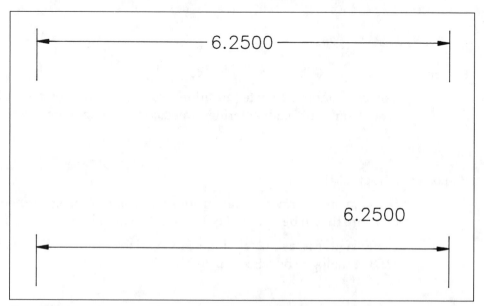

Figure 19-3: Moving dimension text with DIM, Tedit

19.13 **How do you change the orientation of dimension text?**

Trotate lets you rotate the dimension text. You can do the same thing with **Tedit** by using the subcommand **Angle**, but **Trotate** gets you there faster. Also it permits you to use a true **CROSSING** and **WINDOW** to rotate the dimension text of multiple dimensions, whereas **Tedit Angle** allows only one dimension at a time.

Type: `DIM <RETURN>`

Type: `Trotate <RETURN>`

Response: `Enter new text angle:`

Type: `20 <RETURN>`

Response: `Select objects:`

Select dimension objects and confirm. All dimension text selected will be rotated 20 degrees.

NOTE: With Release 12, all dimension variables can be set with the new **DDIM** dialogue box. See Tip 30.21.

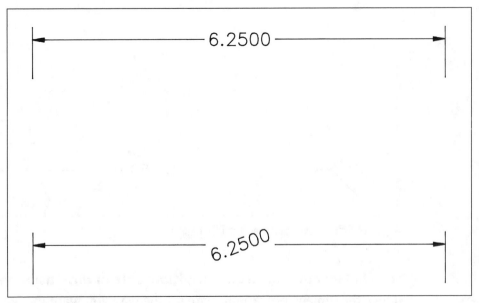

Figure 19-4: Rotating dimension text with DIM, Trotate

19.14 **How do you place dimension extension lines at an angle?**
Oblique allows you to tilt extension lines at any angle.

Type: `DIM <RETURN>`

Type: `Oblique <RETURN>`

Response: `Select objects:`

Select any associative dimensions, and confirm.

Response: `Enter obliquing angle` (<RETURN> for none):

Type: 45 <RETURN>

The extension lines will now tilt at a 45-degree angle.

NOTE: With Release 12, all dimension variables can be set with the new **DDIM** dialogue box. See Tip 30.21.

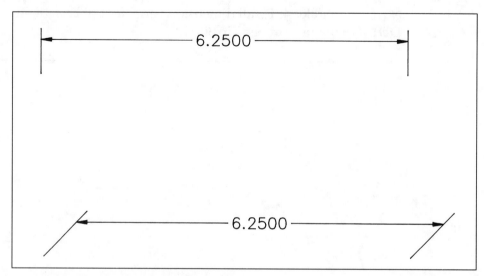

Figure 19-5: Tilting extension lines with DIM, Oblique

19.15 How do you create multiple sets of dimension variables?

Once the dimension variables are set the way you want them, you can save them in what is called a **DIM Style**.

Type: DIM <RETURN>

Type: Save <RETURN>

Response: ?/Name for new dimension style:

Type: ST1 <RETURN>

You've now created a set of dimension variables called **ST1**. You can now change the dimension variables and save them under another name.

NOTE: With Release 12, all dimension variables can be set with the new **DDIM** dialogue box. See Tip 30.21.

19.16 **How do you recall and use various dimension styles?**

Restore permits you to recall and make active a dimension style.

Type: `DIM <RETURN>`

Type: `Restore <RETURN>`

Response: `Current dimension style: ST2`
             `?/Enter dimension style name or <RETURN> to select dimension:`

Type: `ST1 <RETURN>`

This recalls and selects **ST1** as your current dimension style. You could also <RETURN> and then pick an existing dimension. AutoCAD would then read the style of the dimension selected and restore that dimension style.

NOTE: With Release 12, all dimension variables can be set with the new **DDIM** dialogue box. See Tip 30.21.

19.17 **How do you use Ordinate Dimensioning?**

For some, the term *ordinate dimensioning* may not be readily apparent. Simply stated, it produces as the dimension text one of the coordinate values of the point picked. It may be either the value of X or the value of Y.

Type: `DIM <RETURN>`

Type: `Ordinate <RETURN>`

Response: `Select Feature:`

AutoCAD is asking you here to pick a point. You can use your **Object Snap** to secure insertion points for entities as well as any of the **Object Snap** options.

Type: `Pick a point`

Response: `Leader endpoint (Xdatum/Ydatum)`

Type: `X <RETURN>`

Response: `Leader endpoint`

Rubber-band to the endpoint of a leader line, and the **Ordinate Dimension** will be drawn. Rather than entering X or Y at the above response, you could simply point to the endpoint of the leader line. AutoCAD checks the point selected and checks the point picked for the endpoint of the leader line. If the change in X between the two points is greater than the change in Y, it chooses X. Otherwise it chooses Y for you.

NOTE: With Release 12, all dimension variables can be set with the new **DDIM** dialogue box. See Tip 30.21.

19.18 How do you know the status of the dimension variables of a given style?

The **Var** subcommand lets you list the dimension variables of a given style without changing to that style.

Type: `DIM <RETURN>`

Type: `Var <RETURN>`

Response: `Current dimension style: ST2`
`?/Enter dimension style name or <RETURN> to select dimension:`

Type: `ST1 <RETURN>`

The dimension variables of **ST1** will now be listed.

NOTE: With Release 12, all dimension variables can be set with the new **DDIM** dialogue box. See Tip 30.21.

19.19 How do you change the color of various parts of the dimension?

Frequently, it's very important to have different colors for different parts of a single dimension. You can do this by highlighting one part over the other using a different plotting pen. The colors are controlled by different dimension variables. When using these dimension variables outside of **DIM**, you must use the integer color numbers. 0 is **BYBLOCK** and 256 is **BYLAYER**. If you use the dimension variables inside of **DIM** you can specify colors by name.

DIMCLRD   Dimension lines and arrowheads

DIMCLRE   Extension lines

DIMCLRT   Text

NOTE: With Release 12, all dimension variables can be set with the new **DDIM** dialogue box. See Tip 30.21.

19.20 How do you add shading?

Shading is added with the **SHADE** command.

Type: SHADE <RETURN>

Whatever can be shaded will shade. There are no prompts. You can't plot the shading. You can't place light sources. Only solid colors are used. You can make a slide; its color is determined by the color of the entity being shaded.

When **3DFACES** are being shaded, the outlines of the faces are shaded in the background color. Turning off their layers may hide what's behind them but will also prevent them from being shaded. If you want the faces shaded, but you don't want their edges to be visible, use LISP126, which explodes meshes to faces, then makes the faces invisible. Even though the faces are invisible, they still will shade.

19.21 **How do you convert from one unit to another?**

Although **(cvunit)** is an AutoLISP command, it's very convenient to use it to convert a value from one unit to another at the Command line. The units supported and their conversion formula are found in a file called ACAD.UNT, which is supplied with AutoCAD Release 11 and higher. You can add your own units and definitions to this file with a text editor.

Type: `(cvunit 100 "miles" "feet")`

This converts 100 miles to 528,000 feet. Three parameters follow **(cvunit)**: the value to be converted, followed by the "from" unit in quotes, followed by the "to" unit in quotes.

`(cvunit 20 "kilometers" "miles ") 12.4274`

You also can convert the components of a list such as a point.

`(cvunit '(12 24 36) "inches" "feet") (1.0 2.0 3.0)`

More Steps to Success

19.22 **Rename strange XREFs**

When you use the **BIND** command to convert **XREF** blocks to real blocks, AutoCAD inserts $ symbols within the parts of the blocks that have been bound to your drawing. These names can get quite long and strange. Remember, you can always use the **RENAME** command to change the name of any block in your drawing. Now with the new wild card features you can rename large groups of blocks as necessary.

19.23 **BIND XREFs before archiving**

It's generally a good idea to **BIND** all **XREFs** before archiving a drawing. If you don't make the **XREFs** a permanent part of the drawing, the archived drawing will not be complete if it's ever separated from the actual external files.

19.24 **Don't hard-code drives with XREFs**

The actual drive/path/filespec is saved with the **XREF** when it's created. This can cause a problem either on a network or if you move the external file.

It's better to let the **SET ACAD** environment variable do your work for you. This is very useful, since it enables you to set multiple directories.

```
SET ACAD=C:\EXTFILE;C:\LISP;C:\SYMBOLS
```

This command is issued either in your AUTOEXEC.BAT file or in a batch file that brings up AutoCAD. Now when you use **XREF**, you can simply enter the file name. AutoCAD will search through the current directory, then the **ACAD** directory, then begin the search through the directories pointed to by the **SET ACAD** environment variable. This way, you're not hard-coding into the **XREF** file name in your drawing a specific drive or even a specific directory. Therefore, others on your network will be able to find them by setting their own **SET ACAD** to their specific configuration.

19.25 **Don't EXPLODE dimensions**

With all the new capabilities now built in with dimensioning, the need to explode dimensions to move text, change colors, etc., is probably not valid. In fact, you're giving up much more than you're gaining.

19.26 **DIMASO not part of DIM styles**

The dimension variable, **DIMASO**, that turns associative dimensioning on and off is global for all styles. It's not saved with the specific dimension style.

19.27 **Always set DIMASO to 1**

On balance you'll always be better off if you use associative dimensioning than if you don't. Remember, later you can always explode a dimension if there's no other way. Therefore, check each old drawing and make sure that **DIMASO** is set to 1 for all future dimensions on that drawing.

19.28 **Can't CHANGE elevation**

Elevation has been removed as one of the options to the **CHANGE** command. This is unfortunate. Although it can be argued that it was superfluous, it was an easy command that performed a much-needed function for working in 3D. It should be returned as soon as possible.

In the meantime, you'll have to use the **MOVE** command to change the elevation of any entity.

19.29 **Off layers won't work for shading**

One popular trick to make mesh lines invisible and still use them during the **HIDE** command was to place the mesh on a layer and turn the layer off. Note it is off, not frozen. This trick still works, but only for hidden line removal. It doesn't work for shading. The **SHADE** command will not work on entities that are on off layers.

Therefore, the only way to make the mesh lines invisible and still be able to shade the area is to use LISP126, which converts meshes into 3D faces and then makes the 3D faces invisible.

19.30 **Know when to use XREF**

Just because **XREF** is available, you don't have to use it for everything instead of the **INSERT** command. **XREF** saves disk space, not memory. Your drawing won't **REGEN** any faster nor will **OBJECT SNAP** operate any more efficiently. And **XREF**, although useful, carries its own baggage. Here are some hints on when to consider using **XREF** instead of **INSERT**.

1. When the block is used as a base, such as a floor plan or a map, in several drawings.

2. When the block is in excess of 200,000 bytes.

3. When you want any changes to the block to be reflected in all drawings automatically.

4. When you need to make sure you have control over the base block so that no changes can be made accidentally in individual drawings.

If none of these elements are present or you can't justify using **XREF** for any other good reason, you'll probably be better off using **INSERT**.

19.31 **Fewer prototype drawings**

There's now no need to set up prototype drawings for different scales specifically for dimensioning. Since you can now save **DIM Styles** as sets of dimension variables, the same as **Text Styles**, you should set up a **DIM Style** in each prototype drawing for the command plot scales you'll be using.

19.32 **New kind of leader line**

You can use the **ORDINATE DIMENSION** command as a substitute for the **LEADER** command in order to control the direction of your text. Simply override the default **Ordinate** value with your own text at the prompt. Depending on whether you choose **XDATUM** or **YDATUM**, your text will go in the proper direction.

19.33 **Control the degree of shading**

The **SHADEDGE** system variable gives you some limited control over the appearance of the shade. What it looks like on your screen will differ depending on your graphics card. Shade a small area, then experiment by changing the value of **SHADEDGE** from **0** to **3**. **REGEN,** then **SHADE** again each time after you change the system variable.

19.34 **Change unit scale of drawing**

You can easily convert the scale of a drawing by using the **(cvunit)** Auto-LISP function. Let's say you wanted to convert a drawing from inches to metric (meters).

Step 1: Begin by changing your units from architectural to decimal.

Step 2: Rescale your drawing.

Type: `Scale <RETURN>`

Response: `Select objects:`

Type: `Select all entities in your drawing and confirm.`

Response: `Base point:`

Type: `@ <RETURN>`

Response: `<Scale factor/Reference:`

Type: `Reference <RETURN>`

Response: `Reference length <1>:`

Type: `1 <RETURN>` (Your drawing is now in inches and you're going to scale from inches to meters.)

Response: `New length:`

Type: `(cvunit 1 "inch" "meter") <RETURN>`

Step 3: The physical size of your lines have changed. You'll need to do a **DIM Override** on **DIMSCALE** to adjust for the size of the text and other dimension variables.

An alternative to this is to use the **DIMALT**, **DIMALTF** and **DIMA-POST** dimension variables. This permits two dimension units to be shown side by side. You're not actually working in meters using this method and, except for editing the text, there's no way to suppress the actual unit measurement.

19.35 Multicolor layer faces

You can use **PFACE** to make different layers and colors. At any time when asked for Face 1, vertex 1:, you can type **COLOR** or **LAYER**, then change either one for the subsequent sections of **PFACE**.

19.36 Default options

Under the OPTIONS pull-down menu, **POP6**, you're given the ability to create a series of defaults. These defaults include **INSERT**, **DTEXT** and **HATCH**. From each of these choices you can enter defaults for such things as hatch pattern, rotations, scale, size of text, scale of insertion, etc.

These defaults don't work with the regular AutoCAD commands. That is, if you type in the command yourself or choose it from the tablet menu, the defaults will not be active. AutoCAD has written some AutoLISP programming in the other pull-down menus that does recognize these defaults. For example, if you choose the **HATCH** command from the DRAW pull-down, this command becomes an AutoLISP program.

What you were doing when you created the defaults for the **HATCH** options was to simply assign AutoLISP variables with certain values. For example, the following are the variables used by the AutoLISP program:

m:hp   Hatch pattern name

m:hs   Hatch style

m:hsc Hatch scale

m:hr   Hatch rotation

Unfortunately, these variables are alive only during the drawing session. When the drawing is ended, the value of the variables is lost.

If you want to set up these variables so they're the defaults for any drawing when using the pull-down menus, you can assign value to these variables in the ACAD.LSP file, so they will have the same value each time you go into the drawing editor. You don't have to set all the variables for this to work.

The following are the variables used for the other available options.

m:ibn Block name

m:ixs Block X scale

m:iys Block Y scale

m:izs Block Z scale

m:ira Block rotation angle

m:th   Text height

m:tr   Text rotation

19.37 **PEDIT won't work on PFACE**

CAUTION: If you decide to use **PFACE** as one of your meshes, **PEDIT** will not let you edit it in any way.

19.38 **Shade faster**

The **SHADE** command will shade faster as the viewport becomes smaller. Therefore, if you want the shading to take less time so you can preview it, you might consider creating a small viewport for shading purposes.

19.39 **Unshade**

There is no unshade command. And you're not permitted to work on entities while they're shaded. **UNDO** will not unshade it either. The only way to get control back to edit your drawing after a **SHADE** command is to do a **REGEN**.

CHAPTER 20

Intermediate Release 12

How Do You . . .

20.1 How do you change the prototype drawing?

When you create a new drawing you'll be given a dialogue box in which
to name the new drawing. Or, another option is **Prototype...** (See Figure
20-1.) Pick **Prototype...** This brings up a file dialogue box defaulting to the
drive and directory of your current prototype drawing, which is named in
the box to the right of **Prototype...** Use this file dialogue box the same as
any other to find and pick the prototype you want to use.

```
 File Assist Draw Construct Modify View Settings Render Model        AutoCAD
                                                                     * * * *
                                                                     ASE
                                                                     BLOCKS
                                                                     DIM:
                                                                     DISPLAY
                      Create  New  Drawing                           DRAW
                                                                     EDIT
                                                                     INQUIRY
          ┌──────────────────┐  ┌──────────────────┐                LAYER...
          │   Prototype...   │  │  acad            │                MODEL
          └──────────────────┘  └──────────────────┘                MVIEW
            ☐  No  Prototype                                         PLOT...
            ☐  Retain  as  default                                   RENDER
                                                                     SETTINGS
                                                                     SURFACES
          ┌──────────────────┐  ┌──────────────────┐                UCS:
          │ New  Drawing  Name...│  │  FLOORPL      │                UTILITY
          └──────────────────┘  └──────────────────┘
              ┌────────┐          ┌────────┐                         SAVE:
              │   OK   │          │ Cancel │
              └────────┘          └────────┘



 Command:
```

Figure 20-1: Prototype file dialogue box

20.2 How do you begin a drawing without a prototype drawing?

When you create a new drawing, you'll be given a dialogue box in which to name the new drawing. One of the options is a check box called **No Prototype**. Pick this box, and the new drawing will begin without a prototype drawing. This is especially useful if you want to begin a new drawing for the purpose of **DXFIN**, where generally no prototypes are allowed.

20.3 How do you create a library of prototype drawings?

One of the things about a library is that most of the items should be in the same place. Before Release 12, this didn't seem to matter for prototype drawings. When you used the command **NEWDWG=PROTODWG**, AutoCAD couldn't find PROTODWG unless it was your default prototype or you gave it the drive path specifications.

This is no longer the case. Now you can have a whole library of prototype drawings and can keep them in a single directory. Let's assume you call that directory **C:\PROTOTYPE**. Place all of your prototype drawings in this directory.

You must now tell AutoCAD not only where to find your prototype drawings but also which one is to be your default prototype drawing. To do this, begin a new drawing. You are given a **Create New Drawing** dialogue box. See Figure 20-1. Pick **Prototype...** This brings up a file dialogue box. Click in the **Directories** box until you have selected the **C:\PROTOTYPE** directory. This changes the default directory to **C:\PROTOTYPE**. Now pick in the **Files** box the drawing you want to be your prototype, and OK. This returns you to the **Create New Drawing**. Now pick the **Retain as Default** check box. Give the new drawing a name or not, it doesn't matter. What does matter this first time is that you OK the dialogue box.

You have just created a default prototype drawing. This could be ACAD.DWG or any other drawing you might want to be the default prototype. What's important here is that in creating it, you also told AutoCAD where to find all of your prototype drawings—as long as the default prototype drawing is in the same directory as the rest. From now on you can choose any prototype drawing just by picking **Prototype...** and then picking the drawing. The default directory will contain your prototype drawing library.

Remember that any drawing can be the default by picking the **Retain as Default** check box before you OK the new drawing.

20.4 How do you set AutoCAD for noun/verb selections?

The **Noun/Verb** method of selection is the default setting for AutoCAD Release 12. It is controlled by the **Entity Selection Settings** dialogue box. See Figure 20-2. This dialogue box is activated by the **DDSELECT** command. Here you can pick the check box called **Noun/Verb Selection**. If this checkbox is not picked, the pick box on the crosshairs will not be available. This is also your indication that **Noun/Verb Selection** is not available.

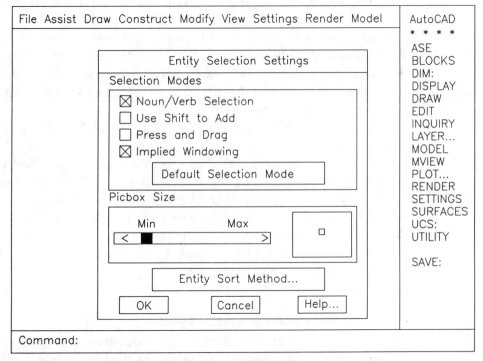

Figure 20-2: Entity Selection Settings dialogue box for DDSELECT

20.5 How do you change the size of the pick box?

You can now do this dynamically through the **Entity Selection Settings** dialogue box. It's activated by the **DDSELECT** command. See Figure 20-2. Look at the slide bar under **Pickbox Size**. As you move it to the left, the pick box in the square to the right gets smaller. As you move it to the right, the pick box in the square to the right gets larger. Once the settings are the way you want them, OK the dialogue box. You'll see the change immediately on the crosshairs.

20.6 How do you use automatic Windows and Crossings?

Creating a **WINDOW** or a **CROSSING WINDOW** are probably the two most common methods of selecting objects for editing. You have the ability to automatically start a **WINDOW** or a **CROSSING WINDOW** without having to pick or type W or C. All you have to do is pick an empty area where you are not picking an entity and you're automatically in the **WINDOW** or **CROSSING WINDOW** mode. If you pick from left to right you're creating a **WINDOW**. And if you pick from right to left, you're creating a **CROSSING WINDOW**. This feature is called **Implied Windowing**, meaning you're implying where the window will begin without having to actually tell AutoCAD you want to begin a window.

Implied Windowing is activated from the **Entity Selection Settings** dialogue box using the **DDSELECT** command. Once checked, **Implied Windowing** is active and ready to use. If **Implied Windowing** is not checked, it works almost as in the past.

If, when selecting objects the first time, you pick in an area without an entity, nothing will happen unless you've checked **Implied Windowing**. AutoCAD will respond with **0** selected. At that time, **Implied Windowing** is activated during this selection-set session only. This means that you can pick twice in an empty area and turn **Implied Windowing** on, even though it's turned off. Remember that you're turning it on only for that one command. You don't have to continually pick twice in an empty area during the command. Once activated, it stays activated during the rest of the command you're working with.

20.7 How do you do a Select All?

If you want to select every entity in your database at the **Select Objects** prompt, use the **All** command. Because of the power of this option you can't use the abbreviation A. Instead, you must spell out the word **All**. This is exactly the same as the AutoLISP function **(ssget"x")**.

There is a severe caution to this command. Unlike other selection set options, **All** has no respect for **Off** or **Frozen** layers. It will select every entity in the database, regardless of whether it's on a **Frozen** or **Off** layer. It will respect a **Locked** layer and not bother it. When you need it, it's a great option. But be careful when using it. The **(ssget"x")** AutoLISP function also respects locked layers.

20.8 **How do you do a Select All Except?**

Actually, there is no such command. But it can be accomplished by using the **All** options at **Select Objects** prompt, then R for Remove. Then you can Remove from the selection set through any of the available methods, such as **FENCE, WINDOW, CROSSING**, etc.

20.9 **How do you select layers in the Layer Control dialogue box?**

The **Layer Control** dialogue box is activated by typing **DDLMODES** from the Command line or choosing it from the SETTINGS pull-down as **Modify Layer....**

In order to operate on any layer you must first select the layer. See Figure 20-3. Notice that the **MECH** layer is highlighted. This is done simply by picking that layer. Every time a layer is picked, it acts like a toggle and highlights or unhighlights the layer. Once a layer is selected, other controls such as **Off, On, Freeze, Thaw, Lock, Unlock, Set Color, Set Linetype, Current** and **Rename** can be used. When any of these operations is used, they affect only the layers that have been highlighted.

You can also select all layers with the **Select All** box and clear all layers with the **Clear All** box.

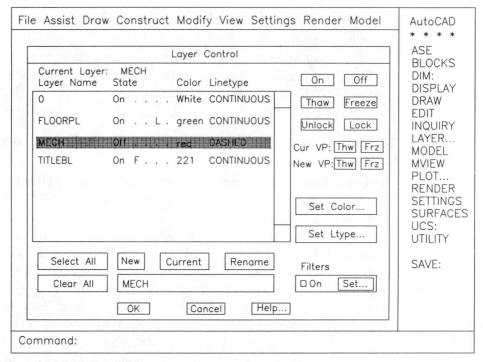

Figure 20-3: Layer Control dialogue box

20.10 **How do you turn layers on and off etc., in the Layer Control dialogue box?**

Once a layer has been highlighted by picking the layer, pick the appropriate operation. See Figure 20-3. You'll notice that the **On** will disappear if you're turning the layer off. An F will appear in one of the dots under **State** if you're freezing the layer, and an L will appear in one of the dots under **State** if the layer is locked.

20.11 **How do you create a new layer in the Layer Control dialogue?**

Pick the box to the right of **Clear All**. See Figure 20-3. Type in the name of the new layer and pick **New** in the box above it. Several layers can be typed at one time with a comma between them. Then pick **New**.

20.12 **How do you make a layer the current layer in the Layer Control dialogue box?**

Select and highlight one, and only one, layer. See Figure 20-3. The name of that layer appears in the box to the right of **Clear All**. Pick **Current** in the box above. The easiest way to do this is to first pick the **Clear All** box, then pick the layer you want to be current. You can't simply type in the name of the layer you want to be current; and if more than one layer has been selected, the layer name box is then empty. If you select the **Frozen** layer, you can't make it the current layer. You can make a **Locked** layer the current layer, but if you try to do so, you receive a warning at the bottom of the dialogue box that says "Warning: Current layer is locked." You can also make an **Off** layer the current layer. If you do so, you receive an Alert as you leave the dialogue box, advising you that the current layer is off.

20.13 **How do you set a layer color in the Layer Control dialogue box?**

Select and highlight the layers for which you want to set the color. Pick the **Set Color...** box. See Figure 20-3. This takes you to the **Color** dialogue box showing you all the colors available for your video card. You can pick other color boxes, and the color number will be selected, even though the specific color is not supported by your video card. If it's one of the colors above 8, the color number, not the name, will be assigned in the layer box.

20.14 **How do you set a layer linetype in the Layer Control dialogue box?**

Select and highlight the layers for which you want to set the linetype. Now pick the **Set Ltype...** box. See Figure 20-3. This takes you to the **Select Linetype** dialogue box, showing you the linetypes that are currently loaded. Linetypes in the ACAD.LIN file aren't available unless they've been loaded. So, you may want to load and then store them in the prototype drawing. If the linetype you want isn't shown, you must exit the **Layer Control** dialogue box and type the **LINETYPE** command, then load the linetypes you want.

20.15 How do you rename a layer in the Layer Control dialogue box?

Select and highlight the one layer you want to rename. Type the new name in the **Layer Name** box and then pick the **Rename** box at the bottom. The layer is then renamed.

20.16 How do you select large groups of layers in the Layer Control dialogue box?

Since layers must first be selected before any operations can be performed, you need procedures that will select layers as a group. This is especially true if you have large numbers of layers in the drawing. The two obvious boxes for doing this are the **Select All** box, which will select all layers available, and the **Clear All**, which will unselect all layers.

You also have the opportunity to select layers depending on their various properties. Let's say you want to select only the **Off** and **Locked** layers, so you can turn them on; but you didn't want to turn on the **Unlocked Off** layers. This is where **Filters** comes in.

First, pick the **Set...** box under **Filters**. See Figure 20-3. This takes you to the **Set Layer Filters** dialogue box. See Figure 20-4. The first five boxes are list boxes. This means that your choices are activated by picking the Down arrow in any of the boxes. Pick the **On/Off:** box and select **Off**. Pick the **Lock/Unlock:** box and select **Lock**. If you want to filter by name of layer, color or linetype, type in the appropriate box using all available wildcard options. If you want everything reset to **Both** and *, pick **Reset**. When your filters are set the way you want them, OK the dialogue. When you are returned to the **Layer Control** dialogue box, only the layers matching the filter criteria are displayed.

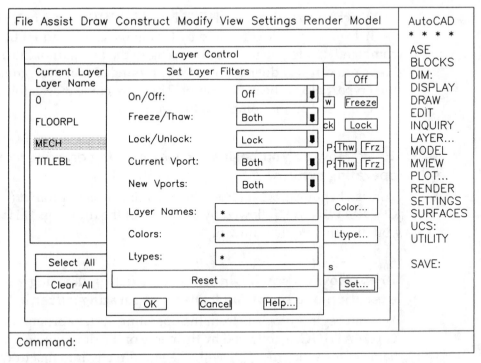

Figure 20-4: Layer Filters box over the Layer Control dialogue box

Once the filters are set, they can be activated or deactivated by picking the **On** check-box in the **Filters** box. If the **On** check-box is checked, the filters will bring up the appropriate layers. If the **On** check-box is not checked, the filters will relinquish control.

20.17 **How do you use the Help option?**

A new **Help** mechanism comes with AutoCAD Release 12. It appears on most of the dialogue boxes. And it's activated by simply typing **HELP** from the Command line.

When the **Help...** box is picked, a screen describing the dialogue box appears. You can then move forward or backward through the entire HELP file, in alphabetical order, by picking the **Previous** or **Next** boxes. If you need help on other things, pick the **Index...** box. This brings up a list of all AutoCAD commands. You can limit the names of the commands available in this list box by changing the pattern. For example, you can make the pattern **DD*** to secure only the dialogue box commands.

You can also activate the HELP by typing **'HELP** or **?**, or **'?**. You can get help on a specific command by typing the command **HELP**, then the command. (Note you're actually typing in the text part of the dialogue box.) You can also do it the other way around. Begin the command and then type **'help** at the next prompt. These are context-sensitive HELP screens based on the command that you're in.

20.18 How do you begin a new or existing drawing from the operating system?

You can begin AutoCAD from the operating system prompt (such as **C:\DRAWING>**), followed by the name of the drawing. This will take you directly into that drawing.

20.19 How do you begin a new or existing drawing with the execution of a script file from the operating system?

You can begin AutoCAD from the operating system prompt (such as **C:\DRAWING>**), followed by the name of the drawing, followed by the name of the script file. This will take you directly into that drawing and begin the script file on that drawing.

20.20 How do you begin an existing drawing with an initial view from the operating system?

From the operating system prompt (such as **C:\DRAWING>**) you can begin AutoCAD followed by the name of the drawing, followed by a comma and the name of the initial view.

CAUTION: When you install AutoCAD Release 12, you have the option of creating a startup BATCH file called **ACADR12.BAT**. This is generally a good idea, but the last statement in the BATCH file is ACAD %1 %2. This permits you to begin the BATCH file with up to two parameters, such as the name of the drawing and the script file. Unfortunately DOS doesn't permit a single name with a comma embedded. It will strip the comma and substitute a space. So, if you use the BATCH file to bring up a named view, it will try to bring up the view as a SCRIPT file—and, of course, not be able to find it.

20.21 **How do you make a drawing read-only after you're in it?**

A drawing can be changed to **read-only** after you're in it by simply changing the status of the system variable, **DWGWRITE**.

Type: `DWGWRITE <RETURN>`

Change the value to **0** and it's now **read-only**. Note: You can't save the drawing under its own name as a **read-only** drawing, because the mere fact that you're saving it under the same name is prohibited as **read-only**. Even if you save it to another name, the **DWGWRITE** variable is not held to **0**.

20.22 **How do you make a drawing available for saving if it's first brought up as read-only?**

Simply change the system variable, **DWGWRITE**, to **1**. You can now save the file under its own name.

20.23 **How do you open a damaged drawing?**

Simply open the drawing as you would any other. If AutoCAD detects that the drawing is damaged in any way, it will alert you to this fact and ask if you want it to try to recover the drawing. If you say **Yes** and the recovery is successful, the drawing will be loaded and displayed. Once it's loaded, save it so the recovery is permanent.

You can also pick **Recover** from the FILES pull-down menu. See Figure 20-5. Choose which file to recover. The only difference between **Recover...** and **Open...** is that **Recover...** goes through the recovery procedure initially, whether it detects anything wrong or not, and provides you with the recovery log.

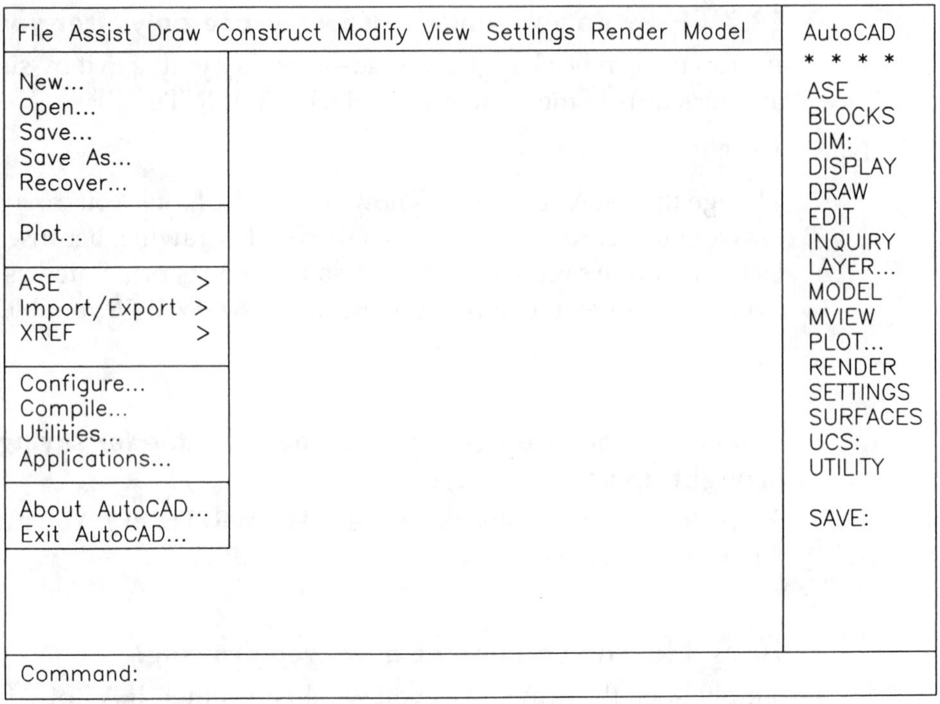

File Assist Draw Construct Modify View Settings Render Model		AutoCAD
New... Open... Save... Save As... Recover...		* * * * ASE BLOCKS DIM: DISPLAY DRAW
Plot...		EDIT INQUIRY LAYER...
ASE > Import/Export > XREF >		MODEL MVIEW PLOT... RENDER
Configure... Compile... Utilities... Applications...		SETTINGS SURFACES UCS: UTILITY
About AutoCAD... Exit AutoCAD...		SAVE:
Command:		

Figure 20-5: Release 12 FILE pull-down menu

20.24 How do you set the time interval for automatic saving?

SAVETIME is a system variable that maintains the automatic time interval between automatic saves. If you don't want AutoCAD to automatically make a saved copy of your current drawing, set this system variable to **0**. The time interval is in minutes. The clock for the **SAVETIME** begins when a change in the drawing is made; it will automatically save the drawing if no save has been made within the interval of time.

The interval between automatic saves can also be set while configuring AutoCAD. This is item number 7 (**configure operating parameters**), then item 7 again (**automatic-save feature**). The system variable, **SAVETIME**, is global in that it's saved to the configuration rather than being local within the drawing.

20.25 How do you set the name of the saved file used for automatic saving?

AutoCAD Release 12 out of the box uses AUTO.SV$ as the default name of the file used for automatic timed saves. You can change this default name with the system variable, **SAVEFILE**. You can also change it during configuration. Item number 7 (**configure operating parameters**), then item number 7 again (**automatic-save feature**). Here you have the opportunity to name the file to be used.

20.26 How do you reconfigure AutoCAD from inside a drawing?

AutoCAD Release 12 gives you the opportunity to configure or reconfigure within the drawing. You can even reconfigure your current video. When you exit the CONFIGURATION menu, AutoCAD will use your new video configuration even on the same drawing. Nothing is lost. And just in case there is an accident and you can't get back into your drawing, Auto-CAD makes sure that the Autosave feature has backed up your drawing one last time before taking you into the CONFIGURATION menu.

To enter the CONFIGURATION menu, type **CONFIG** from the Command line or pick **Configure** from the FILE pull-down menu.

20.27 How do you force a configuration of AutoCAD from the operating system?

You can begin the configuration of AutoCAD without first entering into the drawing editor. This is especially important if you've created a configuration that makes it impossible to enter the drawing editor first. For example, you may have changed your video card, but AutoCAD still thinks you have the old card in your machine.

Type: `ACAD -r <RETURN>`

This will begin AutoCAD at the CONFIGURATION menu. Once you exit the menu, AutoCAD will proceed to bring up the drawing editor.

20.28 How do you unlock files?

Files are locked, as in previous versions of AutoCAD, if file locking is enabled through the configuration of AutoCAD or if you are using the network version of AutoCAD. From time to time, AutoCAD will abort abnormally and leave a lock on a file or files. If you know that no one is currently using that file, you can remove the lock.

This is done by picking **Utilities...** from the FILE pull-down menu or by typing **FILES** from the Command line. This brings up a **File Utilities** dialogue box. Pick the **Unlock File...** box from this dialogue box. You now have a file dialogue box called **File(s)** to unlock. Here you can choose the file, change the directory, select all files or type in the name of the file. This will remove the lock from any files selected.

20.29 How do you rename objects with the dialogue box?

Type **DDRENAME** from the Command line. This brings up a dialogue box from which you can pick any of the following to rename:

Block
Dimstyle
Layer
Ltype
Style
Ucs
View
Vport

Once one of these is chosen, the available names are placed in a list box. Pick one of the available names and fill in the **Rename to:** box.

CAUTION: You must pick the **Rename to:** box after typing in your new name. This does the actual renaming. Now OK the entire box to make it permanent.

20.30 How do you rename files?

This is done by picking **Utilities...** from the FILE pull-down menu or by typing **FILES** from the Command line. This brings up a **File Utilities** dialogue box. Pick **Rename File...** box, and up comes a dialogue box called **Old File Name**. Here you can change pattern, drive and directory. Find the file you want to rename and pick it, then OK. Enter the name of the new file in the dialogue box called **New File Name**.

20.31 How do you enable grips?

Grips are enabled through the **Grips** dialogue box. Activate this either by typing **DDGRIPS** from the Command line or by selecting **Grips** from the SETTINGS pull-down menu. See Figure 20-6.

Check the box to enable grips and/or enable grips within blocks.

20.32 How do you change grip colors?

The actual color of the grips is controlled through the **Grips** dialogue box. Activate this either by typing **DDGRIPS** from the Command line or by selecting SETTINGS from the pull-down menu. See Figure 20-6.

File Assist Draw Construct Modify View Settings Render Model	AutoCAD

```
                                                          AutoCAD
                                                          * * * *
                                                          ASE
                                                          BLOCKS
                              Grips                        DIM:
                                                          DISPLAY
     Select  Settings                                     DRAW
                                                          EDIT
        ⊠    Enable  Grips                                 INQUIRY
                                                          LAYER...
             Enable  Grips  Within  Blocks                MODEL
     Grip  Colors                                         MVIEW
                                                          PLOT...
        Unselected...        5   —   Blue                 RENDER
                                                          SETTINGS
        Selected...          1   —   Red                  SURFACES
                                                          UCS:
     Grip  Size                                           UTILITY

        Min          Max                                  SAVE:
       <                >         □

          OK        Cancel       Help...


Command:
```

Figure 20-6: Grips selection box

There are two types of grips: those that simply show where the grips are, and those that show that a grip has been selected. Pick either the **Unselected...** box or the **Selected...** box, and a color map appears. Any color you pick will be the color used for the grips.

20.33 **How do you change the size of grips?**

The size of the little grip squares is controlled through the **Grips** dialogue box. Activate this either by typing **DDGRIPS** from the Command line or by selecting SETTINGS from the pull-down menu. See Figure 20-6.

At the bottom of the dialogue box is a slide bar labeled **Min** and **Max**. To the right is a picture of the actual size of the grip. Move the slide bar to the left or right, and see the size of the grip change. When the grip is the correct size, OK the dialogue box.

20.34 **How do you use grips, and what are they?**

Grips are little boxes that appear on entities. Depending on the kind of entity, they will be available at different sites. For example, for Lines they appear at the endpoint and the midpoint. For Circles they appear at the center and the quadrants. For Polylines they appear at the vertices, and for Text and Blocks they appear at the insertion point.

Grips are used as a quick base-point for the following commands: **STRETCH, MOVE, ROTATE, SCALE** and **MIRROR**.

20.35 **How do you activate grips?**

First and foremost, grips must be enabled. Do this through the **GRIPS** system variable or the **DDGRIPS** dialogue box. Second you must be using **Noun/Verb Selection** mode. Select this through the **DDSELECT** dialogue box. You know if you're using **Noun/Verb**, because a pick box is always available at the intersection of your crosshairs.

To activate a grip, simply pick an entity. Then the grips appear.

20.36 **How do you get rid of grips once they appear?**

If you've picked an entity and the grips appear, ^c^c will generally turn them off. Also, any other command that modifies the drawing will generally remove the grips from the screen.

20.37 **How do you stretch with grips?**

Begin by picking one or more entities before you enter a command. The grips will then appear. Pick any grip. As you get close to it, notice that you're snapped to the grip. Once you pick a grip, it turns colors to identify that a base point has been selected.

Once a base point has been selected, you're automatically in the **STRETCH** mode. This is something of a misstatement, because the only thing you're stretching is the point where the grip lies. If this happens to be a line, and the base point is the midpoint, simply pick another place on the screen, and the entire line moves. If the base point is the endpoint of the line, pick another point on the screen and the endpoint of the line moves, "stretching" the line to that point and at that angle.

So as you can see, the result differs, depending on which base point you pick. Generally, if you pick the midpoint of a line or the center of a circle or the insertion point of text or block, **STRETCH** has the ability to move the circle or line.

20.38 **How do you copy entities using grips?**

Begin by picking one or more entities before you enter a command. The grips will then appear. Pick any grip. This is the base point.

Before you pick the next point on the screen, hold down the Shift key. Now the entity is copied rather than moved. By picking another point, you're automatically in a **MULTIPLE COPY** mode. This copying will continue until you <RETURN>.

20.39 **How do you copy and offset fixed distances using grips?**

Begin by picking one or more entities before you enter a command. The grips will then appear. Pick any grip. This is the base point.

Before you pick the next point on the screen, hold down the Shift key. Now the entity is copied to the new point. Continue to hold down the Shift key and point to another approximate location. Not only is it copied to that location, but it is automatically copied the same distance as the original offset from the base point. The snap increments are thus set to the same offset.

20.40 How do you move an entity with grips?

Begin by picking one or more entities before you enter a command. The grips will then appear. Pick any grip. This is the base point.

You are automatically in the **STRETCH** mode. Therefore, you must shift to the **MOVE** mode. Do this by typing **MO** or by picking **MOve** from the side-screen menu, or toggle to **MOve** by using <RETURN> or the space bar.

Remember that you can move an entity by picking the center or mid-point while in the **STRETCH** mode and the entire entity will move. The **MOVE** mode on the other hand will permit you to use any base point and will move the entity.

20.41 How do you move and copy using grips?

Begin by picking one or more entities before you enter a command. The grips will then appear. Pick any grip. This is the base point.

This is a combination of **COPY** (remember to hold the Shift key down when you pick the second point) and **MOVE**. Begin by picking the base point. Then pick **MOve**, or toggle to **MOve** by using <RETURN> or the space bar. Before you pick the second point, hold the Shift key down, and the entity will be copied instead of moved.

You can do this with **STRETCH**, but only if the base point is the mid-point or the center. Otherwise it will copy at the stretched angle, depending on which base point is picked.

20.42 How do you rotate using grips?

Begin by picking one or more entities before you enter a command. The grips will then appear. Pick any grip. This is the base point.

Type **RO** or pick **ROtate** from the side-screen menu. You can also toggle through the options by using <RETURN> or the space bar. The entity will rotate around the base point.

20.43 How do you scale using grips?

Begin by picking one or more entities before you enter a command. The grips will then appear. Pick any grip. This is the base point.

Type **SC** or pick **SCale** from the side-screen menu. You can also toggle through the options by using <RETURN> or the space bar. The entity will be scaled relative to the base point.

20.44 **How do you mirror using grips?**

Begin by picking one or more entities before you enter a command. The grips will then appear. Pick any grip. This is the base point.

Type **MI** or pick **MIrror** from the side-screen menu. You can also toggle through the options by using <RETURN> or the space bar. The entity will use the base point as the beginning of the mirror line. If you pick the second point, the entity will be mirrored and the first entity erased. If you hold the Shift key down, the entity will be mirrored, but the first entity will not be erased.

20.45 **How do you change properties with a dialogue box?**

From the Command line, type **DDCHPROP** or pick **Change** from the MODIFY pull-down menu. This is a cascading menu. Pick **Properties** from the submenu.

With this dialogue box you can change color, layer, linetype and thickness. See Figure 20-7. Pick **Color...**, and it brings up the standard color chart for you to pick from. Pick **Layer...**, and you're taken to the standard **Layer** dialogue box. Notice how even stand-alone dialogue boxes can be nested within other stand-alone dialogue boxes for a complete system. Pick **Linetype...**, and you have a list box of the linetypes that are currently loaded. Pick any of these linetypes, and a picture of the linetype is displayed at the top of the box. For **THICKNESS**, just type in the thickness value.

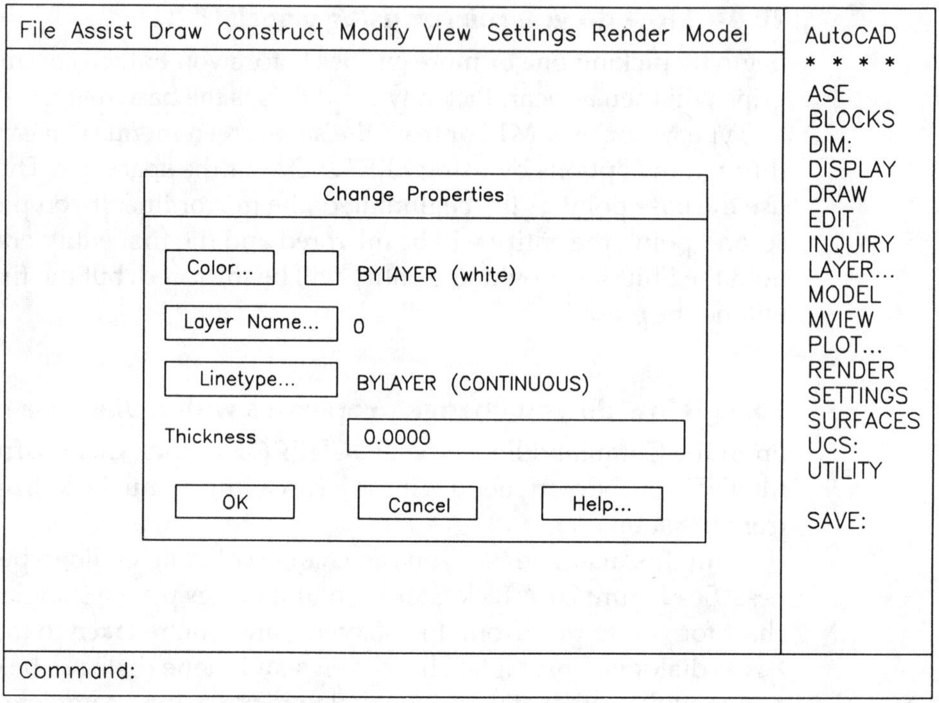

```
  File Assist Draw Construct Modify View Settings Render Model  │ AutoCAD
                                                                │ * * * *
                                                                │ ASE
                                                                │ BLOCKS
                                                                │ DIM:
            ┌─────────────────────────────────────────┐        │ DISPLAY
            │            Change  Properties            │        │ DRAW
            │                                          │        │ EDIT
            │                                          │        │ INQUIRY
            │  ┌──────────┐  ┌──┐                      │        │ LAYER...
            │  │ Color... │  │  │  BYLAYER (white)     │        │ MODEL
            │  └──────────┘  └──┘                      │        │ MVIEW
            │  ┌──────────────┐                        │        │ PLOT...
            │  │ Layer  Name..│  0                      │        │ RENDER
            │  └──────────────┘                        │        │ SETTINGS
            │  ┌──────────────┐                        │        │ SURFACES
            │  │  Linetype... │  BYLAYER (CONTINUOUS)  │        │ UCS:
            │  └──────────────┘                        │        │ UTILITY
            │  Thickness       ┌──────────────────┐    │        │
            │                  │ 0.0000           │    │        │ SAVE:
            │                  └──────────────────┘    │        │
            │  ┌────────┐   ┌──────────┐  ┌─────────┐  │        │
            │  │   OK   │   │  Cancel  │  │  Help...│  │        │
            │  └────────┘   └──────────┘  └─────────┘  │        │
            └─────────────────────────────────────────┘        │
                                                                │
  ───────────────────────────────────────────────────────────────────
  Command:
```

Figure 20-7: DDCHPROP dialogue box

20.46 **How do you create text styles and choose fonts?**

From the DRAW pull-down menu, select **Text**. This is a cascading menu item. Select **Set Style...** from the **Text** submenu. All of the AutoCAD standard fonts are in icons. To the left of the icons is a list box with the names of the fonts. By picking one of the icons, the corresponding item in the list box is chosen. When you have the right font, OK the dialogue box. Also, you could double-click on the icon or the name itself. The rest of the questions are the same style as those in previous versions.

The font and the style now carry the same name. You might want to change the name using the **DDRENAME** command. Pick **Style** and re-name it to something more meaningful and appropriate. By using these two dialogue boxes in combination, you have the ability to pick the font from icons and still give a meaningful name to the style.

20.47 How do you set the current text style?

Pick **Entity Modes...** from the SETTINGS pull-down menu. From this dialogue box you can select the setting for the next entities created by **Color...**, **Layer...**, **Linetype...** and **Text Style....** Pick the **Text Style...** box. All available text styles will be listed in a list box. In the corner is an example of three letters of what the text will look like. You don't have the opportunity here to change any of these items; this only gives you the opportunity to select a text style for the next **TEXT** or **DTEXT** command. The **Show All...** box permits you to see the entire alphabet, using the selected font. The **Sample Text:** box permits you to type in several letters. Although you can type more, it will display only the first three or four.

20.48 How do you insert blocks using a dialogue box?

Pick Insert... from the DRAW pull-down menu or type **DDINSERT** from the Command line. See Figure 20-8. Picking **Block...** will list all of the block definitions in the drawing. Picking **File...** will list all the .DWG files through a standard file dialogue box.

CAUTION: **Pick File...** won't necessarily bring up the block from a file if there's already a block definition by the same name in the drawing. If you want the block brought in already exploded, check the **Explode** box at the bottom. You can also prespecify the scale and insertion point, if the **Specify Parameters on Screen** box is not checked. This is of limited use, since what you really need is the ability to pick the insertion point and then have the predetermined scale and rotation automatically follow. But the **Specify Parameters on Screen** box is an all or nothing.

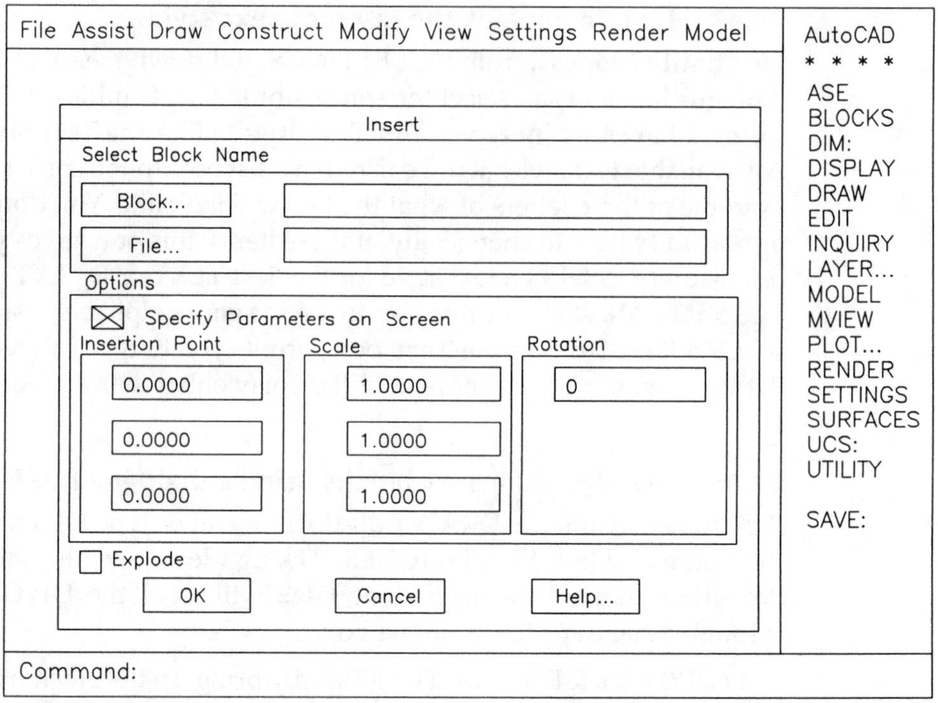

File Assist Draw Construct Modify View Settings Render Model

AutoCAD
* * * *
ASE
BLOCKS
DIM:
DISPLAY
DRAW
EDIT
INQUIRY
LAYER...
MODEL
MVIEW
PLOT...
RENDER
SETTINGS
SURFACES
UCS:
UTILITY

SAVE:

Insert

Select Block Name

Block...

File...

Options

☒ Specify Parameters on Screen

Insertion Point   Scale   Rotation

0.0000   1.0000   0

0.0000   1.0000

0.0000   1.0000

☐ Explode

OK   Cancel   Help...

Command:

Figure 20-8: DDINSERT dialogue box for blocks

20.49 How do you insert a .DWG file into a drawing under a different block name?

From time to time, you may already have a block definition in your drawing by the same name as a .DWG file on disk. The file on disk may look
different from the block definition of the same name. Although inserting
name= will redefine the current block definition with the .DWG file, that
isn't the thing to do in this case.

You want each of the entities, even though they have the same name, to
appear differently in the drawing. Therefore, they must have different
block definition names. But the name on disk is the same as the name in
the current drawing.

Here's how you solve the problem. Pick **Insert...** from the DRAW pull-down menu or type **DDINSERT** from the Command line. See Figure 20-8. Now pick the **File...** box. This will bring up the .DWG files. Pick the one you want to insert. Once it's picked, the same name will be repeated in the **Block Text** area. Now it's a simple case of changing the name of the **Block Text** area. The .DWG file will create a new block definition name in the drawing and proceed to insert the drawing into the current file under a different name.

20.50 How do you create attributes with a dialogue box?

Pick **Blocks** from the side-screen menu, then **ATTDEF**, then **Dialogue** (or type **DDATTDEF** from the Command line). This is simple and straightfor-ward. See Figure 20-9. **Invisible**, **Constant**, **Verify** and **Preset** are check boxes in the upper left. **Tag**, **Prompt** and **Value** are text boxes in the upper right. **Justification** and **Text Style** are pop-up list boxes that limit your choices to predefined options. The **Pick Point <**, **Height <** and **Rotation <** boxes permit you to either type in the information or to pick those boxes individually. Picking the **<** on each box takes you immediately to the drawing, temporarily removing the dialogue box and permitting you to pick the point. Then, after you pick the point, the dialogue box will be returned.

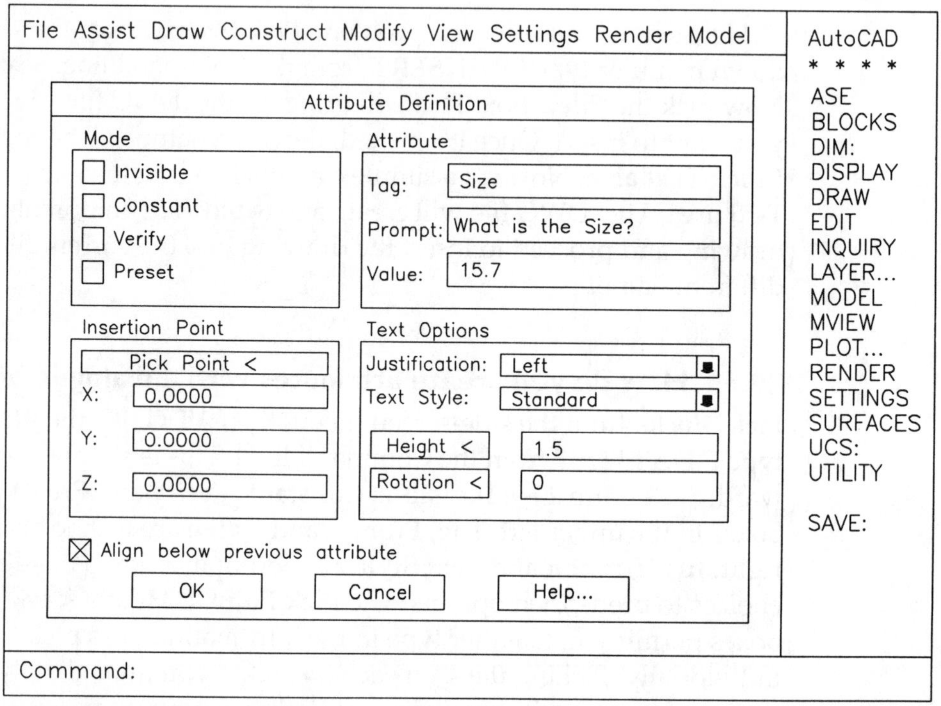

Figure 20-9: DDATTDEF dialogue box for attribute creation

Align Below Previous Attribute will place the attribute text below the previous attribute.

20.51 How do you extract attributes with a dialogue box?

Pick **Utility** from the side-screen menu, then **ATTEXT**, then **Dialogue** (or type **DDATTEXT** from the Command line). See Figure 20-10. The three types of extract files are radio buttons. This means that this is an either/or choice. **Select Objects** < lets you select objects straight from the screen once this box is picked. The < on each box signals that, once the box is picked, the drawing comes up immediately, letting you select the objects. After selection, the dialogue box is returned.

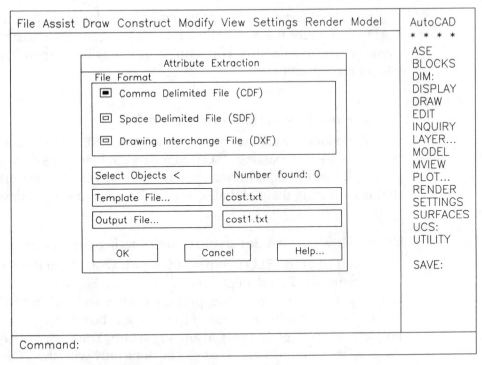

Figure 20-10: DDATTEXT dialogue box for attribute extraction

The **Template File...** is a file dialogue box where you can choose the template file you want to use. You can't create a template file at this point, however; this is done with a text editor.

The **Output File...** is also a file dialogue box. You can choose an existing file or enter a new name.

20.52 How do you name a plotter configuration?

First, let's differentiate between a *plot* configuration and a *plotter* configuration. A plotter configuration is the actual plotter you're going to use, such as a Calcomp 2036 or a Hewlett Packard EXL. The plotter configuration includes serial port selection and other device-specific items of information. The plot configuration, on the other hand, is, collectively, all the parameters you've set. It does not include the plotter you've chosen.

This is done the same as always—through the AutoCAD configuration. Remember that the configuration can be accomplished while you're still in the drawing, by typing **CONFIG** <RETURN> from the Command line.

The only difference is that at the end of the plotter configuration Auto-CAD asks you for the name of the plotter. You can either accept the default name or type in a name of your choice. You may have up to 30 different plotter configurations.

20.53 How do you do a printer plot?

There's no longer a command for printer plot. **PRPLOT** has been replaced with the all-encompassing **PLOT** command. Whether it's a *printer* plot or a *plotter* plot will be determined by which plotter you choose during the plot dialogue. During the plot dialogue you choose your output device.

20.54 How do you determine the plotting output device?

When you enter the **PLOT** command or pick **Plot...** from the FILES pull-down menu, the **Plot** dialogue box appears. See Figure 20-11. For the output device you want to use, pick the **Device and Default Selection...** box in the upper left-hand side of the dialogue box. Here you're given a list box with the plotter that you've already set up. You can't modify any of the available plotters here. That can be done only with the **CONFIG** command.

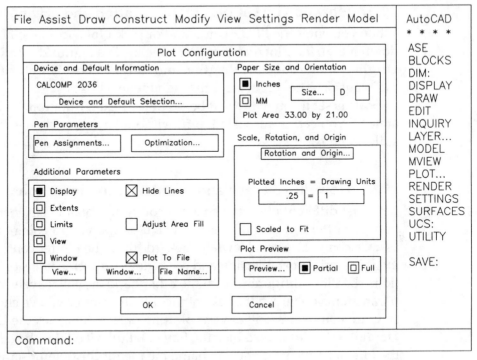

Figure 20-11: Release 12 Plot dialogue box

20.55 How do you set pen assignments?

When you enter the **PLOT** command or pick **Plot...** from the FILES pull-down menu, the **Plot** dialogue box appears. See Figure 20-11. Pick **Pen Assignments...**. A **Pen Assignments** dialogue box is essentially a list box showing the available colors and their pen assignments. If you want to change one, pick the color-pen line; the color, pen, width, linetype and speed appear in the text boxes to the right. Notice that now you can change the pen width for individual colors, if you want to—a feature that finally makes this option useful. The items that are available or grayed out depend on the driver that's in use.

20.56 How do you set the paper size?

When you enter the **PLOT** command or pick **Plot...** from the FILES pull-down menu, the **Plot** dialogue box appears. See Figure 20-11. **Pick Size...** from the **Paper Size and Orientation** area. In addition to the standard paper sizes, you now have a place to store up to five user sizes. The paper sizes available are still limited by the driver in use.

20.57 How do you set plot scale, rotation and origin?

When you enter the **PLOT** command or pick **Plot...** from the FILES pull-down menu, the **Plot** dialogue box appears. See Figure 20-11. **Rotation and Origin** is set through the **Rotation and Origin...** box. Simply set the proper radio button. The origin is set through the text boxes.

Scale is set through the text boxes in the **Scale, Rotation, and Origin** area. Or you can check **scaled to fit** without having to change the other scale text box.

20.58 How do you save and recall plot configurations?

Let's first differentiate between a *plot* configuration and a *plotter* configuration. A plotter configuration is the actual plotter you're going to use, such as a Calcomp 2036 or a Hewlett Packard EXL. The plotter configuration includes serial port selection and other device-specific items of information. The plot configuration, on the other hand, is, collectively, all the parameters you've set. It does not include the plotter you've chosen.

Once you have set all of your plotting parameters, pick the **Device and Default Selection...** box. Pick the **Save Defaults To File...** box. Here, with the **File** dialogue box, you can name the file for the default settings. You can have as many of these files as you want. They all have the extension of .PCP.

In order to recall an existing plot configuration, pick the **Get Defaults From File...** box. Here, with the **File** dialogue box, you can pick the .PCP file that contains your settings.

20.59 How do you preview a plot?

When you enter the **PLOT** command or pick **Plot...** from the FILES pull-down menu, the **Plot** dialogue box appears. See Figure 20-11. First, pick the **Partial** or **Full** radio button. The **Partial** button will give you only an outline of where your drawing will appear on the paper. The **Full** button will give you a picture of your complete drawing as it will actually appear on the paper.

Now pick the **Preview...** box. The drawing will now appear looking exactly as it will on the paper. If you've chosen the **Full** button, you also have the option of ZOOMing around the plotted drawing. Pick **Pan and Zoom**. This works exactly like **Dynamic Zoom**. Your pick button will size your ZOOM window and the <RETURN> button will actually ZOOM. You now have the option of **Zoom Previous** or **End Preview**.

20.60 How do you actually begin the plot from the Plot dialogue box?

This is easy. Pick OK. But be very careful here. OK is the <RETURN> default.

20.61 How do you prevent the Plot dialogue box from coming up?

If you don't want the **Plot** dialogue box to come up each time, and you'd prefer to answer the plot questions the older way, change the value of the **CMDDIA** system variable from **1** to **0**.

More Steps to Success

20.62 Noun/Verb — A different way to choose

Noun/Verb is the reference order you use to either a) choose the command first, then the object; or, b) pick the object first, then the command. Simply put, it refers to the order in which you choose your selection set.

AutoCAD always requires you to issue the command, such as **ERASE**, then **Select Objects**. Well, **ERASE** is the verb, and the objects you select are the nouns. Thus you've been performing all of your editing commands in Verb/Noun order.

AutoCAD Release 12 now permits you to perform your editing commands in Noun/Verb order if you want. What this means is that you can pick the selection set first, then choose the command.

Here's how it works. Begin with some lines on the screen. Now pick those lines. Don't worry about the little squares that appear. They're called grips. Notice that the lines highlight even though you're not in a **Select Objects:** command. Once the objects have been selected, type **ERASE** <RETURN> from the keyboard, and the entities are erased. You can also pick **Erase Select** from the MODIFY pull-down menu.

Noun/Verb will work on the following commands: **ARRAY, BLOCK, CHANGE, CHPROP, COPY, DDCHPROP, DVIEW, ERASE, HATCH, LIST, MIRROR, MOVE, ROTATE, SCALE, STRETCH, WBLOCK** and **EXPLODE**.

Noun/Verb will *not* work on the following commands: **BREAK, CHAMFER, DIVIDE, EDGESURF, EXTEND, FILLET, MEASURE, OFFSET, PEDIT, REVSURF, RULESURF, TABSURF,** and **TRIM**.

Noun/Verb is active only when you have the pick box at the intersection of your crosshairs. This is controlled by the **Selection Mode** dialogue box (**DDSELECT**).

20.63 Select entities in the order of their creation

One of the most frustrating things in AutoCAD is the order in which the **WINDOW** or **CROSSING WINDOW** selects entities. Normally, this is in the reverse order in which they were created. The reason this is frustrating is that, if you're selecting text to write out to an ASCII (DOS text file) file, you generally can't use a **WINDOW** around the text or it will be written out in reverse order. With AutoCAD Release 12 there's a solution. You can set the sort order for the entities in a wide variety of situations.

To get there you have to use the **DDSELECT** command, which brings up the **Entity Selection Settings**. See Figure 20-12. At the bottom of the dialogue box is the **Entity Sort Method**. Once picked, this brings up another dialogue box, as shown in Figure 20-12. If the checkbox is checked, the entities will be sorted in the order in which they were created. For example, if you checked **Redraws**, AutoCAD would redraw the screen with the entities in their creation order.

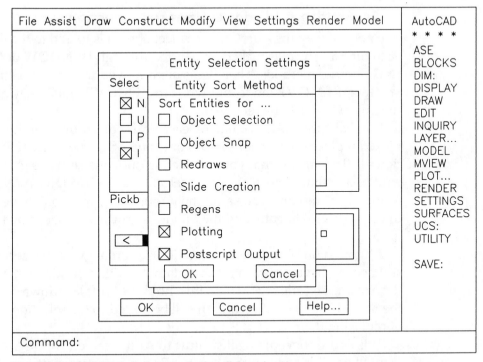

Figure 20-12: DDSELECT Entity Selection Settings dialogue box

For our example, you would want to check the **Object Selection** box. There's one caution. Sorting large numbers of entities every time you redraw the screen or select objects could cost you a lot of time. Therefore these boxes should be checked only when you need them, such as in our example. Then they should be unchecked under normal running.

20.64 **Shift to Add adds entities to a selection set**

The normal way for AutoCAD to select objects is to add to the selection set each time an entity is picked or selected through **WINDOW** or **CROSS- ING** or other methods. Then items are removed from the selection set if you're in **REMOVE** mode, but while in **REMOVE** mode, they're added to the group that is to be removed.

You have the option of having each entity or group of entities you've picked replace the previous entity or group of entities picked in the selec- tion set. This means that you're selecting only one entity or group of entities at a time. This way, if you select by a **CROSSING WINDOW** a group of entities and you select the wrong ones, you don't have to remove them—just select again, and the previous group is replaced by the current group.

Although this can save time and is an alternate way of selecting, you still need to have a way to make certain that other entities can be added to the existing selection set. To do this, hold the Shift key down as you select the next group of entities, and they'll be added to the selection set instead of replacing them.

This entire concept is called **Shift to Add**. You tell AutoCAD that you want to use this concept through the **Entity Selection Settings** dialogue box. This is accessed as **DDSELECT**. See Figure 20-2. If the **Use Shift to Add** box is checked, the **Shift to Add** method of selecting will be used. If **Use Shift to Add** box is not checked, AutoCAD will select objects the same as always.

20.65 **Put a Fence around your objects**

Fence is one of several new selection set options in AutoCAD Release 12. Anytime at the **Select Objects:** prompt, choose or type **F** for **Fence**. A **Fence** is a straight line or a series of straight lines that select any objects that touch the **Fence**. Therefore all you have to do is draw a line (**Fence**) across any entities you want to select. You must <RETURN> after you have drawn your **Fence** line before the entities will be selected. You will still be at the **Select Objects:** prompt.

20.66 Polygon WINDOWS and CROSSINGS

Wouldn't you like to have an irregular-shaped **WINDOW** or **CROSSING WINDOW**? That's what the **Wpoly** and **Cpoly** options for **Select Objects** do. At the **Select Objects:** prompt, choose or type **WP** or **CP**. AutoCAD responds with **First Polygon Point:** This is similar to **First Corner**. Pick a point; then after the second point is picked, AutoCAD closes the polygon. You may continue to pick other points, thus expanding the polygon. This way you can create an irregular-shaped **WINDOW** around the exact entities you want to select. You must <RETURN> after you have drawn your **Wpoly** or **Cpoly** lines before the entities will be selected. You will still be at the **Select Objects:** prompt.

The only difference between **WP** and **CP** is that **WP** works like a **WINDOW** (all entities must be completely inside to be selected), and **CP** works like a **CROSSING WINDOW** (entities may be inside or just cross the window lines to be selected).

20.67 Speed up selecting objects

Every time you select objects by picking, AutoCAD looks through the database to find the entity selected. If you pick 20 entities one at a time in a large drawing, this could be very time-consuming.

The **M** or **Multiple** options at **Select Objects:** permits you to pick as many entities as you want without AutoCAD looking through the database. Once you've picked a group of entities, <RETURN>, and they'll highlight, and the **Select Objects:** prompt will continue. In this way, there is only one check of the database instead of 20. If in a large drawing it takes two seconds to scan the database, this can save some time.

Note that when you use the **M** option, the entities you pick do not highlight. Once you've picked the entities and <RETURN>, they will highlight. Once you're in the **M** option you can't select by any method such as **WINDOW** until you've pressed <RETURN> to leave the **M** option. This method is only for picking entities.

20.68 Not all grips showing are necessarily selected

Just because the grips are showing doesn't necessarily mean that the entities are selected. They must also be highlighted to be selected. If this is the case, **MOVE**, **MIRROR**, **ROTATE** and **SCALE** will operate on all the entities that are highlighted. **STRETCH**, on the other hand, will only move one of the entities—the one with the base point.

20.69 **You can unselect entities with grips**

You turn on the grips by selecting. Remember that this can be done through **Implied Windowing**. Just because the grips are showing doesn't mean that the entities are necessarily selected. But what if you turn the grips on and they are selected, but you don't want them as part of the selection set? How do you turn the selection off? Well, that's easy. Just press Ctrl-C to cancel the selection. The grips will remain on, but the entities are just not highlighted. ^c^c will turn off both the highlighted selections and the **Grips**.

20.70 **UNDO Auto creates groups from menu items**

A new option has been added to the **UNDO** command. This is the **Auto** option under **UNDO**. Your choice is **Off** or **On**. If **Auto** is **Off**, it works the same as previous versions of AutoCAD. If **Auto** is **On**, any item selected from the menu, no matter how complex, will be treated as one group. Therefore, it will take only an **UNDO 1** to undo it.

20.71 **Virtually no more regens while ZOOMing**

The virtual screen in AutoCAD Release 12 has been increased from a few thousand integer pixels to 4,294,967,296. What this means is that you can go almost as deeply as you want **ZOOM**ing into a drawing without kicking in a **REGEN**.

Try this experiment. Start with a **ZOOM All** screen:

Type: Zoom 100 <RETURN>

Keep repeating this by making the number larger and larger. See by how large a **ZOOM** factor you can **ZOOM** before a **REGEN** kicks in. As you **ZOOM** in very deeply you might want to draw something in color on your screen as a future reference point. You should be able to go 500,000 to 750,000 before a **REGEN** kicks in. In AutoCAD Release 11 you would do well to get past 50 to 80 without a **REGEN**.

To have unlimited **ZOOM** you must be using a 32-bit 4.2 video driver.

20.72 **Save your ZOOM All as a view called ZA**

This is an old trick from the days before **ZOOM Vmax** came around in AutoCAD Release 11. Then **ZOOM Vmax** became the **ZOOM All**, but without a **REGEN**. Now, with the increased size of the **Virtual Screen**, the **ZOOM Vmax** is not a **ZOOM All**. It makes the screen too small.

Therefore, a good solution is to first do a **ZOOM All**, which should be about the same as your limits. Then do a **View Save** to **ZA** as the name. Then instead of a **ZOOM Vmax**, do a **View Restore** to **ZA**. Since you're still well inside your virtual screen, this becomes your **ZOOM All** without a **REGEN**.

20.73 **An easier way to HATCH**

There is a new **HATCH** command that can better be described as a complete hatching environment. It's called **BHATCH**. Let's take a look at it one step at a time.

Type: BHATCH <RETURN>

This begins the initial hatching dialogue box. See Figure 20-13. Initially, there are two things you'll want to do. First, you'll want to pick your hatch pattern. So to start things off, pick **Hatch Options....**

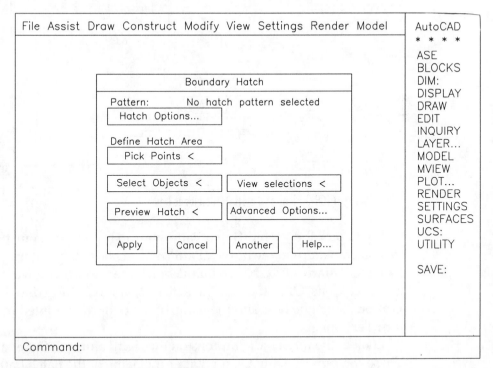

Figure 20-13: Boundary Hatch dialogue box

Now take a look at Figure 20-14. This is your **Hatch Options** dialogue box. Look at the two radio buttons in the top left. **User-Defined Pattern (U)** will automatically choose a U hatch. At that point, **Scale** will not be available but **Spacing** will be. Also **Double Hatch** will be available as a check box if you want cross hatching. You can also change the angle in the **Angle Text** box.

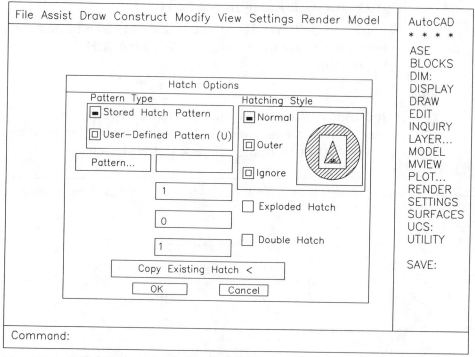

Figure 20-14: HATCH Options of the BHATCH dialogue box

If you pick the **Stored Hatch Pattern** radio button, you must either type in a hatch pattern name or pick **Pattern...** to choose the pattern you want. Pick the **Pattern...** box. Now you may pick the pattern you want from the available icons. Once the pattern is picked, you're returned to the **Hatch Options** dialogue box, and the name of the pattern is printed in the **Pattern Text** box.

Look at the three radio buttons on the right: **Normal, Outer** and **Ignore**. These correspond with ,**O** and ,**I** after the name of the hatch pattern. When you select one of these buttons, the appropriate form of the pattern will appear.

If you don't know the name of a hatch pattern (or you don't want to look it up), and the pattern you want is already in your drawing, pick **Copy Existing Hatch <**. This will exit you to your drawing and permit you to pick the existing hatch. You're then returned to the **Hatch Options** dialogue box, and the name of the pattern is supplied for you.

Once you've selected the hatch patterns, scale and angle, OK this dialogue box. This returns you to the **Boundary Hatch** dialogue box. See Figure 20-13.

Now the real fun begins. You haven't told AutoCAD what to hatch. Pick the **Pick Points <** box. You're taken to the drawing. Unlike the old method of defining your hatch area, simply pick an empty spot inside the boundary. All area boundaries now highlight. It automatically ignores any non-enclosed areas. Not only that but you can continue picking other areas, and their enclosed areas will also highlight. To remove any selected areas, type **U** and they will be removed in the reverse order in which they were selected. Once the areas have been selected, confirm by <RETURN>.

If you're unsure what was selected you can see the selection again by picking the **View Selections <** box. <RETURN> when you're through viewing the selections.

Now here's the important feature. Pick the **Preview Hatch <** box, which then does a temporary hatch of the areas. Let's say the scale wasn't correct; press <RETURN> to return to the dialogue box. Then pick **Hatch Options...** to change the scale and OK. Now do your **Preview Hatch...** again. Continue this until it's right. Once it's correct, pick the **Apply** box. Now your hatch is complete, and you're exited from the dialogue box. Notice that it didn't have to rehatch. It simply used the last **Preview** if no changes were made. The preview became permanent.

If you want to apply the hatch and remain in the dialogue box, pick **Another** rather than **Apply**.

20.74 **BHATCH Advanced Options**

Advanced Options... is a pick box from the **Boundary Hatch** dialogue box. There are four options available. The two radio buttons are **From Everything on Screen** and **From Existing Boundary Set**. It's entirely possible that, in a large drawing, you wouldn't want AutoCAD to search the entire drawing for the necessary boundaries. Therefore, you can limit it to a given area to save time.

To do this you must first create a new boundary set. This is simply the area in which AutoCAD will look for the boundaries, not the boundaries themselves. Pick the **Make New Boundary Set <** box. You can now use a **WINDOW** and outline the area. Confirm when you have finished. When you return to the **Advanced Options** dialogue box, the **From Existing Boundary Set** radio button will be active.

When you hatch, AutoCAD doesn't normally preserve the temporary polyline it used to do the hatch. But you have it saved as a new entity in your drawing. To do this, check the **Retain Boundaries** box.

The final **Advanced** option is **Ray Casting**. Your choices are:

Nearest

X+

X–

Y+

Y–

When AutoCAD looks for the initial boundary, it begins with the closest line to the point you picked. It then turns left and attempts to find an enclosed area. This is the **Nearest** option. This should be suitable under most situations, except in very narrow areas. You have the ability to tell AutoCAD to begin the search by not going to the nearest boundary but to first look to the right, left, up or down. These are the **X+** (right), **X–** (left), **Y+** (Up) and **Y–** (Down) options.

20.75 **Create a polyline from a boundary**

If you don't want to **HATCH** anything using the **BHATCH** command, but you would like to create a polyline using the same rules for boundaries, use the **BPOLY** command. This brings up a dialogue box that's identical to the **Advanced Options...** in the **BHATCH** command. The only difference is that you don't have to hatch anything and retain the polyline in order to get the polyline.

20.76 **New system variables for hatching**

There are several new system variables that maintain the current status of the last hatch. They are:

HPNAME	Pattern name and style
HPSCALE	Scale
HPANG	Angle
HPSPACE	Spacing for U Hatch
HPDOUBLE	**0** for No and **1** for Yes in crosshatch

In addition to these system variables, this information is saved in the extended entity data in the hatching block reference.

20.77 **Be careful with the <RETURN> when plotting**

It's easy to accidentally press <RETURN> and begin the actual plot before you're ready. The only things that will cancel the plot and return you to the drawing screen are Ctrl-C and Esc.

20.78 **Shortcut to plotting**

If you know that all your parameters for plotting are set correctly and that you're using the correct plotter, you don't have to answer a thousand questions and <RETURN> several times to begin the plot.

Type: `Plot <RETURN> <RETURN>`

Your plot is running.

20.79 **Problem with incompatible plotter and file**

You may have saved a plot configuration file that matched a specific plotter. For example, you've saved **pen assignment** while configured under a pen plotter. Now you've changed to a printer as your output device. If you try to load the plot configuration that contains the pen assignment you'll get an error that states that the file and the current plotter are incompatible.

The solution is to set the correct plotter device first before reading in the plot configuration.

20.80 **Plotting without a license**

If you begin AutoCAD from the operating system with **ACAD -p**, you're in **PLOT ONLY** mode. It doesn't count against your number of log-ins. You also don't have to bring up the actual drawing to the screen. Therefore, it doesn't cost you a **REGEN**.

ADVANCED

CHAPTERS 21 - 32

CHAPTER 21

Advanced Drawing

How Do You . . .

21.1 How do you create a new hatch pattern?

Creating your own hatch patterns isn't the easiest thing in the world, but it's by no means impossible. You should usually append any new hatch patterns that you create to the text file ACAD.PAT. This file is supplied to you by AutoCAD and contains all of the standard hatch patterns.

The first line of the text file should begin with an * followed by the name of the hatch pattern. This is the name by which it will be called up. Follow the name with a comma and a brief description of the pattern (these are optional). When you enter ? for **HATCH**, you'll be given the names of all the available patterns in ACAD.PAT. Each name will be followed by a brief, one-line description. The following shows where that description comes from:

```
*dashdots,Series of dashes and dots
```

Dashdots is the name of the new hatch pattern. The next and subsequent lines will describe a single drawing pass over the hatch pattern. In this first simple example, we use only a single pass, so we get only one line. (Each of these passes represents a single line in the pattern text file, and is called a "line family.")

There are four parts to the drawing line:

```
Angle, X,Y Origin, Offset-x,Offset-y, Penlift pattern
```

Let's look at an example:

```
0, 0,0, 0,.5, .5,-.25, 0,-.25, 0,-.25
```

This pattern draws a dash, dot, dot at a 0-degree angle with a .5-unit separation between each line unit. See Figure 21-1.

<u>0</u>, 0,0, 0,.5, .5,-.25,0,-.25,0,-.25

The first 0 (the one underlined above) determines the angle at which the line is to be drawn; in this case, it's to be drawn horizontally. Don't confuse this with the angle of the hatch pattern; that's normally controlled by the **HATCH** command. Think of a hatch pattern as a successive series of lines that is drawn from left to right, then from down to up.

All hatch patterns have a common point of origin. Since this point of origin is the same throughout, you're assured that the patterns will line up.

0, <u>0,0</u>, 0,.5, .5,-.25,0,-.25,0,-.25

The next part, 0,0, indicates the beginning point of origin for the first pass of the hatch pattern (a *pass* is a successive series of lines that fills the entire area to be hatched). All the lines go in the same direction.

Let's assume that you want to draw a pattern of Xs. The first pass would draw lines angled at 45 degrees. Once all of those lines were drawn, the next pass would draw another set of lines angled at 135 degrees through the first set, thus forming a series of Xs. Each pass requires a complete pattern description line of its own. The first pass will almost always be at point 0,0, although this isn't required.

0, 0,0, <u>0,.5</u>, .5,-.25,0,-.25,0,-.25

0,.5 is the offset-x and offset-y (the *AutoCAD Reference Manual* calls these delta-x and delta-y, but "offset" seems more descriptive). Remember that the hatch pattern will begin at an arbitrary origin and proceed to draw a group from left to right, then advance upward in the Y direction. 0,.5 means that each successive line in the pattern will move to the right 0 units and up .5 units. This results in the .5 spacing between the lines. The offset is relative to the initial angle given in the line, so that angle forms the X axis for the offset.

It's easy to understand why you offset the Y value—to give you spacing between the lines. But why would you want to offset the X value and what effect does that have? Imagine a brick wall. Each successive line of bricks is offset to the right a little to create a pattern. So .5,1 would space the bricks upward by one unit and every other line would offset .5 to the right of the origin, creating a stepladder effect.

```
0, 0,0, 0,.5, .5,-.25,0,-.25,0,-.25
```

The final group, underlined above, is the actual dash and dot pattern. It's the same pattern used for creating line types. All positive numbers represent the number of unit spacings that the pen is held down. A 0 represents a dot. The negative numbers represent the number of unit spacings that the pen is lifted up. So in this pattern it's down .5, up .25, down for 0 (which is a dot), up for .25, down 0 and up .25. Therefore, it produces a pattern of dash, dot, dot, dash, dot, dot, etc.

By simply placing the following lines at the end of ACAD.PAT, we've created our own hatch pattern:

```
*dashdots,Series of dashes and dots

0, 0,0, 0,.5, .5,-.25,0,-.25,0,-.25
```

Use this as you would any other standard AutoCAD pattern. If you want, you can make an icon for the pull-down menu (see Tip 23.6) and include this pattern. Figure 21-1 shows what the pattern looks like.

Figure 21-1:
Hatch pattern

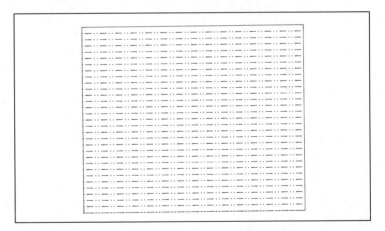

21.2 How do you set an automatic scale for hatch patterns?

Have you ever tried to hatch something, only to find out that it was in the wrong scale? It would be nice to be able to know ahead of time exactly what scale factor you should use for each hatch pattern. By combining LISP63 (see Tip 13.26) with a standard scale factor for each pattern, you'll know exactly what to set it to.

LISP63 lets you measure the area to be hatched and gives you an appropriate scale. The only problem is that it doesn't fit all hatching patterns; the program is designed for a standard of one unit, and some hatching patterns look better if they're larger. LISP63 gives you a factor number that's just fine for a U hatch; but for something like ESCHER you should multiply this number by six.

But how do you discover and remember the factor number for each hatch pattern? In order to find the right number, simply try different ones. The following list gives a suggested factor for each of AutoCAD's standard patterns. The easiest way to keep track of them is to add the factor to each pattern's description line in ACAD.PAT.

Angle	6	Honey	9
Ansi 31-38	6	Hound	12
Box	6	Insul	12
Brass	6	Line	6
Brick	9	Mudst	6
Clay	12	Net	9
Cork	15	Net3	12
Cross	15	Plast	12
Dash	15	Plast1	12
Dolmit	12	Sacncr	12
Dots	6	Square	12
Earth	6	Stars	9
Escher	6	Steel	15
Flex	9	Swamp	6
Grass	6	Trans	9
Grate	18	Triang	9
Hex	9	Zigzag	12

If you've measured the object to be hatched with LISP63, it uses **d** as a global variable. So when **HATCH** asks you for a scale factor, enter **(* d 12)** if the factor is 12.

See LISP97 in Tip 21.14 for a sample program that uses 6 as a scale factor (remember to run LISP63 beforehand). Or you may want to combine LISP63 with LISP97.

21.3 How do you draw a floor plan by only entering the dimensions?

If you're an architect or a builder and you work with floor plans, you often have to draw a series of boxes over and over again. This can be the simplest kind of *parametric processing*—which is where you give AutoCAD the information and it does the drafting.

Of course, AutoCAD depends on AutoLISP to store the information that's given, to ask the questions and then to actually draw the item. Your job is simply to tell AutoLISP where to place the object, and the variations on this are limitless.

See LISP98 in Tip 21.15 for a useful little program that asks you the width and height of a room and then lets you place it anywhere you want, thus building a complete floor plan, room by room.

21.4 How do you generate sequential numbers and save them with a drawing?

A good way to do this is to save the highest number with the AutoCAD user system variable **USER1**, assuming that the numbers you want to generate are integers. You're actually given five integer system variables and five real system variables to use. To secure the last number,

Type: SETVAR <RETURN>

Response: New value for USERI1 <25>

Whatever appears in the brackets is the last number used. Add 1 to this number and press <RETURN>. Now you can use the resulting number.

LISP99 in Tip 21.16 is a program that secures the number, increments by 1, and sets the system variable with the new number.

21.5 How do you digitize with a changed UCS?

You can actually use your digitizer in a UCS. Of course, your digitizer is still a 2D input device. Assume that you've calibrated your tablet in WCS plan view. Now change your **DVIEW** and create an appropriate UCS. Even though you're picking points in what seems to be plan view on your digitizer, you're actually picking points with the appropriate elevation according to the new UCS. This allows you to digitize in 3D.

More Steps to Success

21.6 Directory prefixes

The environment variable **ACAD** lets you call blocks up from a predetermined directory. But if you try to create a block and **WBLOCK** it, you still have to give it a directory prefix name.

Since AutoLISP lets you put strings together, you should create a series of short little programs that will combine the name you give with the directory prefix. See LISP100 in Tip 21.17.

21.7 Combine text with hatches

If you need to put text or other entities inside a hatch pattern, be sure you make room for the text first. Draw a rectangle inside the entity that's to be hatched. Then enter the text and erase the outline of the rectangle; see Figure 21-2 for an example.

This method gives you total control over the size and shape of the blank area around the text. If you write text in first and then hatch, AutoCAD controls the blank area. This method is especially important to follow if you have multiple lines of text.

Figure 21-2: Text
with hatches

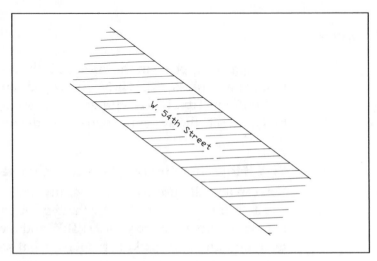

21.8 Hatch files

Although you can create your own files for hatch patterns, we strongly recommend that you add your hatch patterns to ACAD.PAT. If you don't, you must have no more than one hatch pattern per file, and the file and the hatch pattern must have the same name; the file name must end in .PAT.

21.9 Place objects

There's a way to space objects equally along unique curves and areas. By using polylines and polyarcs, you can create a path you want the objects to follow. Then use either **MEASURE** or **DIVIDE** to insert the objects, and they'll follow the path of the polyline. When you're through, erase the polyline.

21.10 Offset PLINE first

If you're using **MEASURE** and **DIVIDE** to insert blocks, you might want to insert the blocks some distance from the polyline. To do this, offset the polyline first and use the second polyline for the **MEASURE** and **DIVIDE**. Then erase the second polyline.

21.11 SPLINE only part of a polyline

Sometimes you want only part of a polyline to be a **SPLINE** curve (of course, if it's a single polyline, all of it will curve). The easiest way is to issue **BREAK @** at the beginning or at the end of the curved area. The curved area will then be a single entity and you can **SPLINE** it.

Then **BREAK @** the splined section somewhere in the middle; this makes it permanent. Otherwise, when you rejoin the lines, AutoCAD decurves the spline when it's joined to the rest of the lines. Finally, join all the segments with **PEDIT**. The entity is now considered both a polyline and a polyarc.

21.12 Be careful with line types

Some early versions of Release 10 have a problem with the dialogue box for **Line Types**. As you go to the second page, AutoCAD may freeze if all the line types aren't loaded. If this is happening to you, the fix is to load all the line types first in all prototype drawings.

21.13 A better way to SKETCH

If you're going to use **SKETCH** to put in contour lines, set the system variable **SKPOLY** to 1. This makes all the segments polylines. Then use a large increment. Finally, curve-fit the entity.

 AutoLISP Programs

21.14 Hatch scale (LISP97)

This program works in conjunction with LISP63. Once LISP63 is run and the entity is measured, a scale factor is produced. This program multiplies that scale factor by 6. We suggest that you write similar programs for **(*d 9)**, **(*d 12)** and **(*d 15)** to cover all of the standard hatch patterns. See Tip 19.2, on automatic scaling for hatch patterns.

Listing:
```
(defun c:lisp97 ()
    (setq hch (getstring "\nHatch pattern "))
    (command "hatch" hch (* d 6) pause pause)
)
```

To Use: Load LISP97.LSP.

Type: LISP97 <RETURN>

Response: Hatch pattern:

Enter the name of the hatch pattern. The rest of the prompts are the same as for **HATCH**, but the scale has been computed.

21.15 Floor plan (LISP98)

This program lets you enter the length and width of a room. The room is drawn, and you can drag it into position. To build a floor plan, repeat the program for each room.

Listing:
```
(defun c:lisp98 (/ pnt1 w has pnt2 pnt3 pnt4)
    (setq os (getvar "osmode"))
    (setvar "osmode" 0)
    (setq pnt1 (getpoint "\nPick a working point "))
    (setq w (getdist "\nWidth "))
    (setq has (getdist "\nLength "))
    (setq pnt2 (list (car pnt1) (+ has (cadr pnt1))))
    (setq pnt3 (list (+ w (car pnt2)) (cadr pnt2)))
    (setq pnt4 (list (car pnt3) (cadr pnt1)))
    (command "pline" pnt1 pnt2 pnt3 pnt4 "c")
    (setvar "osmode" 32)
    (command "move" pnt1 "" pause pause)
    (setvar "osmode" os)
)
```

To Use: Load LISP98.LSP.

Type: LISP98 <RETURN>

Response: Pick a working point:

Pick a point in an empty area of your screen.

Response: Width:

Enter the width of the room.

Response: Length:

Enter the length of the room.

Response: Base point of displacement:

Pick one of the corners of the room at the point you want to move it.

Response: Second point of displacement:

You can now move the room into position.

21.16 **Auto number and store (LISP99)**

This program increments the next available number and stores it with the drawing.

Listing:
```
(defun c:lisp99 ()
    (setq n (getvar "useri1"))
    (setq n (+ n 1))
    (setvar "useri1" n)
    (princ "\n ") (princ "\n ")
    (princ "\nThe next number is ")
    (princ n)
    (princ)
)
```

To Use: Load LISP99.LSP.

Type: `LISP99 <RETURN>`

Response: `The next number is 5.`

21.17 **Directory prefix (LISP100)**

This program lets you enter the name of a **WBLOCK** file or anything else that requires the path to a specific directory. When the name is asked, type (**d**). The name will have the directory path added to it. You should modify this program for your own directory path.

Listing:
```
(defun d ()
    (setq a (getstring "\nName "))
    (setq a (strcat "/detail/" a))
)
```

To Use: Load LISP100.LSP.

Type: `WBLOCK <RETURN>`

Response: `File name:`

Type: `(d) <RETURN>`

Response: `Name:`

Enter the name of the file. The proper directory will be added to it.

CHAPTER 22

Advanced Editing

How Do You . . .

22.1 How do you select only certain entities?

With one line of AutoLISP, you can filter in large groups of entities from the selection set; this is called the *filter option*. Using the proper associative codes and placing your parameter in quotes lets you tell AutoCAD to include all matching entities in the drawing database as part of the selection set. See Tip 31.103 for a list of the associative codes.

Let's say you want all entities on a layer called DIMSX. Any time you are in a command for which AutoCAD asks you to select objects,

Type: `(ssget "x" '((8 . "DIMSX"))) <RETURN>`

Only those on that layer will be highlighted. If you want to further limit the selection set to only the circles on layer DIMSX,

Type: `(ssget "x" '((8 . "DIMSX") (0 . "CIRCLE")))`

If you want multiple AND conditions, simply continue to filter until all entities desired are selected, then confirm. See LISP101 in Tip 22.12 for an automated filtering program.

 RELEASE 12   Gives you the option of **Select All** at the **Select Objects** prompt. This is the same as the AutoLISP filter function of (**ssget "x"**). See Tip 20.7.

22.2 How do you mirror a block so you can explode it?

The problem with mirroring a block is that once it's mirrored, it can't be exploded. If you explode the block first, then mirror the entities, you won't have this problem.

But then the original block is no longer a block. A quick fix for this is to copy the block on top of itself at the same insertion point. Then issue **ERASE Last**. The block will disappear. Explode the original block and mirror it. Be sure to answer Y to the question **Delete old object?** You now have only the exploded and mirrored object. To get the old block back, use **OOPS**. See LISP102 in Tip 22.13.

22.3 **How do you explode a block that's already mirrored?**

If a block is already mirrored, you have a slightly more difficult problem. You can't explode any block whose X, Y and Z values are different. Therefore, you must restore the X, Y and Z values to equality. The figure will flip; explode the object and flip it back.

This sounds easy, but there are really several very complicated steps. It's easier to use LISP103, but here are the procedures if you want to do it by hand or write your own AutoLISP program.

Step 1: Secure the entity list.

Type: `(setq a (entget (car (entsel)))) <RETURN>`

Response: `Select objects:`

Pick the mirrored block you want to explode.

You'll see the entity list on the screen. Associative 41 should be –1.0. This is because 41 is the X, 42 is the Y and 43 is the Z.

Step 2: Make associative 41 equal to 1.0.

Type: `(setq al (subst '(41 . 1.0) '(41 . -1.0) a)) <RETURN>`

Step 3: Update the database with the new entity list.

Type: `(entmod al) <RETURN>`

Your object has now flipped.

Step 4: Explode the object.

Type: `EXPLODE LAST <RETURN>`

Your object is now exploded.

Step 5: Remirror the new object, deleting the old.

Type: `MIRROR <RETURN>`

Response: `Select objects:`

           Select the object with a **WINDOW** or **CROSSING**, and confirm.

Response: `First point of mirror line:`

Type: `(cdr (assoc 10 a1)) <RETURN>`

           This is the old insertion point.

Response: `Second point:`

Type: `(polar (cdr (assoc 10 a1)) (+ (dtr 90) (cdr (assoc 50 a1))) 5)`

Response: `Delete old objects?`

Type: `Y <RETURN>`

           You've now successfully exploded the mirrored object.

22.4 How do you do a BREAK @ on a circle?

Have you ever tried to break a circle into two arcs? Try using **BREAK @** and see what happens. But there are times when you need two arcs instead of a circle, even though the arcs touch.

Break the circle at two points (the break will go counterclockwise). Part of the circle will disappear. Then do an **ARC** using **SEC** (start, end, center) to replace the missing arc area. See LISP104 in Tip 22.15.

22.5 How do you rejoin two arcs back into a circle?

We're assuming that the two arcs make a perfect circle; if they were broken with the **BREAK** tip above, they do. *Don't* try to join them back with **PEDIT JOIN**. Although this seems to work, they can't ever be split, since they won't be a circle but a closed polyarc.

The easiest way to get your circle back is to compute the radius and center point. Then erase both arcs and redraw the circle.

See LISP105 in Tip 22.16.

More Steps to Success

22.6 Make tablet ERASE like pull-down ERASE

One of the conveniences of the pull-down menus is that AutoCAD has programmed the **ERASE** command on the pull-downs as an auto erase. The **ERASE** on your tablet is a large, two-block area. You can easily divide this area into an ordinary **ERASE** on the left side and an auto **ERASE** on the right side.

You'll find two lines in Tablet 4 that look like this:

```
$S=X $S=ERASE ^C^CERASE
```

```
$S=X $S=ERASE ^C^CERASE
```

The first line is the left side of the **ERASE** block, and the second line is the right side. Change the second line to

```
*^C^C$erase si auto
```

22.7 Always place Undo Marks

With all the new features and procedures available, especially since Release 10, it's more important than ever to place **Undo Marks** before beginning a new routine. Getting into the habit of doing this will make your **Undo** much easier.

LISP106 in Tip 22.17 is a quick AutoLISP routine that lets you place an **Undo Mark** by typing M and a space. Then you can go back quickly with an **Undo Back**.

22.8 Scratch pad

If you've ever wanted to bring in another drawing or use a scratch pad to build something without hurting your existing drawing, now you can. Use either **VIEW** or **VPORTS** and create an area far from your drawing and toggle there as necessary.

VPORTS works better because it doesn't reissue a regen, and it's easier to pick things up and move them into position.

22.9 **Strange results with polar array**

You can get unusual results with multiple entities in a polar array if all you do is window them. For best results, first block the group. Then **ARRAY** the block as you like. Finally, explode the block. In this way you maintain the same spatial relationships between the entities.

22.10 **BREAK, TRIM or FILLET**

Here are some general guidelines on when to use **BREAK**, **TRIM** or **FILLET 0**. Use **TRIM** as your first choice when you have a cutting edge; it is the fastest for breaking multiple objects along the same cutting edge. Try **FILLET 0** whenever two straight lines intersect and cross each other, and you want them to stop at the intersection. Use **BREAK** as a last resort, since it takes the most picks.

22.11 **Dangerous CHANGE**

Be careful when using the **CHANGE POINTS** command—make sure **ORTHO** is off. If **ORTHO** is on, the entities will be forced vertically or horizontally, regardless of where you pick.

AutoLISP Programs

22.12 **Entity filters (LISP101)**

This program lets you easily select large groups of entities by filtering. Any time you're asked to select objects, enter **(ss)** <RETURN>. Then enter the associative code and the code parameter. For example, if you wanted everything on layer DIMSX, you'd enter an 8 and then **DIMSX**.

Listing:
```
(defun ss (/ cd par)
    (setq cd (getint "\nEnter Associative Code "))
    (setq par (getstring "\nEnter parameter "))
    (ssget "x" (list (cons cd par)))
)
```

To Use: Load LISP101.LSP.

This program is generally used within an AutoCAD command that asks you to select objects. The items you may filter and their codes are:

0   Entity type
2   Block name
6   Line type name
7   Text style name
8   Layer name

For this example, let's say you wanted to change all entities with dashed line types to layer ALT.

Type: CHANGE <RETURN>

Response: Select objects:

Type: (ss) <RETURN>

Response: Enter Associative Code:

Type: 6 <RETURN> (This is the code for the line type name.)

Response: Enter parameter:

Type: DASHED <RETURN>

Response: 2 found.
        Select objects:

Type: <RETURN> to confirm

Response: Properties/<Change point>:

Type: P <RETURN>

Response: Change what property
        (Color/Elev/LAyer/LType/Thickness)?

Type: LA <RETURN>

Response: New layer:

Type: ALT <RETURN>

All entities that had dashed line types have been changed to layer ALT.

22.13 Mirror block as exploded (LISP102)
Use this routine whenever you mirror blocks so that they're exploded before they're mirrored, without harming the original block.

Listing:
```
(defun c:lisp102 (/ os pt1 a sss)
     (setq os (getvar "osmode"))
     (setvar "osmode" 512)
     (setq pt1 (getpoint "\nPick block "))
     (setvar "osmode" os)
     (setq a (ssname (ssget pt1) 0))
     (command "copy" pt1 "" pt1 pt1)
     (command "erase" "last" "")
     (redraw a 1)
     (command "explode" a)
     (setvar "osmode" os)
     (princ "\n ") (princ "\n ")
     (prompt "\nSelect objects to be mirrored ")
     (setq sss (ssget))
     (command "mirror" sss "" pause pause "Y")
     (command "oops")
)
```

To Use: Load LISP102.LSP.

Type: LISP102 <RETURN>

Response: Pick block:

Pick the block you want mirrored.

Response: `Select objects to be mirrored.`
`Select objects:`

Select the block with **WINDOW** or **CROSSING**. Remember that the block is exploded at this point, but it won't remain that way.

Response: `First point of mirror line:`

Pick the first point of the mirror line just as in the **MIRROR** command.

Response: `Second point:`

Pick the second point of the mirror line just as in the **MIRROR** command.

The block is now mirrored. The original block is still a block, but the mirror image is exploded into its various entities.

22.14 Explode mirrored blocks (LISP103)

This program will explode blocks after they've been mirrored, as long as they weren't mirrored along the Z axis.

Listing:
```
(defun c:lisp103 (/ a a1 ang pt1 pt2)
    (setq a (entget (car (entsel))))
    (setq a1 (subst '(41 . 1.0) '(41 . -1.0) a))
    (entmod a1)
    (command "explode" (cdr (assoc -1 a1)))
    (setq ang (cdr (assoc 50 a1)))
    (setq pt1 (cdr (assoc 10 a1)))
    (setq pt2 (polar pt1 (+ (dtr 90) ang) 5))
    (princ "\n ") (princ "\n ")
    (princ "\nPut a window around the flipped object ")
    (command "mirror" "w" pause pause "" pt1 pt2 "y")
)
(defun dtr (angg)
    (* pi (/ angg 180.0)))
```

To Use: Load LISP103.LSP. Begin with a block that's already been mirrored.

Type: `LISP103 <RETURN>`

Response: `Select objects:`

Pick the block you want to explode. It will be flipped and exploded.

Response: `Put a window around the flipped object.`
`First corner:`

Select the flipped object. Make sure you get all of it, and confirm. The block is back where it was before, but now it's exploded.

22.15 Break @ circle (LISP104)

This program lets you separate a circle into two arcs by picking two points on the circle.

Listing:
```
(defun c:lisp104 (/ os pt1 pt2 a pt3)
    (setq os (getvar "osmode"))
    (setvar "osmode" 512)
    (setq pt1 (getpoint "\nFirst break in circle "))
    (setq pt2 (getpoint "\nSecond break in circle "))
    (setq a (entget (ssname (ssget pt1) 0)))
    (setq pt3 (cdr (assoc 10 a)))
    (command "break" pt1 pt2)
    (command "arc" pt1 "e" pt2 pt3)
    (setvar "osmode" os)
)
```

To Use: Load LISP104.LSP. Begin with a circle.

Type: `LISP104 <RETURN>`

Response: `First break in circle:`

Pick a point on the circle.

Response: `Second break in circle:`

Pick another point on the circle. The circle looks the same, but it's broken into two arcs.

22.16 Restore two arcs to a circle (LISP105)

If you've used LISP104 to break a circle into two arcs, this program joins two arcs back into a circle. It can also complete a circle from an arc.

Listing:
```
(defun c:lisp105 (/ os pt2 a pt1 ra pt3)
     (setq os (getvar "osmode"))
     (setvar "osmode" 512)
     (setq pt2 (getpoint "\nPick one of the arcs "))
     (setq a (entget (ssname (ssget pt2) 0)))
     (setq pt1 (cdr (assoc 10 a)))
     (setq ra (cdr (assoc 40 a)))
     (command "erase" pt2 "")
     (setq pt3 (getpoint "\nPick other arc "))
     (setvar "osmode" os)
     (command "erase" pt3 "")
     (command "circle" pt1 ra)
)
```

To Use: Load LISP105.LSP. Begin with one or two arcs.

Type: LISP105 <RETURN>

Response: Pick one of the arcs:

Pick either arc. That arc will disappear.

Response: Pick other arc:

Pick the remaining arc if you started with two. If you started with only one arc, pick any blank place on the screen or press <RETURN>. Now the circle is restored or the single arc is turned into a completed circle.

22.17 Undo Mark (LISP106)

This is a quick program that lets you place an **Undo Mark** easily by typing M <RETURN>. Use it often. Then when you have to go back to the last mark or marks, use **Undo Back**.

Listing:
```
(defun c:m ()
    (command "undo" "m")
)
```

To Use: Load LISP106.LSP.

Type: M <RETURN>

The mark has been placed. To undo back to the mark,

Type: UNDO B <RETURN>

Notice that you can't type only U.

CHAPTER 23

Advanced Viewing

How Do You . . .

23.1 How do you reprogram digitizer or mouse buttons?

You need to use a text editor in ASCII format. Digitizer and mouse buttons are controlled by the AutoCAD menu, which is in the ACAD.MNU file. Of course, you can do this with any menu file.

The first line of the file is ***BUTTONS**, which denotes the buttons section. The pick button isn't changeable, so the next lines are button 2, button 3, etc. You program buttons the same way as you do any macro. You can also add AutoLISP programs to buttons.

23.2 How do you add an item to the screen menu?

The screen menu is controlled by the menu that's in effect at the time. The screen menu is generally found in the file ACAD.MNU, which you can change with a text editor in ASCII format. Before you begin working with screen menus, you should understand their organization and how one screen menu can call another.

The major sections of the screen menu have headers, each of which begins with *** . The major sections are as follows:

***SCREEN	Screen menu area.
***POP	Pull-down menu area. This is followed by a number from 1 to 10.
***ICON	Icon menu area.
***BUTTONS	Button menu area.
***TABLET	Tablet menu area. This is followed by a number from 1 to 4.
***AUX1	Auxiliary button menu.

You can also create submenus at any place in a file. They must begin with ** . For example, you could create a submenu called **SPECIAL and write it as **SPECIAL 3. The 3 following the name of the submenu tells AutoCAD to begin the menu three lines down. This leaves room for the standard three lines found at the top of most menus. These are

```
[AutoCAD]
```

```
[* * * *]
```

The lines "Previous" and "Last" appear at the bottom of AutoCAD menus. These are found in a submenu called **X. By reserving the top three lines so that a small portion of the main menu remains and by calling the submenu **X each time, you can have these items appear on each of your own submenus.

To add commands to the screen menu, find an existing menu and simply insert or add them after the last item in the menu. Try not to go beyond 15 additional items per menu screen; otherwise you might step on any **X submenu items already in use.

23.3 **How do you chain submenus?**

Let's say you've written a submenu called **SPECIAL** . Somewhere in the menu file is the following:

```
**SPECIAL 3
```

```
[ExMins]^c^clisp52
[AngAra]^c^clisp51
[PolyO]^c^clisp55
[PolyR]^c^clisp56
```

How do you get to it? That's simple. In the menu section is an area that begins ***SCREEN**, which is where AutoCAD's main menu is located. In Release 10, it's at approximately line 429. In Release 11, it's at line 1562. And in Release 12, it's at line 560. Insert the following line anywhere in this section; perhaps after `[UTILITY]$S=X $S=UT` .
```
[SPECIAL]$S=X $S=SPECIAL
```

Let's look at each component part. [SPECIAL] is what actually appears on the screen. If it's within the brackets, it's not executable. $S=X tells AutoCAD to bring menu **X onto the screen. $S=SPECIAL tells AutoCAD to bring the menu that you wrote onto the screen.

Your menu, **SPECIAL, can also call any other submenu that begins with **. Just add a line onto your menu. If the name of the next menu is **SPECIAL2, then, following the text in the brackets, enter:

```
$S=X $S=SPECIAL2.
```

Remember to reserve three lines in the header of each submenu: [AutoCAD], a blank line, and [* * * *]. These let you get back to the main menu and chain you to the OBJECT SNAP menu.

23.4 How do you change pull-down menus?

Pull-down menus are simply menu sections with the headers ***POP1, ***POP2, ***POP3. You can have up to ten pull-down menus, depending on which release you're using; AutoCAD preprograms eight of them. There's virtually nothing in ***POP8, so that's always a good place to begin adding things to a pull-down menu. Be aware, though, that the higher the section number, the narrower the text in the pull-down menu must be.

NOTE: Release 12 has nine pull-down menus that cascade over each subsection.

Each pull-down menu will be as wide as its longest line. The first pull-down (***POP1) has space for up to 80 characters. Each successive pull-down has a shorter line space, since you're approaching the end of the screen. If you exceed the end of the screen, the line will be truncated.

23.5 How do you add items to tablet menus?

Like the pull-down menus, tablet menus have major sections. There are four of them: ***TABLET1, ***TABLET2, ***TABLET3 and ***TABLET4. Except for a few areas or commands you might want to modify, the only true user area is ***TABLET1, where you can use rows A-H and columns 1-25 to modify a total of 200 blocks. (Theoretically, you could configure an unlimited number of blocks, but this uses what AutoCAD provides.)

Since there's nothing to see on the screen for the tablet areas, AutoCAD uses brackets to prenumber the blocks. This makes modifying any of the 200 blocks in Area 1 very easy. ***TABLET1's first lines look like:

```
***TABLET1

[A-1]

[A-2]

[A-3]

[A-4] . . . through [H-25]
```

Place your macros or AutoLISP programs at any block you want to use. There's nothing magical about the numbers in the brackets; that's just a way to reserve space. The blocks are relational, so be very careful not to erase any of the lines in the menu. For example, if you want something at [A-4] and you erased [A-3], then [A-4] would become [A-3], because it's in the third position regardless of its number in the brackets.

23.6 How do you create your own icons?

There's a section on your menu called ***icon** that contains a series of submenu items, each one beginning with **. So far, this is just like any other menu section. But let's digress a second. What are icons and how are they drawn?

To answer this, let's create three separate slides, all about the same size. Make one a line, the second an arc and the third a circle. Call the slide with the line LI, the slide with the arc AR and the slide with the circle CI. Now you have three files called LI.SLD, AR.SLD and CI.SLD.

The next step is to create a slide list. This is an ASCII text file that holds the names of your slides as icons in the order you want to use them. We'll create the following file as SPDRAW.LST. (SPDRAW, a name we made up, contains the list of slides to put into the slide library; the list doesn't have to be in any particular order.) The text file should read as follows:

LI

AR

CI

Notice that extension .SLD isn't used, only the names of the slides.

Next, make a slide library using SLIDELIB. This is an executable file, and it's probably in your AutoCAD directory. Type in the following from DOS or through **SHELL:**

Type: `SLIDELIB SPDRAW <SPDRAW.LST <RETURN>`

Notice the direction of the <. This means "make a slide library called SPDRAW out of SPDRAW.LST." Your slide library file SPDRAW.SLB is now ready.

Since this is only an example, you don't want to hurt your ACAD.MNU file. So before going any further, use DOS to copy ACAD.MNU to ACAD1.MNU and work only with the ACAD1.MNU file.

Now you're ready to attach the new icons to your menu. Let's attach them to ***POP7. (Remember, this is only an example; you wouldn't actually use this pull-down menu.) Find ***POP7. Insert the following in one of the lines:

Type: `[Special Draw]^c^c$i=SPD $i=* <RETURN>`

This gives you access to your icon. When you pull down menu number 7, you'll see **Special Draw** as part of it. When you choose **Special Draw** you'll be transferred to the ***icon section and brought to the submenu **SPD.

Now we need to create the **SPD submenu within the ***icon section. Find ***icon in your menu. You may insert your **SPD submenu after any of the ** submenus. Enter the following.

Type: `**SPD`
```
[Special Drawing Commands]
[spdraw(li)]^c^cline
[spdraw(ar)]^c^carc
[spdraw(ci)]^c^ccircle
```

The first line is a header that will appear in the icon pull-down screen. The other lines activate the icons. The brackets tell which icon to use first.

[spdraw(li)] means, "in a slide file called SPDRAW, use a slide called **li**." Remember that the name of the slide is in parentheses, preceded by the name of the slide file you created.

Now let's try it out. Once you're in an AutoCAD drawing, you'll need to bring up our practice menu called ACAD1.MNU.

Type: `MENU <RETURN>`

Response: `Menu file name or . for none:`

Type: `ACAD1 <RETURN>`

Now pick the seventh pull-down menu. This is the one called FILE. As you can see, you have an additional item called **Special Draw**. Pick it, and your icons should appear.

23.7 **How do you add text entries to the icon menus?**

You can enter text as a header, but this won't let you actually pick it. In order for text to show up, it must be part of an icon. Therefore, if you want to have an item that reads "EXIT," make a slide containing nothing but EXIT and include it as one of the icons. If you want text below each icon, include that text as part of the slide.

More Steps to Success

23.8 **EDLIN warning**

Be careful when using EDLIN or EDIT inside AutoCAD when editing the ACAD.MNU file. The entire file does not load. It's too big. You may need to do a W (Write) and then an A (Append) to find what you need.

23.9 **Begin menus with Ctrl-C**

As you've probably noticed, most of the menu macros begin with Ctrl-C. The reason is that, when you choose a menu item, it's assumed you want to stop whatever you're doing and perform the menu function. One Ctrl-C will cancel most functions in progress. But some functions, such as **DIM**, require two Ctrl-C's. The **CANCEL** command requires three Ctrl-C's.

On the other hand, if a menu function is to be transparent, the last thing you want is to cancel the ongoing function. So those macros should *not* begin with Ctrl-C's.

23.10 **Not all views are the same**

When you save a view, be careful if you're depending on specific coordinates. What you see on the screen may not be what actually plots out; in fact, the same view may produce slightly different coordinates, depending on which graphics card you use.

Therefore, if you're going to plot a view, don't use **VIEW Save**. Use **VIEW Window** instead. **VIEW Window** saves the view as the actual coordinates where the window touches. Of course, you can input these coordinates; also, you don't have to regenerate the screen when the view is being saved. The screen doesn't actually change to the saved view, so you can save several views at once or save them with an AutoLISP program without affecting the current screen.

23.11 **Constant grid**

You should set up a standard for your grid regardless of the zoom level, since it's often difficult to know how deep you are when you zoom. A good constant grid level is the current view size divided by the Y value of the viewing max. These values are found in the system variables **VIEW-SIZE** and **VSMAX**. A good AutoLISP program can help you out too; see LISP109 in Tip 23.19.

23.12 **Polylines can be faster**

Here's a little trick that can speed up your drawings on regens if you use a lot of splines or fit-curves. It takes time for AutoCAD to compute **SPLINE** or **FIT CURVE** every time it regens.

Polylines work a lot faster. One easy way is to do a **BREAK @** on the splines or fit-curves that you know you won't need to de-curve. This makes them permanent polyarcs, and your drawings run a little faster.

23.13 **Set VIEWRES to 2000**

Once a virtual screen is established, you should be able to zoom around anywhere on it without a regeneration. However, if you have **VIEWRES** set to fast zooms and the percentage of circles set to the standard 100 or less, circles and arcs are straight lines. That's inconvenient at best, and you may need to do a **REGEN** to straighten it out.

23.14 **Zoom views for fast zooms**

You should set up your drawing with a standard number of set views. One of the views should be the limits. Do your setup in a virtually empty drawing that's zoomed to the limits. Limit checking should be on, **RE-GENAUTO** should be off, and **VIEWRES** might be set to **2000** percent. The drawing area should be divided into as many as 16 separate viewing areas, so you can recall them quickly with **VIEW RESTORE**.

See LISP112 in Tip 23.22 for a program that partitions your drawing automatically. The program LISP113, described in Tip 23.23, lets you zoom and pan around your drawing by entering Z1-16 or ZA for a **ZOOM All**. If you do happen to zoom in a little too far, **REGENAUTO** set to **Off** will protect you from an inadvertent regen.

The one thing you want to avoid is actually entering **ZOOM All** or **ZOOM Extents**, two commands that don't respect the **REGENAUTO** setting.

23.15 **Use smaller pick and aperture boxes**

If your pick and aperture boxes are too large, the number of possible picks is increased and this may slightly slow down object selection. Also, if boxes are too large, you might select an entity by mistake.

You usually can't tell whether boxes are too large or small until you're in a deep zoom during a command. Remember that the pick box and the aperture box can each be set transparently while you're in another command if you use **'SETVAR PICKBOX** or **'SETVAR APERTURE**. The size of the box is then changed dynamically. Don't forget the apostrophe.

23.16 **More trade-offs with VIEWRES**

If fast **ZOOM** is set to Y, pick selection is slowed. Of course, if you set fast zooms to N, you'll get a regen at every **ZOOM**, so this isn't a valid trade-off. There's one exception, however. If you're using a display-list processing board, you're saving nothing by having fast zooms set to Y, since the software and the board are handling the zooms for you. In that case, it's best to set fast zooms to N so pick selection will be faster.

This tip assumes that you aren't given contrary instructions by your board manufacturer. In all cases, follow the instructions for your particular board.

 **AutoLISP Programs**

23.17 Hide entities (LISP107)

This program lets you temporarily "erase" any entities from the screen. They aren't really erased—they temporarily disappear from the screen and then reappear on the next redraw or regen.

Listing:
```
(defun c:lisp107 (/ blm a n i)
    (setq blm (getvar "blipmode"))
    (setvar "blipmode" 0)
    (setq a (ssget))
    (setq n (sslength a))
    (setq i 0)
    (repeat n
        (redraw (ssname a i) 2)
        (setq i (+ i 1))
    )
    (setvar "blipmode" blm)
)
```

To Use: Load LISP107.LSP.

Type: LISP107 <RETURN>

Response: Select objects:

Use any selection method you like. When you confirm, the objects selected will disappear. This is a good program for viewing what might be under an entity if you've copied over it. All the entities will return on the next redraw of the screen.

23.18 Redraw selected entities (LISP108)

Programs sometimes erase certain entities, and in the process, other entities that weren't erased will disappear from the screen. The only way to get them back is to redraw the whole screen. This can be time-consuming on very large drawings. This program lets you redraw only selected entities or selected parts of the screen without redrawing the entire display. The best way to use it is to put a crossing around the area you want redrawn, and confirm.

Listing:
```
(defun c:lisp108 (/ blm a n i)
    (setq blm (getvar "blipmode"))
    (setvar "blipmode" 0)
    (setq a (ssget))
    (setq n (sslength a))
    (setq i 0)
    (repeat n
        (redraw (ssname a i) 1)
        (setq i (+ i 1))
    )
    (setvar "blipmode" blm)
)
```

To Use: Load LISP108.LSP.

Type: `LISP108 <RETURN>`

Response: `Select objects:`

Use any selection method you like. When you confirm, the objects selected will reappear.

23.19 Set grid standard (LISP109)

This program works in conjunction with LISP110. It's used to set the standard grid width for a **ZOOM A**.

Listing:
```
(defun c:lisp109 (/ ft)
    (setq ft (car (getvar "gridunit")))
    (setvar "userr1" ft)
)
```

To Use: Load LISP109.LSP.

First make sure you're in a **ZOOM All** display. Set your grid to the level you want as standard.

Type: `LISP109 <RETURN>`

This standard level is set and stored with the drawing. This needs to be done only once. You may now change your grid if you want to, and use either LISP110 or LISP111.

23.20 **Grid control decimal (LISP110)**

This program lets you automatically control the density of your grid, no matter how deeply you zoom. It gives you a visible grid without saying that the grid is too dense to display as well as a reference as to how deeply you've zoomed. This program works with decimal units. It defaults to 1 if you haven't run LISP109.

Listing:
```
(defun c:g (/ ft gr)
    (setq ft (getvar "userr1"))
    (if (or (= ft 0) (= ft nil)) (setq ft 1.0))
    (setq  gr (/(getvar"viewsize")  (cadr (getvar "vsmax"))))
    (setq gr (* gr ft))
    (command "grid" gr)
    (princ "\nNew grid setting is ")(princ gr)
    (princ)
)
```

To Use: Load LISP110.LSP.

Type: G <RETURN>

This should be run after you've zoomed. It will restore the grid to the proper level and indicate the current setting. Another way to run it is to first turn your grid off before zooming.

23.21 **Grid control feet/inches (LISP111)**

This program lets you automatically control the density of your grid, no matter how deeply you zoom. It gives you a visible grid without saying that the grid is too dense to display as well as a reference as to how deep you've zoomed. This program works with either architectural or engineering units. It defaults to one foot if you haven't set your grid standard and run LISP109 first.

Listing:
```
(defun c:g (/ ft gr)
    (setq ft (getvar "userr1"))
    (if (or (= ft 0) (= ft nil)) (setq ft 12.0))
    (setq gr (/ (getvar "viewsize")  (cadr (getvar "vsmax"))))
    (setq gr (* gr ft))
    (command "grid" gr)
    (princ "\nNew grid setting is ")(princ (rtos gr))
    (princ)
)
```

To Use: Load LISP111.LSP.

Type: G <RETURN>

This should be run after you've zoomed. It will restore the grid to the proper level and indicate the current setting. Another way to run it is to turn your grid off before zooming.

23.22 Fast zoom setup (LISP112)

This program may very well prevent your having to regen again during zooms. It divides your drawing into 16 separate views and provides an overlay that shows where the sections break. The overlay can be turned off and on. This program also handles setups such as the settings for **VIEWRES, LIMCHECK** and a final creation of the proper virtual screen for your drawing. If you use this program at the beginning of a drawing, it will dramatically increase your ability to zoom around in the drawing at redraw speed. Use of the plus sign at the end of a line in AutoLISP code indicates that line is wrapped.

Listing:
```
(defun c:lisp112 ()
    (setvar "regenmode" 1)
    (setvar "limcheck" 1)
    (command "viewres" "y" "2000")
    (setq limm (list  (+ (car (getvar "limmin")) 0.001) +
      (+ (cadr (getvar "limmin")) 0.001)))
    (setq limax (list (- (car (getvar "limmax")) 0.001) +
      (- (cadr (getvar "limmax")) 0.001)))
    (setq orxa (car (getvar "limmin")))
    (setq orya (cadr (getvar "limmin")))
```

```
(setq orx (car limm))
(setq ory (cadr limm))
(setq x (+ orxa (car limax)))
(setq y (+ orya (cadr limax)))
(setq ofx (/ x 8))
(setq ofy (/ y 8))
(setq v10 (list orx y))
(setq v1b (list (* x 0.25) y))
(setq v2b (list (* x 0.5) y))
(setq v3b (list (* x 0.75) y))
(setq v4b (list x y))
(setq v1a (list orx (* y 0.75)))
(setq v2a (list (* x 0.25) (* y 0.75)))
(setq v3a (list (* x 0.5) (* y 0.75)))
(setq v4a (list (* x 0.75) (* y 0.75)))
(setq v8b (list x (* y 0.75)))
(setq v5a (list orx (* y 0.5)))
(setq v6a (list (* x 0.25) (* y 0.5)))
(setq v7a (list (* x 0.5) (* y 0.5)))
(setq v8a (list (* x 0.75) (* y 0.5)))
(setq v12b (list x (* y 0.5)))
(setq v9a (list orx (* y 0.25)))
(setq v10a (list (* x 0.25) (* y 0.25)))
(setq v11a (list (* x 0.5) (* y 0.25)))
(setq v12a (list (* x 0.75) (* y 0.25)))
(setq v16b (list x (* y 0.25)))
(setq v13a (list orx ory))
(setq v14a (list (* x 0.25) ory))
(setq v15a (list (* x 0.5) ory))
(setq v16a (list (* x 0.75) ory))
(setq v160 (list x ory))
(setq vx (list orx ory))
(setq vy (list x y))
(setq sty (getvar "textstyle"))
(setq crla (getvar "clayer"))
(setq crcol (getvar "cecolor"))
(command "layer" "m" "zoomlin" "c" "yellow" "zoomlin" "")
```

(code continues next page)

```
(setq a (ssget "x" '((8 . "zoomlin"))))
(command "erase" "p" "")
(command "view" "w" "v1" v1a v1b)
(command "view" "w" "v2" v2a v2b)
(command "view" "w" "v3" v3a v3b)
(command "view" "w" "v4" v4a v4b)
(command "view" "w" "v5" v5a v2a)
(command "view" "w" "v6" v6a v3a)
(command "view" "w" "v7" v7a v4a)
(command "view" "w" "v8" v8a v8b)
(command "view" "w" "v9" v9a v6a)
(command "view" "w" "v10" v10a v7a)
(command "view" "w" "v11" v11a v8a)
(command "view" "w" "v12" v12a v12b)
(command "view" "w" "v13" v13a v10a)
(command "view" "w" "v14" v14a v11a)
(command "view" "w" "v15" v15a v12a)
(command "view" "w" "v16" v16a v16b)
(command "view" "w" "v0" vx vy)
(command "view" "w" "v1q" v5a v2b)
(command "view" "w" "v2q" v7a v4b)
(command "view" "w" "v3q" v13a v7a)
(command "view" "w" "v4q" v15a v12b)
(command "line" v10 v4b "")
(command "line" v1a v8b "")
(command "line" v5a v12b "")
(command "line" v9a v16b "")
(command "line" v13a v160 "")
(command "line" v10 v13a "")
(command "line" v1b v14a "")
(command "line" v2b v15a "")
(command "line" v3b v16a "")
(command "line" v4b v160 "")
(command "id" (list (+ (car v1a) ofx) (+ (cadr v1a) ofy)))
(command "text" "s" "standard" "m" "@" (/ ofx 2) "0" "1")
(command "id" (list (+ car v2a) ofx) (+ (cadr v2a) ofy)))
(command "text" "m" "@" (/ ofx 2) "0" "2")
(command "id" (list (+ (car v3a) ofx) (+ (cadr v3a) ofy)))
(command "text" "m" "@" (/ ofx 2) "0" "3")
```

```
(command "id" (list (+ (car v4a) ofx) (+ (cadr v4a) ofy)))
(command "text" "s" "standard" "m" "@" (/ ofx 2) "0" "4")
(command "id" (list (+ (car v5a) ofx) (+ (cadr v5a) ofy)))
(command "text" "m" "@" (/ ofx 2) "0" "5")
(command "id" (list (+ (car v6a) ofx) (+ (cadr v6a) ofy)))
(command "text" "m" "@" (/ ofx 2) "0" "6")
(command "id" (list (+ (car v7a) ofx) (+ (cadr v7a) ofy)))
(command "text" "s" "standard" "m" "@" (/ ofx 2) "0" "7")
(command "id" (list (+ (car v8a) ofx) (+ (cadr v8a) ofy)))
(command "text" "m" "@" (/ ofx 2) "0" "8")
(command "id" (list (+ (car v9a) ofx) (+ (cadr v9a) ofy)))
(command "text" "m" "@" (/ ofx 2) "0" "9")
(command "id" (list (+ (car v10a) ofx) (+ (cadr v10a) ofy)))
(command "text" "s" "standard" "m" "@" (/ ofx 2) "0" "10")
(command "id" (list (+ (car v11a) ofx) (+ (cadr v11a) ofy)))
(command "text" "m" "@" (/ ofx 2) "0" "11")
(command "id" (list (+ (car v12a) ofx) (+ (cadr v12a) ofy)))
(command "text" "m" "@" (/ ofx 2) "0" "12")
(command "id" (list (+ (car v13a) ofx) (+ (cadr v13a) ofy)))
(command "text" "s" "standard" "m" "@" (/ ofx 2) "0" "13")
(command "id" (list (+ (car v14a) ofx) (+ (cadr v14a) ofy)))
(command "text" "m" "@" (/ ofx 2) "0" "14")
(command "id" (list (+ (car v15a) ofx) (+ (cadr v15a) ofy)))
(command "text" "m" "@" (/ ofx 2) "0" "15")
(command "id" (list (+ (car v16a) ofx) (+ (cadr v16a) ofy)))
(command "text" "s" "standard" "m" "@" (/ ofx 2) "0" "16")
(command "layer" "s" crla "")
(command "color" crcol)
(command "style" sty "" "" "" "" "" "" "")
(command "view" "r" "v0")
(setvar "regenmode" 0)
)
```

To Use: Load LISP112.LSP.

NOTE: before you use this program, set **LIMITS** and do all the drawing within those limits. If you ever change your limits, you'll need to run this program again on the new limits.

Type: `LISP112 <RETURN>`

The program will redraw the screen, regen one time if necessary, and divide it into 16 areas. This area outline is found on layer **ZOOMLIN**. LISP114 in Tip 23.24 can turn this layer on and off as necessary. Zoom as you normally would; you'll be able to go as deep as most display processing boards permit. If you try to zoom too deeply or zoom outside of the limits of the numbered boxes, you'll get a regen warning. You may go ahead and regen, but be aware that when you restore view V0, which is a **ZOOM All**, it will regen one more time. As long as you stay within the limits and zoom to a reasonable level, you'll do so at redraw speed.

LISP113, below, helps with **ZOOM All** and quick zooms to each of the numbered boxes (see Figure 23-1).

Figure 23-1: Fast zoom areas

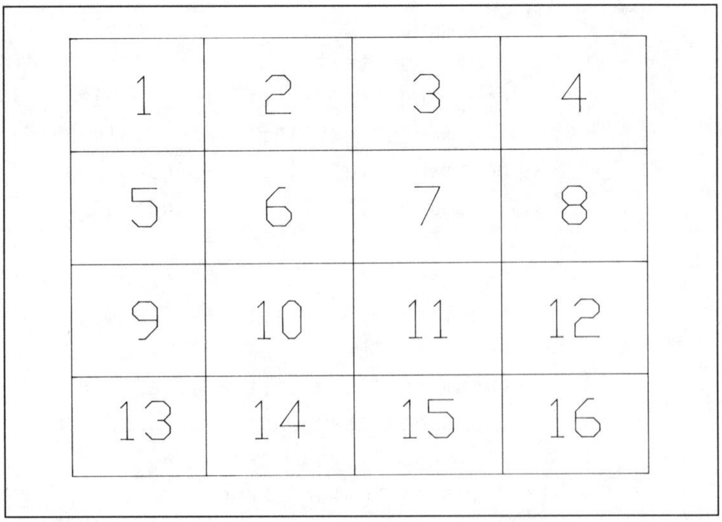

23.23 Fast zooms (LISP113)

This program lets you zoom anywhere in a drawing by entering a short keystroke sequence. Run LISP112 once before you use this. When your drawing is saved, you don't have to run LISP112 again unless you change your drawing limits.

Listing:
```
(defun c:z0 ()
    (command "'view" "r" "v0"))
(defun c:z1 ()
    (command "'view" "r" "v1"))
(defun c:z2 ()
    (command "'view" "r" "v2"))
(defun c:z3 ()
    (command "'view" "r" "v3"))
(defun c:z4 ()
    (command "'view" "r" "v4"))
(defun c:z5 ()
    (command "'view" "r" "v5"))
(defun c:z6 ()
    (command "'view" "r" "v6"))
(defun c:z7 ()
    (command "'view" "r" "v7"))
(defun c:z8 ()
    (command "'view" "r" "v8"))
(defun c:z9 ()
    (command "'view" "r" "v9"))
(defun c:z10 ()
    (command "'view" "r" "v10"))
(defun c:z11 ()
    (command "'view" "r" "v11"))
(defun c:z12 ()
    (command "'view" "r" "v12"))
(defun c:z13 ()
    (command "'view" "r" "v13"))
(defun c:z14 ()
    (command "'view" "r" "v14"))
(defun c:z15 ()
    (command "'view" "r" "v15"))
```

(code continues next page)

```
(defun c:z16 ()
   (command "'view" "r" "v16"))
(defun c:z1q ()
   (command "'view" "r" "v1q"))
(defun c:z2q ()
   (command "'view" "r" "v2q"))
(defun c:z3q ()
   (command "'view" "r" "v3q"))
(defun c:z4q ()
   (command "'view" "r" "v4q"))
```

To Use: Load LISP113.LSP.

Each of the view areas are listed below. If you want to zoom to area 3,

Type: Z3 <RETURN>

and you'll be restored to area 3. The following is a chart of the commands, the actual view names that are being restored and the areas they represent.

Command	Named View	Area
Z1	V1	1
Z2	V2	2
Z3	V3	3
Z4	V4	4
Z5	V5	5
Z6	V6	6
Z7	V7	7
Z8	V8	8
Z9	V9	9
Z10	V10	10
Z11	V11	11
Z12	V12	12
Z13	V13	13
Z14	V14	14
Z15	V15	15
Z16	V16	16

Command	Named View	Area
Z1Q	V1Q	1, 2, 5, 6 (First quadrant)
Z2Q	V2Q	3, 4, 7, 8 (Second quadrant)
Z3Q	V3Q	9, 10, 13, 14 (Third quadrant)
Z4Q	V4Q	11, 12, 15, 16 (Fourth quadrant)
Z0	V0	Zoom All

23.24 **Zoom matrix on and off (LISP114)**

This program gives you a quick way to turn the zoom matrix on and off.

Listing:
```
(defun c:zo ()
    (command "layer" "on" "zoomlin" ""))
(defun c:zf ()
    (command "layer" "off" "zoomlin" ""))
```

To Use: Load LISP114.LSP.

Type: `ZF <RETURN>`

This turns the zoom matrix off.

Type: `ZO <RETURN>`

This turns the zoom matrix on. (Use the letter O, not the number zero.)

CHAPTER 24

Advanced Layers, Blocks, Attributes

How Do You . . .

24.1 How do you create a new line type?

Creating a new line type in AutoCAD is really quite easy. In fact, there's a function that guides you through everything you need to answer except the actual parameters for the line type. Of course, this is the hardest.

A line type is a series of positive and negative numbers that tell a plotter how long to lower or raise the pen. Positive numbers lower the pen and negative numbers raise it. .5 is the normal length of a dash. 0 is a dot. For example, 0, –.25 would produce a series of dots. The first 0 produces the dot; the –.25 raises the pen .25 of a unit. The series then repeats itself.

A dash-dot would be .5, –.25, 0, –.25. And a dashed line would be .5, –.25. You should get the idea—with a little experimentation, you can produce any combinations you need.

Now let's look at how you create a new line type. Let's assume you want the line type to be dash, dot, dot, dot. The format would be .5, –.25, 0, –.25, 0, –.25, 0, –.25. We'll call this new line type **LINEDOT**. To begin, issue the **LINETYPE** command and choose **Create**.

Type: LINETYPE <RETURN>

Response: ?/Create/Load/Set:

Type: C <RETURN>

Response: Name of linetype to create:

Type: LINEDOT <RETURN>

Response: File for storage of linetype <ACAD>:

Type: <RETURN> (ACAD.LIN is the default line type file. But you can create your own file by entering its name here.)

Response: `Wait, checking if line type already defined...`
`Descriptive text:`

Here you can write a description of what the line type looks like. It will appear whenever you use **?** with the line type. You could write, "Dash and three dots." But it would be better if you gave a picture of the line type. To do this, use the underline character for the dash and the period for the dot.

Type: _ . . . _ . . _ . . _ . . _ . . _

Response: `Enter pattern (on next line):`
`A,`

Here's where you type the numeric description of the line type. Begin typing it immediately after the A,

Type: `.5, -.25, 0, -.25, 0, -.25, 0, -.25 <RETURN>`

Response: `New definition written to file.`
`?/Create/Load/Set:`

Press <RETURN> or type **Set** to make your new line type active. Since it's part of ACAD.LIN, you can use this line type as you would any other.

24.2 **How do you change a line type?**

If you've made a mistake or want to change the description or definition, just create a new line type. Give it the same name as the old one. AutoCAD will ask you if you want to overwrite it; answer Y. You can then enter the new definition and description.

24.3 **How do you delete a line type?**

You delete a line type outside of AutoCAD. The line type is stored in ACAD.LIN or in another file you created. These are ASCII text files, so you can use a text editor to delete the lines referring to the file. There are two lines for every file. The first line, the description, begins with an *. The second line is the definition and begins with an A. When these lines are deleted, the line type is gone.

24.4 **How do you insert a 3D block transparently?**

When you're inserting 3D blocks, you usually want them to come in transparently. This means that when they enter the drawing they don't look like they did when they were blocked. They align with the WCS and can be rotated in **DVIEW** with the other entities in the drawing. This applies to all blocks; you want to be able to insert them into a drawing and have them align with the other entities.

The problem with 3D blocks is that they interpret their orientation according to the coordinate system in use when they're created. From drawing to drawing, the only coordinate system you can count on is the World Coordinate System. Therefore, make sure that you're in the WCS when the item is blocked. Then make sure you're in the WCS when the item is inserted, if you want it to retain the same angle it had when it was blocked. If you change the coordinate system, the block will come in at an angle relative to that system.

24.5 **How do you compose multiple 3D drawings on the same sheet?**

This is really a block question. If you want several 3D drawings on the same sheet, you must first compose the **DVIEW** that you want. Next, change your UCS to **VIEW**. Then block the drawing. When it's inserted into the WCS of a new drawing, it will come in looking exactly as it did when it was blocked. This way you can compose several 3D drawings from different angles on the same sheet.

See Tip 27.5 for information on how to bring in a 2D representation of a 3D drawing with hidden lines.

24.6 **How do you create a template text file for extracting attributes?**

Before you can extract information from attributes to a file, you must first tell AutoCAD which fields you want it to use. This is done with a *template text file*. As the name implies, it's an ordinary ASCII text file. It has four parts: tag, character/numeric, width and precision.

An example of a template file might be as follows:

```
BL:NAME      C010000
MATERIAL     C020000
SIZE         N005000
COST         N010002
```

Let's begin with **MATERIAL**. This is the tag name of the attribute. The next non-blank character must be a C or an N. This tells AutoCAD whether it's a number or a character. Numbers can be characters, but they become ordinary text with no numeric qualities. The next three characters tell AutoCAD how wide to make the field. For example, 020 reserves 20 characters. Be sure you fill up all three spaces; 20 wouldn't be valid. The final three spaces determine the precision. This has no meaning for character fields, so it's 000.

Look at **COST**, which is numeric. It allows ten (010) spaces in width and fixes two decimal places of precision (002).

BL:NAME is a special case—it's one of 15 *reserved fields*, which are fields that you don't have to actually put information into to get information out of. For example, AutoCAD already knows the block name if there is one, so you don't need to create an attribute for that. You can access the block name with the reserved field name of **BL:NAME** if you want to use it. Below are listed the other reserved fields. Remember that you don't have to use any reserved fields. But you must have at least one tag in your template in order to pick up any attributes.

BL:LEVEL	Nwww000	Block nesting level
BL:NAME	Cwww000	Block name
BL:X	Nwwwddd	X coordinate of block insertion point
BL:Y	Nwwwddd	Y coordinate
BL:Z	Nwwwddd	Z coordinate
BL:NUMBER	Nwww000	Block counter; same for all members of a MINSERT
BL:HANDLE	Cwww000	Block handle
BL:LAYER	Cwww000	Block insertion layer
BL:ORIENT	Nwwwddd	Block rotation angle
BL:XSCALE	Nwwwddd	X scale factor of block
BL:YSCALE	Nwwwddd	Y scale factor
BL:ZSCALE	Nwwwddd	Z scale factor
BL:XEXTRUDE	Nwwwddd	X component of block's extrusion direction
BL:YEXTRUDE	Nwwwddd	Y component
BL:ZEXTRUDE	Nwwwddd	Z component

When you create the template file, you may use any name you want, but make sure the extension is .TXT. The template doesn't have to have all the tags that are available in the block. An attribute is extracted only if its tag name matches the field name specified in the template file. You don't have to worry about upper- and lowercase, since everything is changed to uppercase for you.

24.7 How do you send attributes out to a file?

First assume that you've made a template file called TEMP1.TXT. You want to create a file of attributes that's readable by another program. The command you use is **ATTEXT**, which stands for "attribute extraction."

You have two basic options. The file format may be either SDF or CDF. SDF means "space-delimited format" and it's a fixed-field format; each field has a fixed number of spaces. Assume that the block name is P1. Then an SDF extracted file might look like this:

```
P1    CLOTH     5    10.00
P1    METAL     8    14.95
P1    PLASTIC   6    12.40
```

The CDF option is "comma-delimited format." The fields are separated by commas. The text is set off with apostrophes. The following is an example:

```
'P1','CLOTH',5,10.00
'P1','METAL',8,14.95
'P1','PLASTIC',6,12.40
```

There's another format, DXF. This is a modified form of AutoCAD's DXF file. It includes the block reference and attribute and end-of-sequence entities.

If you use SDF or CDF, your final finished file will have the extension .TXT. If you use DXF, your final finished file will have the extension .DXX.

Type: ATTEXT <RETURN>

Response: CDF, SDF, OR DXF Attribute extract (or Entities)?

Type: C <RETURN>

Response: Template file:

Type: TEMP1 <RETURN>

Response: Extract file name <Nameofdrawing>:

This response defaults to the name of your drawing. You may change it or press <RETURN>.

Type: <RETURN>

12 RELEASE 12   Gives you the option of extracting attributes by using dialogue boxs. See Tip 20.51.

24.8 **How do you extract certain blocks and not others?**
The **ATTEXT** command has an option that lets you select the object you want included.

Type: ATTEXT <RETURN>

Response: CDF, SDF, OR DXF Attribute extract (or Entities)?

Type: E <RETURN> (This lets you select your own entities for inclusion.)

Response: Select objects:

Select any group of entities, using any selection method, and confirm.

Response: CDF, SDF or DXF Attribute extract?:

The choices continue, as they do with the **ATTEXT** command.

24.9 How do you change the delimiters?

You can use any delimiter you want. You can also get AutoCAD to use quotes instead of apostrophes to denote strings. Simply include the following anywhere in the template file.

```
C:DELIM   *
C:QUOTE   "
```

You may use either of these, or both. **C:DELIM** tells AutoCAD to use *
as the field delimiter. You can use any character you want. /, *, $ are all
valid delimiters; simply follow **C:DELIM** with the character you want to
use. **C:QUOTE** tells AutoCAD what character to use to set off strings.

```
"P1"/"CLOTH"/ 5/ 10.00
"P1"/"METAL"/ 8/ 14.95
"P1"/"PLASTIC"/ 6/ 12.40
```

24.10 How do you convert drawing information to a spreadsheet?

This is only one of many applications for attribute extractions. First, decide
what information you want to send to the spreadsheet. Create a template
file for the columns you want, in the order that you want them. Finally,
extract them in CDF format.

Go into your spreadsheet and use whatever import mode is available
for it. Before you import, you may need to change the file extension. Some
programs may require a special extension, such as .PRN for Lotus. Then
the information will be imported as nice, neat columns. For Lotus, use the
Numbers option.

More Steps to Success

24.11 **Block libraries**

You can create your own block library. Group your blocks by category and keep them as groups in a single .DWG file. This can be a separate file or part of a prototype file. If it's a single file, insert the file. After you give AutoCAD the block name, press Ctrl-C and cancel the function. All of the block definitions that were in the inserted drawing will now be in your drawing. Later, you should purge the definitions you don't need. In this way you don't have to have a lot of .DWG files for every block—it makes organization a lot easier.

24.12 **Recovering a corrupted drawing**

Sometimes when you're bringing in a drawing you've been working on for some time, you get fatal errors while the drawing is coming up. When this happens, AutoCAD aborts and you get none of the drawing.

Don't panic yet. Create a new, blank drawing. Give it the same limits and units as the drawing you want to bring in. Now insert the problem drawing at 0,0. Many times this can save an otherwise dead drawing file.

24.13 **Add Attribute Edit to pull-down menus**

It's strange that AutoCAD gives you a dialogue box to edit attributes, but doesn't give you a way to get to it through pull-down menus. The only way to use the dialogue box is to type **DDATTE** <RETURN>.

Add the following to your ACAD.MNU file in **POP3**. Place it after **[Edit Polylines]**. Be careful: After that line is a continuation of an AutoLISP program, in-line in the menu, that's part of the Edit Polylines entry. Therefore, place this at the end, right before *****POP4**. (Make sure you don't enter a space after the last line of **POP3**.)

```
[Edit Attributes]^c^cddatte <RETURN>
<RETURN>
```

You must leave a blank line after the last entry on a pull-down menu.

24.14 Line up tags

As long as you add attributes one after another, each continues on the next line if you press <RETURN> when asked for a start point. But a problem arises when you've done attributes for another block and want to return to the first block to add more. How do you line up the tags automatically?

First, ID the insertion point of the last attribute text. Now use **DTEXT**. When you're asked for a starting point, press @ <RETURN>. Continue pressing <RETURN> until you receive the **Text:** prompt. Now type in anything.

Next ID the insertion point of the dummy text. Enter **ERASE Last**. This will get rid of the dummy text.

Finally, use **ATTDEF**. When you're asked for a starting point, press @ <RETURN>. Your text will now be at the correct position.

24.15 Turn ATTDISP off

Make sure that **ATTDISP** is off. This will speed up regens and your general work on a drawing.

24.16 Don't forget UNDO for blocks

If you create a block by mistake or change your mind, **UNDO** not only will remove the block but will also totally remove the block definition.

AutoLISP Programs

24.17 **Delete all entities on a layer (LISP115)**

This program lets you quickly erase everything on a given layer.

Listing:
```
(defun c:lisp115 (/ a b)
    (setq a (getstring "\nName of layer "))
    (setq b (ssget "x" (list (cons 8 a))))
    (command "erase" b "")
)
```

To Use: Load LISP115.LSP.

Type: LISP115 <RETURN>

Response: Name of layer:

Enter the name of the layer, and everything on that layer will be erased.

24.18 **Multiple insert (LISP116)**

This program lets you do multiple inserts just as you do multiple copies. The **MINSERT** command isn't really useful here, because it's not a true multiple insert command. It lets you insert only as an array, and when you do, the blocks aren't explodable without our programs.

Listing:
```
(defun c:lisp116 (/ part pt1)
    (setq part (getstring "\nPart name "))
    (setq pt1 (getpoint "\nInsertion point "))
    (command "insert" part pt1 "" "" "")
    (command "copy" "l" "" "m" pt1)
)
```

To Use: Load LISP116.LSP.

Type: LISP116 <RETURN>

Response: Part name:

Type: PART-1 (Enter the name of a block.)

Response: Insertion point:

Pick where you want the first block placed.

Response: Second point of displacement:

Pick where you want the second block placed.

You can keep on inserting the block until you press <RETURN>.

24.19 Exploded MINSERT (LISP117)

This program lets you insert a block as an array. The blocks come in as blocks rather than as an unexplodable **INSERT**.

Listing:
```
(defun c:lisp117 (/ part pt1)
    (setq part (getstring "\nPart name "))
    (setq pt1 (getpoint "\nInsertion point "))
    (command "insert" part pt1 "" "" "")
    (command "array" "1" "" "r")
)
```

To Use: Load LISP117.LSP.

Type: LISP117 <RETURN>

Response: Part name:

Type: PART-1 (Enter the name of a block.)

Response: Insertion point:

Pick a point where you'd like the first block inserted.

Response: Number of rows (---):

Enter the number of rows as in the **ARRAY** command.

Response: Number of columns (|||):

Enter the number of columns as in the **ARRAY** command.

Response: Unit cell or distance between rows (---):

Enter the distance as in the **ARRAY** command.

Response: Distance between columns (|||):

Enter the distance as in the **ARRAY** command.

24.20 **Frozen Layers to Screen (LISP118)**

This program will list to the screen all layers that are either frozen or off.

Listing:

```
(defun c:lisp118 (/ k a b1 th onoff th1 onoff1)
   (textscr)
   (setq k 5)
   (setq a nil)
   (princ "\nLayers          Status")(terpri)(terpri)
   (while (setq b1 (tblnext "layer" k))
      (setq k nil)
      (setq th (assoc 70 b1))
      (setq onoff (assoc 62 b1))
      (setq th1 (cdr th))
      (setq onoff1 (cdr onoff))
      (if (or (= th1 65) (= th1 1))
         (progn
            (setq a 5)
            (princ (cdr (assoc 2 b1)))
            (princ "            ") (princ "Frozen")
            (terpri)
         )
      )
      (if (< onoff1 0)
         (progn
            (setq a 5)
            (princ (cdr (assoc 2 b1)))
            (princ "            ") (princ "Off")
            (terpri)
         )
      )
   )
   (if (= a nil)
      (prompt "There are no Frozen or Off layers in the +
        database \n")
   )
   (prin1)
)
```

To Use: Load LISP118.LSP.

Type: `LISP118 <RETURN>`

The program will run without any further prompts. All layers that are frozen or off will be printed on the screen. If there are no frozen or off layers, you'll get this message:

```
There are no Frozen or Off layers in the database.
```

24.21 **Frozen layers to printer (LISP119)**

This program will list to the printer all layers that are either frozen or off.

Listing:
```
(defun c:lisp119 (/ k a bl th onoff thl onoff1)
     (setq p (open "prn" "w"))
     (princ "          " p)
     (princ "Review of Off or Frozen Layers in the Database\n" p)
     (princ "\n\n" p)
     (setq k 5)
     (setq a nil)
     (princ "Layers          Status\n\n" p)
     (while (setq bl (tblnext "layer" k))
        (setq k nil)
        (setq th (assoc 70 bl))
        (setq onoff (assoc 62 bl))
        (setq thl (cdr th))
        (setq onoff1 (cdr onoff))
        (if (or (= thl 65) (= th 1))
           (progn
              (setq a 5)
              (princ (cdr (assoc 2 bl)) p)
              (princ "          " p) (princ "Frozen\n" p)
           )
        )
```

(code continues on next page)

```
(if (< onoff1 0)
   (progn
      (setq a 5)
      (princ (cdr (assoc 2 b1)) p)
      (princ "              " p) (princ "Off\n" p)
   )
)
)
(if (= a nil)
   (prompt "There are no Frozen or Off layers in the +
   database\n" p)
)
(princ (chr 12) p)
(close p)
(prin1)
)
```

To Use: Load LISP119.LSP.

Type: `LISP119 <RETURN>`

The program will run without any further prompts. All layers that are frozen or off will be sent out to your printer. Make sure that the printer is on. If no layers are frozen or off, you'll get this message:

```
There are no Frozen or Off layers in the database.
```

Advanced Inquiry, Text, Annotation

How Do You . . .

25.1 How do you curve text around an arc?

There is only one way to write text around an arc, and that's one letter at a time. Each letter must be rotated as it goes around the arc. This can be a tedious operation; see LISP120 in Tip 25.10 for a program that makes it easy.

25.2 How do you bring text in and out of an ASCII file?

This is another one of those things that's better left up to an AutoLISP program. There are several commercial programs on the market that do a very good job of this. If you don't use an AutoLISP file, you could always put some script file headers in the file, rename the file with the extension .SCR, and call it in using the **SCRIPT** command. But this is a lot of trouble; you'll be better off using LISP121 and LISP122 in Tips 25.11 and 25.12.

25.3 How do you find the length of an arc?

There are some good formulas for this, but here's a simple way that lets AutoCAD do all the work.

If the arc is a polyline, you can use the **AREA** command and choose **Entity**. AutoCAD will give you the length of the entity. If the arc isn't a polyline, turn it into one with the **PEDIT** command. Then use the **AREA** command to find the length. When you're through, explode the arc to return it to its original entity. See LISP123 in Tip 25.13.

25.4 How do you begin text right under other text that's already been entered?

The problem here is that the last point of text controls where the next line of text is to be written. To override this, first ID the insertion point of the text under which you want to draw. Now use **DTEXT**. When it asks you for a starting point, enter @ <RETURN>. Press <RETURN> until you receive the **Text:** prompt again. It should be lined up.

25.5 How do you pick where a new line of text will be while in DTEXT?

This is a great trick. As you know, if you repeat the **DTEXT** command, text will line up under previous text. But what you probably didn't know is that, while in the **DTEXT** command, you can simply pick another point and the text will continue at the point picked. Try it!

More Steps to Success

25.6 Turn DIMSHO off

Be sure the dimension system variable **DIMSHO** is turned off. Otherwise, as you change or drag items that are affected by associative dimensioning, the dimensions will try to constantly update. This will slow you down.

25.7 New uses for NEWTEXT

After you've already dimensioned part of your drawing, there are times when you'd like to go back and do a continuation using **Continue** or **Baseline** from another dimension. It's still possible to do that.

Choose **HOMETEXT** and select the dimension from which you want to continue. Once it's selected, AutoCAD thinks that it was the last dimensioned item. Begin the dimensioning command. **Baseline** or **Continue** will now work.

25.8 Dimension in 3D

You must take certain precautions when dimensioning in 3D. If you don't, the dimension may seem to work, but you might get the wrong answer—at least in terms of the absolute length of a line. AutoCAD sometimes will give you the apparent length of the line instead.

To get the absolute dimension length, your UCS must be parallel to the entity. To ensure this, use **UCS Entity**. There's only one other minor problem: the dimension text may be going in the wrong direction. If this is the case, use **UCS Y** and rotate the UCS until you have positive X going in the same direction you want your text.

25.9 <RETURN> for an entire line

When you're doing a linear dimension, AutoCAD first asks you to pick the first and second points of the line. If you're dimensioning a single entity, you don't actually have to do that. Simply pick the entity, then press <RETURN>, and AutoCAD will compute the endpoints of the entity for dimensioning purposes. This might save a few picks for object snap, etc.

 **AutoLISP Programs**

25.10 Text around an arc (LISP120)

This program lets you write text around an arc. It's simple to use: pick the place you want the text to begin. Give it a height and pick the arc. If the text isn't positioned correctly, you can rotate it using the base point as the center of the original arc. (Use of the plus sign at the end of a line in Auto-LISP code indicates that line is wrapped.)

Listing:
```
(defun c:lisp120 (/ blm os pt1 sty e tsize siz arc +
  txt r len dia hf int ang cnt ss nang pt tr)
    (setq blm (getvar "blipmode"))
    (setvar "blipmode" 0)
    (setq os (getvar "osmode"))
    (setq pt1 (getpoint "\nBeginning point of text "))
    (setq sty (getvar "textstyle"))
    (setq e (tblsearch "style" sty))
    (setq tsize (cdr (assoc 40 e)))
    (setq siz tsize)
    (if (= tsize 0)
        (setq siz (getdist pt1 "\nText height ")))
    (setvar "osmode" 4)
    (setq arc (getpoint  "\nPick the arc "))
    (setvar "osmode" os)
    (setq txt (getstring 1 "\nText: "))
    (setq r (distance arc pt1))
    (setq len (strlen txt))
    (setq dia (* (/ (* siz len) (* 2.0 pi r)) 360.0))
    (setq hf (/ (* dia pi) 180.0))
    (setq int (/ hf len))
```

(code continues next page)

```
(setq ang (angle arc pt1))
(setq cnt 0)
(setq ss (ssadd))
(while (< cnt len)
(setq nang (- ang (* cnt int)))
    (setq pt (polar arc nang (+ r (/ siz 2.0))))
    (setq tr (- (/ (* 180.0 nang) pi) 90.0))
    (setq cnt (+ cnt 1))
    (if (= tsize 0)
        (command "text" "c" pt siz tr (substr txt cnt 1))
        (command "text" "c" pt tr (substr txt cnt 1)))
    (setq ss (ssadd (entlast) ss))
)
(setvar "blipmode" blm)
(princ)
)
```

To Use: Load LISP120.LSP. First, draw an arc.

Type: LISP120 <RETURN>

Response: Beginning point of text:

Pick a point along the arc for the beginning point of text.

Response: Text height:

This question won't be asked if the height of the text is fixed with the style. Either enter the text height or point to it.

Response: Pick the arc:

Pick any point along the arc. You're set to **Object Snap Center**.

Response: Text:

Now type in your text. When you press <RETURN>, the text will be written along the arc.

25.11 Import text (LISP121)

This program lets you import text from an ASCII text file into your drawing. It also lets you choose the text style you want to use as well as the height and rotation. You can use this AutoLISP program as a sample, since it's in ASCII format. (Use of the plus sign at the end of a line in AutoLISP code indicates that line is wrapped.)

Listing:

```
(defun rtd (angg)
    (/ (* angg 180.0) pi))

(defun c:lisp121 (/ fln sty pt1 hgt rot f e txt)
    (setq fln (getstring "\nFile name to import "))
    (setq sty (getstring "\nEnter text STYLE or <ENTER> +
      for existing style "))
    (setq pt1 (getpoint "\nPick beginning point of text "))
    (setq f (open fln "r"))
    (if (/= sty "") (command "text" "style" sty ^c))
    (setq st (getvar "textstyle"))
    (setq e (tblsearch "style" st))
    (setq tsize (cdr (assoc 40 e)))
    (if (/= tsize 0) (setq hgt nil))
    (if (= tsize 0)
        (setq hgt (getdist pt1 "\nHeight  ")))
    (setq rot (getangle "\nText rotation  "))
    (if (= rot nil) (setq rot 0))
    (setq rot (rtd rot))
    (setq txt (read-line f))
    (if (= hgt nil) (command "text" pt1 rot txt))
    (if (/= hgt nil) (command "text" pt1 hgt rot txt))
    (setq e 1)
    (while e
        (setq txt (read-line f))
        (if (= txt nil) (setq e nil))
        (if (= hgt nil) (command "text" "" txt))
        (if (/= hgt nil) (command "text" "" txt))
    )
    (close f)
)
```

To Use: Load LISP121.LSP.

Type: `LISP121 <RETURN>`

Response: `File name to import:`

Type: `LISP121.LSP <RETURN>`

Response: `Enter text STYLE or <RETURN> for existing style:`

Type: `STANDARD <RETURN>`

Response: `Pick beginning point of text:`

Pick where you want your text to start.

Response: `Height:`

Enter the height of the text. You may also point to the height.

Response: `Text rotation:`

Enter the rotation or press <RETURN> for 0. The text will now start to print on your screen.

25.12 Export text (LISP122)

This program lets you export text to an ASCII file. You must place a window or a crossing around the text, since the program reads the text in reverse order—this is how AutoLISP stores entities in the selection set. Your text file will then come out in the right order.

Listing:
```
(defun c:lisp122 (/ fln f a n index el e txt)
    (setq fln (getstring "\nFile name: "))
    (setq f (open fln "w"))
    (setq a (ssget))
    (setq n (sslength a))
    (setq index (- n 1))
    (repeat n
        (setq el (entget (ssname a index)))
        (setq index (- index 1))
        (setq e (assoc 0 el))
        (if (= "TEXT" (cdr e))
            (progn
                (setq txt (cdr (assoc 1 el)))
                (write-line txt f)
            )
        )
    )
    (close f)
)
```

To Use: Load LISP122.LSP.

Type: LISP122 <RETURN>

Response: File name:

Enter the name of the output file. Use a drive, path specification.

Response: Select objects:

Put a crossing or window around the text you want to export. Don't worry if you capture entities other than text; the program will filter them out. The text will now be written out to disk.

25.13 **Length of an arc (LISP123)**

This program measures the length of an arc.

Listing:
```
(defun c:lisp123 (/ e pt1 e2 e1)
    (prompt "\nPick arc ")
    (setq e (entsel))
    (setq pt1 (cadr e))
    (setq e2 (car e))
    (setq e1 (entget (car e)))
    (if (= (cdr (assoc 0 e1)) "POLYLINE") (command "explode" e2))
    (command "pedit" pt1 "y" "")
    (command "area" "e" pt1)
    (command "explode" pt1)
    (princ "\n ") (princ "\n ")
    (princ "\nLength: ")
    (princ (getvar "perimeter"))
    (princ)
)
```

To Use: Load LISP123.LSP.

Type: `LISP123 <RETURN>`

Response: `Pick arc:`

Pick anywhere on the arc. If the arc is a polyline or part of a polyline, it will be exploded first. The length of the arc will be printed.

CHAPTER 26

Advanced Utilities

How Do You . . .

26.1 How do you save and execute multiple plot configurations?

The ACAD.CFG file is a dynamic, ongoing file—it's where AutoCAD stores a lot of the information that's used from drawing to drawing. When you configure AutoCAD or do a plot sequence, AutoCAD writes that information to the ACAD.CFG file before you even begin to plot. So you can cancel a plot and the information will still be written to this file and used as the parameters for the next plot sequence.

Using the trick of having different ACAD.CFG files in different directories isn't practical, since you would have to exit AutoCAD whenever you wanted to change your plot configuration. In that amount of time, you could just key it in.

Instead, use a script file. This is simply a text file ending in .SCR that holds the actual keystrokes that you'd enter in the plot sequence. In a script file, if you'd normally press <RETURN> you'd need a blank line in the file. Now you can just use a script file for each plot configuration you want to use and simply run the script file by typing **SCRIPT** and the file name.

See LISP124 in Tip 26.11. This isn't actually an AutoLISP program but a script file, so it has the extension .SCR (LISP124.SCR).

RELEASE 12   Gives you up to 29 different plot configurations through the new **Dynamic Dialogue Plot** file. See Tip 20.58.

26.2 How do you plot a .PLT file?

This depends on your plotter; some are easier to work with than others. A plot file is set up to work with XON and XOFF protocol. Some plotters let you use an ordinary communications program and simply send the file using the proper protocol. On other plotters, this won't work.

There are commercial software products on the market that are sold as software plot buffers. Most of the good ones work with .PLT files. These are the best programs to use because they're written specifically to support the most popular plotters. They also let you continue using AutoCAD while you're plotting.

26.3 **How do you put all of your AutoLISP files into one file?**

As you can see in this book, there are an awful lot of AutoLISP files for you to choose from. We don't recommend storing them in one single file. Instead, put a few of those you'll be using the most into the ACAD.LSP file. Group the others into library files to be loaded as needed. But in any event, you need a way to consolidate these files into larger files.

With the word processor, simply bring in each file in turn. While you're in the word processor, feel free to change the name of the program from LISPXX to something more meaningful that you can type in from the keyboard if needed.

There's one other way to put files together. You can use this as a short-cut for a couple of files, but don't use it for a large number of files. In DOS, just add (+) the files together with the DOS **COPY** command. For example, if you wanted to add FILE1.LSP and FILE2.LSP and combine them into TOTALFIL.LSP, you'd enter

```
COPY FILE1.LSP+FILE2.LSP TOTALFIL.LSP
```

There's a space between `COPY` and `FILE1`, but no spaces between the file names and the + sign. If you wanted to add FILE3.LSP and FILE4.LSP to the other two, you'd enter

```
COPY TOTALFIL.LSP+FILE3.LSP+FILE4.LSP TOTALFIL.LSP
```

Notice that TOTALFIL.LSP is copied and appended to itself. Although this will work for any number of files, it's much simpler to use a word processing program or a more sophisticated text editor for a large number of files.

More Steps to Success

26.4 Digitizer and menu configuration

If you use your digitizer a lot, you know that you have to set the tablet to 0 menus. Then when you're through digitizing, you have to reconfigure the tablet. The tablet information is found in ACAD.CFG and stored there until changed.

Consider setting up a directory that will hold the configuration files for the digitizer and for the tablet. Use the same procedure you use when you set up two graphics boards or digitizers. See Tip 18.5 for an example of how to set up and access multiple configuration files.

26.5 Some plot VIEWS may not work

Plotting from a **VIEW** is by far the most efficient method of plotting, since the plot area is composed for you. But many times you want to plot the specific coordinates of your drawing. Be aware that if you zoom to what you want plotted, you might not get on the plot exactly what you see on the screen.

Don't **SAVE** a view of the screen; instead, use the **Window** option in **VIEW**. Then you can either put a window around what you want to plot or give it absolute coordinates. Regardless of what appears on the screen, the plotter will plot only what's within those coordinates.

26.6 Have a .PGP program flip you back to the graphics screen

Have you ever wondered what the last 0 in a .PGP file is for? It's a coded bit that does various things, one of which is to force your drawing back to the graphics screen when the program that's accessing it finishes. Look at the line in ACAD.PGP for EDLIN:

```
EDIT,EDLIN,42000,File to edit: ,0
```

If you change the final 0 at the end of the line to a 4 it will change you to the graphics screen automatically when EDLIN is terminated. This won't work immediately from inside AutoCAD. You must exit your drawing and then go into the drawing editor for AutoCAD to pick up the change in the .PGP file.

26.7 **SAVE can destroy the contents of the backup file**

There's more than one reason to **SAVE** to an alternate file rather than to the current drawing name. First you have to understand how the **SAVE** and **END** commands work. Before they actually save your drawing, they copy the current drawing to the .BAK file. Then they overwrite the current drawing. Thus, you're left with the .DWG file as the edited version of the drawing and the .BAK file as the previous version.

But if you repeatedly **SAVE** a drawing to the same current drawing name, the last save is written to the .BAK file each time. If you need to keep the original drawing before the session begins, save it to an alternate file at the very least.

26.8 **Set up your plotter and go in circles**

Some plotters let you set features such as pen speed, origin plot, etc. But then the plotter seems to do the same old thing and looks as though it's ignoring your signals; and it is. When AutoCAD begins to plot, it sends reset signals to the plotter that reset your commands.

The problem lies in the order in which you do things. One of the last things that AutoCAD displays before it goes to plot is

```
Position page in plotter
Press RETURN to continue or S to Stop for hardware setup
```

This is the only time you can send commands to your plotter that AutoCAD won't override. Type S and proceed to set up the plotter. Then press <RETURN> to continue to plot. Do this each time you plot; it isn't necessary for most plotting operations, but it is when you need to set special commands on your plotter.

26.9 **A precaution on DXFIN**

If a **DXFIN** doesn't seem to work, something in your prototype drawing may be interfering with the import of the .DXF file. Remember that in order to do a **DXFIN** you must start with a new drawing, or you will get only entities.

The only way to assure this is to begin a new drawing as **NAME=**. Assume the name of your drawing is NEWDRAW.DWG. Choose number 1 from the AutoCAD main menu. When AutoCAD asks for the name of the new drawing,

Type: `NEWDRAW= <RETURN>`

This ensures that AutoCAD doesn't use any prototype drawing that might interfere with the .DXF file.

26.10 Chaining AutoLISP

In versions of AutoCAD before Release 10, AutoLISP programs can't load and execute other AutoLISP programs, but script files can load and execute AutoLISP programs, and AutoLISP programs can run script files. Therefore, you can chain AutoLISP programs by having an AutoLISP program call a script file that in turn runs another AutoLISP program, etc.

This method can also be used for those commands that AutoLISP won't let you address directly. If you get the message **Cannot invoke from AutoLISP**, this is where you can chain to a script file.

AutoLISP Programs

26.11 Plot script file (LISP124)

This is a plot script file that automatically sets the plot configuration. You should have one for each type of standard plot configuration you use.

Listing:
```
plot
d
y
y
c7
1
x
n
i
0.00,0.00
```

```
max
n
.010
n
n
f
<RETURN>
<RETURN>
```

To Use:

Type: SCRIPT <RETURN>

Response: Script file:

Type: LISP124 <RETURN>

Save the file as LISP124.SCR. It will run automatically and return you to the drawing editor.

If you enter the script file listing manually, you'll see that each plot question is answered by the script file in detail. No defaults are used because you can't depend on what the previous setting was.

26.12 Purge layers (LISP125)

If you're using prototype drawings correctly, you're probably setting up all the layers you'll need for a drawing. Programs such as AutoCAD AEC also do this. When the drawing is finished, you'll **PURGE** the layers that aren't used. But if you've got a hundred or more, this can take a lot of time. Imagine doing this for 20 drawing files in a project!

This program counts the number of possible layers in your drawing, and it purges the unreferenced ones for you. When it's through, only referenced layers will be in your drawing.

Listing:
```
(defun c:lisp125 (/ flg cnt e)
    (setq flg 1)
    (setq cnt 0)
    (while (setq e (tblnext "layer" flg))
        (setq cnt (+ cnt 1))
        (setq flg nil)
    )
    (repeat cnt
    (command "purge" "la" "y")
    )
)
```

To Use: Load LISP125.LSP.

Type: LISP125 <RETURN>

The program runs automatically.

CHAPTER 27

Advanced 3D

How Do You . . .

27.1 How do you put a 3D face on a complicated object?

A 3D face creates the solid facing necessary to hide lines. The problem is that a 3D face must have four sides. You can make any or all sides invisible; but putting enough faces on a complicated object with curves can be almost impossible.

   The only way to do this is to use a mesh instead of a 3D face. A mesh is really a series of 3D faces, but instead of your having to determine the size and vertices of all the corners, AutoCAD does it for you. Also, you can control the density of a mesh and thus the faces. Unfortunately, meshes leave you with a series of lines—but see Tip 27.2 for a way to make these lines go away.

27.2 How do you make a 3D mesh invisible?

The trick to making a 3D mesh invisible is to explode it. Once the mesh is exploded, it simply becomes a series of 3D faces that you can hide by calling up the entity and changing associative 70 to 15. This can be a tedious process; see LISP126 in Tip 27.13 for a program that handles it.

   If all you want to do is hide the mesh without actually making it invisible, it's much simpler. Place the mesh on its own layer, then turn the layer off. If you freeze the layer, it won't work. By turning the layer off, Auto-CAD will make any object on the layer (such as the mesh) invisible, but it will still hide any entity that's behind it. See Tip 19.20 for making meshes invisible for shading purposes.

27.3 **How do you rotate an object in the Z direction?**

The **ROTATE** command lets you rotate an object only in the X or Y direction. To rotate an object in the Z direction, change the UCS so that the direction you want to rotate is seen as X, Y.

Go into a **DVIEW** camera angle, so you can get a good 3D view of the object such as 45°, 45°. You'll notice that if you try to rotate the object, it's rotating in the X,Y direction.

Type: `UCS`

Response: `Origin/ZAxis/3point/Entity/View/X/Y/Z/Prev/Restore/Save/Del/?`

Type: `X <RETURN>`

Response: `Rotation angle about X axis:`

Type: `90 <RETURN>`

This changes the rotation so that X and Y are now going in the direction of the previous Z. Now when you're rotating the object, it's rotating in the direction of the previous Z.

27.4 **How do you cut a hole in a solid object?**

AutoCAD is a surface-modeling 3D package. If you need a true solid modeler, Autodesk sells AutoSOLID. All the same, AutoCAD users need to create the appearance of solid objects. This is often done with 3D faces and 3D meshes. But there's no real facility for cutting a hole through an object. The best you can do is to create the hole, either with a plain circle or an extruded cylinder. Then put a mesh around the outer portion of the object.

27.5 **How do you create a 2D representation of a 3D drawing with hidden lines?**

The object is to create in AutoCAD a 2D line drawing that's exactly as it would be plotted out. In other words, how do you input as a line drawing the representation of a plot?

AutoCAD makes this easy. Configure the plotter to be an ADI plotter. Select the DXB file output option so that the plotter will plot to a DXB file. To bring in the file, use the **DXBIN** command. Use this file format only for interfaces that need a line drawing representation imported.

More Steps to Success

27.6 Hide in one viewport

In order to avoid having to hide lines over and over, you can choose one viewport and hide the lines. Now draw in other viewports. This gives you a degree of perspective in your drawing without having to constantly rehide the lines.

27.7 Find the center of a rectangle

This is done with a filter command (**.XZ**). Let's say you want to draw a line from the center of a rectangle.

Type: `LINE <RETURN>`

Response: `From point:`

Type: `.XZ <RETURN>`

Pick the midpoint of the lower line of the rectangle.

Response: `Need Z`

Pick the midpoint of the right or left side of the rectangle; this will locate its center.

27.8 UCS for common commands

By changing the UCS, you can affect most of the common commands in AutoCAD. For example, let's say you want to copy one object on top of another that's along the Z axis. The easiest way would be to change the UCS so that Y is pointing above the object (in other words, rotate 90 degrees around X). In this way, Y is pointing toward what was Z. Now you can copy to the second point of displacement by **@4<90**—90 degrees is in the direction of Y, so you're copying above the object.

Almost all commands in AutoCAD are affected this way. If a command is based on X,Y, you can use the command by rotating the UCS in the necessary X,Y direction.

27.9 Use PAN to affect perspective

When you're in **DVIEW** and have set a distance and perspective, you've also set the distance to the object. You can also change your view of an object by using **CAMERA**, **TARGET** or **PAN**.

27.10 Mesh vertices aren't fixed

One advantage of using one of the 3D meshes supplied with AutoCAD is that AutoCAD picks the vertices for you. But be aware that these vertices aren't fixed; you can adjust or add to them with **PEDIT**.

27.11 Spline meshes

Once AutoCAD recognizes that you're working with meshes, it treats the subcommands of **PEDIT** differently. You can use **PEDIT** to create a spline or to decurve a mesh.

27.12 Joining polylines

If you ever need to join polylines that have different Z axes, explode them first. Then use **PEDIT** to join them.

AutoLISP Programs

27.13 Make meshes invisible (LISP126)

One of the main purposes of 3D meshes is to apply a surface to a model. **3DFACE** does this also, but it's difficult to use with irregular or curved objects. A good 3D mesh, applied properly, is an easier way to apply a surface—but it's impossible to get rid of all those lines. This program makes all the lines that form a 3D mesh invisible by exploding them and turning them into a series of 3D faces, then making them invisible.

Listing:
```
(defun c:lisp126 (/ pt1 a n index b1 b c b2)
    (setq pt1 (getpoint "\Pick mesh to make invisible "))
    (command "explode" pt1)
    (prompt "\nThe mesh is now a series of 3dfaces. ")
    (prompt "\nSelect entire mesh area to make invisible ")
    (setq a (ssget))
    (setq n (sslength a))
    (setq index 0)
    (repeat n
        (setq b1 (entget (ssname a index)))
        (setq index (1+ index))
        (setq b (assoc 0 b1))
        (if (= "3DFACE" (cdr b))
            (progn
                (setq c (assoc 70 b1))
                (setq b2 (subst '(70 . 15) c b1))
                (entmod b2)
            )
        )
    )
)
```

To Use: Load LISP126.LSP.

Type: LISP126 <RETURN>

Response: Pick mesh to make invisible:

Pick the 3D mesh.

Response: Select entire mesh area to make invisible:
Select objects:

Now put a window or crossing around the entire mesh. Don't be afraid to include other entities; only the mesh will disappear.

CHAPTER 28

Miscellaneous (Advanced)

How Do You . . .

28.1 How do you control memory?

When using DOS, your main concern is to optimize the available memory in the base 640k area. Any memory you steal for any reason—networks, TSRs (terminate-and-stay-resident programs), pointers to extended memory, AutoLISP, etc.—will reduce AutoCAD's efficiency. Of course, these memory usurpers increase efficiency in other ways. If you have enough memory, shift AutoLISP to extended memory by using extended AutoLISP to free up some of that 640k for other things.

If you want to use a RAM disk, either use VDISK, which is supplied by DOS, or control the beginning address of your extended or expanded memory. The reason for this is that AutoCAD will recognize VDISK and respect the memory that's set aside. AutoCAD may not recognize other programs that set up their own RAM disks, so you must set aside this memory manually; see Tip 18.7.

28.2 How do you right-justify ASCII text for import into AutoCAD?

Most word processors can right-justify text, but AutoCAD can't read this text in a word processing format. Thus, you must trick the word processor into producing a text file that's already right-justified.

The easiest way to do this is *not* to save to a text file; instead, print to disk. When the word processor is printing to disk, it thinks that it's printing to a printer, and will thus right-justify the text. Be sure your printer driver is for a DOS text printer so you don't get any strange printer codes.

Once the file's printed, you can type it out on the screen. It should now be an ordinary, right-justified text file that you can import into AutoCAD.

WARNING: Be sure the text font you're using in AutoCAD has a fixed pitch. Standard-width font MONOTXT will work well; other triplex fonts won't.

28.3 **How do you port AutoCAD to desktop publishing?**

This depends on your desktop publishing software; check the software manual. Different software uses different file formats, which include .PLT (plot files) or DXF—or some may read it in as a DWG file. Regardless of its form, your drawing will come into the desktop publishing software as a unit that can be scaled but not changed.

WARNING: Be very careful that you don't skew the file when you bring your drawing in. When it's scaled, make sure to maintain the X,Y coordinates (the corners).

 RELEASE 12   Gives you the option to create .EPS files with a TIFF or EPSI header, using the new **PSOUT** command.

28.4 **How do you increase environment space?**

If you're working with DOS Version 3.2 or higher, it's not really necessary to increase the environment area. Of course, with more environment variables available and with longer path statements, there's a large demand on the environment area. But the problem isn't *how much* area is set aside, but *when* it's set aside.

Beginning with DOS 3.2, the environment memory size is dynamic; it grows to meet the demand that's created in the AUTOEXEC.BAT file. The environment area will continue to expand until the first program you run. Then it will be fixed in size; if you try to add to it, you'll get an **Out of environment space** error. Make sure that all statements that use the area come at the very beginning of the AUTOEXEC.BAT file. Don't place any programs—even driver programs—before these statements.

In DOS Version 3.2 or earlier, you can use this statement in your CONFIG.SYS file to expand the amount of environment space:

```
SHELL /E:512
```

28.5 **How do you convert a drawing from Release 11 or 12 to Release 10?**

You can't really do this with AutoCAD, but you can **DXFOUT** a Release 11 or 12 drawing. The file must then be stripped of any Release 11 or 12 information that Release 10 doesn't understand. There is a program on your AutoCAD companion diskette called **DXFIX**. DXFIX.DOC is the documentation. This will correct the DXF file for Releases 11 and 12 down to Release 10.

28.6 How do you convert from CAD systems that don't support DXF or IGES?

Commercial programs are available that can convert Hewlett Packard plot files to DXB files so that you can then read in a DXB file. These programs are listed in the AutoCAD applications guide. However, a DXB file that comes from an HP plot file may be just a series of lines. As a result, the conversion might not recognize any entities except lines—and they could be very small ones. Still, this may be your only way to get a facsimile of the conversion into AutoCAD.

Commercial programs are also available that can insert scanned raster files onto their own layer of AutoCAD. These can be useful if you want to trace over them on a real AutoCAD layer.

More Steps to Success

28.7 Network nodes

AutoCAD doesn't directly support networks in Release 10, but it does give you some tools to use when you network. Here are some tips that make networking AutoCAD easier and safer.

First, make sure that every computer on your system has its own copy of AutoCAD on its own hard disk. This shouldn't be a problem, since this is required by the license agreement. Don't try to network AutoCAD with only one copy on the server; that's far too slow.

Since each machine will have its own version of AutoCAD, it will also have its own configuration file. Give each machine a different node name; you'll find this in the configuration routine under Operating Parameters. This will give different names to a drawing's temporary files.

If you have any problems, make sure that drawings aren't called up or created in the same directory. Create a new drawing in another directory and insert the target drawing.

RELEASE 11   Network control under Release 11 is now explicitly supported. See Chapter 9 for a description of the network features available.

28.8 **Unerase files**

Be careful about depending on commercial utilities that say they'll unerase files that are erased by mistake. These programs often won't work with AutoCAD, because they depend on files' sectors being sequential, which is rare with AutoCAD. With some AutoCAD files, it doesn't matter if you get 99 percent of the file, because if you miss that 1 percent, you might as well have given up the entire file.

Only one type of unerase procedure works consistently with AutoCAD. This involves copying the file to another area of disk before the erasure takes place. The temporary file is saved for the number of days designated by the user. Then the file is permanently erased. This procedure isn't really an unerase type of utility; it just copies the temporary file back to its original state. Look very carefully at the procedure used by your utility.

28.9 **Don't use too much memory**

For every megabyte of extended memory you make available to Auto-CAD, you need pointer room in the 640k area. So if you allot substantially more memory than you'd ever use for your largest drawing, you're wasting 640k area to point to that memory. You must limit AutoCAD's access to any excess memory; use the environment variables **ACADLIMEM** for expanded memory and **ACADXMEM** for extended memory.

28.10 **Clearing environment variables**

If you need to clear some of the environment variables, you can use the **SET xxxxxx=** command.

The **xxxxxx** is the name of the environment variable. By setting it equal to nothing, you've effectively erased it. Thus, you can set up dummy environment variables to create available memory, then erase them after at least one program has begun. In this way, space is reserved and other programs can set variables as needed.

28.11 Begin named views

Not only can you bring in AutoCAD to a drawing, you can also bring up AutoCAD to a named view within that drawing. The syntax is as follows:

```
drawingname,view
```

Following the name of the drawing with a command and then the name of the view makes AutoCAD bring up the existing drawing to that view. AutoCAD will tell you if the view doesn't exist and then bring up the drawing to the last view saved.

28.12 Speed up picks

The larger the aperture box, the slower AutoCAD is in picking objects with Object Snap. So always make sure that the aperture box is as small as possible and draw within the limits.

28.13 A trick with XCOPY

Have you ever tried to copy a number of files to a floppy disk, only to fill the disk and have to finish copying the files one by one? If you have Version 3.3 DOS or higher, you can use the **COPY** command, so if you fill a disk, **COPY** will pick up on the next disk right where it left off.

Before you begin the command, add the archive flag to all the files you want to copy:

```
ATTRIB +A C:*.*
```

This adds the archive flag to all files on the C: drive. Of course, you can substitute any path and file spec. Now you're ready to use the **XCOPY** command:

```
XCOPY C:*.* A:/M
```

The **/M** parameter tells **XCOPY** to copy only those files that have the archive flag set. While it's copying, it removes the archive flag. You'll get an **Insufficient disk space** error. Simply put in the next disk and issue the above command. Since the files that have been copied have had their archive flags removed, the routine will pick up where it left off for the next disk. The beauty of this is that the files are copies, not backup versions.

Advanced Release II

How Do You . . .

29.1 How do you know when to work in Paper Space or Model Space?

Let's start with an overview of Paper Space and Model Space. When a new concept is introduced, you suddenly need a name for the old concept. In this case, that name is Model Space. Before Paper Space, all work in Auto-CAD was done in Model Space.

The primary purpose of Paper Space is to open an unlimited number of viewports so you can work in those viewports, arrange the viewports anywhere on the screen, then plot the screen as you see it. Because you're able to toggle back and forth between Paper Space and Model Space with different views, there's the danger of thinking of these two modes as being two different drawings. They are not. Anything done to any view or any part of an entity while in Paper Space is the same as actually editing that entity. Remember, you have only one set of entities. Paper Space just gives you more flexibility in viewing and plotting those entities.

To avoid confusion, you need to think of Paper Space and Model Space as two different modes of viewing and working with your drawing. Within each mode are commands specific to that mode. You must always be in one mode or the other to use specific related commands. The command that toggles you from one mode to the other is **TILEMODE**. This is really a system variable rather than an actual AutoCAD command, but it is used the same way. If **TILEMODE** is set to 1, you're in Model Space mode. If **TILEMODE** is set to 0, you're in Paper Space mode.

Begin by drawing some lines on your screen. At this point you're in Model Space. Once the entities are drawn, change to Paper Space mode.

Type: `TILEMODE <RETURN>`

Response: `New value for TILEMODE <1>`

Type: `0 <RETURN>`

Your screen should go blank. Notice the right triangle in the lower left-hand side of your screen. This is the UCS icon for Paper Space. In order to work in Paper Space, you'll need to create at least one viewport. This is done with the **MVIEW** command.

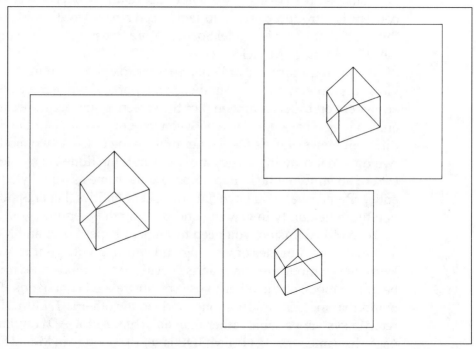

Figure 29-1: Choose viewport size and shape

Type: `MVIEW <RETURN>`

Response: `ON/OFF/Hideplot/Fit/2/3/4/Restore/<First Point>:`

Pick a point on your screen and move your cursor to draw a window. You are creating a viewport. Notice the flexibility you have. You can create the viewport any size or any rectangular shape you want. When you've picked two points that outline the shape of the viewport, the entities from Model Space appear in the viewport.

Repeat the above command and draw two more viewports on your screen.

Notice at this point that you can't enter the viewports to change anything. This is because you're in Pspace rather than Mspace. Pspace and Mspace are two modes within Paper Space mode. This is where the confusion lies. Once you've set **TILEMODE** to 0, you're in Paper Space mode. But there are two modes of operation while in Paper Space mode. They're called Pspace and Mspace. Remember that while working in Mspace within the Paper Space mode, you are *not* working in Model Space mode. Please don't get that confused. Pspace and Mspace are both part of Paper Space, not Model Space. That is, **TILEMODE** is set to 0.

Let's now enter the Mspace mode of operation within Paper Space.

Type: `Mspace <RETURN>`

Notice how the normal UCS icons now appear in each viewport. If you move your cursor outside the viewports, you see the standard inactive arrow. Notice also that one of your viewports seems to be outlined with a double line. This is your active viewport. Move your cursor inside this viewport. See how your crosshairs become active. Move the cursor now to the other two viewports. The crosshairs turn into an arrow, indicating that the other two viewports are not active. Pick while inside one of the other viewports. It now becomes the active viewport.

What this means is that while you're in the Mspace mode of Paper Space, the viewports you created will act the same as the traditional viewports available to you in Model Space. There are two big differences. First, you can have as many viewports as you need. (*NOTE*: only 16 can be visible at any one time.) Second, when you enter Pspace mode within Paper Space, you can move the viewports around, make them larger or smaller, annotate them anywhere on the screen with text, draw from one to another, and plot exactly what you see on the screen.

At any point in time, you can return to Model Space by changing **TILEMODE** from 0 to 1.

Type: `TILEMODE <RETURN>`

Response: `New value for TILEMODE <0>`

Type: `1 <RETURN>`

Your original drawing is now on your screen. Any changes you made to the drawing while in Mspace within Paper Space are reflected when you return to Model Space. Annotations you made while in Pspace within Paper Space are not reflected. You may toggle back and forth at any time.

29.2 **How do you create a Paper Space viewport?**

Viewports are created in Paper Space with the **MVIEW** command. You must first have **TILEMODE** set to 0.

Type: `TILEMODE <RETURN>`

Response: `New value for TILEMODE`

Type: `0 <RETURN>`

Depending on whether you've previously entered and worked in Paper Space, your screen may be blank. You're now ready to use the **MVIEW** command to create up to four viewports at a time.

Type: `MVIEW <RETURN>`

Response: `ON/OFF/Hideplot/Fit/2/3/4/Restore/<First Point>:`

The default is First Point. By picking two points that create a window, you're outlining the size and rectangular shape of the viewport. With the second pick, the viewport is formed and the view from the current Model Space is inserted in it.

29.3 **How do you create multiple viewports in Paper Space at one time?**

You can create up to four viewports each time you use the **MVIEW** command.

Type: `MVIEW <RETURN>` (**TILEMODE** must be set to 0.)

Response: `ON/OFF/Hideplot/Fit/2/3/4/Restore/<First Point>:`

Type: `4 <RETURN>`

MVIEW now creates four viewports, each with the same view of the previous Model Space. Each of these viewports is independent, just as if they were created one at a time. They can be moved, made larger or smaller or activated independently within the **MSPACE** command.

29.4 How do you create viewports in Paper Space with the same configuration as saved viewports in Model Space?

MVIEW lets you restore any previously saved viewport configuration from Model Space. Assume you have a three-viewport configuration in Model Space called V3. This configuration is a top, plan and side view of your object.

Type: `MVIEW <RETURN>` (**TILEMODE** must be set to 0.)

Response: `ON/OFF/Hideplot/Fit/2/3/4/Restore/<First Point>:`

Type: `?/Name of window configuration to insert <*ACTIVE>`

Type: `v3 <RETURN>`

Now choose **Fit** or pick a first and second point. The viewport configuration will be restored within Paper Space.

29.5 How do you hide lines when you plot in Paper Space?

Remember that when you plot in Paper Space, each viewport is treated as a separate entity. You might want one viewport to hide lines, but not another. Therefore, **MVIEW** gives you the ability to choose those viewports where lines will be hidden during the plot and those where the lines will not be hidden during the plot.

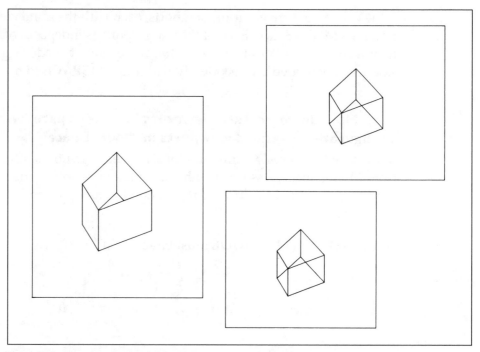

Figure 29-2: Choose viewport(s) to hide lines

    Type: `MVIEW <RETURN>` **(TILEMODE must be set to 0.)**

Response: `ON/OFF/Hideplot/Fit/2/3/4/Restore/<First Point>:`

    Type: `H <RETURN> (Hideplot)`

Response: `ON/OFF`

    Type: `ON <RETURN>`

Response: `Select objects:`

Now pick the viewport(s) where you want the lines to be hidden during the plot. Remember to pick the lines around the viewport, not inside the viewport itself, nor the entities within the viewport. Likewise, you may choose **Off** and pick the viewports where you don't want the lines to be hidden during the plot.

29.6 How do you turn a Paper Space viewport on and off?

There are several reasons why you may want to turn a viewport on or off. First, if you're not working in a viewport currently, it may save you some time to turn the viewport off. This will let you move and change the size of several viewports without having to wait for each one to regenerate. Second, you can have only 16 viewports on at one time. This doesn't mean you can't have more than 16 viewports, but only 16 can be seen on the screen at one time. When you exceed the maximum number, AutoCAD will begin turning off certain viewports automatically. You can choose which will be turned off and which left on.

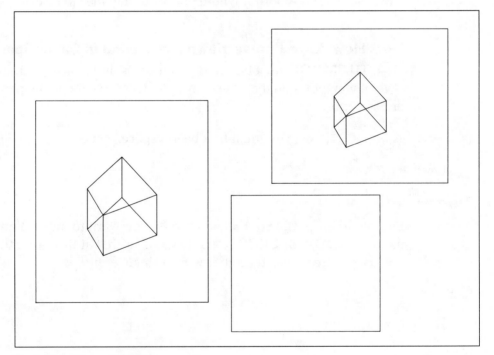

Figure 29-3: Choose viewport(s) to turn off

Type: `MVIEW <RETURN>` (**TILEMODE** must be set to 0.)

Response: `ON/OFF/Hideplot/Fit/2/3/4/Restore/<First Point>:`

Type: `OFF <RETURN>`

Response: `ON/OFF`

Type: `ON <RETURN>`

Response: `Select objects:`

Now pick the viewport(s) where you want the lines to be off.

29.7 How do you move viewports around in Paper Space?

First, **TILEMODE** must be 0 and you must be in Pspace. Assume you have several viewports on the screen and you want to change the position of one viewport.

Type: `Pspace <RETURN>` (You must first be in Pspace.)

Type: `Move <RETURN>`

Response: `Select objects:`

Pick along the outline of the viewport(s) you want to move. You can also use a **WINDOW** or **CROSSING**. Remember that at this point the entire viewport is treated as though it were a single entity.

Response: `1 selected, 1 found`

Type: `<RETURN> This confirms the selection set.`

Response: `Base point or displacement:`

Pick a base point on the viewport to be moved and drag it to the new position, then pick.

You can move the viewport anywhere on the screen. You can even let it overlap other viewports.

29.8 **How do you change the size of the Paper Space viewports?**

First, **TILEMODE** must be 0 and you must be in Pspace. Assume you have several viewports on the screen and you want to change the size of one of the viewports.

Type: Pspace <RETURN> (You must first be in Pspace.)

Type: Scale <RETURN>

Response: Select objects:

Pick along the outline of the viewport(s) you want to scale. You can also use a **WINDOW** or **CROSSING**. Remember that at this point the entire viewport is treated as though it were a single entity.

Response: 1 selected, 1 found

Type: <RETURN> (This confirms the selection set.)

Response: Base point

Pick a base point on the viewport to be scaled. Notice this is the same **SCALE** command you use for any other entity.

Response: <Scale factor>/Reference:

Type: .5 <RETURN>

This makes the viewport half the size. You can also drag the size dynamically or use the **Reference** option. Remember, you're only scaling the viewport, you're not really changing the actual objects inside. So when you return to Model Space they won't be changed. Their size in Paper Space is being scaled accordingly, in relation to the other objects in Paper Space. The size of the viewport is one of the determining factors in the size of the object when it's plotted.

29.9 **How do you plot different entities at different scales using Paper Space?**

Assume you have four viewports and **TILEMODE** is set to 0. You are in Paper Space. What you want to do is to scale four separate views differently at the time of plotting.

The first consideration is the scale factor you're going to use at the time you plot. If it's 1=1, you must do all of your scaling first within the viewports. On the other hand, if the overall scale factor at the time of plotting is 1=50 or 1/4"=1', you can work up a general relationship of the viewports to each other.

Start with the assumption that you are going to be plotting the Paper Space viewports at 1=1 at plot time. Viewport 1 should be plotted 1=50; viewport 2 1=25; viewport 3 1=100; viewport 4 1=1000.

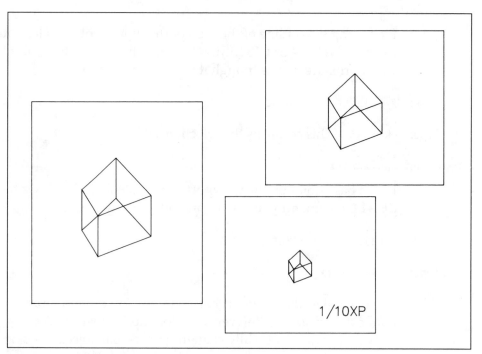

Figure 29-4: Scaling views separately

Type: Mspace <RETURN> (This assumes **TILEMODE 0.**)

Pick and make active viewport 1.

Type: ZOOM <RETURN>

Type: 1/50xp <RETURN>

The XP at the end of the zoom factor scales the image in the active viewport by that ratio. Note that the object is not actually changing size. Only the **ZOOM** view of that object in relation to Paper Space units has changed. This is how different scales are created.

If you're scaling 1/4"=1', you must enter 1/48.

29.10 **How do you control layers in multiple viewports?**

The command **VPLAYER** controls the visibility of layers on individual viewports. The **FREEZE** and **THAW** commands control the visibility of layers in all viewports at once. In order to use **VPLAYER**, you must be in Paper Space. That is to say, the system variable **TILEMODE** must be set to 0. You can be in either Mspace or Pspace at the time you use **VPLAYER**, but the command acts slightly differently depending on which mode you're in.

Begin first with a drawing that has several layers. Set **TILEMODE** to 0.

Type: TILEMODE 0 <RETURN>

Now set up several viewports.

Type: MVIEW <RETURN>

Pick the first and second corner. Repeat this command several times until you have at least two or three viewports on the screen.

Now enter Pspace.

Type: PSPACE <RETURN>

Notice that one of your viewports is the current viewport. You can tell this in the traditional way by moving your crosshairs from viewport to viewport. When the crosshairs change from an arrow to crosshairs, you have the current viewport.

Assume now that the layer you want to freeze is Layer1.

Type: `VPLAYER <RETURN>`

Response: `?/Freeze/Thaw/Reset/Newfrz/Vpvisdflt:`

Type: `Freeze <RETURN>`

Response: `Layer(s) to Freeze:`

Type: `Layer1 <RETURN>` (You may enter layer names separated by commas or use any of the wild card facilities available in Release 11 or Release 12.)

Response: `All/Select/<Current>:`

Type: `<RETURN>`

By pressing <RETURN> at this option, only the current viewport is affected by the **Freeze** option of **VPLAYER**.

Type: `<RETURN>`

This exits you from the **VPLAYER** command and the screen is updated with Layer1 frozen only in the current viewport.

You could have selected the **All** or the **Select** option instead of **Freeze**. If you had chosen **All**, all viewports currently on your screen would have that layer frozen.

But what about new viewports that are created after the **VPLAYER** command? When those viewports are created, the layers previously affected through an **All** option are not affected with a simple **Freeze**.

If you had chosen **Select**, you'd be asked to select objects and the viewports where you wanted the layers frozen.

The **Thaw** option of **VPLAYER** works exactly like the **Freeze** option, except that it makes the selected layers visible.

The **Current** option of **VPLAYER** freezes or thaws the current layer only. This option is valid only if you're in Mspace instead of Pspace.

29.11 How do you create a layer that is already frozen?

An option of **VPLAYER**, **Newfrz**, lets you create a layer that's frozen in all viewports. But why would you want to do this? Assume that you had six viewports on your screen. You are in Pspace and only want information placed in one of the viewports. Use the **Newfrz** option of **VPLAYER** and create a new layer. Now thaw that layer only for the current viewport. Use the regular **LAYER** command and **Set** the new layer as the current layer. Since it was created as frozen in all viewports, what you draw on the new layer will appear only in the current viewport since it was frozen on all the others.

Type:	Mspace <RETURN> (This is easier to illustrate if you are in Mspace.)
Type:	Vplayer <RETURN>
Response:	?/Freeze/Thaw/Reset/Newfrz/Vpvisdflt:
Type:	Newfrz <RETURN>
Response:	New Viewport frozen layer name(s):
Type:	Layer2 <RETURN>
Response:	?/Freeze/Thaw/Reset/Newfrz/Vpvisdflt:
Type:	Thaw <RETURN>
Response:	Layer(s) to Thaw:
Type:	Layer2 <RETURN>
Response:	All/Select/<Current>:
Type:	<RETURN> <RETURN>

Now set yourself to Layer2 using the regular AutoCAD **LAYER** command, and you're ready to draw on that layer only in the selected viewport.

29.12 **How do you set the default visibility of a new layer?**

AutoCAD gives you the ability to set the visibility of any layer to any specified viewports. But what happens when new viewports are created? What layers should be visible and what layers should not?

The **Vpvisdflt** option of **VPLAYER** gives you the flexibility to determine this.

Type: `VPLAYER <RETURN>` (**TILEMODE** must be set to 0.)

Response: `?/Freeze/Thaw/Reset/Newfrz/Vpvisdflt:`

Type: `Vpvisdflt <RETURN>`

Response: `Layer name(s) to change default viewport visibility:`

Type: `Layer1 <RETURN>` (You may enter layer names separated by commas or use any of the wild card facilities available to you in Release 11 and Release 12.)

Response: `Change default viewport visibility to Frozen/Thawed:`

Type: `Frozen <RETURN>`

From now on, any new viewport created will have Layer1 already frozen.

More Steps to Success

29.13 **Scratch pad using Paper Space**

You can use Paper Space to create a scratch pad area to look at other drawings or to bring in other drawings to swap parts.

First, begin by creating a Paper Space viewport. Make sure you're in Mspace. Make your new viewport active. Then you might issue the following **ZOOM** command:

`ZOOM W 10000,10000 10500,10500`

This will create a zoom area in your drawing far away from your real drawing. The actual coordinates can be any distance away from your drawing. Next, insert the drawing you want to work with, or use this viewport as your scratch pad. If you want to move or copy something from your scratch pad, issue the **MOVE** or **COPY** command, then activate a real viewport to move it to.

When you're finished, erase everything by using an **ERASE** crossing with the same coordinates as the zoom area.

This procedure gives DOS users much of the functionality other operating systems enjoy with their windowing capabilities. In fact, since this procedure permits movement of entities between windows, it can actually provide more functionality.

29.14 Viewports 100 percent within viewports

Never put a viewport 100 percent inside another viewport in Paper Space. The reason is that you can then make only one of the viewports active in Mspace. As long as a portion of any viewport is outside another viewport, either viewport can be made active at any time.

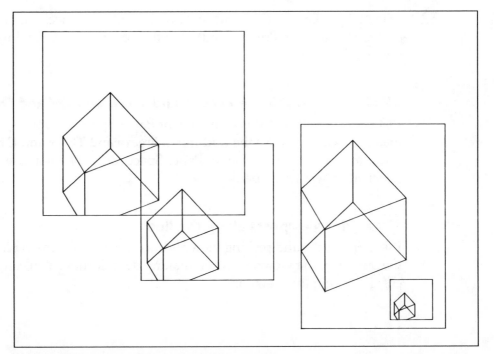

Figure 29-5: Leave portion of any viewport outside of another

29.15 **Drawing in Paper Space**

You can still draw while in Pspace of Paper Space mode. Even though the viewports are not active, you can draw across them. You are not actually touching your Model Space drawing. Instead you're drawing over your drawing. While in Pspace you can plot these out together. This is great for annotation or drawing connecting leader lines. When you return to Model Space, Paper Space entities are not there.

29.16 **Quick check plots**

Here's a trick for using Paper Space entities for marking up check plots. Create Paper Space viewports, and set the drawing to Pspace. Next, begin marking up the drawing as you see fit and on any layer. When the corrections need to be made, change to Mspace within Paper Space mode and make your corrections. Note that you can't Object Snap to Paper Space objects. Toggle back to Pspace and erase the correction note. Toggle back to Mspace and continue making the corrections. This way, you see only the correction notes that are still left to be done. When you return to Model Space at any point in time, none of the correction notes are visible even if they haven't been erased.

 RELEASE 12   Gives you a quicker way to produce a check plot to the screen by using the Preview button of the new **Dynamic Dialogue Plot** file. See Tip 20.59.

29.17 **You can still use Freeze and Thaw and Off and On**

Just because **VPLAYER** is available for Paper Space viewports, this doesn't mean you can't still use the traditional **Freeze** and **Thaw** and **Off** and **On**. These are still available even in Paper Space. But when you use them they affect all viewports globally.

29.18 **Pick viewports along the line**

When in Pspace and picking viewports as entities, be sure to pick along the outline of the viewport when making the selection. You can't pick the entities within the viewport.

29.19 MIRROR and ROTATE viewports are not what they seem

The **MIRROR** and **ROTATE** commands don't really do what they say when you apply them to viewports as entities in Pspace. If you mirror a viewport in Pspace, you've done nothing more than move or copy the viewport. The items in the viewport neither rotate nor mirror. The border of the viewport is still parallel to the view of the screen. The availability of these commands in Pspace may have some value as a method of moving or copying viewports and their creation, but they certainly don't do what their names imply.

29.20 REGENALL and REDRAWALL for Paper Space viewports

Use **REGENALL** and **REDRAWALL** to redraw or regen all of the viewports at one time. **REGEN** and **REDRAW** will regen and redraw only the current active viewport. This is the same as using the regular **VPORTS** command in Model Space.

29.21 DIMSCALE in Paper Space

When dimensioning in Mspace in Paper Space mode, you can make the scale factor of the dimension variables automatically correlate with the scaling between Paper Space and the current viewport by setting **DIMSCALE** to 0,0.

29.22 HATCH scales and Paper Space

When setting the scale factor for a hatch pattern, you can place XP after the scale factor. This tells AutoCAD to calculate the scale factor based on the distance in Paper Space rather than the real distance in Model Space.

29.23 PLOT with and without Paper Space boxes

When you create a viewport in Pspace, the outline of the viewport is created on the current layer. A good tip is to always make sure you create a viewport on a special viewport layer. When you plot, you get exactly what you see on the screen, viewport outlines and all. If you don't want the outlines, **Freeze** the viewport layer. The outlines will be turned off and you'll be left only with the entities you want to plot, properly placed where you need them.

Advanced Release 12

How Do You . . .

30.1 How do you update an open XREF drawing?

Since you can access another drawing on a network through **XREF**, even if that drawing is currently being worked on, you may need to see the updated version of it periodically. If, for example, a designer wanted to see any current, live changes made in an externally referenced drawing, it's a simple matter of using the **XREF Reload** command to import the updated drawing into your current drawing. See Tip 30.11.

30.2 How do you reset your com ports?

A useful trick for resetting the com ports will no longer work in AutoCAD Release 12. From time to time you'll lose your crosshairs because of an interruption of your serial port. Without having to exit AutoCAD, you can reset the com ports by going into the **PLOT** command and then ^C exit back to the drawing. This worked because the **PLOT** command reinitialized all of the AutoCAD settings, including the com ports, as you went back to the drawing editor.

   This trick will no longer work because the **PLOT** command is an integral part of the drawing editor. Therefore, AutoCAD has added a command **REINIT**. This is entered from the Command line. It brings up a dialogue box from which you can choose the kind of reinitialization you want to take place. Pick **Digitizer** and/or **Plotter** under **I/O Port Initialization**.

30.3 How do you reset your video screen?

From time to time your ADI driver might go crazy. You might get stray lines or odd colors even into the menu areas. This can be caused by a bug in the ADI driver or an ill-behaved TSR (terminate-and-stay resident program) you may be using. When this happens, you can reinitialize the screen with the **REINIT** command from the Command line.

   From the dialogue box choose **Display**.

30.4 **How do you reset your mouse or digitizer if you don't have crosshairs to pick with?**

The **REINIT** command works well to reset com ports and devices as long as you have digitizer or mouse control to pick with. If you don't have mouse control, you can still use the dialogue box by using the Tab to highlight the item, and then hit the space bar, which checks the check box. When you have both boxes checked, <RETURN>. **REINIT** provides options for reinitializing either files or I/O ports for devices.

Another way is to use the system variable **REINIT**. The following are the integer numbers to reinitialize each item:

1   Digitizer port
2   Plotter port
4   Digitizer
8   Display
16   PGP file

Type: `SETVAR REINIT  <RETURN>`

Now type in the appropriate number and <RETURN>. If you want to reinitialize more than one, add the numbers of the appropriate items together and enter the sum of the numbers.

30.5 **How do you move a file from one directory to another?**

This is done by picking **Utilities...** from the FILE pulldown menu or by typing **FILES** from the Command line. This brings up a **File Utilities** dialogue box. Pick the **Rename file...** box. In addition to being able to rename a file, this lets you to move the file from one directory to another. The **Old File Name** file dialogue box is brought up. Here you can change pattern, drive and directory. Find the file you want to move and pick it, then OK. Now you're given another file dialogue box called **New File Name**. If you want the file to have the same name when you move it, pick the same file again. But before you OK it, change directories by picking the new directory in the **Directories** list box. The file name will remain in the **File** box. Once you're in the new directory, then OK. The file will be moved.

This will work only as long as you're moving the file from one directory to another on the same drive. It will not work if you try to change drives in the move.

30.6 How do you TRIM multiple objects at one time?

TRIM is one of the most useful commands in AutoCAD. But it has had a severe limitation. Once you've selected the cutting edge, you must select the entities to be trimmed only by picking them one at a time. This can be rather time-consuming if you have several hundred to trim along a single cutting edge. Up until now, you weren't permitted to put a **CROSSING WINDOW** around the entities.

There has been a partial change in Release 12. You still can't select the entities to be trimmed with a **CROSSING WINDOW**, but you can select them with a **FENCE**. Look at Figure 30-1. The dashed line represents the **Fence** line used for the trim selection set.

Type: `Trim <RETURN>`

Response: `Select cutting edge...`
`Select Objects:`

Type: Select your cutting edge or select everything and confirm. In this example, select the arc as the cutting edge.

Response: `<Select object to trim>/Undo:`

Type: `F <RETURN>` (this is the **Fence** selection option)

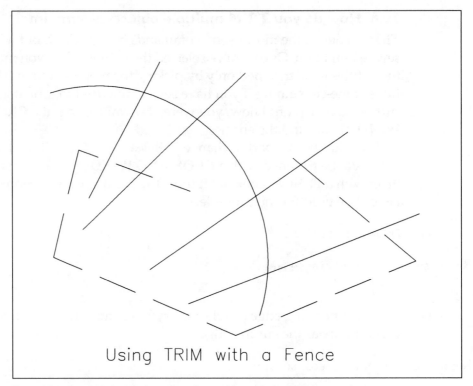

Using TRIM with a Fence

Figure 30-1: Fence (dashed line) used to select entities with the TRIM command

Now draw a **Fence** line across the lines where the dashed line in Figure 30-1 is located and <RETURN>. All the lines will be trimmed at the same time. Notice that you don't have to stop with just one **Fence** line. Figure 30-2 represents the result of the trim.

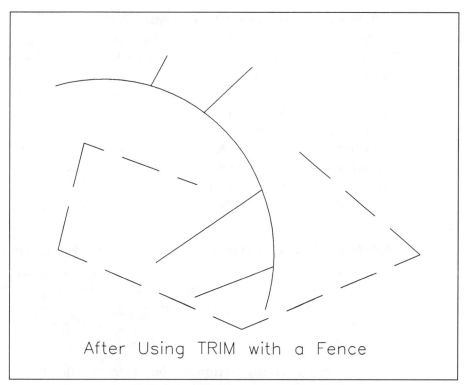

After Using TRIM with a Fence

Figure 30-2: Result of using the Fence to select entities with the TRIM command

30.7 How do you input horizontal and vertical angles with DVIEW CAmera and TArget?

Now that **DVIEW** doesn't use the horizontal and vertical scroll bars for **CAmera** and **TArget**, that doesn't mean it stops asking you the questions at the Command line. You can still enter the angles as before.

30.8 **How do you create PostScript files?**

PSOUT will write out a file. The questions are similar to plot questions in that you can select to write out the **Display**, **Extents**, **Limits**, **View** and **Window**.

You also have the option of including a screen preview. This is useful for desktop publishing programs. This screen preview can be either in TIFF format or EPSI format.

If you've chosen to include a screen preview, AutoCAD wants to know its pixel resolution. The default is 128. This is the most common. It's designed to give a rough indication as to the size and shape of the image. Higher resolution is optional, but will create a much larger and slower file.

30.9 **How do you create a PostScript file with hidden lines?**

Do not use **PSOUT** to create your postscript file if you want a hidden line view. There are no questions about hiding lines. The way you do it is to first create a *postscript plotter configuration*.

Type: `CONFIG  <RETURN>`

Choose **Plotter configuration** and add a new plotter. Choose **PostScript device** ADI 4.2 by Autodesk, and proceed to answer the questions.

Now, using **DVIEW** or other AutoCAD facilities, get the exact 3D view you want on your screen.

Type: `PLOT  <RETURN>`

From the **Plot** dialogue box, choose the **PostScript device plotter**. Check the **Hide Lines** box and the **Plot To File** box. Pick the **File Name...** box and set the name specifically, adding the extension .EPS. Other settings are optional. Now proceed to plot.

If you didn't add the extension .EPS to the file name, shell out of Auto-CAD and rename the file from .PLT to .EPS. Now you can bring the file in to AutoCAD with **PSIN**, and you'll see that the block brought in already has the lines hidden. It will also produce that way for desktop publishing.

If you need a screen preview header, you can then **PSOUT** the current file, since it's really just a block with the lines already hidden.

30.10 **How do you bring in a PostScript file to AutoCAD?**

Use the **PSIN** command. It really works like an **INSERT** command. You are permitted to scale it as it actually comes in. Once in AutoCAD, it's treated as a block.

More Steps to Success

30.11 **Modular drawing using XREF**

The **XREF** command now permits externally referencing a drawing that is currently open by someone else. Conversely, it permits someone else to open a drawing that is being **XREF**ed by another drawing. This opens up a whole new world in modular designing.

In order to make this feasible, you must be on a network. Let's assume that there are three designers working on a single project. Each designer is working on a different part of the overall design. Designer 1 is working on drawing A. Designer 2 is working on drawing B. And Designer 3 is working on drawing C. Designer 1 needs information on drawing B to be available in drawing A in order to complete the design although designer 1 is not responsible for the design in drawing B.

Under the above scenario, designer 1 would **XREF** drawing B and have it available. Designer 1 can still make changes in drawing A.

30.12 **Add aliases on the fly!**

AutoCAD comes with a few abbreviations called *aliases* that are found in the ACAD.PGP file. You, of course, can edit this file and add your own. Nothing in AutoCAD Release 12 has changed that. What has changed is that you can do it while you are in a drawing. If you think of an abbreviation you want to use, simply shell out of the drawing and edit the ACAD.PGP file. This file is now found in the **Support** subdirectory under the **ACAD** directory (if you used the standard installation).

Once the ACAD.PGP file has been modified and you've returned to the drawing editor, you can now reread in the new ACAD.PGP file to make your new abbreviation active. To do this from the Command line

Type: REINIT <RETURN>

In the resulting dialogue box pick **PGP File** and OK. The ACAD.PGP file will be read in again and your abbreviation will now be active.

30.13 **Two kinds of digitizer reinit**

What's the difference between **Digitizer** under **Device & File Initialization** and **Digitizer** under **I/O Port Initialization** under the **RE-INITIALIZATION** dialogue box?

Under the **I/O Port Initialization**, you are only resetting the com port itself. By picking the **Digitizer** under **Device & File Initialization**, it resets the digitizer as appropriate. If you need to reset your digitizer, it's a good idea to reset both.

30.14 **Increase large drawing performance**

There is a growing relationship between the amount of memory available to AutoCAD and the efficiency in handling large drawings. Whenever AutoCAD performs functions such as **REGEN** and **REDRAW** as well as selecting objects or object snapping, it does so within certain areas of the drawing. How efficiently it's able to find those objects depends greatly on its ability to index those entities relative to their position in space and to each other.

A system variable called **TREEDEPTH** controls the level of indexing relative to the amount of memory available in your machine. You should always have **TREEDEPTH** to the highest level possible without creating excessive activity. The indexing system takes up a lot of memory, but it gives you back greatly improved efficiency if you have that memory. On the other hand, if you don't have the proper amount of memory, whatever the indexing system might give you is more than offset by the disk activity that is required to support it.

TREEDEPTH is a four-digit integer number. The first two digits control the maximum depth for model space, and the last two the maximum depth for paper space. AutoCAD out of the box defaults to 3020. If it's a small drawing, what you do with **TREEDEPTH** is immaterial. If you're working with a large drawing and have only 4 megabytes of memory, leave **TREEDEPTH** alone. If it's a large drawing and you have a lot of memory (substantially more than 8 megabytes), raising **TREEDEPTH** can increase your efficiency. Remember, the key is the number of nodes and the average number of entities per node. You want the average number of entities per node to be as small as possible for the most efficient use. That is achieved only by increasing the number of nodes. But remember that each node eats up 80 bytes of RAM. Therefore if you had only 3 megabytes of extended memory and 20000 nodes, then you would be using half of your extended memory just for the index tree. This would not be efficient and would result in an enormous amount of disk access. Therefore you should reduce the **treedepth**.

30.15 **Use TREESTAT to find out your node status**

The command **TREESTAT** will tell you the status of the **treedepth**. The first line is the number of nodes, entities and maximum depth. The second line is the average number of entities per node.

30.16 **How do you select multiple base points with grips?**

After you have selected the entities, pick a base point. If you want to pick other base points at the same time, hold the Shift key down as you pick other base points. Be careful to pick only the base points; otherwise Auto-CAD will think that you're stretching and copying the entity selected.

If you're stretching a rectangle, be sure to first select the three adjacent lines, then Shift, and pick all three of the end line's base points. In order to activate the selection set, again pick one of the base points. Then the stretch will begin.

30.17 **Elevation restored**

Beginning with AutoCAD Release 11, an important option in the **CHANGE** command was removed. That was **Elevation**. The rationale was that the command was superfluous. You could always move the entity to another elevation. But if you wanted an entity to be at an elevation of 5 units, it required you to know the current elevation so that you could move it so many units up or down. And what if you needed to move hundreds of entities of differing elevations to 5 units? It created a nightmare. Of course, if you knew AutoLISP, you could change the Z coordinates to a fixed elevation.

Now, by popular demand, **Elevation** has been restored to the **CHANGE** command. But this also brings back the restriction that the entities selected must be parallel to the current UCS. Otherwise, if you're going to use one of the other options, it would be better to use **CHPROP** instead of **CHANGE**, since it doesn't have a UCS restriction.

30.18 **Smooth out linetype segments around curves**

One of the biggest problems when using linetypes such as dashed lines is that they create a stickish appearance when they're part of curved areas. See Figure 30-3. On the left is the only way dashed lines could be produced with versions of AutoCAD prior to Release 12. On the right is an improved appearance with Release 12. This appearance is caused by a system variable called **PLINEGEN**. When **PLINEGEN** is set to 1 it causes the polyline linetypes to create a continuous curved pattern around the curved area of the vertex. If **PLINEGEN** is set to 0, each linetype line starts and ends at each of the vertices.

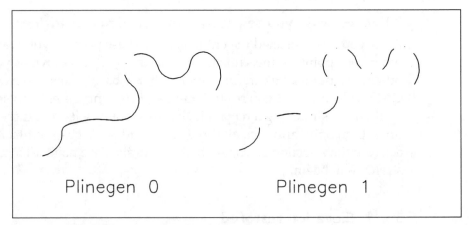

Plinegen 0   Plinegen 1

Figure 30-3: Using PLINEGEN to smooth linetype segments

30.19 **DVIEW easier to use with CAmera and TArget**

DVIEW is now substantially easier to use with the **TArget** and **CAmera** options. Gone are the vertical and horizontal scroll bars. You move the vertical and horizontal rotations simultaneously with one easy movement of the cursor; there's a natural feel to it as it moves.

30.20 **Use Select All with DVIEW**

Using **All** as the option with **Select Objects** for **DVIEW** has really made it very convenient. Especially on smaller objects, you want to select the entire model for **DVIEW**. This becomes difficult if you're currently in a view that doesn't permit this kind of selection. When **DVIEW** asks you to select objects, just answer **All** and <RETURN>.

30.21 Dimension variables are more easily set through a dialogue box

Pick **Dimension Style...** from the SETTINGS pull-down menu or type DDIM from the Command line.

I don't know of anyone who has ever totally memorized the meaning of each of the endless dimension variables. Something needed to be done in some form of plain English to make sense of all the combinations. Finally, AutoCAD has done something about it. The dimension variables are now treated in an organized manner in a dialogue box. See Figure 30-4.

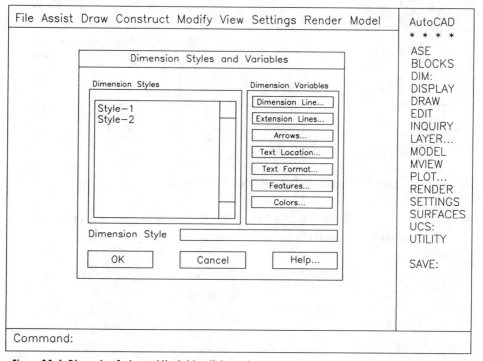

Figure 30-4: Dimension Styles and Variables dialogue box

In the list box to the left are the available dimension styles. To the right are a series of boxes, each of which brings up its own dialogue box. There is one unique box called **Features** that lets you set almost all the dimension variables in one huge dialogue box. See Figure 30-5.

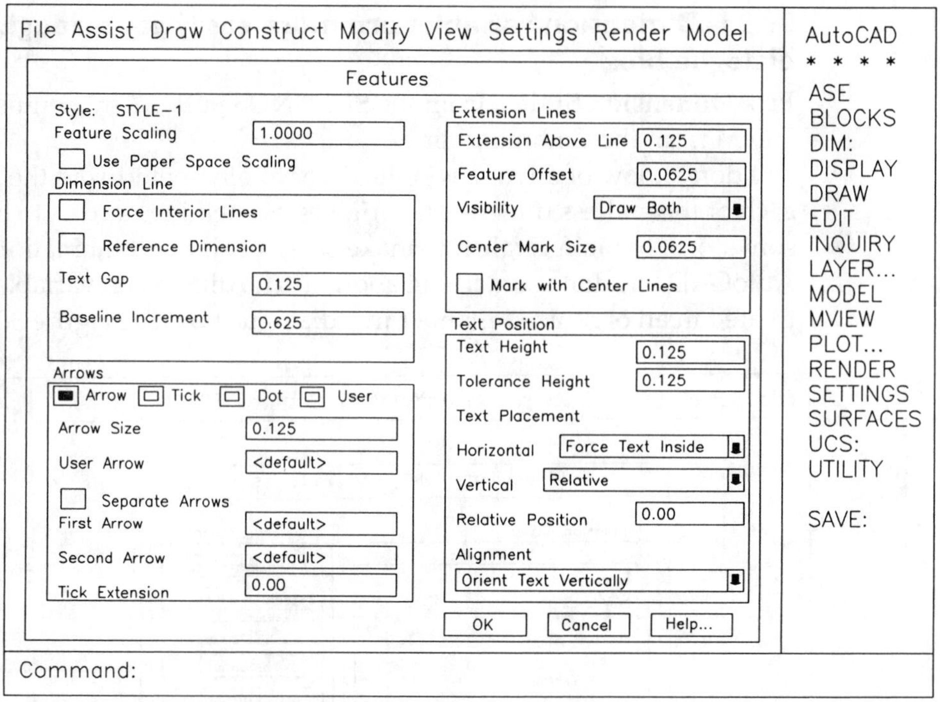

Figure 30-5: Features dialogue box for setting dimension variables

The following is a list of the dimension variables that can be affected by using the dialogue boxes:

Dimension Line ...   **dimscale**

                                                dimclrd

                                                dimoxd

                                                  dimtofl

                                                  dimgap

                                                  dimdli

Extension Lines...   **dimscale**

                                                dimclre

                                                dimexe

                                                dimexo

                                                dimse1

                                                dimse2

                                                dimcen

Arrows...   **dimscale**
dimclrd
dimasz
dimtsz
dimblk
dimblk1
dimblk2
dimsah
dimdle

Text Location...   **dimscale**
dimclrt
dimtxt
dimtfac
dimtix
dimsoxd
dimtad
dimtvp
dimtih
dimtoh

Text Format...   **dimscale**
dimlfac
dimrnd
dimpost
dimzin
dimtol
dimlim
dimtm
dimtp
dimalt
dimaltf
dimaltd
dimapost

Colors... **dimscale**

dimclrd

dimclre

dimclrt

In those dialogue boxes where dimension variables are repeated from other dialogue boxes, such as DIMSCALE or any of the color variables, for example, remember that there is only one dimension variable. Therefore regardless of which dialogue box changes the variable, that variable is changed, and the changed status of the variable will appear in the other dialogue boxes. Therefore, you should not assume that DIMSCALE , for example, applies solely to that one and only dialogue box and that you can have multiple simultaneous scales by changing several dialogue boxes.

30.22 Use Adobe PostScript fonts in AutoCAD

AutoCAD can read-in Adobe Type 1 Postscript fonts directly. These font files have the extension of .PFB. They can be used directly, just like Auto-CAD font files. Simply give it the font name in the **STYLE** command. You can find the Adobe fonts supplied by AutoCAD in the **\ACAD\Fonts** directory. AutoCAD fonts have the extension .SHX. Adobe fonts have the extension .PFB.

If done this way, the font that is referenced by the AutoCAD drawing is recompiled each and every time the drawing comes up. If this font is used a lot, it's more efficient to compile the file to an AutoCAD .SHX file. Although this will save a lot of time, it will cost you a lot of disk space.

30.23 See your PostScript file with PSQUALITY

The system variable **PSQUALITY** determines the quality of the **PostScript** image brought into the drawing. If it's set to 0, the image will be only a box indicating the image that's there and its size. You will not see the actual image. The unit number indicates the number of pixels to each AutoCAD drawing unit. 75 is the AutoCAD default.

The **PSQUALITY** system variable must be set at the time you do a **PSIN**.

30.24 **New device driver variable**

There is a new environmental variable you now have to contend with. If it isn't set right, AutoCAD Release 12 will not run.

AutoCAD now needs to know the directory where it can find all of your device drivers. Therefore, either in your AUTOEXEC.BAT file or in a batch file that calls up AutoCAD, you have to enter the following **SET** statement:

```
SET ACADDRV=C:\ACAD12\DRV
```

This statement assumes the driver files are located in **C:\ACAD12\DRV**. Depending on the answer to the questions you gave on installation, AutoCAD will automatically place the driver files in a subdirectory called **DRV**, under the AutoCAD directory you chose.

30.25 **New required parameters with SET ACAD=**

In addition to other directories you may use with your **SET ACAD=** environmental variable, AutoCAD Release 12 requires that you place in the **SET ACAD=** environmental variable, the name of the directories where it can find the support files, fonts and ADS files. Therefore you must have the following statement in your AUTOEXEC.BAT file or in a batch file that begins AutoCAD:

```
SET ACAD=C:\ACAD12\SUPPORT;C:\ACAD12\FONTS;C:\ACAD12\ADS
```

This statement assumes that the support, font and ADS files are located in the stated subdirectories. Depending on the answers to the questions you gave on installation, AutoCAD will automatically place the driver files in the **SUPPORT**, **FONTS** and **ADS** subdirectories under the AutoCAD directory you chose.

30.26 **Adding your own drivers to the CONFIGURATION menu**

When you configure AutoCAD, a list of drivers for each type is shown on the screen. You no longer set environmental variables such as **DSPAD** for protected mode 386 drivers. Drivers must appear on the configuration screen in order to be used.

If you have a protected mode 386 driver that is not on the menu, you must copy that driver to the **DRV** directory with all the other drivers. In addition, the name of the driver must begin with the proper prefix. For example, video drivers must begin with DS. If your video driver does not begin with the proper prefix, then rename it.

30.27 **Limitation to pre-4.2 ADI video driver**

If you're using a pre-4.2 ADI video driver, you will not get the benefit of **REGEN**-free **ZOOM**s. These drivers are still using the smaller virtual screen. Although they will probably work, you won't get the benefit until you upgrade to the 4.2 or higher video driver.

30.28 **Access PLOT through AutoLISP**

In addition to using script files to automate a plotter, you can also create **LISP** files to access different plotter configurations. To do this, use the system variable **PLOTTER**. This is an integer representing a plotter config-uration starting at 0 (zero) up to 28. (Remember: the new PLOT command can have up to 29 differeent configurations.)

For instance, if you have four **PLOTTER**s configured, the variables are 0 to 6. Do not try to set the **PLOTTER** integer to a higher number—say, to 7—as it will give an error message. If you delete a **PLOTTER** configura-tion, the integers reduce accordingly; they do not stay the same. For example,

```
PLOT-0.LSP

(defun plot-0 ()
   (command "setvar" "plotter" "0")
   (command "plot" " ")
)
```

CHAPTER 31

Advanced AutoLISP

AutoLISP is no longer a mystery known only to those with the computer savvy to discover its power. AutoLISP is now an integral part of Auto-CAD, and everyone should have at least a working knowledge of it.

AutoCAD will never be everything to everyone, and it's not equally useful to every drafting or design discipline. But it's a remarkable engine waiting for you to start it up—and AutoLISP lets you customize this engine for architecture, mechanical and civil engineering, manufacturing, electrical engineering, PC-board layout, construction, mapping and many other disciplines.

Of course, no discipline should use AutoCAD straight out of the box. Each discipline has its own particular needs, and AutoCAD can't be expected to fill all of them. But AutoLISP can help you customize Auto-CAD for specific design, drafting or communication requirements.

Learning AutoLISP is more than learning just a few more AutoCAD commands. The questions, tips and tricks in this section aren't designed to teach you AutoLISP. *AutoLISP in Plain English* (also published by Ventana Press) does a good job of that. This section is designed to answer a range of questions that come up while you're programming in AutoLISP and to give you a wealth of good ideas that will make your programming more efficient and keep you on the right track.

How Do You . . .

31.1 How do you enter an AutoLISP program?

AutoLISP is entered as a regular text file. Use a word processing program or any text editor that doesn't use much RAM space. The real trick is that you want it to work from inside AutoCAD.

EDLIN is an ideal text editor not because it's so good—it's not—but because it's free, readily available and takes up virtually no memory. EDIT from DOS 5.0 or higher also works well. Other editors that come with utility disks are as good, or better.

31.2 **How do you load and run a program?**

An AutoLISP program is stored in a file with the extension .LSP. Before the program can be run, it must be loaded into memory. Let's assume the name of the file is PROG1.LSP and the name of the program is c:prog1. The c: in front of the program name lets you run the program just by typing its name, the same as for any other AutoCAD command.

To load the program, begin at the AutoCAD Command line:

Type: `(load "prog1") <RETURN>`

Once the program is loaded, you can run it by simply typing PROG1 <RETURN>. If you don't put a c: in front of a program name, run it by typing (prog1) <RETURN>. AutoLISP accepts either uppercase or lowercase code.

31.3 **How do you separate functions in the same file?**

Each program is a function or a collection of functions. Unlike BASIC and some other languages, the function (program) and the file that contains it aren't one and the same. In fact, one file may contain many functions. All of the functions are loaded when the file is loaded.

Each function begins with the **(defun** statement and ends with a final closing parenthesis. This determines the limits of the function. The next function can begin on the very next line.

31.4 **How do you enter comments in a file?**

AutoLISP doesn't document itself very well, so you need a way to write notes to yourself when you're working in a file. Comments embedded in a program always begin with a semicolon (;) and end with the end of the line:

```
;This is a comment line
(setq a (getvar "osmode")) ;This begins a comment line
```

Notice in the second example that a comment may begin in the middle of a line. If you need more than one line of comments, you must begin each new line with a semicolon.

31.5 How do you know when a space is required?

Spaces are required between elements of a list, reserved words and variables, and between each variable or variable and number. Spaces aren't required between parentheses and reserved words or between the closing parenthesis of one statement and the opening parenthesis of another.

The trick to this is simple: you can never have too many spaces. AutoLISP ignores extra spaces, so if you're in doubt, put one in.

31.6 How do you make a variable local?

A local variable is one that loses its value when a program ends. It's active only while that particular function is running.

Only variables that are declared are local variables, and you declare them in the **(defun** statement:

```
(defun c:prog1 (/ a j pt1)
```

List all local variables, and place them in parentheses following the function name. The slash tells AutoLISP that all the variables that follow are local.

31.7 How do you make a variable global?

Global means that a variable doesn't lose its value when the program ends; the value can be passed to and shared by other functions while you're in the drawing editor.

To make a variable global, you do nothing. Unless the variable is declared as local, it's global by default. If there are no local variables, use ( ) where the variables would go:

```
(defun c:prog1 ()
```

31.8 How do you create a list?

There are two ways: with the **(list)** command or by using an apostrophe ('). Let's say that you wanted 3 5 7 to be a list. You can't just use parentheses to make a list; the following is an illegal statement:

```
(setq a (3 5 7))
```

In the next example, the command **(list)** tells AutoLISP to make what follows into a list. 3, 5 and 7 are considered expressions. The expressions can be complicated as well:

```
(setq a (list 3 5 7))
```

In the next example, a new list is being made out of the X value of **pt1** and the Y value of **pt2**. This new list is assigned to the variable **a**:

```
(setq a (list (car pt1) (cadr pt2)))
```

When you use an apostrophe to make a list, the items are generally already grouped in parentheses. The apostrophe tells AutoLISP to treat the entire group as a list:

```
(setq a '(3 5 7))
```

31.9 **How do you enter control codes?**

Certain standard control codes can be embedded within the text of a print statement. The most common of these is **\n**, which tells AutoLISP to advance to the next line:

```
(setq pt1 (getpoint "\nPick a point "))
```

Notice that the **\n** comes within the quotation marks.

Other standard codes are also acceptable in this format:

\e	ESCAPE
****	The \ character
\r	<RETURN>
\t	Tab
\nnn	Control code (octal)

31.10 **How do you assign values to variables?**

The basic assignment command in AutoLisp is **(setq)**, which you can think of as **set equal to**. Here's how to assign a value of 10 to the variable **a**:

```
(Setq a 10)
```

This reads, "set a equal to the value of 10."

The value that you assign to a variable doesn't have to be a number or a string. You can assign the results of another command such as

```
(setq pt1 (getpoint "\nPick a point "))
```

The **(getpoint)** command secures the X, Y, Z coordinates, and that result is assigned to the variable **pt1**.

31.11 How do you pick a point?

The basic command for picking a point on the screen is **(getpoint)**. The coordinates of the point picked are then returned, and you have the option of assigning these results to a variable.

The **(getpoint)** command lets you print a message at the Command line as a prompt statement:

```
(setq pt2 (getpoint "\nPick the second point "))
```

You can also rubber-band to the next point by tying the **(getpoint)** command to the first point. Let's assume that the first point is the variable **pt1**—notice its position in this command:

```
(setq pt2 (getpoint pt1 "\nPick the second point "))
```

31.12 How do you enter text?

The command that lets you enter text is **(getstring)**. Its basic syntax is

```
(setq tx (getstring "\nEnter text "))
```

Notice that you can also enter a prompt statement. The text that's entered is assigned to the variable **tx**.

Another fact about **(getstring)** is that if you don't enter anything in the flag position, spaces aren't permitted (the flag position is immediately after **getstring** and before the prompt). This means that if the user enters a space, it acts as a terminator, the same as a <RETURN>. The flag can be any number. Look at the next example:

```
(setq tx (getstring 1 "\nEnter text "))
```

The flag (number 1) follows **getstring**. This means that spaces are permitted and the only terminator recognized is <RETURN>. There's nothing special about the number 1; you could use any number. Remember: if there's no flag, spaces aren't allowed as part of the text, and the text acts as a terminator.

31.13 **How do you issue AutoCAD commands from AutoLISP?**

You can issue virtually any AutoCAD command from inside AutoLISP. Begin the expression with **(command** followed by the AutoCAD command in quotes:

```
(command "line" pt1 pt2 "")
```

All of the required entries must be provided in a **(command** expression. If the user supplies some of the entries, the word **pause** must be placed wherever these user entries are to be:

```
(command "line" pt1 pause "")
```

In this example, AutoLISP begins the **LINE** command and places the first point at **pt1**. The user provides the second point. The " " ends the **LINE** command.

31.14 **How do you see what's in a variable?**

AutoLISP lets you examine the contents of variables from the AutoCAD Command line. Assuming that the variables are global and still contain values, you can examine the contents by preceding them with **!**:

```
!a
```

This will print the contents of the variable **a**.

31.15 **How do you find the X, Y or Z of a point?**

Begin with a list containing the three coordinates:

```
(setq pt1 (getpoint "\nPick a point "))
```

When the point is picked it's assigned to the variable **pt1**. You can now isolate X, Y or Z:

`(car pt1)`	Isolates X
`(cadr pt1)`	Isolates Y
`(caddr pt1)`	Isolates Z

31.16 How do you create your own window effect?

When you issue a command that asks you to select objects, you can follow it with **c** or **w** for **Window** or **Crossing**. AutoCAD then takes over, and the window or crossing effect will be quite natural. Be sure to supply enough pause statements to take into account the first and second corner.

```
(command "erase" "w" pause pause "")
```

This example lets you place a window with a first and second corner. The " " confirm the selection, and everything that's captured inside is erased.

But let's assume that you wanted to select only the coordinates for the window and then to erase everything currently within those coordinates. The following code gives you a visual clue of where the window will be drawn:

```
(setq pt1 (getpoint \nFirst corner "))
(setq pt2 (getcorner pt1 "\nSecond corner "))
```

This draws a window that drags across the screen exactly as the AutoCAD **Window** option does. The corners of the window are now in the variables **pt1** and **pt2**.

Later, you can issue the **ERASE** command as follows:

```
(command "erase" "w" pt1 pt2 "")
```

Remember that this is only an example; actual applications will differ as needed. But it's another example of how a programmer can make sure that an AutoLISP program looks and feels like AutoCAD.

31.17 How do you enter numbers in AutoLISP?

This can be a trap if you're not careful. The rules depend on what kind of number you're entering. Of course, if the program asks for an integer, you can't use a decimal point.

Let's look at some possibilities:

(setq a 4)	Interpreted as an integer
(setq a 4.0)	Interpreted as a real number
(setq a 4.2)	Interpreted as a real number
(setq a .4)	Illegal dotted pair
(setq a 0.4)	Correct way to enter a decimal portion of a number

31.18 **How do you add and subtract?**

These are the arithmetic operators in AutoLISP:

+ Add
– Subtract
* Multiply
/ Divide

The important thing to remember is that these are commands, the same as **(setq)**.

If you want to add 5 and 7,

```
(+ 5 7)
```

reads, "add to 5 the value of 7."

```
(- 8 5) (Returns 3)
```

This reads, "subtract from 8 the value of 5."

```
(* 2 3)
```

This reads, "multiply 2 by the value of 3."

```
(/ 6 2) (Returns 3)
```

This reads, "divide 6 by the value of 2."

31.19 **How do you perform a loop in AutoLISP?**

AutoLISP uses two kinds of loops: **(repeat)** and **(while)**. The **(repeat)** is easy—simply tell AutoLISP how many times you want to repeat:

```
(repeat 5
   (xxxxxxxx)
   (xxxxxxxx)
   (xxxxxxxx)
)
```

Whatever you use for **(xxxxxxxx)** will be repeated five times. The number or variable that controls the number of loops must be an integer. If it's a real number you won't get an error message—it simply won't loop.

The **(while)** loop is a little trickier. Following the **(while** command is a variable or an expression. If this variable or expression is ever nil, the loop stops. The loop will continue as long as the variable or expression is not nil:

```
(setq e 1)
(while e
    (xxxxxxxx)
    (xxxxxxxx)
    (xxxxxxxx)
)
```

If a condition changes the value of variable **e** to nil, the loop will cease.

You may also have an expression after **(while**:

```
(while (setq a (getpoint "\nPick a point "))
    (xxxxxxxx)
    (xxxxxxxx)
    (xxxxxxxx)
)
```

In this example, you continue to pick points until you <RETURN>, which will return nil. Then the loop will terminate.

31.20 How do you make a decision?

The only decisions a computer can make are "yes" for true or "no" for false. This is done through the **(if)** command.

The **(if)** command in AutoLISP is positional; it follows the if-then-else format. The first expression after the **(if** is always the condition. If the condition is true, the next expression **(then)** is executed. If the condition is false, the third expression is executed:

```
(if
    (= a b)
    (prompt "This is true")
    (prompt "This is false")
)
```

In this example, if **a** equals **b** (this is the condition position), it will print "This is true." (This is the **then** position.) If **a** doesn't equal **b**, it will print "This is false." (This is the **else** position; the **else** statement is always optional.) The **(if** is closed with a final parenthesis.

31.21 **How do you make compound decisions?**

(if commands can be grouped with the **(and)** command. Remember that **(and)** is a command the same as **+** or **setq**, so it must come first before the multiple options:

```
(if
    (and (= a b) (> a c))      This is the condition.
    (prompt "Both are true")   This is the then.
    (prompt "One is false")    This is the else.
)
```

You can also use **(or)**; it works the same way as **(and)**. It must come first before the multiple options.

31.22 **How do you have multiple thens?**

If the if-then-else is positional in AutoLISP, how can you perform more than one expression if a condition is true? AutoLISP provides you with a command called **(progn)**.

Start your group of expressions with **(progn**. End the group with a closing parenthesis. Everything within the group is considered to be a single expression, or, in this case, a single **then**, even though the number of expressions within the group can be unlimited.

You can also use **(progn)** for multiple **else**s:

```
(if
    (= a b)
    (progn
        (prompt "a is equal to b")
        (prompt "b is equal to a")
        (prompt "They are both equal to each other")
    )
    (prompt "a is not equal to b")
)
```

Notice that if the condition is true, three statements are performed. They're all grouped within the **(progn**.

31.23 How do you convert radians to degrees?

The **(rtd)** function converts radians to degrees. Place it in your ACAD.LSP file so that other programs can use it readily:

```
(defun rtd (angg)
   (/ (* angg 180.0) pi))
```

Notice in the statement **(defun rtd (angg)** that the variable **(angg)** isn't preceded by a /. This tells AutoLISP that the variable is used to accept value from outside the program. Therefore, **(rtd) 1.5708** would pass the value to the program for conversion.

If the variable **a** contains an angle in radians and you want it changed to degrees, enter

```
(setq a (rtd a))
```

See Tip 31.64.

31.24 How do you convert degrees to radians?

The **(dtr)** function converts degrees to radians. Place it in your ACAD.LSP file so that other programs can use it readily:

```
(defun dtr (angg)
   (* pi (/ ang 180.0)))
```

If the variable **a** contains an angle in degrees and you want it changed to radians, enter

```
(setq a (dtr a))
```

31.25 How do you automatically execute a program in AutoLISP?

Beginning with Release 10, AutoLISP lets you automatically begin an AutoLISP function when you enter the drawing editor. You must precede the function with S::STARTUP and place it in the ACAD.LSP file. You may have only one of these special functions in the ACAD.LSP file, and it will run only when the drawing editor begins:

```
(defun S::STARTUP ()
```

31.26 **How do you make functions common to all programs?**

The mere fact that a function is loaded into memory makes it common to all other programs, but make sure it's loaded as soon as possible. You can do this by including it as a function in the ACAD.LSP file that's always loaded with the drawing editor. Of course, you'll need to consider whether you'll be passing variable data back and forth such as with **(dtr),** or whether the variables will remain global.

31.27 **How do you create defaults as in AutoCAD?**

In many AutoCAD commands, AutoCAD remembers the last entry and puts that entry between angle brackets **(<>)**. Then all you have to do is press <RETURN>, and that value is used. You should use that technique whenever you're creating your own defaults in AutoLISP.

First make sure that you haven't declared as local the variable that will hold the value. Then follow a three-step process: require input from the user and assign that input to a second variable; test to see if the input is nil, and if it is nil, assign the global variable to the real variable. Finally, assign the real variable to the global variable. You're then ready for the next sequence. Here's an example:

```
(defun c:prog1 (/ a)
    (if (= gv nil) (setq gv 1.0))
    (princ "\nEnter distance <")
    (princ gv)
    (princ "> ")
    (setq a (getdist))
    (if (= a nil) (setq a gv))
    (setq gv a)
    (princ "\nThe distance is ")
    (princ a)
    (princ)
)
```

gv is the global variable.

No matter how often you run this program while in the same drawing, it will maintain the last entry as the default. The first time through the program, **gv** is tested to see if it has value. If it doesn't, the program assigns 1.0 as the default value.

31.28 **How do you measure the distance between two points?**

Use the **(distance)** command. If you wanted to measure the distance between two known points assigned to variables **pt1** and **pt2**, you'd use the following:

```
(setq d (distance pt1 pt2))
```

31.29 **How do you derive a point from an angle and a distance?**

Use the **(polar)** command. If the variable **pt1** contained the known point, the variable **ang** contained the angle in radians, and the variable **d** contained the distance, you'd use this syntax:

```
(setq pt2 (polar pt1 ang d))
```

31.30 **How do you know when to convert angles?**

You first must understand why you need to convert angles. Everything involving angles in AutoLISP is done in radians, and in AutoCAD it's done in degrees. You'll often be using an AutoCAD command in an Auto-LISP program, so you'll need to convert the angles.

ang may be the variable that secures an angle in this command:

```
(setq ang (getangle))
```

The value is in radians. But you may want to convert that angle to degrees for use in an AutoCAD command within the AutoLISP program. The following would be the correct way to do this:

```
(command "text" pt1 ht (rtd ang) tex)
```

This assumes that you've created a function called **(rtd)** and that it's been loaded with the ACAD.LSP program. See Tips 31.23 and 31.24.

31.31 **How do you convert angles to different units?**

This is more complex than converting degrees to radians or vice versa. When you use angles in AutoLISP, they're always in radians. But when you print them out, you usually want to see angles in your default units, which might be surveyor's units or degrees, minutes and seconds. The command to convert radians to degrees is **(angtos)**.

Assume **ang** is the variable containing a value in radians and that the default units are degrees, minutes and seconds. **(angtos)** may be used without any other parameters to return a string converted to the default units.

```
(setq a (angtos ang))
```

This might assign 42d58'19" to the variable **a** if **ang** had a value of .75.

You can force the conversion to specific units and specific precision by adding a code number after the variable, followed by the precision:

```
(setq a (angtos ang 0 4))
```

This would force it to 42.9718 (decimal degrees with four units of precision).

The codes are as follows:

0   Decimal degrees

1   Degrees, minutes, seconds

2   Grads

3   Radians

4   Surveyor's units

31.32 How do you convert distances to different units?

Converting distances to different units is much like converting angles to different units. Instead of using **(angtos)** as in Tip 31.31 above, use **(rtos)**, which stands for **real to string**. The procedures are the same:

```
(setq d (rtos dis))
```

Assume that **dis** has a value of 438.5. If your default units were architectural feet and inches it would assign 36'-6 1/2" to the variable **d**.

You can also force the conversion to specific units and precision the same as with **(angtos)**:

1   Scientific

2   Decimal

3   Engineering

4   Architectural

5   Fractional

31.33 **How do you find the value of system variables?**

Use the **(getvar)** command, followed by the name of the system variable in quotes:

```
(setq os (getvar "osmode"))
```

This secures the value of the Object Snap mode and assigns that value to the variable **os**.

31.34 **How do you set system variables?**

Use the **(setvar)** command, followed by the name of the system variable in quotes and then the value you want to assign:

```
(setvar "osmode" 1)
```

This sets the Object Snap mode to 1, which is the endpoint.

31.35 **How do you convert strings to uppercase?**

There are many occasions when you'll need to convert a string variable to uppercase, especially when you've requested a response and need to test it. It's much easier to test it against all-uppercase than to try to test for every combination of upper- and lowercase. The command you use for the conversion is **(strcase)**:

```
(setq uc (strcase t))
```

This converts the value of the string variable **t** to uppercase and assigns the new value to the variable **uc**.

31.36 **How do you enter a <RETURN>?**

There are many times when you'll need the equivalent of a <RETURN> in an AutoLISP program, especially when you want the program to accept certain built-in defaults. In Release 10 and higher, use " " (this might not work in all cases below Release 10).

```
(command "insert" part pt1 "" "" "0")
```

31.37 **How do you enter a Ctrl-C?**

There are many times when you'll need the equivalent of a Ctrl-C in an AutoLISP program. In Release 10 and higher, use **^c**, the same as you do in macros for menus. The ^ is a Shift-6 on the keyboard, not the Ctrl key (this may not work in all cases below Release 10).

31.38 **How do you create a selection set?**

You create an AutoLISP selection set with the **(ssget)** command. You must assign the selection set to a variable when you use this command. Once the command is issued, the user has all of the selection options (**Window, Crossing**, etc.) at his or her disposal:

```
(setq s1 (ssget))
```

31.39 **How do you know how many entities were captured in a selection set?**

You can secure that number with **(sslength)**. Use the variable you assigned for the selection set to let AutoLISP know which selection set you're talking about:

```
(setq n (sslength s1))
```

The variable **n** is assigned the number of entities in the selection set contained in the variable **s1**.

31.40 **How do you select the last entity drawn?**

This is the equivalent to **Last** for **Select objects**, and it's found in the command **(entlast)**. It will give you the entity name for the last entity drawn:

```
(setq na (entlast))
```

The variable **na** now contains the entity name for the last entity drawn.

31.41 **How do you make sure that a user selects only one entity?**

As you saw in Tip 31.38, **(ssget)** lets a user select objects to build an entire selection set. If you want a user to select only a single object, use **(entsel)**. **(entsel)** gives you the entity name followed by the coordinates of the point picked. It lets a user select only one object by picking that object:

```
(setq e (entsel))
```

31.42 **How do you find an entity name?**

An entity name is important, because without it you can't get an entity list. Finding the entity name depends on how the entity was selected in the first place. **(entlast)** gives you only the entity name:

```
(setq na (entlast))
```

The variable **na** contains the entity name.

(entsel) gives you the entity name first, then the coordinates of the point picked. Therefore, you must isolate the first element of this list:

```
(setq na (car (entsel)))
```

The variable **na** contains the entity name.

(ssget) is the most complicated of the three, because you can capture an unlimited number of entity names in a selection set. It's important to realize that the only thing that goes into a selection set is the entity name.

An entity name that goes into a selection set carries with it a relative positional number. The first one to enter is number 0, the second is 1, the third is 2, etc. So you must tell AutoLISP which name you want by giving AutoLISP its index number. The command for this is **(ssname)**:

```
(setq s1 (ssget))
(setq na (ssname s1 5))
```

This will secure the entity name found in the selection set in **s1** at the sixth position (remember, they start at 0). To find a specific entity, put this line of code into a loop and page through all the entities until you find the one you want.

31.43 **How do you use the filter option?**

AutoLISP will let you secure only certain types of entities into a selection set. You can't pick specific entities, though—all entities in the database that match a type's criteria will be secured.

You set up the criteria by listing associatives and acceptable values. For example, if you wanted everything on layer DIMS you could use the following:

```
(setq s (ssget "x" '((8 . "DIMS"))))
```

31.44 **How do you get an entity list?**

Before you can get an entity list, you must have an entity name. Assume that the entity name is in the variable **na**. Use the **(entget)** command followed by the entity name:

```
(setq e (entget na))
```

The variable **e** now contains the entity list.

31.45 **How do you isolate an associative?**

An associative is a list within an entity list that denotes a given field in the drawing database. Each associative has its own code number. See Tip 31.103.

Assume that the entity list is found in the variable **e**. To isolate associative **0**, use the **(assoc)** command followed by the code number **0** and the variable containing the entity list:

```
(setq a (assoc 0 e))
```

The variable **a** now contains an associative denoting the type of entity:

```
(0 . "TEXT")
```

31.46 **How do you change an associative?**

An associative list is just like any other list, but it's called a *dotted pair*—the two elements in the list are separated by a dot and offset with a space on either side. You can change an associative list by typing in another dotted pair and the **(list)** command to tell AutoLISP that the items in the parentheses are part of a list:

```
(setq a (list (40 . 60.0)))
```

Notice that the 60.0 forces the parameter to be a real number. If you don't use a real number, this command line won't work when you try to update the drawing. See Tip 31.104 for more about dotted pairs.

31.47 **How do you use variables to construct a new associative?**

Assume that the variable **t** has a value of 60.0, a real number. You want to construct a new associative list using this value as the parameter and 40 as the associative code number. Use the **(cons)** command:

```
(setq a (cons 40 t))
```

The result to the variable **a** will be (40 . 60.0). Notice that the **(cons)** command includes the dot for you.

31.48 **How do you replace an associative in a list?**

Once you've constructed a new associative, you may want to substitute it for the old associative in the entity list so that you can modify the database. To do this, use the **(subst)** command, which substitutes the new associative for the old one.

Assume that the old associative list is in the variable **oal**. The new associative list has been constructed in the variable **nal**. The entity list containing the old associative list is in the variable **e**. You want to make a new entity list **e1**, with the new associative list replacing the old associative list:

```
(setq e1 (subst nal oal e))
```

You've now created a new entity list as **e1**.

31.49 **How do you update the database with a new entity list?**

Let's say that you have a new entity list called **e1** (see Tip 31.48). You now want to change the database with the new definition found in **e1**. Use the **(entmod)** command, followed by the entity list:

```
(entmod e1)
```

The database will be changed. There's another neat trick about this— it didn't require a regen.

31.50 **How do you find out about the AutoCAD environment?**

The AutoCAD environment includes **ACAD, ACADCFG, ACADFREE-RAM, LISPHEAP** and **LISPSTACK**, among others. AutoLISP has a command that gets the settings for any of these environment variables. That command is **(getenv)** followed by the name of the environment variable in quotes:

```
(setq a (getenv "acadfreeram"))
```

The value assigned to the variable **a** is a string. In the above example, it might be "24."

31.51 **How do you get an entity handle?**

An entity handle is assigned to each entity as it's created, if **HANDLES** is on. Each entity receives its own handle as a unique sequential number. So if you know an entity's handle, you can secure the entity. Note that a handle is not the same as an entity name, which is transient at best. Entity handles are stored in associative **5**.

31.52 **How do you use an entity handle to get an entity?**

If you know an entity's handle, you can get the entity's name; if you know an entity's name, you can get the entity. This is why you can go around in circles. So if you can get an entity in order to get associative 5 to secure the entity handle, you already have the entity—so why do you need the entity handle in the first place?

Entity handles are used in sophisticated programs that can keep track of handles as they're created and can store them in a file. This lets entities be accessed without picking from the screen.

Assume that the handle for a given entity is **3**. To secure the entity, enter

```
(setq e (entget (handent "3")))
```

(handent) followed by the entity handle in quotes gives you the entity name. Use **(entget)** to secure the entity once the entity name is known.

31.53 How do you turn handles on in AutoLISP?

HANDLES On is an ordinary AutoCAD command, so to turn handles on in AutoLISP, enter

```
(command "handles" "on")
```

31.54 How do you know whether handles are on or off?

The status of handles is found in the system variable **HANDLES**. If **HANDLES** is set to **0**, they're off. If it's set to **1**, they're on.

31.55 How do you turn handles off in AutoLISP?

Turning handles on in AutoLISP is simple, but there's really no **Off** command. To turn handles off, you must destroy all handles in the database.

When you try to destroy handles, AutoCAD requires that you enter one of six code phrases. These code phrases are randomly chosen. In AutoLISP the only way around this is to put the command to destroy handles in a loop with GO AHEAD until nil. AutoLISP will repeat the command until it reaches GO AHEAD and destroys handles.

WARNING: Be very careful with this routine—it will destroy all handles in the database.

```
(setq e 1)
(while e
    (command "handles" "destroy" "go ahead")
    (setq h (getvar "handles"))
    (if (= h 0) (setqe nil))
)
```

31.56 **How do you translate coordinate systems?**

Beginning with Release 10, you can have an unlimited number of user-defined coordinate systems. These systems are collectively called the UCS (User Coordinate System). You need to have a way to translate back and forth from a UCS to a World Coordinate System (WCS).

If you have a point in the WCS and you need to translate it to the current UCS, enter

```
(trans pt1 0 1)
```

If you have a point in the UCS and need to translate it to the WCS, enter

```
(trans pt1 1 0)
```

pt1 contains the point to translate. You always enter the code to translate from one system to another; **0** is the WCS and **1** is the UCS.

31.57 **How do you redefine an AutoCAD command?**

Let's assume you have your own special AutoCAD function that draws all lines using polylines. You don't want anyone to use the **LINE** command, and if they do, you want it to automatically be the **PLINE** command, even if **LINE** is picked from the tablet menu or the screen menu. You might enter

```
(defun c:line ()
   (command ".pline"))
```

However, this function has the same name as the AutoCAD **LINE** command until you get rid of the AutoCAD command altogether. To do this, use **UNDEFINE**—either as an AutoLISP function (such as in the S::STARTUP function as you go into the drawing editor) or typed in as an AutoCAD command.

As an AutoCAD command:

```
UNDEFINE LINE <RETURN>
```

As an AutoLISP function:

```
(command "undefine" "line")
```

Now the **LINE** command is out of the way, and only the AutoLISP LINE function is available when the **LINE** command is chosen.

31.58 **How do you use a regular AutoCAD command while it's undefined?**

You can still access an undefined AutoCAD command by putting a dot in front of its name. See Tip 31.57 above—the AutoLISP function that was used in the **LINE** command had to use **.pline** so that AutoCAD could recognize it, since **.pline** was undefined.

31.59 **How do you permanently restore an AutoCAD command once it's been undefined?**

Use the **REDEFINE** command. To bring back the **LINE** command, enter REDEFINE LINE <RETURN>.

When you do this, you cannot use your AutoLISP LINE function.

31.60 **How do you turn virtual memory on?**

AutoLISP will let you load as many programs into memory as you want without having to clear memory space; this is called *virtual memory*. But this doesn't give you unlimited memory for your variables—for that, you need extended AutoLISP.

To activate this procedure, use **(vmon)** without any parameters as the first command in your ACAD.LSP file. (This is not neccessary in the DOS 386 versions of AutoCAD.)

31.61 **How do you look at an atom list?**

An atom list is a collection of all commands available to AutoCAD as well as all the loaded functions. Sometimes this is a good way to see what might have been stuck into AutoLISP but not necessarily documented:

```
!atomlist <RETURN>
```

If you're using **(vmon)**, you can't look at the atom list.

31.62 **How do you control keyboard entry?**

Sometimes you want to limit what a user can enter as a response from the keyboard. This is a two-part command. Let's say you're asking for a Yes or No answer. First you must set up the acceptable answers. Use **(initget 1)** to do this, followed by the acceptable answers in quotes separated by spaces:

```
(initget 1 "Y N")
```

Now ask your question. Use **(getkword)**—this means "get key word." If the user puts in anything but Y or N, AutoCAD automatically indicates that it's a wrong response and lets the user repeat the answer until an acceptable response is given:

```
(setq y (getkword "\nIs this correct "))
```

Note one little trick here. You can't just repeat **(getkword)** and assume that **(initget 1)** is still in effect. **(initget 1)** and **(getkword)** must be used as a pair each time.

31.63 **How do you suspend a program for user input?**

This is done with a **pause** within a **(command)** expression:

```
(command "line" pt1 pause "")
```

This example suspends a program and lets the user input a second point.

31.64 **How do you pass information in and out of a program?**

To share variables, simply make them global. But you can pass data directly into a program variable and have the program return the results by declaring the receiving variable(s) without a / in front of them. For example, look at the **(dtr)** function:

```
(defun dtr (angg)
   (* pi (/ angg 180.0)))
```

This function can be called from the Command line or from another AutoLISP program. Notice that **(angg)** doesn't have a / in front of it, so this variable is declared not as a local variable but as an argument-passing variable. Thus **(dtr 90)** returns the radian equivalent of 90 degrees.

31.65 **How do you check to see whether a file exists?**

Beginning with Release 10, the command to use is **(findfile)**, followed by the name of the file in quotes. It can't use wild cards and it searches for only one file. The file must also exist in the current directory, in the Auto-CAD directory where the programs reside, or in the directory set up in the ACAD= environment variable. If the file exists, **(findfile)** returns the drive path specification for the file. If it doesn't exist, it returns nil.

31.66 **How do you flip the screen?**

We're assuming that you're using a single-screen monitor. To flip to graphics, use **(graphscr)**. To flip to text, use **(textscr)**. If you're on the correct screen or are using a dual-screen monitor system, these commands do nothing.

31.67 **How do you keep from loading a program if it's already loaded?**

Before you can use a function, you must load it—but you don't want to waste time loading a function every time you use it. Assume that function name **prog1** is located in a file called FILE1. Use this as part of your menu macro for executing the file:

```
(if (not prog1) (load "file1"))^c^cprog1
```

31.68 **How do you know what kind of variable it is?**

One great thing about AutoLISP is that you usually don't have to worry about what type of variable or data you're working with. AutoLISP keeps track of the type of data stored in a variable and adjusts the variable accordingly.

But from time to time, especially for debugging, you'll need to know a variable's type. Use the **(type)** command:

```
(type a)
```

This will give you the type of variable **a**.

31.69 **How do you know which way slashes go?**

This is becoming a tricky question to answer. The slashes we're referring to are path slashes, normally backslashes (\). AutoLISP interprets a backslash as the beginning of a control code such as \n. Therefore, it uses a forward slash for the path. This is especially evident in the **(load)** command:

```
(load "/lsprog/file1")
```

If you insist on using backslashes, use two of them for every one you need. The following is also correct:

```
(load "\\lsprog\\file1")
```

Now comes the tricky part. If you're in AutoCAD instead of AutoLISP, use regular backslashes:

```
EDIT \LSPROG\FILE1.LSP
```

The above is strictly in AutoCAD.

```
(command "insert" "/detail/part" pt1 "" "" "0")
```

Even though this is an AutoCAD statement, it's inside AutoLISP—so you must use forward slashes.

```
INSERT \DETAIL\PART <RETURN>
```

This **INSERT** command is totally in AutoCAD.

31.70 **How do you get out of a 1> error?**

This error is usually caused by a missing parenthesis or quotation mark. It was a big problem in versions before Release 10, but AutoCAD has corrected it. If you're using an earlier version, you must supply AutoLISP with the missing **)** or **"** or **'** or some combination of the three, mixed in with a few Ctrl-Cs—and you *may* get out. For Release 10 and higher, just press Ctrl-C, and you'll be returned immediately to the Command line.

31.71 **How do you get into extended AutoLISP?**

Extended AutoLISP is a memory-resident TSR (terminate-and-stay-resident), and it requires a minimum of 512k of extended memory. Before going into AutoCAD, type **EXTLISP** <RETURN>. This loads the TSR. To remove the TSR and free up memory for other programs, type **REMLISP** <RETURN>. This will restore the memory if extended AutoLISP was the last TSR to be loaded.

Extended AutoLISP will work only with 80286-class machines and higher; it won't work with 8088- or 8086-class machines, and is not needed with the DOS 386 versions of AutoCAD.

31.72 **How do you open a file?**

AutoLISP uses the **(open)** command to open a file, and the files must be sequential. AutoLISP doesn't support random-access files.

```
(setq fh (open "filename" "w"))
```

The variable **fh** is called a *file handle*. You refer to an open file by this variable.

There are three modes you can use when you open a file:

w   Write to the file

r   Read from the file

a   Append to the end of the file

31.73 **How do you write to a file?**

First, open the file under **w** mode for **write** or **a** mode for **append**. Once the file is opened, use **(princ)** to print to the file. Follow what you want to print with the file handle that was used when the file was opened; this points to the correct file:

```
(princ "\nWe are writing this to the file" fh)
```

The string in quotes will be written to the file that has the handle **fh**.

31.74 **How do you read information from a file?**

First, open the file under **r** mode for **read**. Once the file is opened, you have a choice of two commands:

> **(read-char)**   This reads a single character from the file. Each **(read-char)** will read the subsequent character.
>
> **(read-line)**   This reads an entire line from the file. A line is read until a <RETURN> is found.

In the following example, a line of data is read from the file with the file handle **fh**. The data is assigned to the variable **a**:

```
(setq a (read-line fh))
```

31.75 **How do you print to a printer?**

Printing to a printer is really the same as writing or printing to a file, except that the file name is always **prn**. You must first open the file for **w** (write to **file**). Secure the file handle and issue **(princ)** using that file handle:

```
(setq fh (open "prn" "w"))
(princ "\nWe are printing to the printer" fh)
```

31.76 **How do you know when to use radians and when to use degrees?**

This is simple: everything you do when using an AutoLISP command is in radians. This includes everything produced or used by **(getangle)**, **(angle)**, **(polar)**, etc. However, when you use **(command)**, for all practical purposes you're using AutoCAD, not AutoLISP. In that case all angles must be measured in degrees, since that's what AutoCAD requires.

31.77 **How do you know when to use an apostrophe?**

Both the apostrophe (**'**) and the **(list)** command create lists. The difference is that **(list)** uses values as its parameters, and the apostrophe treats anything within parentheses as a list:

```
(list 5.0 7.25 3.9)
'(5.0 7.25 3.9)
```

31.78 **How do you find a single entity in a selection set?**

Whenever you use **(ssget)**, you can capture an unlimited number of entities as part of a selection set. Here's a way to pull out and work with only the entity you want to use.

Let's say you want to isolate text and change its size after putting a window around an area (of course, if you wanted to change all text in the drawing, you'd use the filter system). The following is a model for searching the selection set for just text and discarding everything else.

First look at the variables you're going to use:

- **s1** The variable containing the selection set.
- **i** The variable used as the index counter, so you can page through each entity in the selection set one at a time to find the one you're looking for.
- **n** The number of entities captured in the selection set. **n** is also the variable controlling the number of times you page through the loop.
- **oal** An associative list that's isolated and tested to see if it's for text.

```
(setq s1 (ssget))
(setq n (sslength s1))
(setq i 0)
(repeat n
   (setq e (entget (ssname s1 i)))
   (setq i (+ i 1))
   (setq oal (assoc 0 e))
   (if (= "TEXT" (cdr oal))
      (progn
          (Now that you've found the entity,)
          (these are the lines where you)
          (manipulate the entity depending)
          (on the nature of your program)
      )
   )
)
```

This is the basic program you'll use each time you page through a selection set looking for an entity or group of entities.

31.79 **How do you find the target position?**

The target position in 3D is located as a coordinate in the system variable **TARGET**. This is a read-only system variable that maintains the coordinates of the target for **DVIEW**.

31.80 **How do you find the camera position?**

This is a little harder than finding the target position in 3D. There's no simple system variable that tells you these coordinates.

The coordinates of the camera position are the sum of each of the coordinates of the target position and the viewing direction found in the system variable **VIEWDIR**. This means that the Xs, Ys and Zs of each system variable are added together to create the coordinates of the camera position.

Fortunately, there's an AutoLISP function that adds each of the respective elements; it's called **(mapcar)**. The following expression will assign to the variable **cam** the coordinates of the camera position:

```
(setq cam (mapcar '+ (getvar "target") (getvar "viewdir")))
```

31.81 **How do you temporarily use an AutoCAD function after it's been undefined?**

Once an AutoCAD command has been undefined, it doesn't exist. In order to tell AutoCAD to use it within an AutoLISP program anyway, place a dot in front of the command. Enter **(command ".line")** instead of just **line**.

31.82 **How do you know where parentheses go?**

First, you must have as many closed parentheses as you have open parentheses. You must also always begin an AutoLISP command with an open parenthesis. If that command uses the value of another command, it's not closed immediately. Think of this nested command as simply providing value to the first. Only when all of the values required of the first command are satisfied will it be closed. The most striking example of this is the **(defun** command, which isn't closed until the end of the entire function.

31.83 **How do you get rid of the value in a variable?**

The only way to get rid of the value in a variable is to **(setq)** it to **nil**. Even then, **nil** can be tested, but it basically means that the variable is empty. Unless a variable is global and has been set by another program, it begins with **nil** and doesn't necessarily need to be initialized before the program begins.

31.84 **How do you turn off background scrolling?**

This is controlled by the system variable **cmdecho**. If it's set to **1**, scrolling is turned off. If it's set to **0**, scrolling continues.

31.85 **How do you search a file?**

Searching a file is similar to searching a selection set. Remember that AutoLISP supports only sequential files. It doesn't support random-access files. To search a sequential file, you must start at the beginning of the file and read in everything until you've found what you're looking for. You then either continue reading the file or break out and do something else.

Place continuous reads in a **(while)** loop and set the controlling variable to **nil** when the search is completed or when you reach the end of the file.

31.86 **How do you test for an end-of-file?**

As you're reading in the data either with **(read-line)** or **(read-char)**, read in a **nil** that you can test for when you reach the end of a file.

31.87 **How do you recover node space (memory) if you don't use (vmon)?**

First, always use **(vmon)**. But if you don't, there's a little routine that removes unused functions from memory and lets you recover the node space. This routine is from the *AutoCAD Programmer's Reference Manual*. It should never be used if **(vmon)** is on. It will remove any routines that were loaded after it was loaded, and it will protect any routines that were loaded before.

```
(defun C:CLEAN (/ i item)
    (setq i 0)
    (while (not (equal (setqitem (nth i atomlist)) 'C:CLEAN))
        (if (= (type (eval item)) 'FILE)
            (close (eval item)))
        (setq i (1+ i))
    )
    (setq atomlist (member 'C:CLEAN atomlist))
    'DONE
)
```

See Tip 31.110.

CAUTION: Do not use **(vmon)** or **C:CLEAN** with the DOS 386 versions of AutoCAD.

31.88 **How do you draw on the screen without hurting the current drawing?**

First, you can use **(grclear)** to clear the screen or viewport. A **REDRAW** or **REGEN** will bring the original drawing back at any time.

Another way is to use **(grdraw)** as if it were a **LINE** command. Give it two points and a color number with or without a flag value in the highlight position, and it will draw lines on your screen.

First, assign coordinates to the variables **pt1** and **pt2**:

```
(grdraw pt1 pt2 2)
```

This will draw a yellow line between the two points.

Add a non-nil value such as 1 in the **highlight** position at the end, and it will highlight the lines:

```
(grdraw pt1 pt2 2 1)
```

REGEN or **REDRAW** will bring your original drawing back.

31.89 How do you find the sublists of a block or a polyline?

When you use the **(entget)** command, you're bringing up only the parent entity list at first. If it's a block or a polyline, it will have other entity lists below it. You must use the command **(entnext)** to bring these up:

```
(setq e2 (entget (entnext (entlast))))
```

You can continue to add **(entnext)** for as many parts as the block or polyline has. When you reach the end, associative **0** will return **SEQEND**. As a shortcut, you can do an **(entnext)** on the previous entity name:

```
(setq e3 (entget (entnext (cdr (assoc -1 e2)))))
```

31.90 How do you know which units are currently in use?

This information is stored in the following system variables:

aunits	Angular units	
	0	Decimal degrees
	1	Degrees, minutes, seconds
	2	Grads
	3	Radians
	4	Surveyor's units
auprec	Precision for angular units	
lunits	Basic unit style	
	1	Scientific
	2	Decimal
	3	Engineering
	4	Architectural
	5	Fractional
luprec	Precision for unit style	

31.91 How do you know the current layer?

The current layer is found in the system variable **CLAYER**. This is a read-only system variable.

31.92 How do you know which way an angle was picked and measured?

How a user picks the two points of an angle will determine the degrees. You can test for this by seeing if the angle is greater than, equal to, or less than 180 degrees. This will help you determine whether you should subtract 180 degrees to compensate for picking the other direction. Of course, there are more considerations, but this will give you a start.

31.93 How do you load an AutoLISP file within an AutoLISP program?

This is no problem with Release 10 and later. **(load "file1")** can now be placed directly in an AutoLISP program. For earlier versions of AutoCAD, you can run a script file from inside AutoLISP and then have the script file load the AutoLISP file.

31.94 How do you say "not equal"?

When testing for equality, use =. When testing for inequality, use /=.

31.95 How do you check to see whether a variable is a list?

Use the **(type)** command, which returns a variable's type. But since this isn't a string, to test it you must enter

```
(if (= (eval v) LIST) . . .
```

You could also use **(listp)** to see whether a variable is a list:

```
(if (= T (listp a)) . . .
```

(listp) returns **T** if it is a list and **nil** if it isn't.

31.96 How do you check to see whether a variable is a number?

Follow the same test as in Tip 31.95, but test for **REAL** or **INT**. You can also use **(numberp)**, which works the same way as **(listp)** on lists. If the variable is a real number or an integer, it returns **T**. If not, it returns **nil**.

31.97 **How do you check for positive or negative?**

The command for this test is **(minusp)**. It returns **T** if a number is negative and **nil** if it's positive.

31.98 **How do you set object snap modes in AutoLISP?**

This is done through the system variable **OSMODE**. The following are the codes for this system variable:

0	None
1	Endpoint
2	Midpoint
4	Center
8	Node
16	Quadrant
32	Intersection
64	Insert
128	Perpend
256	Tangent
512	Nearest

31.99 **How do you set multiple object snaps?**

If you want to set multiple object snaps, simply add the numbers together for the groups you want (see Tip 31.98 for the codes). For example, if you want to set endpoint and intersection, use 33—the sum of the intersection (32) and the endpoint (1).

31.100 **How do you control pull-down menus from AutoLISP?**

Pull-down menus can be activated with the **(menucmd)** command. Each menu is numbered P1 through P8 or possibly through P10, depending on your system. If you want P3 to be pulled down, enter

```
(menucmd "P3=*")
```

More Steps to Success

31.101 **Sum of the bits**

The *AutoCAD Reference Manual* or *AutoCAD Programmer's Reference Manual* sometimes refer to "the sum of the bits." This means that you can derive other functions by adding certain function codes together.

The codes for object snap are listed in Tip 31.98 of this chapter. By adding any or all of the codes together you can combine multiple object snaps. You can also combine the codes that control the visibility of the **3DFACE** lines:

0	All on
1	Side 1
2	Side 2
4	Side 3
8	Side 4

These codes are accessible through associative **70** of the entity list for a **3DFACE**. If you wanted sides 2 and 3 to be invisible, you'd use code **6**—the sum of the codes for the two sides.

Just remember that whenever AutoCAD or AutoLISP refer to the sum of the bits, you need to add codes together to derive or combine functions.

31.102 **Facing East**

AutoLISP gives you two commands to use to secure angles: **(getangle)** and **(getorient)**. Before AutoCAD let you change the direction of 0 degrees, it was always East. **(getangle)** will secure an angle based on wherever 0 degrees is. **(getorient)** will always assume that 0 degrees is East when measuring an angle. This will give you consistency in your programs regardless of how a user has changed the units.

31.103 List of associatives

Below are a few of the more common associative code numbers:

- −1   Entity name
- 0   Type of entity
- 1   Description (string of text)
- 2   Block name
- 7   Text style
- 8   Layer name
- 10   Beginning X, Y, Z coordinate
- 11   Ending X, Y, Z coordinate
- 40   Size

31.104 The dotted pair

Because associatives use dotted pairs (see Tip 31.46), you must be careful where you put in the dot and how you extract elements from the entity list. When creating a dotted pair, use the **(cons)** command. When **(cons)** puts together two parts of the list, it automatically creates them as a dotted pair and places the dot between them.

When you're writing a decimal number, make sure you put a 0 in front of the decimal point if there's no whole number. If you start a number with a decimal point, you'll get an "illegal dotted pair" error.

One final tip about dotted pairs is that a dot is used only if there are exactly two elements in the associative list. For example, **(40 . 60.0)** has a dot but **(10 3.25 4.80 0.0)** doesn't, because it has more than two elements.

31.105 FLATLAND for now

FLATLAND is a Release 10 system variable that aids the transition to a full 3D database. Some programs simply won't run if the UCS is changed or if the Z coordinate is part of the database.

If **FLATLAND** is set to **1** (on), AutoCAD operates as it did in Release 9. If it's set to **0** (off), AutoCAD has all the facilities of Release 10.

In Releases 11 and 12, **FLATLAND** can be set only to **0**.

31.106 **The fudge factor**

Many computer languages have problems when testing for equality between two variables. When a computer is doing numeric data conversions, numbers that actually equal each other might be slightly off by some insignificant degree of accuracy. When this happens, a test for absolute equality will often fail.

To correct this problem, you can add a fudge factor to a test for equality. This is a real number set to the number of decimal places of precision required for evaluating equality. If the two numbers are equal within this degree of precision, the test will succeed:

```
(if
   (equal a b 0.001) . . .
```

If **a** is equal to **b** within **.001**, the test will work.

31.107 **Short variable names save memory**

Even though AutoLISP lets you use long variable names (such as **first-point**), they're an enormous waste of memory. If a variable name has six or fewer characters, it fits into the symbol name node. If the name is longer than six characters, it will point to string space, which eats away at total memory.

31.108 **Take a look at your AutoLISP memory**

If you ever need to see your memory statistics to check memory available, especially for large programs with lots of variables, use the AutoLISP memory statistics command **(mem)**.

31.109 **(vmon) pages only (defun functions**

You can write functions that weren't defined with the **(defun** command. **(vmon)** can only page out functions written with **(defun**, so if you don't use **(defun** for a lot of your functions, you may run out of memory space.

(vmon) is not used with DOS 386 versions of AutoCAD.

31.110 **Leave the atom list alone**

If you use **(vmon)** (and you should), *never* touch the atom list, even if you figure out a way to get to it. One way you might accidentally modify the atom list is by using a **CLEAN** program to recapture memory. This can destroy the paging and lock up your programs. See Tip 31.87.

31.111 **A quick way to look at your programs**

Once a program is loaded into memory, you can print out its contents. This might be easier than looking through the file, especially if it's as long as an ACAD.LSP file.

All you have to do is use the AutoLISP **(print)** command, followed by the name of your program. If it was created with a **c:** be sure to use the **c:** too:

```
(print c:prog1)
```

The only problem is that statements within the parentheses will be printed after each other without carriage returns, but the printout is readable.

31.112 **Proper settings for Lispheap and Lispstack**

Under normal circumstances, **Lispheap** should be set to **39000** and **Lispstack** should be set to **5000**.

31.113 **Where to put AutoLISP programs?**

AutoLISP programs are really text files, so they can't be called up with the ordinary path facilities found in DOS. Only real, executable programs are affected by the DOS path command. But starting with Release 10, you can set aside a directory for blocks and AutoLISP programs. You set up this directory with the **ACAD** environment variable:

```
set acad=c:\lisprg
```

If you want to put all of your AutoLISP programs in a directory called **c:\lisprg**, you can set the environment variable equal to that directory; then AutoCAD will always be able to find them.

31.114 **(getreal) or (getdist)**

Never use **(getreal)** when you can use **(getdist)**, which you can do most of the time. The reason is that **(getreal)** lets you enter data only as real numbers, while **(getdist)** lets you enter data as real numbers, in default units, or by pointing to a distance on the screen.

31.115 **(getreal) or (getangle) and (getorient)**

Never use **(getreal)** when you can use **(getangle)** or **(getorient)**. The reason is that **(getreal)** lets you enter data only as real numbers, while **(getangle)** and **(getorient)** let you enter angles as real numbers, as default angles, or by pointing to angles on the screen.

31.116 **(initget 16) obsolete**

Before Release 10, **(initget 16)** was used to access 3D coordinates. Now it's no longer needed, and you shouldn't use it—most coordinates are 3D unless **FLATLAND** has turned them off.

31.117 **Reset OSMODE**

Nothing is more infuriating than to begin drawing and have that little square appear on the screen indicating that a running object snap is in effect. This is usually caused by AutoLISP programs that don't reset **OSMODE** before they run. Resetting it is a simple procedure.

`(setq os (getvar "osmode")`	This saves the initial object snap setting.
`(setvar "osmode" 1)`	This sets the object snap according to the needs of the program.
`(setvar "osmode" os)`	This sets the object snap back where it was before the program began.

31.118 **Elegant exit**

Always try to provide an exit from an AutoLISP program; Ctrl-C by a user isn't an elegant exit. And when the rest of the program scrolls by on the graphics screen, it makes the user feel that something's wrong.

One solution might be to place the entire program in a huge loop that exits upon some condition. The loop is the last thing in the program; so when it exits, the program terminates gracefully.

31.119 Dividing by 0

You can write a program that requests data from a user, and that works fine when the data are given. But if AutoLISP won't load such a program, it sees that you're trying to divide by 0, and you get the message **error: divide by 0**.

The solution is to initialize the variable with a real number at the beginning of the program. This number will be replaced during the program, but it gives AutoLISP a chance to load it.

31.120 Repeat loops use integers

One bug that's especially hard to find is when a loop doesn't loop even once. This is generally caused because the variable controlling the **(repeat)** loop is a real number, even though it wasn't entered that way. This can occur if you **(setq)** the variable from another number; so make sure that all **(repeat)** loops use integers only.

31.121 Dotted pairs use real numbers

In associative lists, the data parameters for dotted pairs that require numbers always use real numbers. Integers are usually accepted, but they won't work.

31.122 Use post-processing

Make sure that all of your individual AutoLISP programs are small and uncomplicated. Don't try to write great works of genius; AutoLISP is just too slow to handle an enormous amount of data and calculations.

This is where pre- and post-processing come in. Heavy number crunching should be done by other programs outside of AutoCAD. Their answers should be written as data and either imported into AutoLISP or from AutoLISP. Don't make AutoLISP do more than it was designed to do.

31.123 Error-check as needed

Error-checking is a good thing, but it can be a time-consuming process for a programmer. Error-check only to the needs of the end user. If you know what needs to go into a program, you rarely make certain types of errors, and if you're the end user, don't bother writing error-checking routines, especially if the program is short. If you make an error, just repeat the program.

31.124 **Menu AutoLISP**

AutoCAD now puts a lot of AutoLISP inline in the AutoCAD menu, but don't add to it. First, it makes the menu incredibly large. Second, the lines of code that are executed are often not written with **(defun** and won't be paged out by **(vmon)**. Third, you can't call them up from the keyboard or other menus unless they're copied—which can take up even more space and memory.

NOTE: Release 12 has a companion memory file for AutoLISP programs called ACAD.MNL.

31.125 **Debug first, then declare**

Here are two important rules: Never use global variables unless you really need them to be global. Never declare variables as local until a program is completely debugged and in production. If you do, you won't be able to see their values when you're debugging the program.

But the really insidious bug is when a global variable's value depends on the program that came before it, and that value isn't consistent. This means that the program works only some of the time.

Always start a program out with ( ) in the variable section. When the program is ready for production, go back and declare all the variables local unless they really must be global.

31.126 **Multiple (setq)**

You can make multiple assignments using only one **(setq)** expression. Both methods below produce the same results:

```
(setq a 1 b 2 c 3)
```

is the same as

```
(setq a 1)
(setq b 2)
(setq c 3)
```

31.127 **Use Box instead of Crossing**

Whenever you're starting a window or crossing for a user, use **Box** instead of **Window** or **Crossing**. This lets the user choose whether to use **Window** or **Crossing**, depending on where he or she begins the first corner:

```
(command "erase" "box" pause pause "")
```

If the first corner is left and goes to the right, **Window** has been chosen. If the first corner is right and goes to the left, **Crossing** has been chosen.

31.128 **Variables and subroutines**

Whenever you use functions as subroutines, make sure the variables that the routines will share aren't declared as local. Keep them global.

31.129 **Set global variables to nil**

When you're deliberately using global variables, it's a good idea to set them to **nil** when you know that their values are no longer needed. This will help protect unsuspecting programs from disaster.

31.130 **Global variables for prior layers**

Global variables are very good for remembering previous layers. Let's say you have a program that requires you to change layers for construction lines, so you need to let the user change back to the previous layer.

If you store the name of the layer in a global variable, the value of the variable is saved when the program ends. That value remains as long as the user is in the drawing editor. When the next program begins, it can restore the user to the previous layer.

31.131 **Ring the bell**

You can make the bell on the computer sound in AutoLISP. Include the command **(princ "\007")** or **(prompt "\007")** in the program. **(print)** and **(prin1)** won't work. Also make sure that the user is on the text screen; the bell won't sound on the graphics screen.

31.132 **Unfinished (command)**

You don't have to finish a **(command)** expression if it's the last expression in a program; an unfinished **(command)** expression will automatically exit AutoLISP and continue in the AutoCAD command. But when the Auto-CAD command is completed, you won't be in your AutoLISP program:

```
(command "line" pt1 pause "")
(command "line" pt1 pt2 "")
```

Each of these is a completed **(command)** expression.

```
(command "line")
```

This is not a completed **(command)** expression. You'll continue in the **LINE** command, but no other expressions in the program will be executed.

31.133 **Use (princ)**

Try to use **(princ)** instead of **(prin1)** unless you must. **(prin1)** doesn't accept control codes such as **n** for line feed; so if you do use **(prin1)**, make sure you use **(terpri)** as needed for line control.

31.134 **Get (polar) in the right order**

Be careful not to reverse the command **(polar point angle distance)**. If you use **(polar point distance angle)** instead, AutoLISP won't know it's an error; it will just evaluate the numbers as it sees them and give you the wrong point.

31.135 **(ssget) parameters**

You can use parameters with the **(ssget)** command. For example:

```
(setq s (ssget "L"))
```

This will give you the last entity drawn. It's similar to **(entlast)** except that **(ssget)** actually puts the entity into its own separate selection set. So **s** is a selection set.

```
(setq s (entlast))
```

Here, one entity was also selected. It's the same entity. The difference is that **s** isn't a selection set but the entity name.

31.136 **Automatic crossing**

You can build your own selection set with automatic crossing by varying the available parameters with **(ssget)**. If you simply enter **(setq s (ssget))**, the user has to decide what selection method to use.

Look at this sample program. It performs crossing without making the user enter **c** for **Crossing**:

```
(setq pt1 (getpoint "\nFirst corner "))
(setq pt2 (getcorner pt1 "\nSecond corner "))
(setq s (ssget "c" pt1 pt2))
```

Now all the user has to do is pick the two corners. The box temporarily drawn gives the same look and feel as if he or she had chosen **c** for **Crossing**. It also eliminates the need to confirm the choice and the need for any other choices.

 RELEASE 12   Uses Implied Windowing automatically. Just pick where there is no entity, and a window will form. See Tip 20.6.

31.137 **Pick an entity**

Many times, such as in a **FILLET**, you need to pick an entity in order to select it, and you want AutoLISP, not the user, to pick the entity.

One way to do this is through the entity list. You might use the coordinates of associative **10** to select the object, since these are its beginning X,Y coordinates. Still, many entities don't have an associative **10**, and other entities may lie at the exact same coordinates. So the entity list isn't a foolproof way to pick an entity.

The best way is to reference the entity name. Look at this example:

```
(setq e1 (entlast))
(setq e2 (ssname s 3))
(setq e3 (assoc -1 e))
```

These are three possible ways that an entity name can be assigned to a variable.

Assume that **e1** and **e2** are variables that contain the names of two distinct entities:

```
(command "fillet" e1 e2)
```

This is an example of how entity names can be used to pick the entities for the **FILLET** command.

31.138 **Use extended LISP if possible**

Even if you aren't planning to write programs that can't run in regular AutoLISP, extended LISP offers an advantage, if you have the memory available. It frees up the 640k normally used by regular AutoLISP and thus makes AutoCAD run faster.

31.139 **Get rid of quotation marks**

If you use **(prompt)** or **(princ)**, you can get rid of the quotation marks around strings. Quotation marks can be especially confusing around **(angtos)** when you're using degrees, minutes and seconds.

   If you use **(print)** or **(prin1)**, the quotation marks remain.

31.140 **The difference between (equal) and (=)**

At first glance, you might think that **(equal)** and **(=)** can pretty much be used interchangeably. But **(=)** doesn't recognize **(fuzz)** and **(equal)** does. If this is important to you, use **(equal)**.

31.141 **cmdecho caveat**

Although **cmdecho off** has some advantages, be careful using it. Some programs depend on it being on to work, so know when you can turn it off and when you can't. If a program doesn't seem to work, try **cmdecho on** and see if that helps.

31.142 **Menu control**

You can place instructions in the screen menu area without actually touching the menu file itself. This is done with the **(grtext)** command.

(grtext) lets you write on any line of the menu area and highlight that line if you want to:

```
(grtext 1 "     ")
(grtext 2 "     ")
(grtext 3 "Pick")
(grtext 4 "     ")
(grtext 5 "SETUP")
(grtext 6 "     ")
(grtext 7 "from the")
(grtext 8 "     ")
(grtext 9 "Tablet")
(grtext 10 "Menu")
(grtext 5 "" 1)
(grtext 11 "     ")
(grtext 12 "     ")
(grtext 13 "     ")
(grtext 14 "     ")
(grtext 15 "     ")
(grtext 16 "     ")
(grtext 17 "     ")
(grtext 18 "     ")
```

(grtext 5 " " 1) highlights **SETUP**.

Note that these don't pick anything from the menu, nor are they menu items. This is text, used for instructions only.

31.143 **Get your menu back**

If you've used **(grtext)** to overwrite a menu for special instructions, you can get the previous menu back by using **(grtext)** without any parameters.

31.144 **Get rid of the final nil**

To get rid of the final **nil** in a program, make **(princ)** the last statement.

31.145 **Find any element in a list**

(car), (cadr) and (caddr) are fine for finding the first, second and third elements in a list. But what about the others? A quick and easy way to get to any element in a list is with the **(nth)** command:

```
(setq a (nth 4 b))
```

This will find the fifth element in the list (remember that the elements begin with number 0). You could also use this instead of **(car)**, **(cadr)** or **(caddr)** by finding the 0, 1 or 2 element in the list.

This method also prevents a **bad argument** error message if there's no element; you'll only get a **nil**.

31.146 **Blank out entities**

You can blank from the screen any entity or group of entities you want. Use **(redraw)** followed by the entity name and the code number **2**.

Assume that **e1** is the name of an entity:

```
(redraw e1 2)
```

will erase that entity from the screen. On the next regular **REGEN** or **REDRAW**, it will be returned.

Or you can bring it back with

```
(redraw e1 1)
```

31.147 **Highlight entities**

You can highlight any entity by using **(redraw)** and changing the code number to **3**.

```
(redraw e1 3)
```

Code **4** de-highlights the entity.

On the next regular **REGEN** or **REDRAW**, the entities will be returned to their previous state.

31.148 **Don't forget to configure extended AutoLISP**

It's not enough to simply load extended AutoLISP as a TSR (see Tip 31.71); you must tell AutoCAD that it's there. This is done when you configure AutoCAD. Item number 8 is the OPERATING PARAMETERS menu and item number 7 of this menu is **AutoLISP Feature**. You're asked if you want AutoLISP enabled. Answer Y. You're then asked if you want to use extended AutoLISP. Answer Y if you're using it.

31.149 **Don't make your ACAD.LSP file too large**

Although AutoLISP can handle it, you shouldn't make your ACAD.LSP file too large. Because it loads automatically, it's tempting to put all of your programs into this file, but this can cause a lengthy delay every time a drawing comes up, even a new one. This will happen even if you have absolutely no intention of using AutoLISP programs.

How large is too large? Well, that depends on how long you want to wait.

31.150 **A simple way to append program files to a larger file**

You'll often want to append your most recent program to the ACAD.LSP file or to another file. Of course, you can use a word processing program, but sometimes this is inconvenient. A quicker way is through DOS. Let's say that you want to append FILE20.LSP to ACAD.LSP. From the DOS prompt, type

```
copy acad.lsp+file20.lsp  acad.lsp <RETURN>
```

This adds the two files together and rewrites the new longer file back to itself.

Remember to make a backup; if something goes wrong, you could lose the longer file. Try writing it temporarily to a third file for safety's sake.

CHAPTER 32

System Variables

More and more system variables are added with each release of AutoCAD, and each release offers unique and useful functions. But many users are aware of only the more common system variables. This chapter describes how most of the current variables can best be used.

You might think that most system variables are used mainly in AutoLISP, but some of them are used straight from AutoCAD. Still, it's often faster to use an AutoLISP program rather than **SETVAR**. System variables are divided into two classes: those that are read-only and those that you can change. Regardless of a system variable's type, you can always view it with **SETVAR**.

Type: `SETVAR BLIPMODE <RETURN>`

Using this command with any system variable will return its value.

Type: `SETVAR ? <RETURN>`

This will give you a list of all the available system variables and their values.

Type: `SETVAR MIRRTEXT 1 <RETURN>`

When you follow the name of the system variable with a value, you can change the variable if it isn't read-only.

Steps to Success

32.1 ACADPREFIX (String variable, read-only)

This system variable returns the directory path designated by the environment (ACAD). This is a good one to use with the **WBLOCK** command. If you don't use this variable, AutoCAD will store WBLOCKs in the current drawing directory. The following example shows how **ACADPREFIX** can be used in an AutoLISP routine:

```
(setq sv (getvar "acadprefix"))
(setq bl (getstring "\nName of file "))
(setq bf (strcat sv bl))
```

You can now use this in a **WBLOCK** command:

```
(command "wblock" bf pause)
```

32.2 **ACADVER (String, read-only)**

This system variable returns AutoCAD's current version number. This can be used in error-trapping routines to test for Release 10; for example,

```
(if (/= (getvar "acadver") "10")
    (princ "\nThis routine requires Release 10"))
```

32.3 **AFLAG (Integer)**

Four modes let you work with attributes in AutoLISP: **1**–Invisible; **2**–Constant; **3**–Verify; and **4**–Preset. If the system variable is **0**, all of the modes are set to N.

You can combine any of these modes by adding their code numbers together. For example, if you want attributes to be defined as **Invisible-Y** and **Preset-Y** and all other attributes set to N, enter

```
(setvar "aflags" 5)
```

5 is the sum of the codes for **Invisible** and **Preset**. You can use **AFLAG** only for initial **ATTDEF**; it can't be used for editing.

32.4 **ANGBASE (Real)**

This system variable holds the angle base used for 0 degrees. You can use it to test whether a user has changed it from 0. If your routine requires the angle base to be 0 degrees, store the old angle base and then restore it when the program exits.

```
(setq angb (getvar "angbase"))
(setvar "angbase" 0)
(XXXXX)
(XXXXX) These lines represent your program.
(setvar "angbase" angb)
```

Before the program exits, the angle base returns to its original setting.

32.5 ANGDIR (Integer)

This system variable determines whether angles are measured clockwise or counterclockwise. You can use it to test whether a user has changed the counterclockwise default of AutoCAD. If necessary for your calculations, you can change it, then return it to its original value before the program exits.

```
(setq angd (getvar "angdir"))
(setvar "angdir" 0)
(XXXXX)
(XXXXX) These lines represent your program.
(setvar "angdir" angd)
```

The original angle direction is restored to its original setting before the program exits. **0** represents counterclockwise and **1** represents clockwise.

32.6 APERTURE (Integer)

This system variable controls the size of the box used in **Object Snap**. Use this one interactively with **SETVAR** or within an AutoLISP program.

Often while you're in a command you'll find that the aperture is set too large or too small. These routines can be used within these other commands to reset the size of the aperture.

Type: `'SETVAR APERTURE 30 <RETURN>`

This is an AutoCAD command.

```
(defun ap ()
   (setq apt (getint "\nEnter size of object snap box"))
   (terpri)
   (setvar "aperture" apt))
```

Now anytime you need to, type **(ap)** and answer the question. When you're through, you can continue with the command you're in.

32.7 AREA (Real, read-only)

This system variable contains the last area computed. You can use it to check on the minimum or maximum sizes that you want to permit in an area, thus giving the program a chance to warn the user.

32.8 **ATTDIA (Integer)**

This system variable determines whether the dialogue box will be used for attributes during the **INSERT** command. The setting is either **1** (use the dialogue box) or **2** (don't use the dialogue box).

This can be controlled individually per insert macro, depending on the number of attributes and use of presets. A user can customize this.

32.9 **ATTMODE (Integer)**

You can use this system variable to quickly turn the visibility of attributes on or off or return them to normal. Look at the following programs:

```
(defun c:aton ()
    (setvar "attmode" 2))        Turns on
(defun c:atof ()
    (setvar "attmode" 0))        Turns off
(defun c:atn ()
    (setvar "attmode" 1))        Returns to normal
```

32.10 **ATTREQ (Integer)**

This system variable controls whether attribute questions will be asked at all. Attributes can be very troublesome in some third-party software and even in Autodesk's own AEC packages, especially if you don't want to use them. By setting **ATTREQ** to **0**, you can bypass questions about inserted blocks. Constants and presets will still be added. Use this system variable with **ATTMODE** set to **0** (invisible), and you won't even know you're using attributes. Set **ATTREQ** to **1** for normal prompting.

32.11 **AUNITS (Integer)**

This system variable controls angle units. You can use it to test to see what the current units are. If necessary for your calculations, you can change the units, then return them to their original value before the program exits.

```
(setq angu (getvar "aunits"))
(setvar "aunits" 4)
(XXXXX)
(XXXXX) These lines represent your program.
(setvar "aunits" angu)
```

The units are reset before the program exits. These are the available codes:

  0   Decimal

  1   Degrees/minutes/seconds

  2   Grads

  3   Radians

  4   Surveyor's units

This system variable is especially useful for temporarily changing to surveyor's units for survey input.

32.12 **AUPREC (Integer)**

This system variable determines the decimal-place precision of angle units. It's useful to change this precision if the display is getting in the way. Setting the system variable is easier than going through the entire set of questions for the **UNITS** command.

32.13 **AXISMODE (Integer)**

This system variable turns the axis on and off. You should use this in an AutoLISP program only when you need to control the visibility of the axis. In ordinary operation, most users would rather use the **AXIS** command.

32.14 **AXISUNIT (2DPOINT)**

This system variable controls the spacing between the tick marks on the outside axis. It requires an X distance and a Y distance, which control the units between the ticks along each axis.

32.15 **BACKZ (Real, read-only)**

This system variable is used mainly for 3D operations, to control the back-clipping plane. You can find the distance of the camera to the back-clipping plane by subtracting the distance of the camera to the object from the value of **BACKZ**. The larger the value of **BACKZ**, the less back clipping takes place.

32.16 **BLIPMODE (Integer)**

This system variable is the counterpart of an AutoCAD command by the same name. If it's set to **1**, the little blips you see on the screen when you pick a point will continue. If it's set to **0**, the blips won't appear.

CURRENT SETTINGS (Read-only)

Items 17 through 22 below are a series of system variables that can tell you various current AutoCAD settings. You can change the settings by using the system variables. Most of them can also be changed with the related AutoCAD commands.

32.17 **CDATE (Real, read-only)**

This system variable always contains the current time and date, assuming that your system date was set correctly. The date's format is unique: it's a real number with each position to the left and right of the decimal point representing an aspect of the date.

```
YYYYMMDD.HHMMS Smsec
```

YYYY	=	Year (1989)
MM	=	Month (01-12)
DD	=	Day (01-31)
HH	=	Hours (00-23)
MM	=	Minutes (00-59)
SS	=	Seconds (00-59)
msec	=	Milliseconds (000-999)

For example, 3:15:24 p.m., November 22, 1989, becomes:

```
19891122.151524892
```

This format allows comparison of one date as greater than or less than another date. If you use AutoLISP and **(getvar)**, you'll also need to use **(rtos)** to see the entire decimal number.

```
(rtos (getvar "cdate") 2 9)
```

32.18 DATE (Real)

Like **CDATE**, this system variable maintains the current time and date. The difference is that this date is a Julian-and-fraction version of the day and time. A Julian date is a number from 1 to 366 representing each day of the year (e.g., February 1 is 32). Therefore, **DATE 32.5** represents noon on February 1.

The format uses three decimal places for time of day. As such it can be added and subtracted. This is the ideal system variable to use in determining the most recent save of a drawing. If you use AutoLISP and **(getvar)**, you'll also need **(rtos)** to see the entire decimal number. For example:

```
(rtos (getvar "date") 2 4)
```

32.19 CECOLOR (String, read-only)

This system variable reflects the current entity color. You can use it to test and save the value. To change color, use this format:

```
(command "color" "green")
```

32.20 CELTYPE (String, read-only)

This system variable reflects the current entity's line type. You can use it to test and save the value. To change the line type, enter

```
(command "linetype" "dashed")
```

32.21 CLAYER (String, read-only)

This system variable reflects the current layer. You can use it to test and save the value. You can write any of a number of programs to change to a temporary layer, then change back when a function has terminated. Layers are changed using the **LAYER** command.

32.22 **CVPORT (Integer)**

This system variable controls the active viewport. It's an integer that not only tells you which viewport is active but also lets you switch viewports by changing the variable.

32.23 **CHAMFERA, CHAMFERB (Real)**

These system variables control default distances for the two **CHAMFER** values. Setting these values lets AutoLISP preset them, bypassing the **CHAMFER** command. You can also test these values as previous **CHAMFER** values.

32.24 **CMDECHO (Integer)**

This system variable is set to **0** for **echo** off and **1** for **echo** on. This controls whether AutoLISP commands will be echoed to the screen. Be very careful with this one: it's not saved with a drawing, but must be reset each time you enter the drawing editor. Ideally, each AutoLISP program should do its own setting; some programs won't work if this variable is set to **0**.

32.25 **COORDS (Integer)**

If the value is **0**, the coordinates are updated only when points are picked. If the value is **1**, the absolute coordinates are displayed constantly. If the value is **2**, the distance and angle are displayed from the last point picked. At the very least, **2** should be the setting. This lets you use coordinates for measuring from the last point, even if you're not interested in seeing the absolute coordinates.

Whether coordinates are on or off isn't of great importance with today's faster machines. Formerly, coordinates weren't usually on unless it was necessary, since that slowed cursor response.

32.26 **DISTANCE (Real, read-only)**

This system variable produces the last distance measured with the **DISTANCE** command. You can test it the same way as the **AREA** system variable.

32.27 **DRAGMODE (Integer)**

Dragging can be controlled directly from AutoLISP with this system variable. If it's set to **0**, no dragging will occur. If it's set to **1**, dragging will occur only if the user types **drag** during the command. If it's set to **2**, dragging will occur automatically when appropriate.

32.28 **DRAGP1, DRAGP2 (Integer)**

These two system variables control the frequency of a drag's redraw. **DRAGP1** controls how often a drawing's image is to be redrawn as it's being dragged across the screen. This variable should be larger if you're dragging very large images. Otherwise, leave the setting alone. **DRAGP2** controls how often AutoCAD checks the cursor position when an object is being dragged.

At first glance, these two variables seem the same, but there's a subtle difference. If you change **DRAGP2** without changing **DRAGP1**, the drag will seem jerky on large drawings; the frequency of redraw doesn't change, but AutoCAD won't check the cursor position often enough.

32.29 **DWGNAME, DWGPREFIX (String, read-only)**

These two variables are similar and can be used together. **DWGNAME** is the name of the current drawing. If the user provides a directory prefix when the drawing is called up, the prefix is included here. **DWGPREFIX** is the directory path for only the current drawing. You can use it to place or retrieve other items from the current drawing's directory.

32.30 **EXPERT (Integer)**

This system variable gives you control over the prompts that AutoCAD provides before a procedure is continued. The level of **EXPERT** is like an insurance policy. It alerts you to possible danger before a function proceeds. If you turn any of these alerts off—because you simply don't want to be bothered with warnings—be sure you know what you're doing.

0   Issue warnings.

1   Suppress **About to regen, proceed?** and **Really want to turn the current layer off?**

2   Suppress all of the above, plus **Block already defined. Redefine it?** and **Drawing with this name already exists. Overwrite it?**

3   Suppress all of the above, plus the warning about loading a line type that's already loaded or creating a line type that already exists.

4   Suppress all of the above, plus warnings for **UCS**s and **VPORTS** that already exist.

WARNING: Never globally set **EXPERT** and leave it. It may temporarily be set for specific operations, but remember to set it back immediately.

32.31 EXTMIN, EXTMAX (3DPOINT, read-only)

These two system variables contain the coordinates for the lower left-hand corner and the upper right-hand corner of a drawing's extents. By using **ZOOM Window** with these system variables instead of **ZOOM Extents**, you may avoid a regen.

The one thing to remember about these system variables is that they expand outward as a drawing expands. But they don't expand inward until the next real **ZOOM All** or **ZOOM Extents**. So if you use the above technique, recognize the limitations.

32.32 FILLETRAD (Real)

This system variable maintains the current radius for the **FILLET** command. Rather than setting the fillet radius with the **FILLET** command and repeating the command, you can set the fillet radius directly.

32.33 FILLMODE (Integer)

This system variable sets **FILL** on or off. As a rule, don't use it except through AutoLISP, since the command **FILL On** or **FILL Off** is available through AutoCAD. If **FILLMODE** is set to **1**, **FILL** is on. If it's set to **0**, **FILL** is off.

32.34 **FLATLAND (Integer)**

This was a temporary system variable available only in AutoCAD's Release 10. It let Release 10 work the same as Release 9 so that AutoLISP programs stayed compatible. The purpose of the system variable was to aid the transition into a full 3D database. If the system variable was set to **0** (off), all of the facilities of Release 10 were available to the user. If **FLAT-LAND** was set to **1** (on), Release 10 operated the same as Release 9.

Release 12 users will find that **FLATLAND** can be set to 0 (off) only.

32.35 **FRONTZ (Real, read-only)**

This system variable is similar to **BACKZ** except that it maintains the offset of the front clipping plane. The distance of the front clipping plane from the camera can be computed by subtracting the value of **FRONTZ** from the camera-to-target distance. **FRONTZ** is used primarily in 3D. The larger the variable, the more the object is clipped.

32.36 **GRIDMODE, GRIDUNIT (Integer, 2DPOINT)**

Both of these let you control the grid from AutoLISP. **GRIDMODE** lets you turn the grid on and off. If it's set to **1**, the grid is on for the current viewport. If it's set to **0**, the grid is off for the current viewport. **GRIDUNIT** maintains the grid spacing.

32.37 **HANDLES (Integer, read-only)**

This system variable lets you test whether handles have been turned on. If they haven't, they're turned on with the AutoCAD **HANDLES** command. A protection sequence makes it difficult to turn handles off in AutoLISP; but it can be done by placing one of the coded phrases in a continuous loop. Then each time through the loop, test this system variable to see if it's been turned off. If it hasn't, continue the loop until it returns to 0.

CAUTION: this will destroy all the handles in the database.

If the system variable is **0**, handles are off. If it's **1**, handles are on.

32.38 **HIGHLIGHT (Integer)**

When AutoCAD asks you to select objects, this system variable controls whether objects selected will be highlighted. Set it to **1** to have an object highlighted or to **0** to suppress highlighting. Unless you have a good reason, don't turn off highlighting. Generally, **HIGHLIGHT** should be reserved for the special needs of an AutoLISP program.

32.39 **INSBASE (3DPOINT)**

This system variable maintains the coordinates of the base point. You can set the base point with this variable and the AutoCAD **BASE** command; you usually do this to create an insertion point for a drawing if the point wasn't created through a **WBLOCK** drawing.

With this knowledge, you can test for the base point. If **INSBASE** is **0,0,0** (the default), you know that a base point hasn't been assigned.

32.40 **LASTANGLE, LASTPOINT, LASTPT3D (Real, 3DPOINT)**

LASTANGLE is a read-only variable that contains the ending angle of the last arc entered. This ending angle is used as the continuation angle for the **ARC** command.

LASTPOINT is the last point selected. This system variable is not read-only and it can be set, although not while you're in another command. By then, **LASTPOINT** has already been read and any change to it won't affect the current command.

Use **LASTPOINT** to set a last point in an AutoLISP program. If you want to set the last point without AutoLISP, use the **ID** command and simply pick the point.

32.41 **LENSLENGTH (Real, read-only)**

This system variable determines the lens length in millimeters. The lens length affects the field of view, which determines how much of a drawing can be seen. Increasing the lens length is like adding a telephoto lens; decreasing the lens length is like using a wide-angle lens.

Since this is a read-only system variable, you can't use it to change the lens length, but you can change the lens length by using the **Zoom** suboption of **DVIEW** with **Perspective On**. If **Perspective** is off, the **Zoom** suboption is the equivalent of a **Zoom Center**.

The default lens length is 50. You can use this system variable to check the current lens length and thus make any adjustments necessary.

32.42 **LIMCHECK (Integer)**

This system variable controls whether AutoCAD will check to see if you're drawing outside your drawing limits. If **LIMCHECK** is set to **1**, limits checking is on. If it's set to **0**, limits checking is off. You can also control limits checking with the AutoCAD **LIMITS** command by entering **On** or **Off**.

Limits checking has several advantages. First, it protects you from entering points outside the drawing limits. It also controls the limits of **ZOOM All**. Finally, it lets you effectively use the **LIMMIN** and **LIMMAX** system variables and measure with them. See Tip 32.43.

32.43 **LIMMIN, LIMMAX (2DPOINT)**

These system variables contain the X, Y coordinates for the lower left-hand corner and the upper right-hand corner of the drawing limits. Many of the AutoLISP programs that measure the scale of a drawing for hatching patterns, text and line type scale depend on these limits for the measurable size of a drawing.

You can also perform a **ZOOM All** without necessarily causing an automatic regen. Enter

```
(command "zoom" "w" (getvar "limmin") (getvar "limmax"))
```

32.44 **LTSCALE (Real)**

This system variable controls your line type scale. It lets AutoLISP control the scale directly as well as query the current scale. You can enter the scale directly to the system variable, or use the AutoCAD command **LTSCALE**.

32.45 **LUNITS, LUPREC (Integer)**

These system variables let you save the current units and precision and temporarily change them according to the needs of your AutoLISP program. Since these can be changed through AutoLISP, they can also be changed back or controlled.

LUNITS controls the units as follows.

1   Scientific
2   Decimal
3   Engineering
4   Architectural
5   Fractional

LUPREC controls the decimal places or the denominator, depending on the setting of **LUNITS**.

32.46 **MENUECHO (Integer)**

This system variable controls whether menu items are repeated on the screen when they're picked from the tablet or screen menu. Normally this isn't employed by a user. It's a good idea to have the menu items echoed at the Command line to confirm that the correct item was chosen. Don't turn off the system prompts; you wouldn't know what you were choosing. Regardless of the level of echo you choose, it can be controlled with a Ctrl-P from the keyboard.

1   Suppress echo of menu items.
2   Suppress prompts during menu.
4   Disable Ctrl-P toggle of menu-item echoing.

As for many system variables, these codes are additive; if you want to combine any of these three levels, add their numbers together.

The real usefulness of **MENUECHO** is that it lets you make choices through AutoLISP and not have them echoed at the Command line.

32.47 **MENUNAME (String, read-only)**

This system variable lets you query which menu is in effect. This prevents your reloading a menu if it's already loaded.

32.48 **MIRRTEXT (Integer)**

It's amazing how many AutoCAD users don't know that **MIRRTEXT** exists. Unfortunately, this system variable comes set to **1**, which automatically mirrors text.

 MIRRTEXT controls whether text will be mirrored along with other entities during the **MIRROR** command. Setting this variable to **1** mirrors text, and setting it to **0** keeps text as is.

32.49 **ORTHOMODE (Integer)**

This system variable toggles **ORTHO** on and off. **ORTHO** is on if set to **1** and off if set to **0**.

32.50 **OSMODE (Integer)**

One of the main system variables used with AutoLISP, **OSMODE** sets your **Object Snap**. One thing to remember when using this system variable is that these are running modes—they remain set until you reset them.

Example: `(setvar "osmode" 32)`

1	Endpoint
2	Midpoint
4	Center
8	Node
16	Quadrant
32	Intersection
64	Insertion
128	Perpendicular
256	Tangent
512	Nearest
1024	Quick

These modes are additive; add the codes together if you want to combine any of the modes.

32.51 **PDMODE (Integer)**

This system variable controls the shape of points and nodes in a drawing. Figure 32-1 illustrates the available options. Notice the symmetry. Items **0** through **4** are basic shapes. Items **32**, **64** and **96** add to those shapes. By adding 0 through 4, you vary the shapes.

Figure 32-1:
PDMODE options

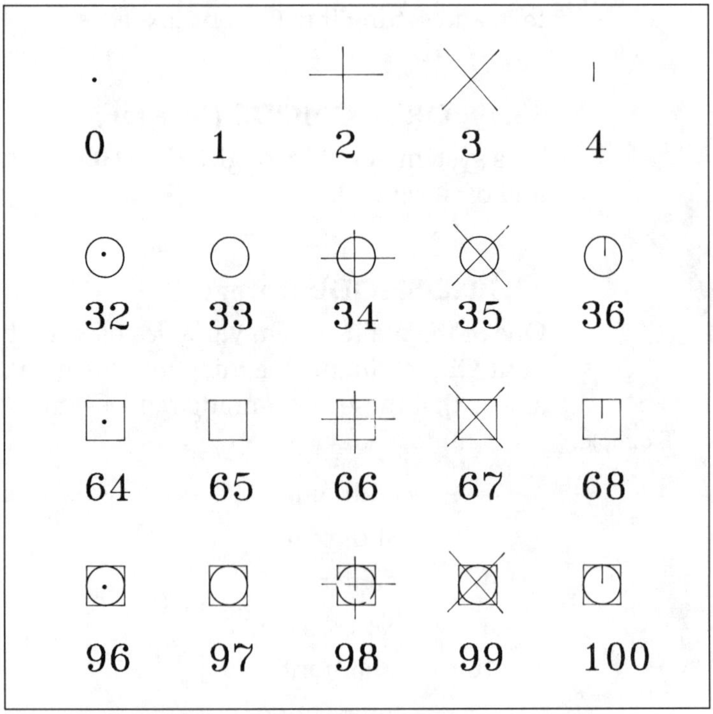

32.52 **PDSIZE (Real)**

This system variable simply controls the size of a point or node, and can be useful in making a point large enough to see and use. Later, you can make these points invisible by changing **PDSIZE** to **0**. Remember that a change in either **PDMODE** or **PDSIZE** affects all points or nodes in the next regen of a drawing.

32.53 **PERIMETER (Real, read-only)**

This system variable contains the last perimeter computed. This can be useful when you're checking on the minimum or maximum size that you want to permit for a perimeter; thus, your program can warn the user.

32.54 **PICKBOX (Integer)**

Often you'll find that the pickbox is set either too large or too small. You can use **PICKBOX** routines while you're in other commands, to control the size of the box used in object selection. Use it interactively with **SETVAR** or within an AutoLISP program.

Type: `'SETVAR PICKBOX 30 <RETURN>`

The above method is an AutoCAD command. Here's the AutoLISP routine:

```
(defun pk ()
    (setq pkb (getint "\nEnter size of selection box"))
    (terpri)
    (setvar "pickbox" apt))
```

Type **(pk)** and answer the question. When you're through, you can continue with the command you're in.

32.55 **POPUPS (Integer, read-only)**

This system variable will tell you whether pull-down menus are available with the current graphics card (obviously, this is useless to an end user). If you want to know, just move your cursor to the top of the screen and try it. **POPUPS** can be useful in AutoLISP to check whether the user has pull-down menus.

32.56 **QTEXTMODE (Integer)**

This system variable turns **QTEXT** off and on. If it's set to **1**, **QTEXT** is on. **0** is for off. **QTEXT** is affected only by the next regen.

32.57 **REGENMODE (Integer)**

This is an important system variable, since it controls **REGENAUTO**. In most situations you'll want to set it to off so that AutoCAD will prompt you before it regens. If **REGENMODE** is set to **1**, **REGENAUTO** is on (regens automatically). If it's **0**, **REGENAUTO** is off (asks before regen). Certain commands will regen even if **REGENAUTO** is off; these include **ZOOM All**, **ZOOM Extents**, **VPORTS** and **DVIEW**.

32.58 **SCREENSIZE (2DPOINT, read-only)**

This system variable maintains the size of the current viewport. This is expressed as an X, Y value. The X value reflects the number of pixels to the right and the Y value is the number of pixels up from the lower left-hand corner. The screen size is a result of your graphics screen and can't be controlled by the user. It varies, depending on the size of a viewport.

32.59 **SKETCHINC (Real)**

If you must use **SKETCH**, use it in polyline mode and set the increment as high as possible. This system variable lets you set the increment as the default.

32.60 **SKPOLY (Integer)**

This system variable controls whether lines drawn with the **SKETCH** command are treated as ordinary lines or as polylines. If **SKPOLY** is set to **0**, lines are drawn. If it's set to **1**, polylines are drawn.

32.61 **SNAPANG (Real)**

This is an extremely useful system variable; it's the basis of a wide variety of AutoLISP programs. **SNAPANG** lets you rotate the crosshairs to any angle. (Often, angles are secured from another entity and the crosshairs are rotated to the entity's angle.)

Make sure that the angle that's transferred to this system variable is in decimal angles, not radians as is usually the case in AutoLISP.

32.62 **SNAPBASE (2DPOINT)**

This system variable moves the grid to a specific point on the screen, when it's necessary to align the grid with the endpoint or intersection of entities on the screen. Once the point is picked, it's set to **SNAPBASE**, and the grid moves. This variable also controls the base point for **HATCH**.

32.63 **SNAPISOPAIR (Integer)**

In AutoCAD you use Ctrl-E to control the current isometric plane; this is a toggle. If you want to control the current isometric plane in AutoLISP, this is the system variable to use:

0 Left

1 Top

2 Right

32.64 **SNAPMODE (Integer)**

This system variable simply toggles **SNAP** on or off. If it's set to **1**, **SNAP** is on and if it's set to **0**, **SNAP** is off. Remember that you can set this independently for each viewport.

32.65 **SNAPSTYL (Integer)**

This system variable controls whether you're in isometric mode or regular mode. Set it to **1** for isometric and to **0** for regular.

32.66 **SNAPUNIT (2DPOINT)**

This system variable controls the distance between snap points. Remember that, in the X direction, a snap point can be different from what it is in the Y direction. For example, if the snap distance is **1**, it would be set to **1,1**. But if you wanted the X distance to be 1 unit and the Y distance to be 2 units, you'd set the system variable to **1,2**.

32.67 **SPLFRAME (Integer)**

This system variable has only two values, **0** and **1**, but it controls a variety of things. If it's set to **1**, it will display the original straight polylines from vertex to vertex, even though the lines are spline-fitted. Only the defining mesh of a surface-fitted mesh is displayed; the fit surface isn't displayed. Finally, the edges of a 3D face are displayed, even though they're invisible.

If **SPLFRAME** is set to **0**, the control polylines aren't displayed. The fitted surface of a mesh is displayed and the invisible edges of 3D faces aren't displayed.

32.68 **SPLINESEGS (Integer)**

This system variable controls the number of segments for each **SPLINE** group. Obviously, the higher the number, the smoother-looking the spline curves, but the regeneration time is longer. The settings for this system variable affect only future splines. If you want to affect a current spline, issue **PEDIT** and re-spline the line.

32.69 **SPLINETYPE (Integer)**

AutoCAD currently has two types of **SPLINE** curves: quadratic B-splines and cubic B-splines. Set this system variable to **5** for quadratic and to **6** for cubic. The settings for this system variable affect only future splines. If you want to affect a current spline, issue **PEDIT** and re-spline the line.

32.70 **SURFTAB1, SURFTAB2 (Integer)**

These two system variables control the density of a mesh. **SURFTAB1** controls **RULESURF** and **TABSURF** as well as one direction of **EDGE-SURF** and **REVSURF**. Since **EDGESURF** and **REVSURF** have meshes that go in a second direction, **SURFTAB2** controls the density of the second mesh direction.

   WARNING: you can't readjust the density of a mesh once it's drawn. You can erase and redo the mesh while these system variables are set to a different density.

32.71 **SURFTYPE, SURFU, SURFV (Integer)**

If you use **PEDIT** on a surface mesh, you get a different set of options. Instead of **SPLINE** and **DECURVE**, you can choose **SMOOTH** and **DESMOOTH**. How these are controlled depends on the **SURFTYPE** system variable:

   5   Quadratic B-spline surface
   6   Cubic B-spline surface
   8   Bezier surface

   The density of these smoothed surfaces is controlled by **SURFU** and **SURFV** in a way that's similar to **SURFTAB1** and **SURFTAB2**.

32.72 **TARGET (3DPOINT, read-only)**

This system variable gives you the 3D coordinates of the current target. This can be useful in determining a current target point if you want to change the camera view.

32.73 **TDCREATE, TDINDWG, TDUPDATE, TDUSRTIMER (Real, read-only)**

Each of these system variables is read-only, letting you check on aspects of a drawing's time. Each is also a real number with its own format.

TDCREATE	Time and date of a drawing's creation. This uses a Julian date and a fraction.
TDINDWG	Total time spent in a drawing. The format is the number of days and a fraction.
TDUPDATE	Date and time of the last update as determined by the last save. This uses a Julian date and a fraction.
TDUSRTIMER	Maintains the user-elapsed time, which can be reset with the **Reset** option of the **TIME** command. The format is the number of days and a fraction.

32.74 **TEMPREFIX (String, read-only)**

This system variable maintains directory paths of temporary files; you could use it to determine whether a RAM disk is in use, for example. These temporary files are placed in the directory noted during AutoCAD's configuration.

The variable isn't actually saved anywhere. Its value is read from the AutoCAD configuration file and stored in this system variable. This is important to note if you use varying configurations and want to check which configuration file is in use.

32.75 **TEXTEVAL (Integer)**

Entering information in response to string requests can cause problems. It's valuable to be able to use an AutoLISP command before inputting text. But how does AutoCAD know whether the first parenthesis is the beginning of an AutoLISP command or part of the text you're entering?

If **TEXTEVAL** is set to **0**, all responses are taken literally, as part of the string. If it's set to **1**, strings starting with **(** or **!** are interpreted as the beginning of AutoLISP code or as an AutoLISP value. For example, **!a** will help you input the value of the variable **a** if **TEXTEVAL** is set to **0**.

DTEXT always interprets strings literally, regardless of the status of **TEXTEVAL**.

32.76 **TEXTSIZE, TEXTSTYLE (Real, string)**

Of course, these system variables control the size and style of text. But more important, they let you write programs and know what the last text size and style were so you can set these in your AutoLISP programs.

32.77 **THICKNESS (Real)**

This is becoming a more important system variable than ever. The **ELEV** command lets you set thickness and elevation of an entity. A useful command for those users who need to convert 2D to 3D drawings.

32.78 **TRACEWID (Real)**

This system variable controls width for the **TRACE** command. However, it's not a good idea to use **TRACE**; use **PLINE** with width instead.

32.79 **UCSFOLLOW (Integer)**

This system variable can be confusing if you don't thoroughly understand it. As you know, you can shift the view of an object to the plan view of the current UCS. (Plan view is the view of an object as though you were looking at the current X and Y from the viewpoint of Z.)

Of course, whenever you want to shift to the plan view of the current UCS, you can use the **PLAN** command, then choose **Current UCS**. What this system variable does is shift you to the plan view of the current UCS automatically, whenever you change UCS. This occurs if it's set to **1**. If it's set to **0**, the view doesn't change.

32.80 **UCSICON (Integer)**

The explanation of **UCSICON** in the *AutoCAD Reference Manual* is a bit confusing. This simple system variable controls the visibility of the UCS icon. Here are the settings:

0   Off

1   On

2   Off

3   Placed at the origin if possible

32.81 **UCSNAME (String, read-only)**

This system variable gives you the name of the current UCS. Being able to retrieve this name lets you use several UCSs in your AutoLISP programs and then return to the current UCS.

32.82 **UCSORG (3DPOINT, read-only)**

This system variable provides you with the 3D point of the current origin. As with **UCSNAME**, you're able to save the coordinates of the origin and then restore it later in an AutoLISP program.

32.83 **UCSXDIR, UCSYDIR (3DPOINT, read-only)**

These system variables control the positive direction of X and Y for the current UCS. By securing information from **UCSNAME**, **UCSORG** and these system variables, you have all the information you need to establish a UCS. Assume that you've saved the following information in these variables:

UO	UCSORG
UX	UCSXDIR
UY	UCSYDIR

You can then restore the UCS as follows:

```
(command "ucs" "3" uo ux uy)
```

32.84 **USERI1-5, USERR1-5 (Integer, real)**

Ten system variables are available strictly for the user to store and retrieve information with each drawing. Five are used as integer variables and five are used as real variables. It's possible to store defaults with these variables, which are saved with the drawing and are not global.

32.85 **VIEWCTR (3DPOINT, read-only)**

This system variable maintains the center of the view in the current viewport expressed in the current UCS. One application of this system variable is in **PAN**—use the coordinates and increment X by a given amount, then **PAN** from **VIEWCTR** to the new coordinate.

32.86 **VIEWDIR (3DPOINT, read-only)**

This system variable maintains the viewing direction of the current viewport expressed in World Coordinates. Its main use is to locate the camera position. The following is the formula for locating the camera position:

```
(setq cam (mapcar '+ (getvar "target") (getvar "viewdir")))
```

32.87 **VIEWMODE (Integer, read-only)**

This system variable gives you the status of the current viewport:

1 Perspective is on

2 Front clipping is on

4 Back clipping is on

8 UCS Follow is on

16 Front clip not at **Eye**. If on, **FRONTZ** determines the front-clipping plane. If off, **FRONTZ** is ignored and the front-clipping plane is set to pass through the camera point.

VIEWMODE uses the sum of the codes to determine which modes are on.

32.88 **VIEWSIZE (Real, read-only)**

This system variable gives you the height of the current viewport, expressed in the current drawing units.

32.89 **VIEWTWIST (Real, read-only)**

This system variable gives you the angle of twist for the current viewport. This is controlled by the **TWIST** subcommand of **DVIEW**.

32.90 **VSMIN, VSMAX (3DPOINT, read-only)**

These system variables give you the lower-left and upper-right coordinates of AutoCAD's virtual screen at any point in time. This is important to know since the size of the virtual screen affects how far you can **ZOOM** without a regen.

32.91 **WORLDUCS (Integer, read-only)**

This system variable lets you know if the current UCS and the World Coordinate System are the same. If the value of the system variable is **1**, they're the same. If it's **0**, they're different.

This can be very useful in determining whether a drawing is in a UCS or WCS. In Release 12, **FLATLAND** can be set to 0 only. In Release 10, **FLATLAND** lets a programmer know whether the WCS is in effect. If it isn't in effect, the AutoLISP program can set it properly.

32.92 **WORLDVIEW (Integer)**

This important system variable is originally set to **1**. When you go into **DVIEW**, you'll never get any consistency if every view is relative to the current UCS, because the numbers will keep changing; **WORLDVIEW** fixes that. With a value of **1**, the variable makes AutoCAD change to the WCS when entering **DVIEW** and returns you to your current UCS when you leave **DVIEW**.

If your **DVIEW** command ever starts acting strangely, make sure that no one has changed this system variable to **0**.

WINDOWS

CHAPTER 33

AutoCAD for Windows

How Do You . . .

33.1 How do you increase the resolution of AutoCAD for Windows?

The Windows version of AutoCAD doesn't have its own driver as do other platforms of AutoCAD. It uses the resolution of the general Windows driver. This is changed through Windows setup. If you're using the standard VGA 640 x 480 Windows driver, AutoCAD will be 640 x 480 resolution. On the other hand, if your video card manufacturer has furnished you with a higher driver specifically for Windows (not AutoCAD), AutoCAD will use the higher resolution.

Video card and software driver manufacturers have developed their own drivers specifically for AutoCAD for Windows. These drivers have their own specific installation instructions.

33.2 How do you use the digitizer and mouse at the same time?

First, there are a very limited number of digitizers supported. Most of these digitizers have the ability to also emulate a Microsoft mouse. This means that they can be used as part of both Windows and AutoCAD. But if you choose this option, remember that your digitizer is no longer a digitizer, it's a mouse. This means that you cannot pick menu items from the tablet template. You can use only the pull-downs and the screen menu.

On the other hand, you can configure your digitizer as a digitizer and have a real mouse hooked up to another serial port or use a bus mouse. Now you actually have two input devices, the mouse and the digitizer. If this is your configuration, you'll need to tell AutoCAD that you want your mouse and digitizer to act together. To do this, pick the FILE pull-down menu and choose **Environment**. See Figure 33-1.

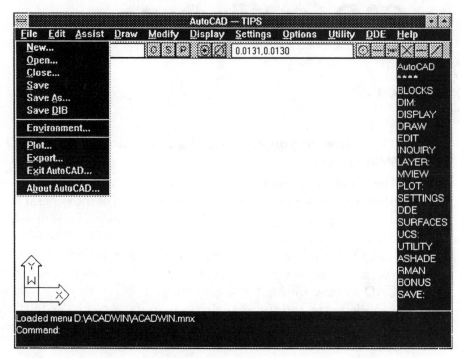

Figure 33-1: FILE pull-down menu of AutoCAD for Windows

You should now choose the Digitizer/Mouse arbitrate. See Figure 33-2. This lets you use your mouse for the Windows operations and the digitizer for the tablet. You may use either the mouse or the digitizer for the cross-hairs and AutoCAD picks.

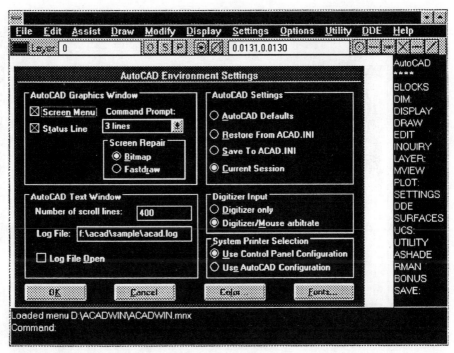

Figure 33-2: AutoCAD for Windows Environment Settings box

Remember that, until the technology changes (and they're working on it), your digitizer can't be a mouse and a digitizer at the same time.

33.3 How do you change the color of the screen?

Pick the FILE pull-down menu and choose **Environment**. See Figure 33-1. Now choose **Color...** at the bottom of the dialogue box. See Figure 33-2. You now can choose from a complete dialogue box that gives you access to most parts of the AutoCAD screen. See Figure 33-3. You may either pick the screen representation on the left or pull down the list box and choose the aspect of the screen you want to change. Once the part of the screen is chosen, you can point to the color directly.

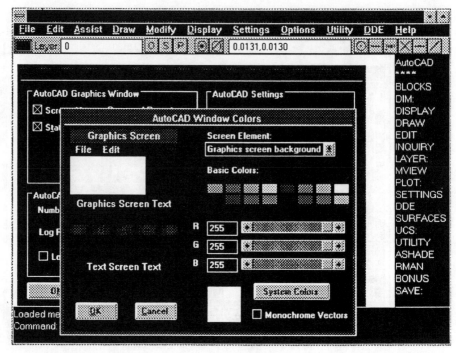

Figure 33-3: Color sub-option of the Environment Settings box

33.4 How do you flip back and forth to the text and graphic screen?

If you try it the old way, with F1, you'll find that it doesn't work. What you get is the Help options. This is to conform with the way other Windows programs work. The flip screen toggle is now F2.

33.5 How do you make the environment settings permanent?

As you can see from Figure 33-2, there are a lot of things you can change from the **Environment** settings. If you don't save the settings to the ACAD.INI file, they will be valid only for the current session.

33.6 **How do you record the text screen to a file?**

You can save for viewing on screen as many as 1500 lines of text. When you flip to the text screen, you can scroll back and forth through the previous text. But you also have the option of saving all the text to a file. This is called the log file. See Figure 33-2. Here you can determine the number of scroll lines and the name of the log file to be used. If you want to actually save to the log file, you must check the **Log File Open** box.

33.7 **How do you get AutoCAD for Windows to recognize text fonts?**

If you have to ask this question, you have not installed AutoCAD for Windows correctly. AutoCAD for Windows is not a complete version of AutoCAD. It still uses some support files, such as .SHX font files from the DOS version of AutoCAD. You must tell AutoCAD for Windows where the DOS version of AutoCAD is located. This is done in the **Properties** setup for the ACADWIN icon in Windows.

You can find this by picking once on the ACADWIN icon. (Yours may be called something different.) Pick FILE from the drop-down WINDOWS menu; then pick **Properties**. The Command line should read as follows (this will not be exact, as your directories will probably be different):

```
c:\acadwin\acad.exe /s c:\acadwin;c:\acad386
```

It's the last part of the line that is important. The **c:\acad386** is the directory where the DOS version of AutoCAD is located.

33.8 **How do you plot to a printer?**

You can of course configure AutoCAD for printer operations. But you also have the option of having AutoCAD use the **Control Panel Configuration**, which is the printer you chose for Windows. This is the easier way. If your printer driver is working for Windows, it will work for AutoCAD. You tell AutoCAD which you want to use through the **Environment** settings. See Figure 33-2.

33.9 **How do you begin a new drawing or start an existing drawing?**

This is very similar to Release 12. Pick the FILE pull-down menu and choose either **New** for a new file or **Open** in order to work in an existing drawing. See Figure 33-1.

See Figure 33-4. The file dialogue box is a typical Windows file box. This is the same for both the **New** and the **Open** options. Although it is similar to Release 12, there are some major differences. First the **File Name** and **Directories** are on different sides compared with Release 12. The **New** option doesn't give you the ability to pick from a prototype library, or **Open** in read-only mode. These are Release 12 options. Finally, when AutoCAD for Windows first comes up, you can't begin drawing immediately; first, you must open a file, either a new one or an existing one.

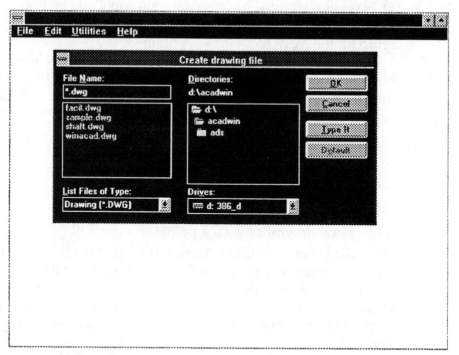

Figure 33-4: File Directory dialogue box

33.10 How do you transfer an image to another program?

The easiest way to transfer your drawing to another program is through the **Copy Image** option found on the EDIT pull-down menu. See Figure 33-5. When you pick this option, your crosshairs turn into a cross. Now pick the first corner, as you do when you start an AutoCAD window. Finish the window around the area you want to transfer. Remember, what you're transferring is the bitmap image, not the vectors. Therefore, you can transfer not only the drawing but part of the AutoCAD screen as well.

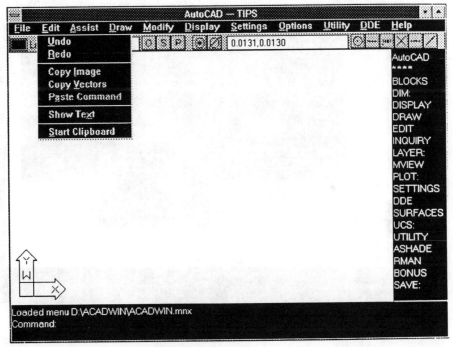

Figure 33-5: AutoCAD for Windows EDIT pull-down menu

This method transfers the image to the clipboard. Once on the clipboard, you can enter another program using that program's EDIT pull-down; then paste your drawing from the clipboard into the new program.

33.11 How do you create a metafile file from your drawing?

If you want the metafile vector image of the drawing sent to a file, you should choose **Export** from the FILE pull-down menu (see Figure 33-1). The **File** dialogue box on Figure 33-6 permits you to name the file. When you pick OK in the **File** dialogue box, you can then select the objects to be sent to the file.

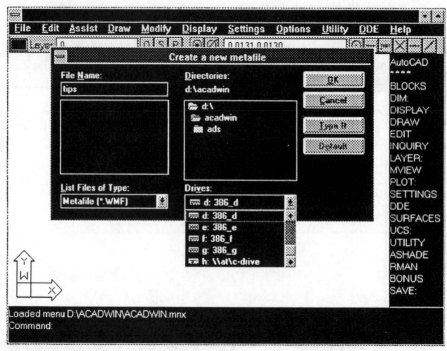

Figure 33-6: Metafile dialogue box

33.12 How do you change the color of the next entity drawn?

Pick directly on the color in the left-hand corner of the Toolbar. See Figure 33-7. The **Entity Creation** dialogue box appears. See Figure 33-8. This is a similar dialogue box to the one found in Release 12.

Figure 33-7: AutoCAD for Windows Toolbar

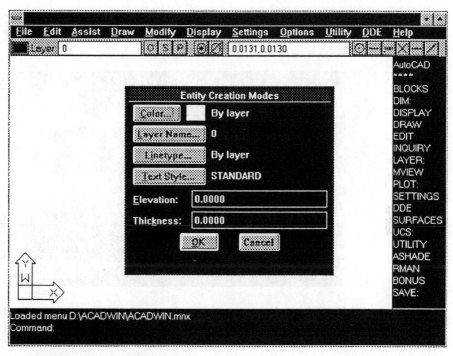

Figure 33-8: Entity Creation dialogue box

33.13 How do you bring up the Layer dialogue box?

Simply pick on the **Layer** part of the Toolbar (see Figure 33-7). You may pick on either the word **Layer** or the name of the layer. The **Modify Layer** dialogue box will appear. See Figure 33-9. This is similar to the dialogue box found in Release 12, except Release 12 has **Lock** and **Unlock** layers.

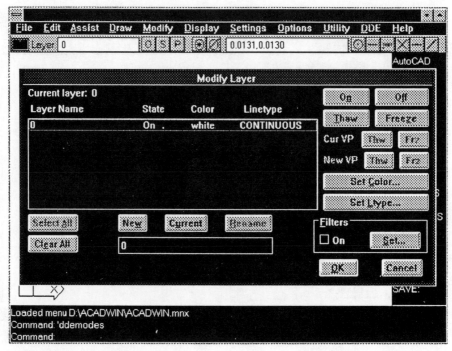

Figure 33-9: Modify Layer dialogue box

33.14 How do you customize the push buttons on the Toolbar?

Any of the buttons on the Toolbar can be customized except the **Snap**, **Ortho** and **Pspace**. To customize a button, pick it with the second button of your mouse or digitizer. Let's change the **Object Snap Intersection** button to an **ARC** command. See Figure 33-10. The **Toolbar** dialogue box appears. See Figure 33-11.

Figure 33-10: AutoCAD for Windows Toolbar

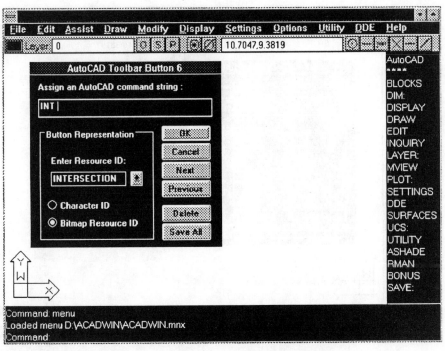

Figure 33-11: Object Snap intersection choice in AutoCAD for Windows dialogue box

You have two options. You can make the button character-based (simply type in the character you want to appear on the button) or you can use one of the predefined bitmap icons provided.

If you choose bitmap, you can choose from the bitmap options in the pull-down list. See Figure 33-12. In our case, we've picked the arc icon.

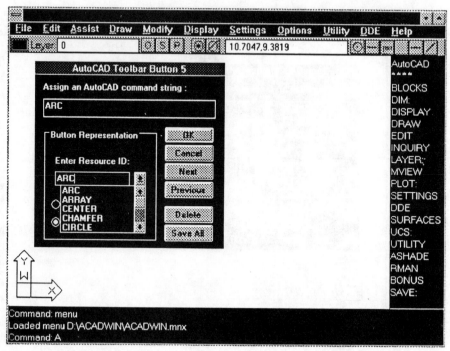

Figure 33-12: Bitmap options showing Arc choice

The important thing to remember is that there are two major parts of this dialogue box. The resource ID is only the bitmap icon that will be the picture that appears on the button. This in and of itself doesn't actually issue the AutoCAD command. That is done at the top, in the text box labeled "Assign an AutoCAD command string:." This is where you actually type in the AutoCAD command. It can be anything, even AutoLISP commands. Notice that the icon doesn't have to match the AutoCAD command string that you type.

When you OK the dialogue box, the icon changes. See Figure 33-13. Where there was the icon for the **Object Snap Intersection**, it is now the picture of an arc.

Figure 33-13: Changed icon from Object Snap Intersection to Arc

33.15 **How do you get more buttons on the Toolbar?**

The number of buttons that appear on the Toolbar is directly dependent on the resolution of your display. The maximum number of buttons available is 26. Also, if the window is reduced in size, buttons begin to disappear.

33.16 **How do you configure AutoCAD for Windows?**

The **Configure** option is available only before you actually bring up a drawing. It's in the UTILITIES pull-down menu. See Figure 33-14. If you've already brought up a drawing, you can simply close it; you don't have to actually exit AutoCAD.

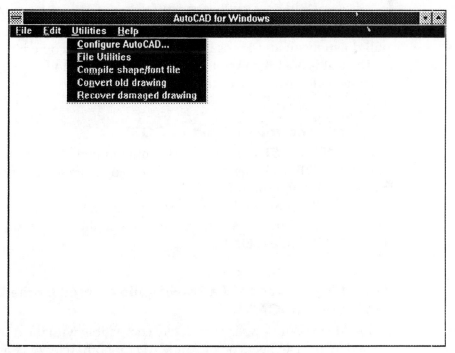

Figure 33-14: AutoCAD for Windows UTILITIES pull-down menu

33.17 **How do you unlock locked files?**

Before you begin a drawing, pick the UTILITIES pull-down menu. Then choose **File Utilities** (see Figure 33-14). Now the **Unlock Files** option is the same as AutoCAD Release 11.

33.18 **How do you see what's on the Clipboard?**

You can bring up the Clipboard at any time. From the EDIT pull-down menu, choose **Start Clipboard**.

33.19 **How do you bring in text from a word processor?**

Begin in a Windows version of any word processor or text editor. Highlight the text in the word processor by picking the beginning of the text. Continue to hold down the pick button. As you move across the text and down, it will highlight. Once the text is highlighted, pick the EDIT pull-down menu of the word processor and choose **Copy**. Now leave the word processor and enter the drawing in AutoCAD for Windows.

Begin either the **TEXT** or **DTEXT** command in AutoCAD. Answer all the options until AutoCAD asks you for **Text:**. At this point, pick the EDIT pull-down menu and choose **Paste**. The text will be copied in at that time.

The text is not bitmapped; it's real text. This method can be used at anytime AutoCAD asks for text information.

33.20 **How do you shell out to DOS?**

You can still type **SHELL** from the Command line, as with other versions of AutoCAD. But a better way would be to open another window and use the DOS **Prompt** options from Windows.

The **SHELL** command won't work unless you have correctly installed AutoCAD for Windows so that it's pointing to the support directory where the ACAD.PGP file is located.

33.21 **How do you load a drawing file created by the DOS version of AutoCAD?**

AutoCAD for Windows is completely compatible with the drawings created by the DOS version of AutoCAD for both Release 11 and Release 12. In fact, it's probably best to develop your drawing in the DOS version of AutoCAD.

When you open a drawing that was created with AutoCAD Release 11 or Release 12, it will try to bring up the menu file with which it was saved. You'll need to choose the **MENU** command after the drawing is brought up so that you can choose the ACADWIN.MNX menu for windows.

33.22 **How do you adjust the speed of your mouse?**

The mouse can't be adjusted from the AutoCAD CONFIGURATION menu. It can be adjusted only from the **Windows Control** panel. This adjusts the mouse not only for AutoCAD but also for all of the Windows environment.

More Steps to Success

33.23 **Speed will increase with the AutoCAD for Windows Release 12**

When Autodesk ships the 32-bit Release 12 version of AutoCAD for Windows, speed will not be a problem. AutoCAD for Windows will cease being an extension and will be a completely independent platform. It will run on Windows 3 (and its successors). But, meanwhile, there are a few things you can do to increase efficiency and speed.

33.24 **More memory will increase speed**

Put more memory in your machine. This is the single most important thing you can do, short of getting a faster machine. The more memory, the faster it will run generally. This is especially important if you're going to be using AutoCAD for Windows as it was intended to be used—that is, for communicating with other programs. It will totally bog down if you don't have enough memory. Although AutoCAD for Windows will run with 4 megabytes, 8 should really be considered the minimum.

33.25 **Use display list processing**

Purchase a special display list-processing driver specifically for AutoCAD for Windows. This will cut down tremendously on the **REGEN**s and dramatically speed up the **ZOOM**s. This will make the speed almost acceptable for actual development.

33.26 **Don't resize windows**

Stop resizing the window and changing the environment. This is going to activate a **REGEN** every time.

33.27 **Get completely out of Windows from time to time**

Periodically get out of Windows completely and come back in. This will refresh the memory for Windows and speed up all of your programs.

33.28 **Optimize your hard disk**

Make certain that your hard disk is optimized. Fragmentation can dramatically slow down your entire computer.

33.29 **Create a permanent swap file**

Create a permanent Windows swap file. This permits Windows to do its swapping directly rather than going through the DOS file system.

33.30 **Use Bitmap instead of Fastdraw**

If you have a 1024 display, you might want to change the Environment Settings for Screen Repair to **Bitmap** instead of **Fastdraw**. See Figure 33-2.

33.31 **Use metafile method of transfer**

If all you want to do is copy the drawing to the Clipboard, you're better off using a metafile rather than a pixel-image copy. To do this, choose the **Copy Vectors** option from the EDIT pull-down menu. See Figure 33-5. This permits you to put an AutoCAD type of window or use any selection set options available. The vectors are then copied to the Clipboard. Once on the Clipboard, you can enter another program using that program's EDIT pull-down and paste your drawing from the Clipboard into the new program.

33.32 Toggle Snap, Ortho, Coordinates and Pspace with Toolbar buttons

The Toolbar permits you to toggle on **Snap, Ortho, Pspace** and **Coordinates**. O=Ortho; S=Snap; P=Pspace. See Figure 33-15. Activate any of these by simply picking the Toolbar button. The Coordinates are turned on and off by picking directly on the coordinates themselves.

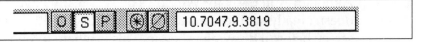

Figure 33-15: Toolbar allows you to toggle Ortho, Snap, Pspace and Coordinates

33.33 Remember to SAVE programmed buttons on the Toolbar

Changing the button definitions on the Toolbar will be in effect only during the current drawing, unless you pick **Save All**. See Figure 33-12. This saves the current definition to the ACAD.INI file.

33.34 How do you activate menu and dialogue boxes without a mouse?

If for some reason your mouse is not working, or you simply find this method faster, you can use what are known as accelerator keys. The pull-down menu words each have an underscore. Use Alt + the letter that is underscored, and the pull-down menu will be visible. Submenu items also have underscored letters. You don't need to use the Alt key with submenu items. Simply press the letter of the underscore to activate the command.

33.35 Inactive areas

AutoCAD for Windows is smart enough to know when an option should be available and when it shouldn't. If an option isn't available, it will still be visible but will be grayed out. This means that you're not able to pick it.

33.36 Conventions not completely consistent

Up until now, the conventions used by AutoCAD for Windows haven't been completely consistent. This has been corrected in Release 12. For example, a menu item followed by ... means that the item has a dialogue box behind it. The **Plot...** on the FILE pull-down menu, however, doesn't bring up a dialogue box. It is the straight text-based plot command.

33.37 **Toggle text with Show/Hide**

In addition to being able to toggle between the text screen and the graphics screen with F2, you can also choose **Show/Hide Text** from the EDIT pull-down menu.

33.38 **END and QUIT do not exit AutoCAD**

Although AutoCAD for Windows doesn't really have a main menu, it doesn't really act the same as AutoCAD Release 12. It starts from a neutral screen before a drawing is begun. This is where it returns after a **QUIT** or an **END**. You must then exit from this screen to exit back to the program manager.

33.39 **Think twice before installing enhanced Help**

Although the enhanced Help available through AutoCAD for Windows is quite impressive, it takes a lot of disk space: 15 additional megabytes. Even if you don't install the enhanced Help, you'll still have a very good help facility, but without wasting all that disk space.

33.40 **Save more often**

Windows applications aren't really as stable as straight DOS applications. This, though, isn't an indictment of AutoCAD for Windows or other Windows applications. Inevitably, as programmers and users alike stretch the limits of the current technology, there are more crashes as programs conflict. Do yourself a favor and save often.

Appendix A

Creating and Loading AutoLISP files

Most of the chapters in this book end with a series of ready-to-run Auto-LISP programs. If you have the optional *1,000 AutoCAD Tips and Tricks* companion diskette, you'll find each program in a separate file ready to be loaded. (To order the diskette, complete the form in the back of this book.) Otherwise, you must create the file before you can run it.

Although *1,000 AutoCAD Tips and Tricks* is filled with more than 100 useful AutoLISP routines, it's not the purpose of this book to teach you AutoLISP. For a beginning and easy-to-understand tutorial on AutoLISP, please read *AutoLISP in Plain English* (Ventana Press).

An AutoLISP program is created as an ordinary text file. You may use EDLIN.COM or your favorite word processor to create the file. If you use a word processor, be sure the file is saved in ASCII or as a DOS text file, not as a word processor file.

If you don't have the optional diskette, type the programs in exactly as they are in the book, using a text editor. If you see a plus sign at the end of a line of code, it indicates a wrap-around line. Don't type the plus sign; it's simply there because the line of code wouldn't fit on one line. Save the program under its file name plus the extension .LSP; all AutoLISP program files must have this extension. For example, the LISP1 program should be typed in and saved as LISP1.LSP.

Once created, the file must be loaded before it can be used. AutoLISP files are loaded from inside the AutoCAD drawing editor. Before each program, you'll see a line like this that reminds you to first load the file. We're using the program name LISP1 as an example.

To Use: Load LISP1.LSP

This statement means that you're to load the LISP file. Type in the following at AutoCAD's Command line:

```
(load "lisp1") <RETURN>
```

Notice that the extension isn't included. Once the program is loaded, it can be executed the same as an ordinary AutoCAD command. Just type its name and press <RETURN>.

Each of the more than 100 AutoLISP programs in this book is sequentially numbered. Each number, such as LISP14, is a program's name. Choose the programs you want to use. You can then change their names to be more meaningful to you, combine them all in the ACAD.LSP file so that they'll be loaded automatically, and/or add them to your menu.

The programs you choose will become an integral part of your AutoCAD system and your work. As your productivity increases, you'll begin to wonder how you ever got along without them.

Appendix B

Companion Diskette

Congratulations on your success in beginning to learn AutoLISP. After having completed the lessons in this book, you have come a long way toward reaching your goal. Not only are these programs useful but they're also meant to serve as examples of how what you have learned can be put into real practice.

What's on the Companion Diskette?

The companion diskette contains the programs ready to load for all of the programs found at the end of each lesson. There is also a drawing file with the appropriate units and limits already set, as well as the entities and blocks used as examples in the lessons.

When you receive your companion diskette, all you have to do is type **A:INSTALL** to copy the AutoLISP files and drawing files onto your hard disk. Then they are ready to use.

Bonus Programs

The companion diskette offers more than ease of use; it also provides useful bonus programs that are not listed in the book. These three programs are fully documented, like those in these pages. The additional program examples will accelerate your learning process and, also, bolster your AutoLISP library.

NOTE TO THE USER: One of the most frustrating things that can happen to a new student trying to learn AutoLISP is to try to debug simple typing errors. I can't tell you how many people have called me to say that they've had as many as five people check their code and proclaim that it's perfectly correct—yet the programs still don't work. Then, when a hard copy of the code is faxed to me, I've found as many as three major errors preventing the programs from working. The problem is that most AutoCAD users aren't expert typists. Autodesk has done everything possible to keep you from having to type. So why impede your progress by typing and debugging the programs in the book—and possibly increasing your frustration level?

This listing contains cross-referenced tips only.

INDICES

INDICES

INDICES

ALPHABETICAL INDEX

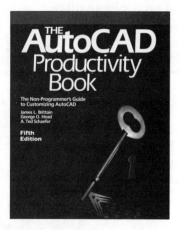

TO ORDER additional copies of *1000 AutoCAD Tips & Tricks, Third Edition,* or other books in the Ventana Press AutoCAD Reference Library, please fill out this order form and return it to us for quick shipment.

	Quantity		Price		Total
1000 AutoCAD Tips & Tricks	_____	x	$27.95	=	$_____
1000 AutoCAD Tips & Tricks Disk	_____	x	$49.95	=	$_____
AutoCAD: A Concise Guide	_____	x	$24.95	=	$_____
AutoCAD: A Concise Guide Disk	_____	x	$19.95	=	$_____
AutoLISP in Plain English	_____	x	$23.95	=	$_____
AutoLISP in Plain English Disk	_____	x	$19.95	=	$_____
Solid Modeling With AutoCAD	_____	x	$29.95	=	$_____
Solid Modeling With AutoCAD Disk	_____	x	$49.95	=	$_____
The AutoCAD Productivity Book	_____	x	$27.95	=	$_____
The AutoCAD Productivity Book Disk	_____	x	$49.95	=	$_____
Outside AutoCAD	_____	x	$29.95	=	$_____
Outside AutoCAD Disk	_____	x	$49.95	=	$_____
The AutoCAD 3D Companion	_____	x	$27.95	=	$_____
The AutoCAD 3D Companion Disk	_____	x	$49.95	=	$_____
All seven books & seven disks (30% off!)	_____	x	$317.00	=	$_____

Please specify disk size: ___3 1/2"   ___5 1/4"

Also available from Ventana Press: best-selling presentation and desktop publishing design titles:

	Quantity		Price		Total
The Presentation Design Book	_____	x	$24.95	=	$_____
Harvard Graphics Design Companion	_____	x	$23.95	=	$_____
Looking Good in Print	_____	x	$23.95	=	$_____

Shipping: Please add $4.50/first book for standard UPS, $1.35/book thereafter; $8.25/book UPS "two-day air," $2.25/book thereafter.
For Canada, add $8.10/book.   = $_____

Send C.O.D. (add $4.50 to shipping charges)   = $_____

North Carolina residents add 6% sales tax   = $_____

Total   = $_____

Name _____

Company _____

Address (No P.O. Box) _____

City_____ State_____ Zip _____

Daytime Phone _____

___ Payment enclosed ___VISA ___MC Acc't # _____

Expiration Date_____ Signature _____

Please mail or fax to:
Ventana Press, P.O. Box 2468, Chapel Hill, NC 27515; 919/942-0220; FAX: 919/942-1140
FOR FASTER SERVICE, CALL TOLL-FREE 800/743-5369.

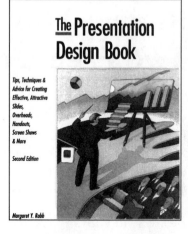

Return This Card For Two Free Updates!

Let us keep you up-to-date on the latest techniques for maximizing AutoCAD's power. Complete the card below, mail it to us, and we'll send you two issues full of never-before-published techniques to help you continue to get the most out of AutoCAD.

Please send your request to
Ventana Press
P.O. Box 2468
Chapel Hill, NC 27515
919/942-0220; Fax 919/942-1140

Yes, please send me two free issues of *Tips & Tricks, The AutoCAD Update.*

Name _____

Company _____

Street address (no P.O. box) _____

City _____ State _____ Zip _____

Daytime telephone _____

Signature _____

Return to: Ventana Press, P.O. Box 2468, Chapel Hill, NC 27515
FAX 919/942-1140
(Please don't duplicate your fax requests by mail.)

Become Even More Productive . . . With This No-Risk Disk

Order the *1000 AutoCAD Tips & Tricks Disk*, which allows you to enter the AutoLISP programs and drawings featured throughout the book directly into your computer. Completely self-installing, the disk gets you up and running immediately for enhanced productivity. In addition to saving you typing time, these programs can provide instant shortcuts that save you time week after week.

To order your copy, please complete the form below, detach and mail to

Ventana Press, P.O. Box 2468
Chapel Hill, NC 27515
800/743-5369 for orders only; 919/942-0220; Fax 919/942-1140

Please be sure to specify disk size.

Yes, please send ___ copies of the *1000 AutoCAD Tips & Tricks Disk, Third Edition,* at $49.95 per disk. Add $3.90/disk for normal shipping; $7.00/disk for UPS "two-day air"; $11.50/disk for overnight and international shipping. NC residents add 6% sales tax. Immediate shipment guaranteed.

Please specify disk size: ___3 1/2"   ___5 1/4" (Disks are IBM-compatible only.)

Name _____

Company _____

Street address (no P.O. box) _____

City _____ State _____ Zip _____

Daytime telephone _____

___ Payment enclosed ___VISA ___MC Acc't # _____

Expiration Date_____ Signature_____

Return to: Ventana Press, P.O. Box 2468, Chapel Hill, NC 27515
800/743-5369 for orders only; 919/942-0220; FAX 919/942-1140
(Please don't duplicate your fax requests by mail.)